Consumer Math and You

R. ROBERT ROSENBERG
euben

Educational Consultant
Former President of Jersey City Junior College
Jersey City, New Jersey

JOY RISSER

Instructor, Victor Valley College
Victorville, California

Consultant
JOHN E. WHITGRAFT

Former Director, Division of Occupational Instruction
The State Education Department
Albany, New York

Gregg Division/McGraw-Hill Book Company

New York / St. Louis / Dallas / San Francisco / Auckland
Bogotá / Düsseldorf / Johannesburg / London / Madrid
Mexico / Montreal / New Delhi / Panama / Paris / São Paulo
Singapore / Sydney / Tokyo / Toronto

Sponsoring Editor: Susan Schornstein
Senior Editing Supervisor: Pamela M. Nugent
Editors: Dale Ramsey, Nancy Sorensen, Marie Spano
Senior Production Supervisor: Robert Sánchez
Art Director: Frank Medina
Design Supervisor: Karen Miño
Design: A Good Thing, Inc.
Cartoons (chapter openers):   Janice Stapleton

The photographs and illustrations in this book appear courtesy of the following:

New York Convention and Visitors Bureau, 6.
Burlington Industries, Inc., 15.
American Cancer Society, 27.
Alexander Deutsch, 40.
Jeanne Strongin, 45.
Jeanne Strongin, 66.
Ford Motor Company, 90.
Jeanne Strongin, 109.
Bettmann Archive, 118.
Howard Johnson's, 125.
New York Knickerbockers, 134.
New York Convention and Visitors Bureau, 147.
Jeanne Strongin, 153.
David Harbaugh, 158.
Macy's, 175.
State University of New York at Stony Brook, 187.
Jeanne Strongin, 223.
The Port Authority of New York and New Jersey, 242.
Tom Stratton, 248.
State University of New York at Stony Brook, 262.
New York Stock Exchange, 280.
American Cancer Society, 305.
New York Philharmonic, Martha Swope, 321.

Library of Congress Cataloging in Publication Data

Rosenberg, Reuben Robert, date
    Consumer math and you.

    Includes index.
    SUMMARY: A high school textbook discussing such
topics as budgeting, banking, borrowing, obtaining
credit, investing, and other aspects of consumer
mathematics.
    1. Finance, Personal.   2. Consumer education.
[1. Finance, Personal.   2. Consumer education]
I.   Risser, Joy, joint author.   II.   Title.
HG179.R678   640'.42   78-12238
ISBN 0-07-053641-4

Consumer Math and You

1 2 3 4 5 6 7 8 9 0   VHVH   7 8 7 6 5 4 3 2 1 0 9

Preface

Math skills are important to each of us. Why? Because each of us needs to function in society as a wise consumer. *Consumer Math and You* has been designed as a vehicle for teaching these essential math skills in a relevant and interesting fashion. As the students gain mastery of math, they secure the knowledge they will need as consumers in the marketplace.

To meet these objectives, the book covers the math skills and activities that apply to all areas of consumer mathematics—earning money, budgeting, banking, purchasing consumer goods, obtaining consumer credit, renting and buying, saving, investing, paying taxes, using public and private transportation, and using the metric system. A lively style, numerous cartoons and photographs, an easy reading level, and an open design further help to meet the objectives of *Consumer Math and You*.

Components of the Program

The *Consumer Math and You* program includes a textbook, an activity guide with problems supplementing those in the text, and a teacher's manual and key that includes tests for duplication.

Textbook. The textbook focuses on the kinds of computations that today's students will need to perform effectively as consumers. Numerous exercises are provided—both math problems that emphasize basic skills and narrative problems that stress the application of these skills. The textbook also contains extensive sections on basic math skills and on the metric system. (The math skills sections can be covered all at once or on a point-of-need basis as the students proceed through the book.)

For easy manageability, the textbook is divided into five parts. Performance goals introduce each part. Chapters within each part are divided into sections. Short segments within each section provide immediate reinforcement of key concepts and applications.

Activity Guide. The *Activity Guide* follows the textbook's format and is divided into corresponding sections. Performance goals and appropriate page references are given at the beginning of each section. The *Activity Guide* contains completely different problems (along with answer space) that parallel those in the basic textbook. Working papers for all textbook exercises are also included. The activity guide includes these special features: "Refresh Your Skills"—exercises that build basic math skills; "Apply Consumer Math"—word problems that reinforce textbook concepts; "Consumer Challenge"—opportunities for students to make wise consumer decisions; and "Take a Break"—light-hearted looks at math.

Teacher's Manual and Key. The *Teacher's Manual and Key* contains teaching suggestions, scheduling options, keys for all exercises in the text and in the activity guide, and transparency masters. In addition, there is a testing program that includes tests on each chapter, a diagnostic test on basic math skills, plus keys for the tests.

Features

Consumer Math and You contains many special features.

- ◻ A criterion-referenced testing program is provided in the *Teacher's Manual and Key*. The testing program includes a pretest on basic math skills that can be used at the beginning of the course as a diagnostic test. Full-page chapter tests can be used to measure the students' mastery of performance goals.
- ◻ Performance goals begin each part of the textbook and each section of the *Activity Guide*.
- ◻ The text is written in a lively, easy-to-read style. Many cartoons and photographs are included.
- ◻ Marginal notes highlight important information.
- ◻ "Do You Know" features offer valuable consumer tips and advice.
- ◻ Basic math problems plus practical narrative problems follow each short section of the textbook.
- ◻ Two special features—"Consumer Challenge" and "For You to Solve"—are found at the end of each part of the textbook. "Consumer Challenge" presents a case study in which students must exercise judgment and make a wise consumer choice. "For You to Solve" consists of problems that apply the concepts learned in that part of the textbook.

◻ Each part of the text covers a different topic and is largely independent of the other parts. This offers the teacher the flexibility to emphasize those topics deemed most essential for each particular class and to cover any other topics as time permits. Such scheduling options are covered in the *Teacher's Manual and Key.*

Acknowledgments

The authors would like to thank those educators and members of the business community who have reviewed and commented upon *Consumer Math and You.* Much valuable assistance was provided by Dr. Barry Siebert, assistant professor of business education, Florida Technological University, and Rosemary Stroer, a former teacher with the New York City school system.

The Authors

A note from the publishers

It is with deep regret that the publishers must add that Dr. Rosenberg passed away just before this book went to press. His qualities as an outstanding educator, consultant, writer, and gentleman will be sorely missed.

Contents

Who Is a Consumer?

The dictionary says that a consumer is one who buys goods and services. Consumers are people who buy items in a small general store on Main Street, in a giant department store, or through a mail-order catalog. You, members of your family, and your friends are consumers. The vacationer using a credit card at a hotel is a consumer. The musician who buys new sound equipment is a consumer. The nine-year-old who purchases a pack of bubble gum is a consumer. Anyone, at any time, in any place, who is buying any number of things is a consumer.

It sounds easy to be a consumer, and it's *very* easy to spend money. But to do it wisely takes some thinking and some work. Consumers need to be informed so that they can exercise good judgment. They need to compare carefully many aspects of the goods or services that they plan to buy. No one wants to be cheated.

What does the consumer need to know before deciding to buy an item? Jane Watkins considered a list of things when she bought her new car. Quite by accident, she discovered six major areas of consumer math. These are budgeting, consumer credit, shopping for goods, savings, taxes, and insurance. All of these are in the following description of Jane's purchase. See if you can spot them.

Jane needed a car to get to her job about ten miles from home. A compact car—one that offered good mileage and would hold up for several years—was her choice.

Jane decided upon a price range that she was both willing and able to pay for the car. She wisely timed her shopping to get the best value for her money. Jane found that September is the month when cars are often sold below regular prices. Car dealers showed her a number of models selling at 20 to 40 percent below regular prices. She bought one of these cars.

Jane got a bagain, but she now had to pay for the car, plus the sales tax on it. She had saved enough money for the down payment, but she needed to borrow the rest. So she went to a local bank and got a loan. She would repay the loan with interest in two years. Next, she purchased automobile insurance.

You can see that Jane had a lot to consider in making her purchase. Her ability to do some quick computing helped in her decision making. Jane was using *consumer math*. You'll find consumer math important too. Suppose you want to buy a bicycle, go on a plane trip, or get new clothes. There's an old saying: "Let the buyer beware." This means you should stop, think, and compute.

In the next year or so, you will undoubtedly make a number of money decisions. You may decide you want something badly enough that you will sacrifice some other things for it. Essentially, this will mean planning and controlling your spending. *Consumer Math and You* will give you the skills you'll need for your important money decisions.

Earning and Budgeting

Performance Goals

When you finish work on this part, you should be able to:

- [ ] Compute earnings when an employee is paid hourly, by the piece, or on commission.
- [ ] Determine the wages an employee paid on an hourly basis loses because of lateness.
- [ ] Compute overtime wages.
- [ ] Compute earnings combining piece-work earnings plus an hourly rate and combining salary plus commission.
- [ ] Compute earnings in different commission plans.
- [ ] Compute net pay.
- [ ] Determine amounts of federal income tax, state income tax, and social security tax (FICA) withheld from a paycheck.
- [ ] Compute voluntary deductions.
- [ ] Prepare a balanced budget by estimating monthly net income, fixed expenses, and variable expenses.
- [ ] Select the amounts to budget when expenses are paid in different ways (quarterly, bimonthly, and so on).
- [ ] Adjust budgets.
- [ ] Apply percents to budgeting.

Earning an Income

Becky Smith works in a day-care center and is paid by the hour. Ed Santiago is a bank teller and earns a weekly salary. Nora Sweeney paints country scenes and is paid for each painting she completes. William Janovic sells copying machines and is paid a percentage of his total sales.

What do all these people have in common? All are earning some kind of income. *Income* is the money you receive for work or services that you perform. Most people earn an income by working at a regular job where they receive steady pay. Workers are paid in different ways. (Four possible ways were mentioned in the first paragraph.) It is important for you to understand how people are paid. Pay adds up to income, and, as consumers know, income means money to spend and save.

Section One
Wages by the Hour

Wages for most employees are based on the number of hours they work and the hourly rate of pay. A company and an employee usually agree on the number of hours and the hourly rate, or a

Regular salary: money earned for working normal hours.

Overtime pay: money earned for working extra hours.

contract may be drawn up between a company and a labor union. The contract is an agreement that sets the hourly wage for certain jobs.

When employees complete a normal work week, usually 35 or 40 hours, they earn a *regular salary*. (If they work more than 40 hours in one week, they earn extra money. This is called *overtime* pay. Overtime rates will be discussed on pages 5 to 8.)

Computing Regular Weekly Earnings

Becky Smith works 35 hours each week at the Bryant Avenue Day-Care Center. She earns $4.40 an hour as a teacher's aide. What are her regular weekly earnings?

Hourly rate of pay	$4.40
Hours worked weekly	35
Earnings for a week	$4.40 × 35 = $154

Exercises
Find the amount earned during one week by each of the following employees.

Employee	Hourly Rate	Hours Worked	Weekly Earnings
1. C. Judson	$2.45	34	$ 83.30
2. R. Lum	6.51	39	_____
3. M. Weiss	4.25	40	_____
4. J. Jackson	5.08	38	_____
5. L. Kanner	2.45	40	_____
6. T. Tully	3.62	36	_____
7. J. Tate	2.75	40	_____
8. M. Ortiz	3.18	37	_____
9. S. Skoll	4.50	36	_____
10. D. Meyer	2.93	35	_____

Losing Wages Because of Lateness

Rules about lateness.

Although Becky likes her job working with children, she doesn't like it when wages are subtracted because of lateness. Becky's union has strict rules about lateness. These are the rules.

1. *For the first 10 minutes of lateness, no wages are subtracted.*
2. *For each following 10-minute period, or for any part of that period,* 15 minutes' worth of wages are subtracted. (Remember that 15 minutes is equal to $\frac{1}{4}$, or .25, of an hour.)

One day Becky was 20 minutes late. Here is how she computed the amount of wages that she lost.

Number of minutes late	20
Number of minutes for which wages are lost	20 − 10 = 10
Number of 10-minute periods	10 ÷ 10 = 1
Number of hours of wage loss	1 × .25 = .25
Hourly rate of pay	$4.40
Wages lost	$4.40 × .25 = $1.10

Suppose Becky had been 40 minutes late. Here is how she would have computed the amount of wages that she lost.

Number of minutes late	40
Number of minutes for which wages were lost	40 − 10 = 30
Number of 10-minute periods	30 ÷ 10 = 3
Number of hours of wage loss	3 × .25 = .75
Hourly rate of pay	$4.40
Wages lost	$4.40 × .75 = $3.30

If Becky had been 35 minutes late, she would have lost the same amount of wages. Explain why this is so.

Computing Weekly Earnings Minus Wages Lost Because of Lateness

If Becky has worked a normal week, she can easily compute her weekly earnings, even when she has lost wages because of lateness. She merely takes her regular weekly earnings and subtracts the amount lost.

Regular weekly earnings	$154
Wage loss due to 20 minutes of lateness	$1.10
New weekly earnings	$154 − $1.10 = $152.90

Exercises

1. The following employees are supposed to arrive at the Bryant Avenue Day-Care Center at 8 a.m. How many minutes late is each employee? For how many 10-minute periods will wages be lost? For how many hours?

Employee	Time of Arrival	Minutes Late	10-Minute Periods for Which Wages Are Lost	Hours of Wage Loss
a. C. Judson	8:15	15	1	.25
b. R. Lum	8:30	————	————	————
c. J. Tate	9:10	————	————	————
d. M. Ortiz	8:48	————	————	————
e. S. Skoll	8:05	————	————	————

2. The hourly rates of pay for some of the employees at the Bryant Avenue Day-Care Center are listed below. The number of hours of wage loss are also given. How much did each employee lose in wages? (If necessary, round off to the nearest cent.)

Employee	Hourly Rate of Pay	Hours of Wage Loss	Loss in Wages
a. M. Weiss	$5.00	1.5	$ 7.50
b. L. Kanner	4.80	.5	————
c. T. Tully	2.75	.75	————

3. Each of the employees named above works a normal 35-hour week. Use the information given in Exercise 2 to compute the regular weekly earnings. Then compute the earnings minus the loss of wages due to lateness. (Assume that, except for being late one morning, each of the employees worked normal hours.)

Employee	Regular Weekly Earnings	Loss in Wages	New Weekly Earnings
a. M. Weiss	$ 175.00	$ 7.50	$ 167.50
b. L. Kanner	————	————	————
c. T. Tully	————	————	————

Overtime Wages

Regular and overtime rates.

Ed Santiago works as a bank teller at the Buckley Savings Bank. Sometimes he works overtime, especially at the end of the month. The chart below is a guide to the rates of pay—regular and overtime—at the Buckley Savings Bank.

35-hour work week.........	paid at regular hourly rate
35- to 40-hour work week.....	paid at regular hourly rate
Hours after 40	paid at time-and-a-half rate

Note that even though the normal work week is 35 hours, Ed's overtime hours don't begin until 40 hours have passed. When Ed works more than 40 hours before the week has come to an end, he starts to earn a higher rate of pay. This rate is called *time-and-a-half*.

Suppose Ed works 45 hours one week. His 5 extra hours will earn him $1\frac{1}{2}$ times as much as 5 of his regular hours.

Going to work each day doesn't always mean reporting to an office or a factory. This employee works at an aquarium. Other people may work at ball parks, airports, or beaches. Can you think of any other unusual places to work?

Ed earns $3.95 an hour during a normal work week. His time-and-a-half rate is computed by first changing $1\frac{1}{2}$ to a decimal: 1.5.

Regular hourly rate $3.95

Time-and-a-half rate $1.5 \times \$3.95 = \$5.925$ *or* $5.93

For our purposes, the overtime hourly rate is rounded off to the nearest cent.

Exercises

Compute the time-and-a-half hourly rate that these people earn. If necessary, round off your answer to the nearest cent.

Employee	Regular Hourly Rate	Time-and-a-Half Rate
1. K. Bailey	$3.38	$ 5.07
2. C. Fischer	2.75	_____
3. E. Gallagher	4.92	_____
4. P. Mueller	4.85	_____
5. C. Rodriguez	6.07	_____
6. A. Bonomo	3.45	_____
7. F. Fletcher	5.12	_____
8. M. Gomez	4.56	_____
9. E. Schroeder	2.87	_____
10. S. MacDonald	2.65	_____

Computing Weekly Earnings Plus Overtime

During the December holiday season, Ed often works late. In one week he worked 45 hours. What were his earnings that week?

Regular hourly rate	$3.95
Time-and-a-half rate	$5.925 *or* $5.93
Number of hours at time-and-a-half rate	$45 - 40 = 5$
Regular earnings for week	$40 \times \$3.95 = \$158$
Time-and-a-half wages	$5 \times \$5.93 = \$29.65$
Total weekly earnings	$\$158 + 29.65 = \$187.65$

Exercises

1. Compute the overtime earnings for the following employees at Buckley Savings Bank. Each earns time-and-a-half pay for every

hour worked beyond 40 hours during one week. You will need to find the number of hours for which each employee received the time-and-a-half rate.

Employee	Time-and-a-Half Rate	Total Hours Worked	Hours at Time-and-a-Half Rate	Overtime Earnings
a. R. Carter	$ 7.25	52	12	$ 87
b. C. Ming	6.37	49		
c. D. Hume	11.25	57		
d. A. Gomez	8.40	53		
e. P. Keefe	5.95	46		

2. What is the total amount earned last week by the following employees of Toy City? Note that, at Toy City, time-and-a-half rates are paid after an employee works a total of 38 hours.

Employee	Regular Hourly Rate	Total Hours Worked	Regular Earnings for Week	Time-and-a-Half Rate	Time-and-a-Half Wages	Total Weekly Earnings
a. J. Allison	$2.76	47	$ 104.88	$ 4.14	$ 37.26	$ 142.14
b. S. Vegas	7.35	53		11.03		
c. K. Landau	4.15	36		6.23		
d. B. Luce	3.27	39		4.91		
e. B. Locke	2.93	49		4.40		

Computing Weekly Earnings Plus Double Time

Double time: twice as much as a regular hourly rate.

Phyllis Sawyer is an auto mechanic who works a regular 40-hour week. If Phyllis works on Sundays or holidays, she earns *double time,* or twice as much as her regular hourly rate. Her regular hourly rate is $4.75 an hour. How much will Phyllis earn if she works 5 hours on a Sunday?

Regular hourly rate	$4.75
Double time rate	$4.75 × 2 = $9.50
Number of hours at double time	5
Double time wages	5 × $9.50 = $47.50
Regular earnings for week	40 × $4.75 = $190
Total weekly earnings	$190 + $47.50 = $237.50

Part 1   EARNING AND BUDGETING

Exercises for Section One

1. Find the double time rate and the double time earnings for the following employees.

Employee	Regular Hourly Rate	Double Time Rate	Double Time Hours	Double Time Earnings
a. D. Stokes	$4.49	$ 8.98	6	$ 53.88
b. R. Palmer	2.95	_____	7	_____
c. J. Horne	3.84	_____	9	_____
d. V. Garcia	5.38	_____	5	_____
e. A. Flynn	3.75	_____	8	_____

2. Find the total weekly earnings for the following employees.

Employee	Regular Weekly Earnings	Regular Hourly Rate	Double Time Rate	Double Time Hours	Double Time Earnings	Total Weekly Earnings
a. C. Levine	$150.00	$3.75	$ 7.50	3	$ 22.50	$ 172.50
b. G. Bauer	174.80	4.37	_____	8	_____	_____
c. J. Moran	114.40	2.86	_____	6	_____	_____
d. M. Cruz	168.80	4.22	_____	2	_____	_____
e. W. Lloyd	157.60	3.94	_____	9	_____	_____
f. C. Camero	126.00	3.15	_____	7	_____	_____

3. Rod Parks earns $2.40 an hour working as a gardener. During one busy week last summer, he worked 28 hours. What were Rod's total earnings?

4. Anne Goldstein earns time-and-a-half pay for hours worked beyond 40 each week. Her hourly rate is $4.21. What did she earn during one 43-hour work week? (Round off the time-and-a-half rate to the nearest cent.)

5. Mel Cooper is a clerk at a store which is open on Sundays and holidays. He earns double time pay when he works on these special days. His regular hourly pay is $2.58. What were his earnings during one week when he had 38 hours of regular pay and 8 hours of double time pay?

6. Kay Lader works 7 hours each day and earns $2.80 an hour. Yesterday she arrived at her job 35 minutes late. What were her earnings for the day? (Kay's company uses the same rules regarding lateness as those used by the Bryant Avenue Day-Care Center on page 3.)

7. Franklin Jones earns time-and-a-half pay for hours worked beyond 38 each week. His hourly rate is $4.74. What did he earn during one 41-hour work week?

DO YOU KNOW

how to change weekly earnings to an hourly rate? Suppose you see an ad in a newspaper for a part-time job and call the company. You are told that the job pays $49 a week for 20 hours of work. You might wonder, "How much would I make an hour?" To find out, you can do some fast figuring.

Total weekly salary $49
Total weekly hours   20
Hourly rate $49 ÷ 20 = $2.45

You can do the same type of figuring to find out the weekly rate of a job that pays $6,200 a year.

Total yearly salary $6,200
Total weeks in year   52
Weekly rate $6,200 ÷ 52 = $119.23

To find out the hourly rate when your weekly salary is $119.23, simply divide by the number of work hours in the week, 35.

Total weekly salary $119.23
Total weekly hours   35
Hourly rate $119.23 ÷ 35 = $3.406 *or* $3.41

Section Two
Earnings by the Piece

Nora Sweeney is a good artist and always liked to paint. Her job with the Bargain Art Company requires that she paint small country scenes. Her paintings are then sold to stores.

Earning on a piece-rate basis: earning money for each item produced.

The Bargain Art Company pays Nora $4.50 for each scene she paints. We say Nora is paid on a *piece-rate basis* because she is paid for each "piece," or item, she completes. She does not receive a regular salary.

Computing Daily Earnings by the Piece

Nora painted seven farm scenes yesterday. How much did she earn?

Paintings completed	7
Pay per painting	$4.50
Daily wages	$7 \times \$4.50 = \$31.50$

Computing Weekly Earnings by the Piece

One reason Nora likes her job is because she has a lot of freedom. She can work wherever she pleases—at home or by a brook. She can also work whenever she likes—in the evenings or on weekends.

Last week Nora completed the following number of paintings. Monday, 7; Tuesday, 9; Wednesday, 0; Thursday, 3; Friday, 12; Saturday, 6. How much did she earn?

Paintings completed	$7 + 9 + 0 + 3 + 12 + 6 = 37$
Pay per painting	$4.50
Weekly wages	$37 \times \$4.50 = \$166.50$

Combining Piece-Rate Earnings and an Hourly Rate

Many companies don't pay their employees on a straight piece-rate basis. At Banya Television Company, employees receive an hourly wage *plus* a bonus for each item they complete above a certain number. For example, Ben Bryan receives an hourly wage of $4.35 for wiring TV receiver components. In addition, he earns a bonus of $.42 for each component over 120 that he wires. Yesterday Ben worked 7 hours and wired 131 components. How much did he earn?

Hourly wages	$7 \times \$4.35 = \$30.45$
Bonus pieces	$131 - 120 = 11$
Bonus wages	$11 \times \$.42 = \$4.62$
Total earnings	$\$30.45 + \$4.62 = \$35.07$

Exercises for Section Two

1. Compute the total daily earnings for the following employees. (These employees are working on several different types of

products, which explains the differences in the pay per piece and the number of pieces completed.)

Employee	Pieces Completed	Pay per Piece	Total Daily Earnings
a. S. Campbell	18	$2.07	$ 37.26
b. P. Martinez	264	.16	_____
c. W. Watson	47	.58	_____
d. H. Ishikawa	28	1.65	_____
e. N. Jarman	56	.43	_____

2. At Stone Cookware Company, Jane Silva runs a machine which fastens handles onto frying pans. Jane earns $3.87 an hour plus a bonus of $.26 for each frying pan she completes above 190 a day. Find her weekly earnings. (Round off to the nearest cent.)

	Hours Worked	Daily Wages	Pieces Completed	Bonus Pieces	Bonus Wages	Total Daily Earnings
a. Monday	8.0	$ 30.96	207	17	$ 4.42	$ 35.38
b. Tuesday	3.5	_____	81	_____	_____	_____
c. Wednesday	8.0	_____	190	_____	_____	_____
d. Thursday	8.0	_____	241	_____	_____	_____
e. Friday	8.0	_____	236	_____	_____	_____
f. Total	_____	_____	_____	_____	_____	_____

3. Martha Haynes earns $.185 for each box of fruit she picks. What were her earnings on a day when she filled 136 boxes?

4. Lee Yama works for a flower shop where he earns a regular weekly salary of $85.40. He also receives $.45 for each flower arrangement he completes. This week he arranged 58 special flower orders. What are Lee's total weekly earnings?

5. Every day Paula Christensen receives $1.26 for each piece she completes over 48 pieces. She also earns a regular daily wage of $27.48. Paula completed 62 pieces today. What are her total earnings for the day?

6. Stanley Newton has a job at which he hand-paints dishes. He earns $.37 for each dish he paints. He also earns $2.55 an hour. During one 7-hour work day, Stanley painted 47 dishes. What were his earnings for the day?

7. Besides earning $2.85 an hour, Cliff O'Neill receives bonus pay for fast work. For items packaged each day beyond 105, he earns $.19 per package. What were his total earnings during one 8-hour day in which he packaged 142 items?

Section Three
Earning by Selling on Commission

Commission:
a certain
percentage of
total sales.

Many salespeople earn a *commission*, which is a certain percentage of their sales. William Janovic sells copying machines. Others sell cars, vacuum cleaners, magazine subscriptions, or other products that consumers want and need.

Computing a Straight Commission

William Janovic is paid a *straight commission*. This means that his weekly earnings are based on a certain percent of his total sales. Since he receives no regular salary, he must depend on his sales each week to earn a worthwhile living.

Daily Earnings on Commission

William's commission is 12.5 percent on each machine he sells. One day he sold a machine for $1,750. What was his commission that day? (Remember to change the percent to a decimal before you multiply: 12.5% = .125.)

Sales commission $1,750 × .125 = $218.75

Copy Center Inc. 391 Fourth Ave. Chicago, IL 60603				May 19, .19. —		
				SALES SLIP NO. 613		
Name *Central Alarm Co.*						
Address *4193 Elm Ave.*						
Chicago, IL 60607						

Clerk *W.J.*	Cash	C.O.D.	Charge ✗	On Acct.	Retd.	Paid Out
QTY.	DESCRIPTION			UNIT PRICE		AMOUNT
1	#3264			1,750 00		1,750 00

Sales slips, such as the one shown above, make it easier to keep track of William Janovic's sales.

Weekly Earnings on Commission

William Janovic sold several copying machines last week. Here are his sales: Monday, $575; Tuesday, 0; Wednesday, 0; Thursday, $2,490; Friday, 0. Since his commission rate is 12.5 percent, what were his earnings for the week?

Total sales $575 + $2,490 = $3,065

Commission $3,065 × .125 = $383.125 *or* $383.13

Exercises

1. The salespeople listed below work on commission at Cromwell Discount Store. Compute the amount of commission each earned yesterday.

Employee	Department	Total Sales	Commission Rate	Commission Earned
a. P. Brady	Appliances	$1,156	7%	$ 80.92
b. T. Diaz	Shoes	408	11%	_____
c. R. Hampton	Carpeting	1,694	8%	_____
d. M. Miller	Auto supplies	1,828	4.5%	_____
e. L. D'Arcy	Stereo	2,472	3.5%	_____

2. Compute the weekly commissions earned by the employees of Cromwell Discount Store. Use the commission rates shown in Exercise 1 for these salespeople. (If necessary, round off the weekly commission to the nearest cent.)

Employee	Mon.	Tues.	Wed.	Thurs.	Fri.	Total Sales	Weekly Commission
a. P. Brady	$385	$ 739	$1,045	$ 74	$ 962	$ 3,205	$ 224.35
b. T. Diaz	639	128	457	83	706	_____	_____
c. R. Hampton	455	0	638	1,146	257	_____	_____
d. M. Miller	347	298	936	458	1,267	_____	_____
e. L. D'Arcy	573	1,599	2,836	996	1,645	_____	_____

Salary Plus Commission

Maria Cruz, a friend of William Janovic, works for another company and sells radios. Maria receives a regular salary plus a commission. Her commission rate is 4.5 percent on all sales over $500 a week. (A salesperson who earns a regular salary works for a lower commission rate than someone who works on a straight commission rate.)

Maria receives a regular salary of $200 a week. Her total sales during the first week of November were $1,275. How much did she earn that week?

Total weekly salary	$200
Total sales over $500	$1,275 − $500 = $775
Commission rate on sales	4.5%
Commission on sales	$775 × .045 = $34.875 *or* $34.88
Total earnings	$200 + $34.88 = $234.88

Skilled employees are required in many factories to ensure that a quality product is produced.

Exercises

The employees listed below all receive a weekly salary. They also receive a 5-percent commission on sales over $550 a week. What were the weekly earnings for these employees? (If necessary, round off the commission to the nearest cent.)

Employee	Weekly Salary	Weekly Sales	Sales over $550	5-Percent Commission on Sales	Weekly Earnings
1. A. Casey	$225	$1,810.35	$1,260.35	$ 63.02	$ 288.02
2. K. Weber	220	1,296.70	_____	_____	_____
3. D. Payne	225	862.55	_____	_____	_____
4. L. Jahnz	145	2,477.25	_____	_____	_____
5. N. Nunez	215	1,465.75	_____	_____	_____
6. J. Simon	230	1,902.45	_____	_____	_____
7. M. Gibbs	145	1,602.40	_____	_____	_____
8. A. Stein	155	2,961.85	_____	_____	_____
9. J. Cleary	205	2,116.35	_____	_____	_____
10. E. Jensen	195	2,375.60	_____	_____	_____

Comparing Earnings

Suppose Maria and William each have the same amount of total sales during one month. Which of them will earn more money?

Maria Cruz had total monthly sales of $7,730 in December. Shoppers bought her company's new line of inexpensive radios for holiday presents. In addition, she received her regular salary of $200 per week. How much did she earn for that month? (Remember that she receives a commission of 4.5 percent on sales over $500 a week. Since we will work out this problem on the basis of four weeks in the month, we will deduct $2,000—or $500 × 4—from Maria's total sales.)

Total weekly salary	$200
Total monthly salary	$200 × 4 = $800
Total sales over $2,000	$7,730 − $2,000 = $5,730
Commission rate on sales	4.5%
Commission	$5,730 × .045 = $257.85
Total earnings for month	$800 + $257.85 = $1,057.85

William Janovic also had total sales of $7,730 during December. Remember that he is paid a straight commission of 12.5 percent of his total sales. What were his earnings for that month?

		Total sales	$7,730		
		Commission	$7,730 × .125 = $966.25		

Do you think that a person who receives a salary plus commission would always earn more than someone who receives a straight commission? Why or why not? How could the amount of salary make a difference? The rate of commission?

Exercises for Section Three

1. Compute the monthly earnings of the following salespeople who receive a salary plus commission on sales. (In this and the following exercises, round off the commission earned to the nearest cent, if necessary.)

Employee	Regular Monthly Salary	Total Sales	Commission Rate	Commission Earned	Total Monthly Earnings
a. T. Roe	$350	$ 7,615.40	6.5%	$____495____	$____845____
b. J. Hoke	504	6,157.50	8.0%	_____	_____
c. K. Conrad	415	4,035.75	7.0%	_____	_____
d. B. Seals	730	27,145.20	3.5%	_____	_____
e. D. Dove	645	19,328.00	2.5%	_____	_____
f. S. Jones	340	12,040.85	4.5%	_____	_____
g. R. Cortez	610	8,615.30	4.5%	_____	_____
h. P. Ponti	504	14,910.25	3.5%	_____	_____
i. F. Martin	520	17,053.00	2.25%	_____	_____
j. L. Billings	472	8,919.90	3.75%	_____	_____

2. Ned Blanton receives a salary of $275 a week plus a commission of 3.7 percent on sales over $350 a week. His sales totaled $1,132 this week. How much did he earn on commission? What were his total earnings this week?

3. Peg McCall receives a straight commission of 10 percent. Hy Ramos receives a salary of $250 a week plus a commission of 2.5 percent on sales over $300 a week. Compute their monthly earnings if each totals $27,000 in monthly sales.

4. Art Baldwin receives a regular $135 weekly salary plus 5.5-percent commission on monthly sales over $23,000. Rod Greene earns a $615 monthly salary plus a 3-percent commission on monthly sales over $25,000. Compute their monthly earnings if each totals $30,381 in monthly sales.

5. Jim Lee earns a 6.5-percent straight commission on monthly sales. Sue Kane earns a weekly salary of $124 and a 9-percent commission on monthly sales over $12,000. Compute their monthly earnings if each totals $15,976 in monthly sales.

REVIEW FOR CHAPTER 1
EARNING AN INCOME

1. Last week Gary Allen baby-sat for 16 hours. If he received $1.15 an hour for his work, what were his total earnings?
2. As a clerk in a hardware store, Phil Markovits earns $2.63 an hour. What were his total earnings for the week if he worked for 38 hours?
3. Henry Rowe was among the workers who repaired power lines damaged by a storm. His weekly earnings during this crisis period were based on the following hours of work.
   a. First week: 40 hours at regular hourly rate ($5.07)
   b. Second week: 40 hours at regular hourly rate
                     16 hours at time-and-a-half
                     11 hours at double time

   What amount did Henry earn each week? (Round off his time-and-a-half rate to the nearest cent.)
4. Wally Goodman worked 9 hours on Monday, 9 hours on Tuesday, 10 hours on Wednesday, and 11 hours on Thursday, but he didn't go to work on Friday. His hourly rate is $3.48. He earns time-and-a-half pay for any hours worked beyond 40 in one week.
   a. What was the amount of Wally's earnings for the week?
   b. If Wally had worked 8 hours on Friday, what would have been his total weekly earnings?
   c. What additional amount would Wally have earned by working that one extra 8-hour day?
5. Peg Murphy is paid monthly on a straight commission basis. During a 4-week month, her weekly sales figures were $5,320, $3,578, $6,630, and $4,685. What were her total earnings at a 7.5-percent commission rate? (If necessary, round off the commission to the nearest cent.)
6. The base weekly salary for Jim Torre's job is $115. For sales over $750 a week, he earns 4.5-percent commission. What did Jim earn during a week in which his total sales were $3,849.80? (If necessary, round off the commission to the nearest cent.)

7. Sam Knox works 7 hours a day and earns $3.18 an hour. Sam was late on three mornings out of five: 22 minutes on Monday, 14 minutes on Tuesday, and 24 minutes on Friday. Altogether, Sam had five quarter-hours of pay deducted from his weekly paycheck.

   a. What amount of pay did Sam lose because of his lateness? (Round off to the nearest cent.)
   b. What amount did Sam receive for the week's work?

8. Rita Ortega is helping take the local census. She earns $.45 for each census form she completes. Today she went to 51 homes and completed 36 forms. What were Rita's earnings for the day?

9. At Daley's Radio and TV Repair Shop, Alice Moto earns $4.28 an hour plus $2.15 for each electrical appliance she repairs. What are Alice's earnings for a week in which she worked 40 hours and repaired 34 appliances?

10. Max Goldblatt earns a $560 monthly salary plus a 13.5 percent commission on his weekly sales over $1,825. Here are Max's sales for the month of February: $2,176, $1,643, $1,963, $2,748. What did Max earn in February? (If necessary, round off the commission to the nearest cent.)

CHAPTER

2 Your Paycheck

After Jack Victor had worked a week at his new job, he went to the office to pick up his paycheck. As he waited, two other employees, Joan and Marty, examined the checks they had received.

"I would be much happier," said Joan, frowning, "if I could stop paying these taxes."

Her co-worker, Marty, pretended not to understand. "Which taxes do you mean, Joan? The federal taxes, the state taxes, or the social security taxes?"

"All of them," she said. "I'm not choosy."

Jack smiled. But he knew that taxes would affect his paycheck too. Jack's employer would *deduct*, or subtract, certain amounts of money from his total earnings. These amounts are usually called *deductions*. The money deducted from Jack's pay would be held aside in order to pay his taxes. Like his co-workers, Jack wasn't happy about this, but he knew that the government required the deductions. He also knew that the deductions would determine exactly how much money he could spend as a consumer. All employees should be aware of the ways their earnings are handled by their employers.

Section One
Gross Earnings and Net Pay

Jack looked at his paycheck. It said, *Pay to the order of Jack Victor $158.87.* This is the amount he received for his week's work, even though his salary is $222 per week. What happened to the rest of his money?

Period Ending	Hours Worked	Rate	Regular	Overtime	Total	Federal Withholding	FICA	State Withholding	Savings	Insur.	Total	Amount	Ck. No.
2/20/--	40	5.55	222.00	--	222.00	34.40	13.43	8.80	5.00	1.50	63.13	158.87	6418
			Earnings			Deductions						Net Pay	

Employee's Pay Statement
Detach and retain for your records.

Name Jack Victor

NORTH ATLANTIC TELEPHONE
490 W. Howell St.
Beaufort, New York 11801

50-2781
213

Payroll Check No. 6418

February 20, 19 --

Pay To
The Order Of Jack Victor - $ 158.87

One hundred fifty-eight and 87/100 - Dollars

FIRST NATIONAL BANK
Beaufort, New York

Anne Jackson
Treasurer

⑆0213 ⑈2781 4310 ⑇ 264⑈

Attached to his check was his *pay statement,* a list of his earnings and deductions. It explained where his money went. Look at Jack's gross earnings, the total amount of money earned during the pay period. Jack did earn $222 that week. But Jack, like his friends and all wage earners, had deductions taken from his gross earnings. These amounted to $63.13. *Net pay,* also called *take-home pay,* is the income left after all deductions have been subtracted from the gross earnings.

Gross earnings: total amount of income earned.

Net pay: income left after all deductions have been subtracted.

Total gross earnings	$222
Total deductions	$34.40 + $13.43 + $8.80 + $5 + $1.50 = $63.13
Total net pay (take-home)	$222 - $63.13 = $158.87

Exercises for Section One

1. Compute the net pay for the employees whose gross earnings and total deductions are given on page 22.

Employee	Gross Earnings	Total Deductions	Net Pay
a. H. Booth	$378.95	$108.84	$ 270.11
b. V. Lin	287.22	73.91	_____
c. E. Sherman	926.40	366.30	_____
d. G. Schaefer	103.65	18.50	_____
e. M. Reyes	247.80	91.79	_____
f. C. Tibaldi	315.00	103.15	_____
g. K. McMillan	285.75	99.43	_____
h. T. Jacobson	308.20	100.78	_____
i. F. Snyder	525.82	226.94	_____
j. E. Fitzgerald	146.77	24.07	_____

2. Mark Callahan earns $78.35 each week, but $12.48 is taken out for deductions. What is Mark's weekly net pay?

3. Valerie Porter has the following amounts deducted from her weekly earnings: $5.38, $12.87, $2.76, $.45, $2.50. What are her total deductions?

4. Polly McClellan earns $247.85 a week. These are the amounts of her deductions: $14.99, $35.80, $8.65, $1.25, $7.50. What is the amount of Polly's weekly net pay?

5. Kevin Berg earns almost as much each week as Polly does, but Kevin doesn't have so many deductions. These amounts are deducted from Kevin's earnings: $14.52, $33.40, $6.02. What is Kevin's weekly net pay if he earns $239.95 a week?

6. Richard Rivera has a full-time job and a part-time job. He earns $92.43 on one job, and his weekly deductions are $14.79. He earns $38.70 on the other job, and his deductions are $5.81. What are Richard's total earnings? What are his total deductions? What is Richard's total weekly net pay?

Section Two
Required Deductions

In Chapter 1, when you computed weekly earnings by the hour, by the piece, or by a commission on sales, you were figuring gross earnings. Now you know that all wage earners, no matter how they are paid, have certain amounts deducted from their gross earnings. Of course, deductions such as those for income taxes are required by the government. (In the next section, you'll see that other deductions, such as for insurance, are chosen by the employee.)

Federal Income Tax

Withhold: to deduct for tax purposes.

34.40
Federal Withholding

Withholding allowance: amount of income freed from taxes.

Federal income tax must be paid by all employees. In some cases, state and city income tax must also be paid. For this purpose, an employer must *withhold* money that is deducted from an employee's gross earnings. The withholding is treated as an advance tax payment and sent to the government.

Look again at Jack's statement of gross earnings and deductions. Notice the deductions withheld by his employer. One of these amounts is for federal income tax: $34.40.

Each year, the government sets a minimum amount for incomes that can be taxed. Only people with incomes above this minimum pay federal income tax. Taxes provide a large part of the federal government's money. They help pay the costs of national defense; the salaries of government employees; the costs of transportation, housing, education; and many other government expenses.

Withholding Allowances. The amount of taxes withheld by an employer is based on the employee's gross earnings, marital status, and the number of withholding allowances claimed. A *withholding allowance* frees a certain amount of income from being taxed. When the number of withholding allowances increases, the amount of taxable income decreases. The number of allowances claimed depends on answers to the following questions, among others.

1. Does the employee hold one or more than one job?
2. Does the employee pay for the support of any other person?
3. What is the employee's age?

When Jack first began work at his new job, he filled out an Employee's Withholding Allowance Certificate, also known as a *Form W-4.*

Form W-4

Department of the Treasury
Internal Revenue Service

Employee's Withholding Allowance Certificate
(Use for Wages Paid After May 31, 19—)

This certificate is for income tax withholding purposes only. It will remain in effect until you change it. If you claim exemption from withholding, you will have to file a new certificate on or before April 30 of next year.

Type or print your full name
Jack Victor

Your social security number
320-61-8626

Home address (number and street or rural route)
133 Maple Avenue

Marital Status
☒ Single ☐ Married
☐ Married, but withhold at higher Single rate

Note: If married, but legally separated, or spouse is a nonresident alien, check the single block.

City or town, State, and ZIP code
Beaufort, New York 11801

1 Total number of allowances you are claiming **1**
2 Additional amount, if any, you want deducted from each pay (if your employer agrees) . . . . $
3 I claim exemption from withholding (see instructions). Enter "Exempt" . . . .

Under the penalties of perjury, I certify that the number of withholding exemptions and allowances claimed on this certificate does not exceed the number to which I am entitled. If claiming exemption from withholding, I certify that I incurred no liability for Federal income tax for last year and that I anticipate that I will incur no liability for Federal income tax for this year.

Signature ▶ **Jack Victor**   Date ▶ **February 12** , 19 —

Dependent: person who receives more than one-half of his or her financial support from the taxpayer.

On Jack's Form W-4, he claimed one allowance. Jack is single, so he claims only himself as a dependent. If Jack were married with two children and if his wife were not employed, he would claim himself, his wife, and both children—a total of four dependents. A *dependent* is one who relies on the taxpayer for over half of his or her financial support. The taxpayer pays for most of the dependent's food, clothing, shelter, and other expenses.

SINGLE Persons — WEEKLY Payroll Period

And the wages are—		And the number of withholding allowances claimed is—					
		0	1	2	3	4	5
At least	But less than	The amount of income tax to be withheld shall be—					
$ 94	$ 96	$ 10.40	$ 7.80	$ 5.40	$ 3.00	$ .70	$ 0
96	98	10.70	8.10	5.70	3.40	1.10	0
98	100	11.10	8.50	6.00	3.70	1.40	0
100	105	11.70	9.10	6.60	4.20	1.90	0
105	110	12.60	10.00	7.40	5.00	2.70	.40
110	115	13.50	10.90	8.30	5.80	3.50	1.20
115	120	14.40	11.80	9.20	6.60	4.30	2.00
120	125	15.30	12.70	10.10	7.50	5.10	2.80
125	130	16.20	13.60	11.00	8.40	5.90	3.60
130	135	17.10	14.50	11.90	9.30	6.70	4.40
135	140	18.00	15.40	12.80	10.20	7.60	5.20
140	145	18.00	16.30	13.70	11.10	8.50	6.00
145	150	20.00	17.20	14.60	12.00	9.40	6.80
150	160	21.60	18.60	16.00	13.40	10.80	8.20
160	170	23.80	20.60	17.80	15.20	12.60	10.00
170	180	26.00	22.80	19.70	17.00	14.40	11.80
180	190	28.30	25.00	21.90	18.80	16.20	13.60
190	200	30.70	27.20	24.10	20.90	18.00	15.40
200	210	33.10	29.60	26.30	23.10	19.90	17.20
210	220	35.50	32.00	28.60	25.30	22.10	19.00
220	230	38.10	34.40	31.00	27.50	24.30	21.20
230	240	40.90	36.80	33.40	29.90	26.50	23.40
240	250	43.70	39.60	35.80	32.30	28.80	25.60
250	260	46.50	42.40	38.40	34.70	31.20	27.80
260	270	49.30	45.20	41.20	37.20	33.60	30.20
270	280	52.10	48.00	44.00	40.00	36.00	32.60
280	290	54.90	50.80	46.80	42.80	38.70	35.00
290	300	57.70	53.60	49.60	45.60	41.50	37.50
300	310	60.80	56.40	52.40	48.40	44.30	40.30
310	320	64.00	59.40	55.20	51.20	47.10	43.10
320	330	67.20	62.60	58.00	54.00	49.90	45.90
330	340	70.40	65.80	61.20	56.80	52.70	48.70
340	350	73.60	69.00	64.40	59.70	55.50	51.50
350	360	76.80	72.20	67.60	62.90	58.30	54.30
360	370	80.40	75.40	70.80	66.10	61.50	57.10
370	380	84.00	78.80	74.00	69.30	64.70	60.10
380	390	87.60	82.40	77.20	72.50	67.90	63.30
390	400	91.20	86.00	80.80	75.70	71.10	66.50
400	410	94.80	89.60	84.40	79.20	74.30	69.70
410	420	98.40	93.20	88.00	82.80	77.60	72.90

Using an Income Tax Withholding Table. Jack's employer assigns the job of computing the employees' weekly withholdings to the payroll clerk, Sandra White. Sandra begins with federal income tax withholdings. She uses a wage bracket table like the one shown on page 24. These rates may change from year to year as tax laws change. (Note that this table is for single persons who are paid once a week. Different tables are used for married persons, and for persons who are paid twice a month, once a month, and so on.)

Sandra uses Jack's gross earnings as a guide to the withholding for his federal income taxes. Sandra looks under the At Least column for wages and finds the figure $220. That's pretty close to Jack's weekly wage of $222. She then checks the But Less Than column next to the $220. It reads $230. Is $222 at least as much as $220, but less than $230? Yes. Sandra has found the correct column. Now Sandra looks to the right. She finds the column for one withholding allowance. The amount to be withheld is listed as $34.40. This is the same amount shown on Jack's statement of gross earnings and deductions.

Exercises

Determine the federal income tax withheld from the gross earnings of the employees listed below. Assume that all are single and paid weekly. Use the wage bracket table illustrated on page 24.

Employee	Weekly Gross Earnings	Withholding Allowances	Federal Income Tax Withholding
1. M. King	$137.45	1	$ 15.40
2. S. Gross	185.40	3	
3. K. Ramirez	326.17	5	
4. B. Seig	247.63	2	
5. L. Shelton	115.34	4	
6. V. Wong	175.00	1	
7. T. Kyle	147.54	3	
8. H. Graves	361.83	5	
9. I. Sedasky	178.36	4	
10. J. Short	281.90	3	

State Income Tax

Many states also require wage earners to pay state income taxes. These help pay the costs of hospitals, schools, highways, parks, and other state expenses. State taxes are also withheld from employees' paychecks. In most states, tax laws permit the same allowances as the federal tax laws. Tax rates are different, however, from state to state.

Now Sandra uses a state income tax table like the one following. (You can see that state taxes are much less than federal taxes.) The state tax is found in the same way that the federal tax is found. Sandra again uses Jack's gross earnings of $222 a week as a guide. She reads across the $220 line to the column for one exemption. ("Exemption" is sometimes used in the same way as "withholding allowance".)

Sandra finds the amount of $8.80. This is the same amount shown on Jack's pay statement.

| 8.80 |
| State Withholding |

STATE WEEKLY WITHHOLDING TAX TABLE

WAGES		EXEMPTIONS CLAIMED					
At Least	Less Than	0	1	2	3	4	5
		TAX TO BE WITHHELD					
$86	$88	$2.50	$2.00	$1.50	$1.10	$ .70	$ .40
88	90	2.60	2.10	1.60	1.20	.80	.40
90	92	2.70	2.20	1.60	1.20	.90	.50
92	94	2.70	2.20	1.70	1.30	.90	.50
94	96	2.80	2.30	1.80	1.40	1.00	.60
96	98	2.90	2.40	1.90	1.40	1.00	.70
98	100	3.00	2.50	2.00	1.50	1.10	.70
100	105	3.10	2.60	2.10	1.60	1.20	.80
105	110	3.40	2.80	2.30	1.80	1.40	1.00
110	115	3.60	3.00	2.50	2.00	1.50	1.10
115	120	3.90	3.30	2.70	2.20	1.70	1.30
120	125	4.20	3.50	2.90	2.40	1.90	1.40
125	130	4.40	3.80	3.10	2.60	2.10	1.60
130	135	4.60	4.00	3.40	2.80	2.30	1.80
135	140	4.90	4.20	3.60	3.00	2.50	2.00
140	145	5.10	4.40	3.80	3.20	2.60	2.10
145	150	5.30	4.70	4.00	3.40	2.80	2.30
150	160	5.70	5.00	4.30	3.70	3.10	2.60
160	170	6.20	5.50	4.80	4.10	3.50	2.90
170	180	6.80	6.00	5.20	4.60	3.90	3.30
180	190	7.30	6.50	5.70	5.00	4.40	3.70
190	200	7.90	7.00	6.30	5.50	4.80	4.20
200	210	8.50	7.60	6.80	6.00	5.30	4.60
210	220	9.10	8.20	7.30	6.50	5.80	5.00
220	230	9.70	8.80	7.90	7.10	6.30	5.50
230	240	10.30	9.40	8.50	7.60	6.80	6.10
240	250	11.00	10.00	9.10	8.20	7.30	6.60
250	260	11.70	10.70	9.70	8.80	7.90	7.10
260	270	12.50	11.50	10.50	9.50	8.60	7.70
270	280	13.30	12.30	11.30	10.30	9.40	8.50
280	290	14.20	13.10	12.10	11.10	10.10	9.20
290	300	15.20	14.00	12.90	11.90	10.90	9.90
300	310	16.10	14.90	13.80	12.70	11.70	10.70
310	320	17.00	15.90	14.70	13.50	12.50	11.50

Exercises

Compute the state income tax withheld from the gross earnings for the following employees. Use the tax table shown above.

Part 1 EARNING AND BUDGETING

Employee	Weekly Gross Earnings	Withholding Allowances	State Income Tax Withholding
1. R. Dahl	$156.00	3	$ 3.70
2. P. Webster	290.00	1	_____
3. A. Jacobs	118.45	4	_____
4. G. Sanchez	173.80	2	_____
5. R. Yang	202.05	3	_____
6. E. Davidson	210.45	2	_____
7. P. Hernandez	241.57	4	_____
8. L. Morgan	196.40	3	_____
9. S. O'Brien	259.65	5	_____
10. A. DuPont	134.35	2	_____

The money deducted from an employee's paycheck is spent in many different ways. For example, the government often uses taxes to provide funds for medical and scientific projects. This young woman is involved in medical research.

FICA: Federal
Insurance
Contributions
Act. Also known
as *social security*.

Another deduction required by law is the social security withholding. The law is known officially as the Federal Insurance Contributions Act (FICA). During the years people work, they pay taxes into a social security fund. The Social Security Administration also requires employers to contribute the same amounts to the fund. These amounts are collected by the employer and sent to the government. The withholding rate is set by law and can be changed by Congress.

When Jack was hired, the rate was 6.05 percent on the first $17,700 of his earnings for the year. This means that if he reached the $17,700 mark, no more FICA taxes would be withheld until the next year. (The $17,700 amount can also change from time to time.)

How social
security helps
taxpayers.

The social security number assigned to Jack sets up an account with the U.S. Treasury Department for the rest of Jack's life. All withholdings from his earnings for social security will be deposited to the account. This government account will provide him with retirement pay, benefits for his dependents when he dies, income if he becomes disabled, and medical help when he retires.

The social security tax recorded on Jack's statement of gross earnings and deductions is $13.43. Payroll clerks have tables to compute these deductions. However, using the rate of 6.05 percent, one can find the tax simply by multiplying. First, the tax rate is changed to a decimal: .0605. Then the decimal is multiplied by his weekly gross earnings.

13.43
FICA

Weekly gross earnings	$222
Social security tax rate	.0605
Social security tax	$222 × .0605 = $13.431 *or* $13.43

DO YOU KNOW

that the federal government budgets its income from your tax dollars? Each year, the President's Office of Management and Budget has a plan that shows how each federal tax dollar is spent. The pie graph below is an estimate for a recent year. Notice that the pie graph representing a dollar is sliced up with the largest part, $.38, going for direct benefit payments to individuals. Another big part of the tax dollar, $.26, is spent on national defense. Also, the government pays out interest, such as on savings bonds. The interest payments will be $.07 of each dollar. When planning your budget, it might be helpful to estimate what part of *your* dollar income will be spent for major items, such as rent, transportation, clothing, taxes, and so on.

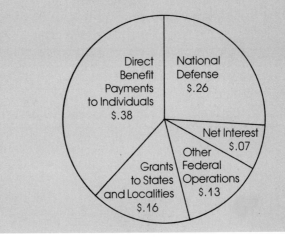

Exercises for Section Two

1. Compute the social security (FICA) tax deductions for each of these employees. Use .0605 as your tax rate. (If necessary, round off to the nearest cent.)

Employee	Weekly Gross Earnings	FICA Tax
a. S. Phillips	$119.00	$ 7.20
b. D. Neffman	231.00	_____
c. C. Craig	92.65	_____
d. R. Moore	182.19	_____
e. P. Agnelli	193.70	_____

2. Compute the total tax withholdings and the net pay for the following employees. Assume that the tax withholdings are the only amounts deducted from their gross earnings.

Employee	Weekly Gross Earnings	Federal Income Tax	State Income Tax	FICA Tax	Total Tax Withholdings	Net Pay
a. C. Johnson	$104.63	$ 9.10	$ 2.60	$ 6.33	$ 18.03	$ 86.60
b. S. Foster	223.82	31.00	5.50	13.54		
c. B. McDaniels	94.75	7.80	1.80	5.73		
d. R. Gonnelli	143.38	16.30	5.10	8.67		
e. W. Mathis	285.01	42.80	11.10	17.24		

3. Steve Silva's gross earnings are $370.20 each week. His net pay, the amount he takes home, is $288.10. What is the amount of Steve's weekly deductions?

4. Terry McFarland earns $195.30 a week. For federal income taxes, $27.20 is withheld. For state taxes, $6.30 is withheld. For social security (FICA) taxes, $11.82 is withheld. What is the amount of Terry's net pay after taxes are deducted?

5. If during one pay period Carl Brand earns $257.65, what amount is withheld for FICA taxes? (Use the rate of .0605. Round off to the nearest cent.)

6. On one of her part-time jobs, Anne Roe earns $121.40 a week. On another job, she earns $34.85 a week. What is Anne's gross pay each week for the two jobs combined? Compute her weekly net pay after the following taxes have been withheld.

	Job A	Job B
Federal income tax	$12.70	$ 0
State income tax	2.90	.10
FICA tax	7.34	2.11

7. Dan Hendricks earns $178.45 a week. Compute Dan's weekly net pay, using these deductions: federal income tax—$19.70, state income tax—$4.60, FICA—$10.80.

Section Three
Voluntary Deductions

Voluntary deductions: deductions an employee chooses to take.

One's net pay may be reduced by additional deductions from the gross pay. An employee may ask his or her employer to deduct certain amounts for various purposes. These are called *voluntary deductions.* Look again at Jack's statement of gross earnings and deductions. He has two voluntary deductions: for insurance, $1.50,

5.00	1.50
Savings	Insur.

Premium: money paid for insurance coverage.

and for savings, $5. To find the total cost of Jack's voluntary deductions, simply add them together: $1.50 + $5 = $6.50.

Many wage earners are covered by medical insurance plans that are set up for groups of people. The cost for this group insurance (and other kinds of insurance too) is called a *premium*. Employees' premiums are based in part on the number of dependents covered in their insurance programs. Jack's insurance plan covers himself only. His weekly premium is $1.50. How much is his monthly premium? His yearly premium?

Another deduction on Jack's weekly pay statement is $5 for savings. Jack has this amount withheld from his paycheck each week, and it is deposited directly into a savings account he has with his company's credit union. (You'll learn more about credit unions in Chapter 6.) How much will Jack save in a year?

Some other payroll deductions that employees request are for (1) life insurance, (2) savings bonds, and (3) charity contributions.

Fringe Benefits

Fringe benefits: goods and services that employers often give employees at low cost or for free.

Whether you're hunting for a job or have one, you will want to know what *fringe benefits* an employer offers. These are various goods and services that employers often provide employees for free or at a low cost. These goods and services cost less when purchased by an employer for groups of employees. What are some of the fringe benefits you should consider when choosing a job?

1. *Pension funds.* Most companies have plans to cover an employee's retirement, usually at age 65. A certain amount of money is deducted monthly from an employee's paycheck and set aside in a retirement fund. Employers sometimes contribute an equal, or matching, amount to the fund.
2. *Group health insurance.* Health insurance does not always require deductions. Many companies pay for all or most of the health insurance coverage for their employees. When purchased by the individual, health insurance is much more expensive than when purchased through a company, or group, plan.
3. *Educational benefits.* Quite a number of employers pay the tuition costs for further education and training of employees.
4. *Moving expenses.* If a company asks its employees to move to a new location, most of the moving expenses are frequently paid for by the company.
5. *Paid vacations and holidays.* The average vacation is two weeks, and most employers offer ten paid holidays.
6. *Profit-sharing plans.* Some companies offer a part of their profits to employees each year. Others set up a profit-sharing fund, free of federal income taxes, for employees. When employees retire

or leave the company, employees withdraw their shares and pay taxes at that time.

Of course, you may not wish to take part in all these plans. You would select the ones most important to you. If you are to pay any part of the cost, it will be handled through payroll deductions. In many cases, your employer will pay the entire cost.

In recent years many people have recognized that fringe benefits are as important as pay increases. For example, a person with high medical bills would benefit greatly by being enrolled in a good health insurance plan.

Exercises for Section Three

1. Compute the total voluntary deductions for each employee.

Employee	Life Insurance	Medical Insurance	Savings Bonds	Community Fund	Total Voluntary Deductions
a. J. Patrick	$ .55	$ 5.50	$ 3.50	$ .50	$ 10.05
b. G. Randall	1.65	24.00	75.00	5.00	
c. H. Colona	.85	11.00	0	0	
d. A. Ellis	.75	16.00	25.50	2.10	
e. M. Munez	.25	5.50	4.50	.75	

2. Compute the total deductions and the net pay for each of the following employees. (There are two rows for this exercise; don't forget the bottom row.)

Employee	Monthly Gross Earnings	Federal Income Tax	FICA Tax	Medical Insurance
a. J. Webb	$ 751.68	$ 69.00	$45.48	$12.00
b. T. Oakes	1,135.50	118.50	68.70	8.00
c. O. Golden	862.82	90.60	52.20	0
d. R. Kovac	1,076.93	115.30	65.15	12.00
e. C. Morrow	483.45	15.40	29.25	12.00

Employee	Savings Bonds	Community Fund	Total Deductions	Net Pay
a. J. Webb	$ 6.50	$1.50	$ 134.48	$ 617.20
b. T. Oakes	50.00	.75		
c. O. Golden	35.50	2.00		
d. R. Kovac	0	5.00		
e. C. Morrow	5.00	0		

3. Besides the amount withheld for taxes, Anita Montez has asked to have the following amounts deducted from her gross earnings: $.75 for life insurance, $11.50 for medical insurance, and $25 for a pension plan. What is the total of Anita's voluntary deductions?

4. Randy McBride earns $231.75 each week. These are his deductions: federal income tax—$36.80, state income tax—$7.30, FICA—$14.02, insurance—$.50, savings bonds—$3, community fund—$1.50. What is the total amount of Randy's deductions?

5. Neal Adams' weekly deductions are as follows: federal income tax—$20.60, state income tax—$4.20, FICA—$9.95, life insurance—$.75, medical insurance—$6, credit union—$12.50, community fund—$1.25. Neal's gross earnings are $164.50.
   a. What are Neal's total required deductions?
   b. What are Neal's total voluntary deductions?
   c. What is Neal's weekly net pay?

6. Sue Kaup's weekly earnings are the same as Neal's, $164.50, but Sue declares more withholding allowances than Neal does. She declares two allowances. Use the tables on pages 24 and 26 to find the following deductions for Sue, then compute her net pay. (If necessary, round off to the nearest cent.)
   a. Total required deductions (federal income tax, state income tax, FICA).
   b. Total voluntary deductions (credit union—$1.50, savings bonds—$.75).
   c. Net pay.

7. Bob Austin saves $12.50 a week. Rick Elliott saves $.75 a week. What amount will each save in a year?

DO YOU KNOW

how to protect yourself and your budget against rising costs? Balancing your income and your spending doesn't have to be a constant battle. Smart consumers use tested weapons such as the checklist below to stretch their dollars.

1. The item is really needed.
2. The item is of good quality.
3. The price is fair and reasonable.
4. No other item is less expensive and available.
5. The item is properly labelled.
6. The seller is reliable and reputable.
7. Special services are offered by the seller.
8. The item requires little maintenance.

Section Four
Inflation and Your Paycheck

Prices have been rising for everything. Social security taxes are climbing steadily. Wages are higher than ever, but you pay more income tax as your income increases. This is known as *inflation.* What does it mean to the wage earner?

Sally Williams, for example, earns more money now than she did three years ago. But she doesn't feel that she has any more money to spend.

Sally earned $8,000 three years ago. By now, she has received pay increases amounting to 30 percent. How much more does she earn now than she earned three years before? What is her new yearly income?

Income three years before	$8,000
Percent of increase	30%
Amount of increase	$8,000 × .30 = $2,400
New yearly income	$8,000 + $2,400 = $10,400

To find out why Sally doesn't feel that she has more money now, we need to ask some questions.

1. Does Sally actually have $10,400 to spend? No. Her new income is her gross pay. What she can actually spend is the net amount after taxes.
2. Is $10,400 worth the same amount as it was three years ago? No. If prices rise faster than Sally's income increases, then her new income may actually be worth *less* than her $8,000 was worth three years before. This would mean that she can buy less even though she has additional money.
3. Does Sally have the same needs and wants that she had three years ago? No. Like many other consumers, she now wants some of the luxuries she used to do without. And they now cost more than ever before.

Loss in Buying Power

One way to learn what Sally's dollar is worth in buying power is to use the *Consumer Price Index,* or *CPI.* The CPI measures the costs of goods and services in a given year. This kind of data is expressed in index numbers. An *index number* pinpoints an amount, such as a price, at a definite time. To see how amounts change over a space of time, we simply compare index numbers. A base number of 100 is usually used as a reference point.

Index number: pinpoints an amount, such as a price, at a definite time.

In the Consumer Price Index, the year 1967 is used as a base of comparison. That year is given the index number of 100. This means that for 1967, we will say that $100 bought goods and services worth $100. In other words, the buying power of $1 was $1.

Comparisons show that, in later years, this has changed. Today, the buying power of $1 is less than $1.

Look at the index below. It shows the values (by 1967 standards) for $1 in the years 1973 to 1976.

1967   100 cents
1973   75 cents, or 75% of its 1967 value
1974   68 cents, or 68% of its 1967 value
1975   62 cents, or 62% of its 1967 value
1976   59 cents, or 59% of its 1967 value

In a manner of speaking, 100 cents in 1976 was worth only 59 cents. The buying power of $1 has fallen drastically since 1967. So our money doesn't go as far as it once did. To understand the loss in buying power, let's compare two years—1973 and 1976—with the base year 1967.

In 1967, Sally could buy 50 candy kisses for $1. How many could she buy for $1 in 1973?

Number for $1 in 1967	50
Buying power of $1 in 1973	$.75 *or* .75
Number (rounded off) for $1 in 1973	$50 \times .75 = 37.5$ *or* 38

Let's see how many candy kisses Sally could buy for $1 in 1976.

Number for $1 in 1967	50
Buying power of $1 in 1976	$.59 *or* .59
Number (rounded off) for $1 in 1976	$50 \times .59 = 29.5$ *or* 30

Now you understand why Sally feels that her dollar doesn't go as far as it once did.

Almost every day, newspapers carry articles about worldwide inflation. How many articles can you find in your daily newspaper?

2033772

Exercises for Section Four

1. Each of the following wage earners has received raises over the past five years. For each one, compute the amount of the increase and the new yearly income.

Employee	Income 5 Years Before	Percent of Increase	Amount of Increase	New Yearly Income
a. M. Chandler	$6,700	34%	$ 2,278	$ 8,978
b. E. Ward	8,150	25%		
c. F. Perez	7,245	37%		
d. S. Schwartz	6,150	29%		
e. L. Ophus	9,430	32%		
f. G. Hoffman	5,965	41%		
g. V. Garrett	8,746	26%		

2. Compute the effect that inflation has had on each of the following items. Use the index on page 35 showing the buying power of $1 for the years 1973 to 1976. (Round off if necessary.)

Item	Number Bought for $1 in 1967	Number Bought for $1 in 1973	Number Bought for $1 in 1976
a. Raffle tickets	10	8	6
b. Thumbtacks	200		
c. Pencils	20		

3. Dale Morris earned $3,178 on his part-time job three years ago. Now his earnings have increased 17 percent. What is the amount of Dale's increase? How much does Dale earn now?

4. Don Petri's annual salary was $8,395 four years ago. His present salary shows an increase of 28 percent. What is the amount of Don's salary this year?

5. Last year, Rosa Tieg was earning $7,346. Her salary now has increased 8 percent. What is Rosa's present annual salary?

6. In 1967, Julie Jones could buy 4 loaves of bread for $1. How many loaves of bread could she buy in 1974 when $1 bought only a $.68 value? (Round off your answer.)

7. Debbie Green could buy 5 little house plants for a dollar in 1967. How many such plants could she buy for a dollar in 1976 when $1 was worth $.59? (Round off your answer.)

REVIEW FOR CHAPTER 2
YOUR PAYCHECK

1. Ned Gomez's gross earnings are $240.80 each week. His net earnings are $189.41. What is the amount of Ned's weekly deductions?

2. Dawn Farrell's weekly earnings and deductions statement shows her gross earnings as $164.50. Her federal income tax deduction is $20.60, her state income tax deduction is $5.50, and her social security deduction is $9.95. What is the amount of Dawn's net pay?

3. If Fred Foley's weekly gross earnings are $138, what amount will be deducted for his social security taxes? (Use the rate of 6.05 percent and round off your answer to the nearest cent.)

4. Bill Levin's weekly gross earnings are $221.80. Bill, who is single, claims only one withholding allowance—for himself. Sheila Besnier is also single and gets weekly gross earnings of $221.80. Sheila, however, claims three withholding allowances. Use the tables on pages 24 and 26 to answer these questions.
   a. What amount does Bill have deducted for federal income tax? Sheila?
   b. What amount does Bill have deducted for state income tax? Sheila?
   c. What amount does each have deducted for social security tax? (Use the rate of 6.05 percent, and round off your answer to the nearest cent.)
   d. What is Bill's weekly net pay?
   e. What is Sheila's weekly net pay?
   f. How much more is deducted for taxes from Bill's gross earnings than is deducted from Sheila's?

5. Helen Bridges is paid semimonthly, or twice a month. From each of her semimonthly paychecks the following amounts are withheld: federal income tax—$143.90, FICA—$44.31, medical insurance—$.65, credit union—$40. Helen's semimonthly gross earnings are $732.45. What is the amount of her net pay?

6. Karen Griffin's weekly gross earnings are $156.80. Her federal income tax is $21.60. Her state income tax is $5.
   a. Using the rate of 6.05 percent, compute Karen's social security tax deduction to the nearest cent.
   b. Compute her total deductions.
   c. Compute her total net pay.

7. These are the amounts deducted from Lee Gennaro's weekly salary: Insurance—$.75, FICA—$12.10, federal income tax—$31.40, state income tax—$7.60, credit union—$13, community fund—$50.
   a. What is the total of Lee's required withholdings?
   b. What is the total of his voluntary deductions?

8. In 19X4, Roger Turner earned $8,900 a year. By 19X7, his annual salary had increased to $11,800. The 6.05 percent FICA rate was in effect throughout this four-year period. How much more did Roger pay in social security taxes in 19X7 than he did in 19X4?

9. Jennifer Wolfe earned $5,624 five years ago. Her annual salary now has increased by 29 percent. What is Jennifer's present annual salary?

10. Annette Minsky earned $7,550 three years ago. Her annual salary has increased by 14 percent. What is the amount of the increase? What is Annette's present annual salary?

3

Budgeting Your Income

Money is earned mostly to be spent. Many people do not have enough money to buy all the things they want and need. They must spend carefully. But spending with care is something that every consumer should practice. Every day, we must all make good decisions about how to spend the money we have.

A decision to spend or not to spend can affect your life for months or even years. For example, you may decide to save your money for schooling a few years from now, instead of buying a costly stereo today. This kind of decision can bring you closer to your goals in life. Of course, your goals are the things that you aim toward, because they are really important to you.

Section One
Preparing a Budget

The most sensible spending is done by consumers who organize their money. Their secret is simple: they plan ahead. Planning ahead means making a *budget,* a financial plan. There are three steps to making a budget:

1. Decide what goals are important.
2. Estimate—or judge the amount of—monthly income after taxes.
3. Estimate expenses and savings.

Want to travel to faraway lands? If a vacation trip is one of your goals, careful budgeting can help you get there sooner than you think. Keep track of your spending, and maintain a strict savings plan. A good budget can help you visit unusual places, such as Asia Minor (shown here), or anyplace else you'd like to go.

When people clearly know their goals, they can make better decisions about spending and saving money. Goals are usually determined by a person's values, that is, by the way a person thinks he or she can get the most out of life. For example, William Janovic is twenty-three and works as a copying machine salesman. He attends college in the evening and plans to start his own mail-order business after college. Diane Perez is eighteen and a senior in high school. She works part-time in sales at the Century Department Store. Diane plans to go to medical school. Harvey Bellows, twenty, a real estate agent for Meadows Limited, has recently gotten married. Harvey and his wife Jill want to buy a home.

Getting an education, getting married, owning a business, and owning a home are all goals that require money. You can see that all of these young adults have defined their goals. Later you will examine the budgets prepared by William and Diane. You will see different approaches to making budgets.

Estimating Income

Budgets are usually set up on a monthly basis. The first step in setting up a budget is to estimate your monthly income; you must know how much income you expect to earn each month. List only the net amount of your regular pay, that is, your income after taxes and other deductions. For example, you may remember that Becky Smith earns $154 per week as a teacher's aide. After taxes and other deductions are taken out, she is left with a net of $128.28. To find her monthly net pay, simply multiply by 4: $128.28 \times 4 = $513.12. (Assume that there are 4 weeks in a month.)

Many people are paid semimonthly, or twice a month. If you are paid twice a month, simply multiply your net semimonthly pay by 2. The product will be your net monthly pay.

Maybe you do not receive regular weekly or monthly wages. You may receive your income in different ways, such as commissions, tips, fees, or an allowance.

William Janovic sells copying machines on commission. His income varies from week to week. William estimates his net monthly pay by taking an average of his net pay from last year. (He rounds off to whole dollar amounts.) He totals his monthly earnings. Then he averages the total.

Total monthly earnings	$726 + $520 + $611 + $788 + $641 + $595 + $320 + $651 + $643 + $721 + $980 + $1,109 = $8,305
Average monthly income	$8,305 \div 12 = $692.083 $ or $ $692.08

William earns, on the average, $692.08 a month. Some months he makes less, and other months he makes more. The average tells him what he needs to know for the purpose of budgeting. He can now plan ahead.

Exercises

1. Find the estimated monthly net income for each person listed below. Each is paid weekly. Assume that there are four weeks in a month. (If necessary, round off to the nearest cent.)

Name	Job	Weekly Net Pay	Estimated Monthly Income
a. M. Hill	Reporter	$224.25	$ 897.00
b. R. Jackson	Lawn mowing, baby-sitting	35.00	_____
c. J. Durey	Payroll clerk	176.35	_____
d. L. Ralston	Receptionist	106.75	_____
e. A. Zamora	Store clerk	195.50	_____
f. K. Davis	Gas station attendant	139.40	_____
g. S. Hastaja	Delivery truck driver	218.85	_____
h. R. Limon	Librarian	302.53	_____

2. Find the estimated monthly net pay for each person listed below. None of these people receive a regular salary. (If necessary, round off to the nearest cent.)

Name	Job	Monthly Net Pay			Average Monthly Income
a. E. York	Waiter	$ 649	$ 601	$ 544	$ 679.83
		808	543	598	
		710	688	650	
		903	713	751	
b. L. Flores	Lawyer	$2,593	$2,730	$2,262	_____
		2,475	1,945	3,891	
		1,428	2,356	1,740	
		1,659	3,385	1,465	
c. B. Clark	Electrician	$1,807	$ 960	$1,750	_____
		2,215	1,240	2,365	
		1,085	1,356	1,637	
		894	2,162	1,742	

William Janovic has broken his income down into a monthly average, as we have seen. His next step in setting up a budget is to estimate his monthly expenses. There are two types of these: fixed expenses and variable expenses.

Fixed expenses: expenses that don't change during the year.

Fixed Expenses. Fixed expenses are definite amounts that must be paid at certain times. These expenses are nearly the same every month. For example, William rents an apartment for $225 a month. In the future, his rent may go up, but for more than a year now it has stayed the same. Another fixed amount he pays each month is $58.21 for an automobile loan. William will have to pay the same amount every month for the next 15 months, until the car is completely paid for. His budget will help him do this.

Other expenses William has each month do change slightly. These are his telephone, electric, and gas bills. William knows, for example, that his telephone bill will be around $12.25 each month. Of course, it varies according to the number of telephone calls he makes. One month he made several long-distance calls, which cost more than local calls, and his bill was $19.48. But on the average, William must plan to pay the phone company $12.25 a month.

William also averages his electric and gas bills. Electricity costs him roughly $15 a month. His expense for gas is $8.50 a month on the average.

William cannot plan other kinds of expenses until he has budgeted for these fixed expenses. He has to be sure he can pay his rent, his auto loan, and his other bills first. He totals his monthly fixed expenses.

Auto loan	$ 58.21
Electricity	15.00
Gas	8.50
Rent	225.00
Telephone	12.25
Total	$318.96

William has now estimated his monthly fixed expenses. But he isn't finished. There are other fixed expenses he has to pay at different times during the year. These are not monthly payments. But William's plan is to set money aside for them each month.

One such expense is tuition. He will pay the college $90 in tuition twice this year, or semiannually. At both times that he pays tuition, he will need roughly $30 for books and $8 for supplies. William totals these costs and divides by 12 months.

Tuition plus books plus supplies	$90 + $30 + $8 = $128
Number of payments	2
Total amount	$128 \times 2 = $256
Amount budgeted monthly	$256 \div 12 = $21.333
	or $21.33

William also has to pay a $27 premium 4 times a year to insure his car. He includes the insurance costs in his budget too.

Insurance premium	$27
Number of payments	4
Total amount	$27 \times 4 = $108
Amount budgeted monthly	$108 \div 12 = $9

For his nonmonthly fixed expenses, William will set aside $21.33 for schooling and $9 for auto insurance each month. For his monthly fixed expenses, he will set aside $318.96. As we saw earlier, William earns around $692.08 a month. He now subtracts all his fixed expenses from his income. The net amount tells William how much money he has once his fixed expenses are taken care of.

Monthly income	$692.08
Total fixed expenses	$318.96 + $21.33 + $9.00 = $349.29
Net amount	$692.08 - $349.29 = $342.79

William has now budgeted his average monthly income to cover his fixed expenses. He learns that he has about $342.79 to spend or save.

Here's another way he budgets for nonmonthly payments. Suppose a payment of $51.39 is due quarterly. "Quarterly" means 4 times a year. And 4 times a year is *every 3 months*. To budget for these payments, he would plan to set aside one-third of the payment each month. So he would divide the quarterly payment by 3: $51.39 \div 3 = $17.13. By setting aside $17.13 each month, he would be fully prepared to meet the quarterly payment when 3 months have gone by. The trick is not to think of "quarterly" as meaning 4 months, because it doesn't.

Some payments are bimonthly. Bimonthly payments come along every 2 months. So, each month half the payment would be set aside.

Exercises

1. The people listed on page 45 have fixed expenses that are paid in various ways. Compute the amount each person should budget each month for the expense. (Round off to the nearest cent.)

Name	Expense	When Paid	Amount of Each Payment	Amount To Be Budgeted Monthly
a. P. Moore	Life insurance	Quarterly	$ 60.00	$ _20.00_
b. J. Dorsey	Magazine subscriptions	Yearly	24.00	_____
c. D. Groves	Gardening	Bimonthly	35.00	_____
d. D. Novotny	Cable television	Quarterly	25.52	_____
e. H. Baum	Disposal service	Bimonthly	10.84	_____
f. R. Day	Tuition	Quarterly	228.00	_____
g. E. Sartisian	Health insurance	Bimonthly	180.00	_____
h. M. Montini	Automobile insurance	Bimonthly	141.68	_____
i. S. Brill	Tuition	Bimonthly	350.70	_____
j. K. Simms	Automobile insurance	Semiannually	313.76	_____

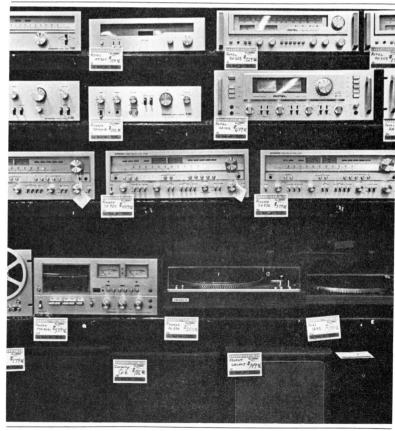

Whether you buy stereo equipment for $100 or $1,000, financial planning is a must. In fact, your ability to stick to your budget can affect the amount you plan to spend.

Variable Expenses. Our general expenses are called variable expenses. They vary from day to day according to our needs and wants. Food, clothing, transportation, and entertainment are variable expenses. Each time you shop for groceries, for instance, the amounts you spend are different. Also, there are some variable expenses you can't predict. They are special or sudden, as in the case of emergencies. And the money you save is an amount that changes at times.

Some variable expenses can be labeled "miscellaneous." They can be expenses for just about anything such as postage stamps, shampoo, laundry, and record albums.

Of course, some unplanned expenses are emergencies. Suppose you come down with a serious cold and have to visit a doctor. Have you budgeted to pay for the doctor's bill or for medicine? In other words, do you have a plan for expenses you could not plan for?

We've all been told that it's a good idea to save money. Savings are important to have for unplanned expenses. If you set money aside "for a rainy day," the expenses you couldn't predict won't take you too much by surprise.

How much should you budget for savings? Most people agree that 5 percent of your total net income is a good start. You may not be able to save that much. If you can't afford 5 percent, try to save 3 percent. Even 2 percent a month will add up fast.

The last time we saw William Janovic, he had budgeted for his fixed expenses. Now he turns to his variable expenses. (Refer to William's budget on page 47 as you read.) First, he decides to save 5 percent of his income. On page 41 we found his earnings to be around $692.08 a month. He computes his savings this way:

Monthly income	$692.08
Percent of savings	5% *or* .05
Monthly savings	$692.08 × .05 = $34.6040 *or* $34.60

By setting aside $34.60 each month, William prepares himself for unplanned expenses. Now he must examine his other variable expenses.

William has kept a list of his living expenses for the last four weeks. It gives him a clear idea of how much he spends and what he buys in goods and services. For example, here are his expenses for food for the four weeks: Week 1—$19.36, Week 2—$15.60, Week 3—$20.97, Week 4—$13.15. When he adds these amounts, William sees that he spends roughly $69.08 a month for food. He decides that $70 would be a wise amount to budget for food each month.

William Janovic
MONTHLY BUDGET

Estimated Income

Net pay	$692.08	
Total Estimated Income		$692.08

Estimated Expenses

Fixed Expenses:

Auto insurance	$ 9.00	
Auto loan	58.21	
Electricity	15.00	
Gas	8.50	
Rent	225.00	
Schooling (tuition, books, and supplies)	21.33	
Telephone	12.25	
Total Fixed Expenses		$349.29

Variable Expenses:

Clothing	$ 48.00	
Entertainment	54.00	
Food	70.00	
Miscellaneous	42.00	
Music lessons	32.00	
Savings	37.79	
Transportation	59.00	
Total Variable Expenses		$342.79
Total Estimated Expenses		$692.08

Let's look at the variable expenses budget William decides to use.

Clothing	$ 48.00
Entertainment	54.00
Food	70.00
Miscellaneous	42.00
Music lessons	32.00
Savings	34.60
Transportation	59.00
Total	$339.60

We have followed William step by step as he has made his budget. First, he estimated his monthly income. Then he budgeted for his fixed expenses. He computed that $342.79 was left after fixed expenses. This amount would cover his variable expenses. His variable expenses came to a total of only $339.60. William sees that he still has money left in his budget.

Budget after fixed expenses	$342.79
Total variable expenses	$339.60
Net amount	$342.79 − $339.60 = $3.19

William has planned his expenses well. He has $3.19 still in his budget. This means he is not spending more than he earns. If he sticks to his plan, he can afford what he needs and wants. He decides that the $3.19 should be added to his savings: $34.60 + $3.19 = $37.79.

Balanced budget: budget in which expenses and savings equal the amount of income.

Look at William's completed budget on page 47. The amount he spends and saves is the same as the amount he earns. William's budget is said to be *balanced*.

Exercises

1. The variable expenses for the following people are listed below. What is the total amount of each person's variable expenses?

Name	Variable Expenses		Total Variable Expenses
a. N. Forrest	Clothing	$20.00	$ 111.75
	Entertainment	8.00	
	Food	25.00	
	Miscellaneous	23.00	
	Savings	15.00	
	Singing lessons	20.75	

b. M. Hale	Automobile fuel	$53.00	_____
	Clothing	14.00	
	Entertainment	26.00	
	Food	76.00	
	Miscellaneous	19.50	
	Savings	26.00	
c. D. Horowitz	Clothing	$27.00	_____
	Dry cleaning	9.00	
	Entertainment	31.00	
	Food	96.00	
	Miscellaneous	23.25	
	Savings	48.00	
	Tennis lessons	17.50	
d. J. Nelson	Clothing	$31.00	_____
	Entertainment	19.00	
	Food	54.00	
	Savings	30.00	
	Swimming lessons	13.00	
e. A. Gonzales	Driving lessons	$45.00	_____
	Entertainment	12.00	
	Food	68.50	
	Miscellaneous	8.50	
	Savings	50.00	
	Sewing lessons	22.50	
	Sewing materials	37.00	

2. The net incomes of the following people for October are listed below. The percent of income saved is also given. What amount did each person save in October? (If necessary, round off to the nearest cent.)

Name	Net Monthly Pay	Percent Saved	Amount Saved
a. N. Roberts	$440	2%	$ 8.80
b. P. Ward	425	5%	_____
c. L. Nanni	583	4%	_____
d. R. Chin	510	4.5%	_____
e. P. Monet	487	3.5%	_____
f. G. Ellison	462	3%	_____
g. P. Lawson	531	2.5%	_____
h. R. Fiazza	608	2%	_____
i. C. O'Mara	486	6%	_____
j. R. Miller	707	4.5%	_____

When you start to work on your own budget, you may face different decisions than those William faced. Your finances may be less than his, while your goals are greater.

Diane Perez, whom you read about earlier, goes to high school and has a part-time job. And even though Diane's income is much smaller than William's, her goal—to go to medical school—is more expensive than his business college goals. She carefully follows her budget, which is shown on this page. One reason it is so unlike William's budget is that Diane lives at home. Her parents pay such expenses as rent, telephone, electricity, and major food costs.

After you've taken a close look at Diane's budget, go on to the exercises for Section One.

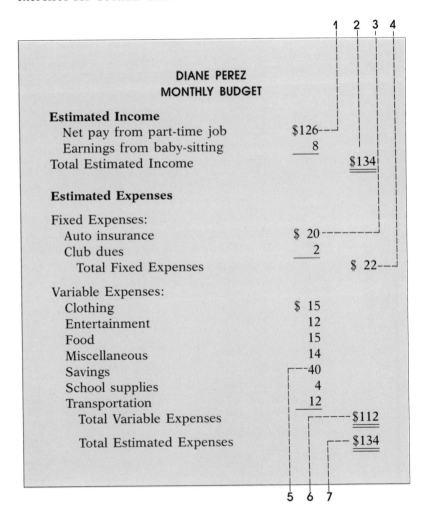

DIANE PEREZ
MONTHLY BUDGET

Estimated Income
    Net pay from part-time job $126
    Earnings from baby-sitting   8
Total Estimated Income $134

Estimated Expenses

Fixed Expenses:
    Auto insurance $ 20
    Club dues   2
        Total Fixed Expenses $ 22

Variable Expenses:
    Clothing $ 15
    Entertainment   12
    Food   15
    Miscellaneous   14
    Savings   40
    School supplies   4
    Transportation   12
        Total Variable Expenses $112

    Total Estimated Expenses $134

1. Diane got this figure by dividing 12 into her $1,512 yearly net pay ($1,512 ÷ 12 = $126).
2. Diane added the amounts of her estimated income to find the total ($126 + $8 = $134).
3. Diane got this amount by dividing 3 into her $60 quarterly premium for auto insurance ($60 ÷ 3 = $20).
4. Diane added the amounts of her estimated fixed expenses to find the total ($20 + $2 = $22). These expenses will remain the same every month.
5. Diane is saving money for books and tuition, so she budgeted almost 30 percent, far more than 5 percent, of her net income for savings.
6. Diane added the amounts of her estimated variable expenses to find the total ($15 + $12 + $15 + $14 + $40 + $4 + $12 = $112). These expenses may change from month to month.
7. Diane added the totals of her fixed and variable expenses to find her total estimated expenses ($22 + $112 = $134). Note that the total of her estimated expenses is the same as that of her estimated income. Her budget is balanced.

Exercises for Section One

1. Penny Lance pays $390 each quarter for college tuition. How much should she budget each month for tuition?

2. Jasper and Marie Danzia's annual insurance premium for their home is $174. Their annual car insurance premium is $219, and their annual life and health insurance premiums total $417.60. What is their yearly total for insurance premiums? What should they budget monthly for insurance premiums?

3. Set up a monthly budget for Walt Bauer. Model it after Diane Perez's. These are the amounts of Walt's estimated monthly income and estimated monthly expenses.
   Estimated income: net pay from job after school—$162.50, net pay from weekend job—$59.25.
   Estimated fixed expenses: auto insurance—$95.50, magazine subscriptions—$1.25, gym membership dues—$8.50.
   Estimated variable expenses: clothing—$13, entertainment—$22, food—$14, miscellaneous—$11.50, savings—$20, transportation—$36.

4. Kay Doyle is saving now in order to buy a piano as soon as she gets out of school. Kay is budgeting her income to ensure saving at least $550 for a down payment. She graduates in 15 months. Kay's estimated monthly income and estimated monthly expenses are given on the next page.

a. Prepare a budget for Kay. Kay plans to save any money remaining after she pays her expenses. How much does Kay plan to save each month?

b. If she follows her budget, what amount will Kay have saved by graduation?

Estimated income: net pay from part-time jobs—$185.

Estimated fixed expenses: auto insurance—$23, auto loan—$28, athletic club dues—$6.

Estimated variable expenses: entertainment—$23, clothing—$17, food—$13, miscellaneous—$14, transportation—$21.

5. Carol and Ken Kursch plan to buy a house next year. For a down payment they will need an additional $2,100 to add to their present savings. This means they must save $175 each month for a year. The Kursches have adjusted their variable expenses in order to save this monthly amount. Prepare their monthly budget based on the following income and expenses.

Estimated income: Carol's annual net pay—$6,300, Ken's annual net pay—$9,750, quarterly stock dividends—$63.

Estimated fixed expenses: auto insurance (quarterly)—$219, auto loan (monthly)—$253, furniture loan (monthly)—$77, life insurance (quarterly)—$51, medical insurance (bimonthly)—$18, rent (monthly)—$325, utilities (monthly)—$54.50.

Estimated variable expenses: entertainment (monthly)—$50, food (monthly)—$230, miscellaneous (monthly)—$25, savings (monthly)—$175, transportation (monthly)—$70.

Section Two
Keeping Your Budget Realistic

A few months ago, Bert Spangle moved from the suburbs to the city. He continues to work in the suburbs. So when Bert prepared a new monthly budget, he decided to spend $436 for variable expenses, including transportation. The next month he found he was spending about $25 *more* for gas and oil than he had budgeted. He had underestimated the costs of driving to and from his job every day. Bert had to *adjust*, or change, his budget to make it more realistic. He added $25 to his transportation expenses. He decided to spend $25 less for entertainment than the amount he had budgeted.

Bert tried to stay within his budget the following month. But he spent $15 more for clothing than he had estimated. He'd bought a shirt he really didn't need. This time he decided not to change his budget. It wouldn't happen again. By keeping good records, by watching his expenses carefully, and by shopping wisely, Bert will make a realistic attempt to stay within his budget in the next few months. He has learned that his budget must be followed if he is to live within his income.

Reasons for Adjusting Budgets

There are several reasons for adjusting budgets listed below.

1. Inflation, or sharp rises in consumer prices, may drive up the costs of food, clothing, transportation, and so on. You would have to budget higher amounts to pay for these necessities.
2. The loss of your job or a pay increase would alter the amount of your net income.
3. Emergencies or crises, such as a long hospital stay after an accident or illness, would reduce your income.
4. Additions to your family would increase your variable expenses.
5. Changes in tax rates or new taxes would affect the amount of your net income.
6. Underestimating or overestimating your expenses would require you to make adjustments.

Balancing Your Budget

Harvey Bellows is newly married. He and his wife Jill have vowed that their monthly budget will be realistic and always balanced. They have set up the system below.

1. They have estimated their total net monthly income.
2. They have listed all estimated fixed expenses as accurately as possible.
3. They have listed all variable expenses. At first, they listed everything they wanted to buy, even though they knew they couldn't afford some items. Then they cut down their spending on some variable items until the amount of their expenses equaled the amount of their incomes.
4. Jill keeps accurate records of all expenses. Small cash expenses are written in a notebook. Larger expenses are recorded on check stubs.
5. They add up their expenses each month and compare the expenses with the total amount of income available.

If you follow these rules, your expenses should come out less than or equal to your income. If they do not, some expenses must be reduced or cut out altogether.

	Balance Brought Forward		748	50
November Expenses	No. *342*			
	Date *Nov. 1,* 19 __			
Movie $ 7.00	Pay To *Jerome Ryan*			
Restaurant 11.50				
Pair of gloves 8.00				
Shampoo 2.50	For *Rent expense*			
Basketball game 6.00	*for the month*			
Bus fare to game 3.00	*of November.*			
Haircut for Harvey 5.25				
Charity 5.00				
Batteries 1.25	Total		748	50
Total $49.50	Amount This Check		320	00
	Balance Carried Forward		428	50

Above you can see a sample of Jill and Harvey Bellows' notebook record for November. What other types of expenses might they have included in their notebook? Would you include the same types of expenses in your own notebook? Also shown is a sample of a check stub for their rent expense. What other expenses might they record on their check stubs?

Using Percents in Budgeting

It is sometimes helpful to use percents when you want to see quickly what you are spending on an item in relation to your income. Harvey and Jill earn $690 in monthly net income. They budget $128 for their food expenses each month. What percent of their net income are they budgeting for food? To find out, divide the amount of the monthly income into the amount of the food expense.

Monthly income	$690
Food expenses	$128
Percent of income spent for food	$128 ÷ $690 = .185 *or* 19%

Exercises for Section Two

1. During a storm, a falling tree damaged Pat Reed's car. Since he doesn't have proper insurance, he has to save $405 to pay for repairs. Illustrated on the opposite page is Pat's present budget. He will have to make a number of adjustments to his budget in order to save the $405.

a. Make up a new budget for Pat using the following adjustments. Clothing—originally $25, subtract $10; entertainment—originally $49, subtract $29; food—originally $165, subtract $60; miscellaneous—originally $5, add $9; savings—originally $5, add $130; transportation—originally $75, subtract $40.

b. Be sure that Pat's budget is still balanced.

c. Find the number of months it will take Pat to save the $405.

2. Rather than live on such a restricted budget, Pat Reed found a part-time job. It pays $62 in monthly net pay. He also bought additional car insurance. Refer to Pat's original and adjusted budget figures in Problem 1.

   a. Make up a new budget for Pat using the figures given here. Auto insurance—originally $57, add $3; entertainment—originally $49, subtract $19; food—originally $165, subtract $35; miscellaneous—originally $5, add $13; transportation—originally $75, subtract $20.

   b. Be sure that Pat's budget is still balanced.

PAT REED
MONTHLY BUDGET

Estimated Income

Net pay	$497	
Total Estimated Income		$497

Estimated Expenses

Fixed Expenses:

Auto insurance	$ 57	
Medical insurance	3	
Rent	90	
Utilities	23	
Total Fixed Expenses		$173

Variable Expenses:

Clothing	$ 25	
Entertainment	49	
Food	165	
Miscellaneous	5	
Savings	5	
Transportation	75	
Total Variable Expenses		$324
Total Estimated Expenses		$497

3. Harvey and Jill Bellows have the following expenses recorded in their notebook for expenses in July. Compute the amounts by which they are under the budget or over the budget.
   a. *Clothing:* tie for Harvey—$5.50, shoes for Jill—$17, robe for Harvey—$15.75. *Clothing budget:* $35.
   b. *Entertainment:* movie—$12, dinner out—$15.50, circus—$23. *Entertainment budget:* $35.
   c. *Food:* Wednesday shopping—$54.40, Saturday shopping—$38.95, Tuesday shopping—$32.15. *Food budget:* $128.
   d. *Miscellaneous:* dental bill—$27, gift—$2.75, dry cleaning—$4. *Miscellaneous budget:* $50.

4. A camera that Lisa Bennet wants to buy costs $180. She hopes to save the amount by the end of five months. These are her income and expense amounts from January through May. What amount did she save each month? Is Lisa over or under in her savings toward the camera? By what amount?

Month	Income	Expenses	Savings
a. January	$76.50	$39.52	$ 36.98
b. February	69.25	31.30	_____
c. March	74.20	36.22	_____
d. April	71.64	32.90	_____
e. May	68.60	29.57	_____
f. Total	_____	_____	_____

5. What percent of her total income does Diane Perez budget for the following? (Use Diane's budget on page 50. If necessary, round off to the nearest whole percent.)
   a. Automobile insurance
   b. Entertainment
   c. Food
   d. Miscellaneous
   e. Savings
   f. School supplies

REVIEW FOR CHAPTER 3 BUDGETING YOUR INCOME

1. Fran Hudson wants to save for a new electric typewriter. In setting up her budget, she estimated that she has the following monthly income: baby-sitting—$30; mowing the lawn—$2.50; Saturday job—$41.65. Fran listed the following estimated expenses: clothing—$11.25; entertainment—$6; lunches—$8; miscellaneous—$8.50; school activities—$3.50. If Fran stays within her budget, what amount should she be able to save each month for her typewriter?

2. In preparing a monthly budget, Ross Price realized that his total estimated expenses were greater than his total estimated income of $638.50. Therefore, he adjusted his budget. Ross's original and adjusted budget allowances are given below.

   Original expenses: auto insurance—$29.50, auto loan—$126.80, clothing—$65, entertainment—$60, food—$85, miscellaneous—$42, personal improvement—$60, rent—$165, transportation—$55, utilities—$25.

   Adjusted expenses: auto insurance—$29.50, auto loan—$126.80, clothing—$40, entertainment—$45, food—$65, miscellaneous—$37, personal improvement—$35, rent—$165, transportation—$45, utilities—$25.

   a. By what amount is the original expense total greater than Ross's $638.50 income?

   b. What is the total of Ross's adjusted expenses?

   c. What amount should Ross be able to save each month if he stays within his budget?

3. By spring Amanda Ryan wants to have saved $1,000, part of the cost of her living room furniture. If she saves $143 a month for 7 months, she will have enough. Amanda has decided which variable expenses she will adjust. Use the income and expenses given here to prepare Amanda's adjusted monthly budget. The original amounts are given, plus the adjustments. You will have to compute the new amounts. For example, if Amanda's savings were originally $50 and she is now saving an additional $93, the adjusted amount is $143 ($50 + $93 = $143).

   Estimated income: monthly net pay—$645.

   Monthly estimated fixed expenses: auto insurance—$34, medical insurance—$3, rent—$215.

   Monthly estimated variable expenses: clothing—originally $42, subtract $14; dry cleaning—$10; entertainment—originally $65, subtract $25; food—originally $135, subtract $20; miscellaneous—originally $40, subtract $18; savings—originally $50, add $93; transportation—originally $50, subtract $15.

4. Jim Harrison wants to take an art course which begins next summer. The cost for the course will be $185. What amount should Jim budget each month if he has 8 months in which to save the $185?

5. Stewart Cohen has set up the following budget.

   Fixed expenses: auto insurance—$27.25, auto loan—$39.40, electricity—$24, rent—$182, tuition and books—$53.40, vacation loan—$22.50.

   Variable expenses: clothing—$20, entertainment—$30, food—$65, miscellaneous—$34, savings—$31.45, transportation—$36.

   a. What is the total of Stewart's fixed expenses?

b. What is the total of Stewart's variable expenses?

c. If Stewart's monthly net pay is $565, what percent of his earnings has he decided to save each month? (In this exercise and those following, round off to the nearest percent, if necessary.)

6. These are the totals of Al Worth's budget: Fixed expenses— $469; Variable expenses—$377. (Savings are not included in these figures.) Al's monthly net pay is $920.

a. What percent of his net pay does he budget for fixed expenses? (Hint: To find the percent he budgets for fixed expenses, divide the amount of his fixed expenses by the amount of his net pay.)

b. What percent of his net pay does he budget for variable expenses?

c. What amount of money can he save each month?

d. What percent of his net pay would his savings be?

7. Sid and Sandy Leffer's monthly net pay is $685. Each month they budget 49 percent of their income for fixed expenses and 51 percent for variable expenses, of which $34.25 is for savings.

a. What amount do they budget for fixed expenses?

b. What amount do they budget for variable expenses?

c. What percent of their earnings do they set aside for savings?

8. The Ericksons and the Bryans each have a total monthly net pay of $980. The Ericksons live in Minnesota, and the Bryans live in Florida. The Ericksons budget 5.5 percent of their monthly net pay for heating fuel; the Bryans budget only 1.5 percent.

a. What is the monthly amount budgeted by the Ericksons for heating fuel? By the Bryans?

b. By what amount is the Ericksons's annual estimated heating expense greater than the Bryans's?

9. In the summer, the Bryans use electricity for air conditioning. The Bryans' monthly electricity allowance is 5 percent of their $980 monthly net pay. The Ericksons' monthly allowance for electricity is 3 percent of their net pay.

a. What is the monthly amount budgeted by the Ericksons for electricity? By the Bryans?

b. How much more each month do the Bryans budget for electricity than the Ericksons do?

10. Even though the Bryans' and the Ericksons' expenses vary, both families save 7 percent of their monthly net pay. What amount does each family save monthly?

Consumer Challenge

Larry Gordon's income as a hair stylist has been growing steadily since he began work five years ago. The first year, he earned $855 a month, the second year $920 a month, the third year $1,066 a month, the fourth year $1,280 a month, and the fifth year $1,500 a month. Larry is very thrifty and has been able to save 15 percent of his gross income each year.

Larry has always wanted to own a hair salon in the city where he lives. This would cost about $28,000. He figures he will need most of the money he has saved these past five years to start a business. (He will leave some money in the bank for emergencies—an amount equal to two months' gross income for the fifth year plus all the interest his savings have earned.)

Larry has some ideas about how to go about getting his own business. These are some of the things he has thought of.

- Take additional courses in France and Italy in order to become even more accomplished.
- Speak to owners of hair salons about the problems involved in owning such a business, read any material that's available, and consult small business agencies.
- Go into business with one or more partners.
- Wait until he has saved more money.
- Borrow the additional money he needs.

To make a wise decision, Larry has to know how much money he has and what he can afford to spend. Do the following computations and answer the questions. Explain your answers.

1. How much money did Larry save during the first year? The second year? The third year? The fourth year? The fifth year? What is the total amount of his savings?
2. How much money did Larry decide to leave in his savings account for emergencies (not including the interest his money earned)?
3. How much money is left over? How much more money would he need to buy his own business?
4. What are the advantages and disadvantages of each of Larry's ideas?
5. Which idea or ideas do you think Larry should put into action?
6. Why do you think some people prefer to own their own business? Why do some people prefer to work for others?

For You To Solve

1. Harold Brown, Ronda Sullivan, and Fred Amato just graduated from Plainview High School. They each plan to work for a year, save some money, and then decide whether to go to college or continue working. Harold got a job working in a supermarket 40 hours a week at $3.20 an hour, with time-and-a-half for overtime over 40 hours. Ronda took a job in a factory stamping metal plates for highway signs. Her salary is based on piece work of $.15 per piece beyond a weekly quota of 1,000 pieces in a 40-hour week, for which she is to receive $2.80 an hour. Fred Amato's job is to sell shoes in a large discount store. He works on a straight commission of 12 percent on total weekly sales. Look at the work reports below for the week ending July 30.
   a. Harold Brown worked a total of 44 hours. What were his gross weekly earnings?
   b. Ronda Sullivan worked 40 hours and stamped 1,240 metal plates. What were her gross weekly earnings?
   c. Fred Amato's shoe sales for the week amounted to $1,260. What were his gross weekly earnings?

In Exercises 2 to 5, round off your answers to the nearest cent or nearest percent, when necessary.

2. When Harold, Ronda, and Fred received their first weekly paychecks, they saw that deductions had been made for federal income taxes and Social Security (FICA) taxes. In addition, each had chosen to have 10 percent of their gross earnings deducted for savings. Using the federal weekly withholding tax table on page 24, and the FICA tax rate of .0605 on gross earnings, compute the net pay each received. (Since all are single with no dependents, all took only one allowance on their Form W-4s.
   a. What was Harold Brown's net pay for the week?
   b. What was Ronda Sullivan's net pay for the week?
   c. What was Fred Amato's net pay for the week?

3. The three graduates have prepared budgets. Since all have different fixed and variable expenses, their budgets differ. Use the answers you obtained in question 2 and the budgets on the next page to compute the following for each employee.
   a. The monthly net pay (assume 4 weeks in a month).
   b. The total fixed expenses.
   c. The 10-percent savings for each.
   d. The total estimated variable expenses.
   e. The amount that remains that can be used for additional savings (net pay minus variable and fixed expenses).
   f. The adjusted percent of gross income put into savings.

	Harold Brown	Ronda Sullivan	Fred Amato
Monthly net pay	_____	_____	_____
Fixed expenses			
Installment purchases	$25.00	$23.00	$26.00
Insurance premiums	20.00	11.00	19.00
Room and board	90.00	98.00	100.00
Total fixed expenses	_____	_____	_____
Variable expenses			
Clothing	30.00	32.00	40.00
Entertainment	36.00	38.00	40.00
Food	28.00	30.00	30.00
Miscellaneous expenses	37.00	30.00	38.00
Personal care	15.00	25.00	24.00
Savings	_____	_____	_____
Transportation	26.00	35.00	38.00
Total variable expenses	_____	_____	_____
Additional savings (if any)	_____	_____	_____
Percent of gross income in savings	_____	_____	_____

4. Helen Taylor took a civil service job as a stenographer at $7,500 a year. She is paid weekly.
   a. What is her weekly gross rate of pay?
   b. Using the Income Tax Withholding Table on page 24, compute how much federal income tax is withheld. (She takes only one withholding allowance.)
   c. Using the social security withholding tax rate of .0605, and other voluntary deductions of an additional $40 per week, determine what Helen Taylor's weekly net pay will be.

5. Helen has begun to make a monthly budget. Make the calculations required to complete Helen Taylor's monthly budget.
   a. What is the amount of her monthly net pay? (Assume 4 weeks in a month.)
   b. Her fixed expenses are: installment payments—$15, life insurance—$10, music lessons—$12, room and board—$100, U.S. savings bond—$18.75. What is the total of her fixed expenses?
   c. What amounts should be budgeted if she plans to spend the following percents of her monthly net pay on the following variable expenses? Charitable donations—3%, clothing—10%, education—6%, entertainment—8%, gifts—4%, medical expenses—5%, miscellaneous—7%.
   d. What amount remains that can be used for additional savings?
   e. What percent of Helen's net income is the additional savings?

Banking and Credit

Performance Goals

When you finish work on this part, you should be able to:

- ☐ Compute bank service charges using various plans.
- ☐ Prepare deposit slips, checks, check registers, and reconciliation forms.
- ☐ Compute the cost of credit and the monthly and annual interest rates for loans.
- ☐ Compute simple interest.
- ☐ Compute monthly principal payments, monthly interest payments, total interest payments, and actual annual interest rates for add-on loans.
- ☐ Compute total interest and proceeds for discount loans.
- ☐ Compute interest charges for loans based on 360- and 365-day years.
- ☐ Determine annual interest rates by using an annual interest rate table.
- ☐ Compute total interest charges and actual annual interest rates for loans from credit unions, cash advances on credit cards, and loans from finance companies.
- ☐ Select loans that offer the best terms.
- ☐ Compute amounts of down payments, loans, and total finance charges of items bought on the installment plan.
- ☐ Compute charge account finance charges and balances.
- ☐ Identify minimum payment from a schedule of payments.
- ☐ Compute credit fees for a charge account purchase.

Using a Checking Account

Imagine tuning in a local department store with your Picturephone hookup. You dial the sporting goods department. In a flash, a whole selection of skis is running across your screen along with prices and identification numbers. You punch the number of the skis you want to order, and within hours they're delivered at your doorstep. How do you pay? The store dials the bank and charges your account for the amount you owe.

Or what about placing a specially coded plastic card in a slot on your telephone? You dial your bank's computer number, then you dial the amount of money you owe the supermarket. Presto—in seconds, an electronic voice tells you the exact amount you spent and how much is left in your account.

Far out? Not really. These two forms of banking are called EFT (Electronic Funds Transfer). EFT is a way to bank without writing a check. But widespread use of EFT is still in the future. So, until consumers have these new ways of handling their money, most of them will continue to use checking accounts. A *checking account* is a bank deposit against which the depositor writes checks. Checking accounts provide consumers with the following advantages.

1. A safe and convenient way of paying bills.
2. A record of paid expenses.
3. Proof that bills have been paid.

Section One
Selecting and Opening a Checking Account

There are a number of different types of checking accounts available. Tina Katz visited the local banks to select the checking account that would be best for her. Some of them had a monthly service charge plus a charge for each check. Some of them were free. Some plans included a credit line, which is a plan for borrowing money. Tina decided to look closely at two kinds of checking accounts—regular and special.

Regular Checking Accounts

Minimum balance: specified amount of money that must be kept in a bank account.

Service charge: bank fee for handling a customer's account.

Interest: money that banks pay customers for the use of the money they deposit in savings accounts.

In a regular checking account, Tina would have to keep a certain amount of money, called a *minimum balance,* in the account. At one bank, The First City Trust Company, the balance must be no less than $500 for each day of the entire month. If it ever drops below $500, the depositor must pay a service charge. A *service charge* is a fee charged by a bank for handling a customer's account. The service charge will be $2 if the monthly balance drops to between $300 and $499, and $3 if it goes below $300.

Tina didn't want to place $500 in a checking account. That's why she became interested in a plan at The Harrison Bank. This bank offers depositors a free checking account if they keep a minimum monthly balance of $500 in a *savings* account. If Tina were to let her savings account fall below $500 one month, the bank would make a service charge on her checking account. However, the money in her savings account would always be earning interest. *Interest* is money that banks pay customers for the use of the money they deposit in savings accounts.

Exercises

1. The people listed below have checking accounts at The First City Trust Company. Use the information above to find what service charge (if any) these people have to pay.

Name	Minimum Balance	Service Charge
a. M. Gleason	$450	$ 2.00
b. T. Stanton	264	_____
c. B. Albert	305	_____
d. A. Lopez	742	_____
e. T. Dana	497	_____

2. Morgan City Bank has a checking account plan with various service charges depending on the minimum balance. The minimum balances and service charges are listed on page 66.

Minimum Balance	Service Charge
0 to $ 99.99	$2.00
$100 to $199.99	1.50
$200 to $299.99	1.00
$300 and over	0

Find the service charge (if any) that the following customers at Morgan City Bank have to pay.

Name	Minimum Balance	Service Charge
a. L. Panzo	$432.00	$ 0
b. J. Henderson	87.50	_____
c. L. Lantelli	284.60	_____
d. V. Jensen	211.75	_____
e. L. Watkins	179.42	_____

Tina Katz pays for her exercise classes by check. Paying by check is convenient. It gives her a record of the payment. It's also safe. She doesn't have to carry a great deal of cash. Tina uses checks to pay for numerous goods and services. How many of these goods and services can you think of?

Special Checking Accounts

Tina also looked into the special checking account at The Harrison Bank. With a special checking account, the depositor is not required to keep a minimum balance. However, there is a monthly service charge. At The Harrison Bank, there is a monthly service charge of $.75 plus a charge of $.10 for each check written. If a depositor writes more than ten checks in one month, the bank does not charge the $.75. Instead, the depositor is charged only for the checks that are written. Here is how the charge is computed for one month during which a depositor writes 8 checks.

Charge for 8 checks	$8 \times \$.10 = \$.80$
Monthly service charge	$.75
Total charge	$\$.80 + \$.75 = \$1.55$

Here is how the charge is computed for one month during which a customer writes 11 checks.

Charge for 11 checks	$11 \times \$.10 = \$1.10$
Monthly service charge	0
Total charge	$1.10

Tina selected the special checking account. Since she has just started to work full-time, she knows it will be hard to keep the $500 minimum balance needed for the regular checking account plan. As soon as Tina has saved $500, however, she wants to change over to the regular checking account plan that requires that she keep $500 in a savings account.

Exercises for Section One

1. The people listed below have special checking accounts at The Harrison Bank. Use the information above to find the total charge each customer must pay.

Name	Checks Written	Monthly Service Charge	Total Charge
a. M. Wong	7	$ .75	$ 1.45
b. L. Quinn	4		
c. M. Noble	18		
d. C. Ricci	9		
e. J. Barth	6		

2. The Washington State Bank has no service charge for its special checking account. Instead, it uses the monthly schedule below, based on the number of checks written.

Number of Checks Written	Monthly Charge Per Check
The first 10 or fewer (1 to 10)	$.15
The next 10 (11 to 20)	.10
All checks over 20 (21 and over)	.05

The people listed below have special checking accounts at The Washington State Bank. Compute the monthly charge for each person.

Name	Checks Written	Monthly Charge
a. B. Remo	14	$ 1.90
b. C. Barry	8	_____
c. P. Divina	26	_____
d. R. Hopkins	12	_____
e. J. Lee	6	_____

3. During the last six months Ed Shelburn has had the following service charges: $3, $3, $3, $3, $2, and $3. What amount has Ed paid during this period for checking account services?

4. Ed could have had his checking account at a neighboring bank. In that bank, he would have had the following service charges: $1, $1.50, $1.50, $2, 0, and $1. What total amount of service charges would Ed have paid during the same six-month period at the neighboring bank?

5. Regina Watts has a special checking account. She pays an $.80 regular monthly charge plus $.10 for each check she writes. This month she wrote 8 checks. What was her total service charge?

6. Last month Lucy Barra wrote 7 checks. She paid $.15 for each check written but paid no monthly service charge. Her minimum balance for the month was $167. How much more or less would Lucy's service charge have been at a bank which charges a monthly service charge of $1.50 for accounts with a monthly balance below $199?

7. Joe Rasco wrote 19 checks during the past 3 months and kept a minimum balance of $225. At Central Savings Bank he would pay $.75 monthly plus $.10 for each check he writes. At Morgan City Bank he would pay $1 monthly if his minimum balance fell

below $300. How much would Joe pay in checking fees at Morgan City Bank? At Central Savings Bank? How much more would Joe pay at Central in service charges for the 3-month period than he would have paid at Morgan City?

Section Two
Your Checking Account

When Tina opened her account, Ms. Dixon, one of the bank officials, welcomed her. She accepted Tina's first deposit, which was $90. Ms. Dixon then helped her select the type of checkbook she wished to use. The bank would have Tina's name, address, and account number printed on her checks and on a set of deposit slips. These would be mailed to her.

Depositing Money

Deposit slip: list of the total amount of cash and checks deposited.

Every time Tina deposits money in her account, she must turn in a deposit slip with the money. The *deposit slip* lists the total amount of cash and checks deposited. Here is how Tina fills out a deposit slip.

1. She fills in the date. (Her name, address, and account number are already printed.)
2. She fills in the amount of cash—the paper money (also called currency) and coins she is depositing.
3. She fills in the amount of each check she is depositing.
4. She totals the cash and check amounts.

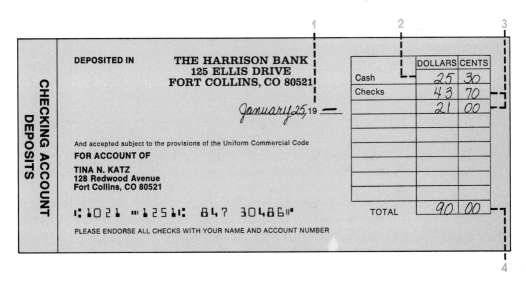

Exercises

1. Look at the deposit slip on page 69.
   a. How much cash did Tina deposit?
   b. How many checks did she deposit?
   c. What was the total amount deposited?

2. Terry Parsons made a deposit for his employer. There was a cash deposit of $32.25, and there were ten checks for the following amounts: $25.60, $10.55, $4.64, $5.98, $32.10, $11.12, $3.92, $14.90, $17.45, $7.85. What was the total amount of the deposit?

3. Robert Grady had a balance of $223.70 in his checking account. He made the following deposit: five $5 bills, $7 in nickels, and a check for $170.75.
   a. How much cash did he deposit?
   b. What was the total amount deposited?
   c. What was the new balance?

4. Laurie Billot had a balance of $104.53 in her checking account. She made the following deposit: Two $10 bills and one $5 bill, a check for $41.35, and another check for $33.11.
   a. How much cash did she deposit?
   b. What was the total amount deposited?
   c. What was the new balance?

Writing a Check

Check register:
place to record
checks, deposits,
and the account
balances.

A week later Tina received a box of 200 checks printed with her name, address, and account number. She also received a check register. A *check register* is a place to record checks, deposits, and balances in your account. For each check Tina writes and for each deposit she makes, she records an entry in her register.

The first check Tina wrote was to pay for a toaster at Harvey's Hardware. Note that when Tina wrote this check she used a pen. Also, she didn't erase or cross out anything. If she had made a mistake, she would have written another check. Here is how Tina writes a check.

1. She fills in the date of the check by writing the month, the day, and the year.

Payee: person or
business to
whom a check is
made out.

2. She writes the name of the payee. The *payee* is the business or person to whom the check is made out. Any blank space after the payee's name is filled with a wavy line.

3. She writes the amount of the check in figures. The figures are clearly written. They are placed right next to the dollar sign so that no one can write another number in front of the figures. Cents are written as a fraction of 100.

$$\frac{01}{100} \quad or \quad \frac{78}{100} \quad or \quad \frac{00}{100} \quad or \quad \frac{No}{100}$$

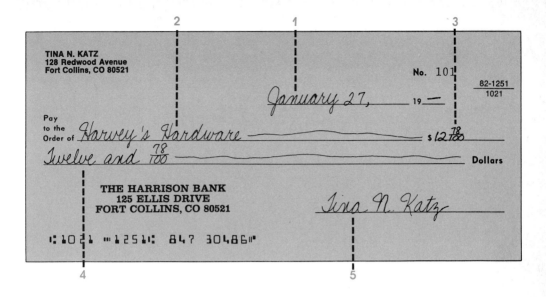

4. She writes the amount of the check in words. Cents are again written as a fraction of 100. She writes clearly and fills in any blank space after the amount with a wavy line.
5. She looks over the check to make sure it is correct before she signs it.

Tina followed all these steps when she wrote her first check to Harvey's Hardware. She also made sure she recorded the check in check register, which appears on the next page.

Recording a Check in the Check Register

Tina prefers to enter information about each check in her check register *before* she even writes the check. Also, as soon as she makes a deposit, she writes this amount in her check register.

Tina follows these steps to record her checks and deposits in her check register, which appears on the next page.

1. She writes the number of the check. Tina finds the check number on the upper right corner of the check. Her checks were sent to her with numbers already printed on them. Some people, though, number their own checks.
2. She writes the date.
3. She writes the payee's name and, on the next line, the reason for the check.
4. She writes the amount of the check, $12.78. Some people also write the amount of the service charge. Tina decides to deduct the service charges later. The bank will notify her of the total charge for the entire month.

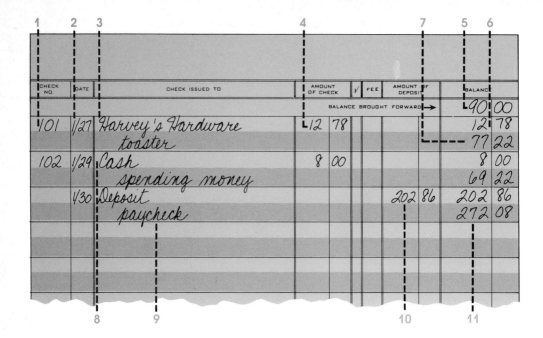

CHECK NO.	DATE	CHECK ISSUED TO	AMOUNT OF CHECK		√ FEE	AMOUNT OF DEPOSIT	BALANCE
				BALANCE BROUGHT FORWARD→			90 00
101	1/27	Harvey's Hardware	12 78				12 78
		toaster					77 22
102	1/29	Cash	8 00				8 00
		spending money					69 22
	1/30	Deposit				202 86	202 86
		paycheck					272 08

5. Her balance of $90, the amount deposited when she opened the account, is already entered.

6. She writes the amount of the check under the balance.

7. She subtracts the amount of the check from her old balance. Now she has a new balance of $77.22.

8. In order to get some spending money out of her account, Tina wrote a check with the word *Cash* on the line where the payee's name is normally written. She does not fill in her own name on that line. The amount was $8.

9. Tina deposited her paycheck by mail. She recorded the date and the description of her deposit.

10. She wrote the amount of the deposit, $202.86, in two columns.

11. She added the deposit, $202.86, to the previous balance, $69.22, to get a new balance of $272.08.

Exercises for Section Two

1. The checks Tina wrote and the deposits she made during February are listed on page 73. Complete Tina's check register for February. You may draw a check register or use the one in the activity guide. The first check is recorded in the activity guide as an example.

Check 103, February 1, to Ross Massero, for rent, $150.

Check 104, February 1, to *Cash*, for spending money, $10.

Check 105, February 1, to S. & W. Electric Corporation, for electricity bill, $12.13.

Check 106, February 3, to United Telephone Company, for phone bill, $6.48.

Check 107, February 9, to King Market, for groceries, $26.70.

Check 108, February 14, to John Katz, for John's eleventh birthday, $11.

February 14, deposit of paycheck, $202.86.

Check 109, February 16, to Lucille's Hair Styles, for hair trim, $5.75.

Check 110, February 19, to Berryhill Gift Shop, for parents' anniversary gift, $10.28.

Check 111, February 21, to *Cash*, for spending money, $20.

Check 112, February 25, to King Market, for groceries, $52.

Check 113, February 26, to Roland's Department Store, for sheets and pillowcases, $24.32.

February 28, Deposit of tuition refund, $45.

Check 114, February 28, to Robert MacIver, D.D.S., for dental work, $44.59.

2. Clyde Morrison made a deposit for his mother's dry cleaning shop. There was a cash deposit of $230.50, and there were seven checks for the following amounts: $2.75, $10.80, $3.50, $17.90, $21.25, $6.50, $14.75. What was the total amount of the deposits?

3. Prepare deposit slips for the following deposits. Refer to the example on page 69. Use your own name and address. Your account number is 8472681. For this and the next two exercises, you can draw forms like those on pages 69, 71, and 72 of the textbook. Or, you may use the forms in the activity guide.

Date	Currency, Coins	Checks
a. April 19, 19—	$36, $.75	$18.43, $6.56, $24.90,
b. May 13, 19—	$18, $1.34	$7.85, $53.40, $14.35, $5.62

4. Now prepare checks for the following payments in the same manner as you did the deposit slips. Refer to the example on page 71.

Check No.	Date	Payee	Amount
a. 331	January 14, 19—	Sandra Nunez	$ 93.45
b. 332	February 8, 19—	Robert Prince	148.50

5. Record the following checks and deposit in your check register. On March 4, your balance was $214.81.
   a. March 6, issued Check 314 for $19.03 to Lido Shoes for boots.
   b. March 6, issued Check 315 for $28.34 to High Light Shop for jacket.
   c. March 10, issued Check 316 for $2.67 to King Radio and TV for cassettes.
   d. March 15, deposited paycheck for $17.50.
   e. March 27, issued Check 317 for $24.62 to National Oil Company for gasoline credit card bill.
   f. April 3, issued Check 318 for $67 to Statewide Insurance Company for quarterly auto insurance payments.

DO YOU KNOW

the checklist for check writing?

1. Write checks in ink.
2. Fill out your check register first, and then write your check.
3. Check your math on the check register.
4. Write figures next to the dollar sign on each check.
5. Start the written amount of the check at the beginning of the line, and draw a wavy line to fill any space that is left.
6. Never sign a check on which the payee is left blank. Anyone can cash such a check.
7. Make no changes on a check once it's written.
8. Protect your checks as if they were cash. Keep them safe.
9. As soon as it arrives, reconcile your bank statement with your checkbook register.
10. Save your canceled checks as proof of payment.

Section Three
Balancing Your Checkbook

Bank statement: record that a bank sends the depositor.

Canceled check: check that the bank has deducted from the depositor's account and returned to the depositor.

Each month the bank sends Tina a bank statement. The *bank statement* is a record of check payments, deposits, and service charges, if there are any. Banks send these statements so that customers can keep their account records accurate. The bank also sends Tina canceled checks for each month with the monthly statement. A *canceled check* is a check that the bank has paid and deducted from a depositor's account. Canceled checks provide proof that an amount has been paid. They are usually stamped *Paid*. Tina compares the canceled checks with the bank statement. She makes sure that the bank has returned all the checks listed on the statement. Tina's statement gives the following information.

			THE HARRISON BANK 125 ELLIS DRIVE FORT COLLINS, CO 80521		

TINA N. KATZ
128 REDWOOD AVENUE
FORT COLLINS, CO 80521

ACCOUNT NUMBER   847-30486

PERIOD ENDING   FEBRUARY 28, 19--

Checks	Checks	Deposits	Date		Balance
			FEBRUARY	1	77.22
8.00				3	69.22
		202.86		4	272.08
150.00	10.00			7	112.08
12.13				8	99.95
6.48				10	93.47
26.70				16	66.77
		202.86		16	269.63
11.00				21	258.63
5.75				23	252.88
20.00				25	232.88
1.65 SC				28	231.23

Beginning Balance	Total Amount of Deposits	Total Amount of Checks Paid	Total Charges	Ending Balance
77.22	405.72	250.06	1.65	231.23

	Number of Deposits Made	Number of Checks Paid	Number of Other Charges	
	2	9	1	

Codes: CC Certified Check   OD Overdrawn
DM Debit Memorandum   RI Returned Item
EC Error Correction   SC Service Charge

Please examine this statement upon receipt and report at once if you find any difference. If no error is reported in ten days, the account will be considered correct. All items are subject to final payment.

1. The balance of Tina's account at the beginning of February. Tina had a balance of $77.22 on February 1.
2. Each check paid from Tina's account during February.
3. All deposits received from Tina during February.
4. The dates on which the bank paid the checks and received the deposits.
5. The balances during February. Each time a deposit was received or a check was paid, the bank computed a new balance.

6. The service charge for February, including the $.10 charge for each check. The bank deducted the amount ($1.65) from Tina's account. The service charge is labeled *SC*.
7. The balance in Tina's account at the end of the month. Tina had a balance of $231.23 on February 28.
8. The totals of the deposits received, checks paid, and charges made during February. Also the number of other charges.

Tina compared the last balance in her check register with the balance shown at the bottom right of the bank statement. The bank's balance is a higher amount. But she knows there are a number of possible reasons for the difference. It takes time for a check to be processed at a bank. So a check she has subtracted from her register may not be subtracted on the bank statement. Also, Tina may have made a mistake in computing her register. Or she may have forgotten to enter a deposit she made.

Sometimes the bank statement shows a lower balance than Tina's register. In this case, she may have forgotten to enter a check she wrote. And finally, she knows she has chosen to wait till she gets her statement to deduct the service charge.

Tina sets to work to *reconcile* the differing balances—that is, to make them agree with each other. She uses a reconciliation form, which is supplied as a helpful tool by the bank (see page 77). To reconcile her bank statement balance with her check register balance, Tina follows the steps below.

To reconcile balances: to make the bank statement balance agree with the checkbook balance.

1. She enters the final balance on the bank statement, $231.23.
2. She enters the balance shown in her checkbook register, $146.59.
3. Tina compares her copies of this month's deposit slips with the entries for deposits on the bank statement. Sometimes deposits are made too late to appear on the statement. These deposits are called *deposits in transit*. Tina has a deposit in transit of $45 which she enters on the reconciliation form. She enters the total deposits in transit, $45.
4. She adds the deposits in transit to the bank statement balance for a subtotal of $276.23.
5. She arranges the canceled checks by check number. In her checkbook, she puts a check mark (✓) next to each entry for which she has received the canceled check. Those she does not check off were not paid or not received by the bank in time to appear on the statement. They are called *outstanding checks*. Tina had four outstanding checks: Check 110—$10.28, Check 112—$52.00, Check 113—$24.32, Check 114—$44.59.
   Tina enters each of the check numbers and amounts on the reconciliation form. She fills in the total of her checks outstanding, $131.19.

Deposit in transit: deposit that was made but that does not appear on the bank statement.

Outstanding checks: checks that have not yet been paid by the bank when the monthly statement is prepared.

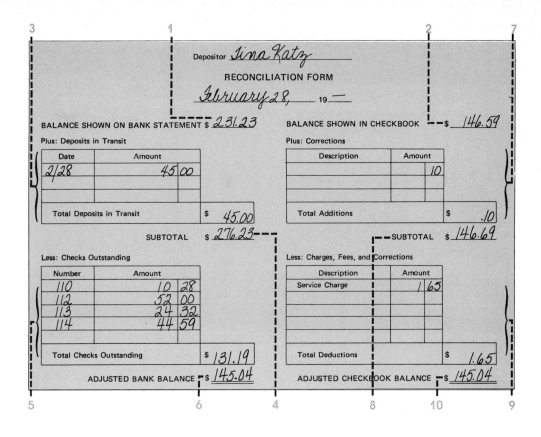

3   1   2   7

Depositor *Tina Katz*

RECONCILIATION FORM

February 28, 19 —

BALANCE SHOWN ON BANK STATEMENT $ *231.23*

BALANCE SHOWN IN CHECKBOOK --$ *146.59*

Plus: Deposits in Transit

Date	Amount
2/28	45 00
Total Deposits in Transit	$ *45.00*

SUBTOTAL $ *276.23*

Plus: Corrections

Description	Amount
	10
Total Additions	$ *.10*

SUBTOTAL $ *146.69*

Less: Checks Outstanding

Number	Amount
110	10 28
112	52 00
113	24 32
114	44 59
Total Checks Outstanding	$ *131.19*

ADJUSTED BANK BALANCE --$ *145.04*

Less: Charges, Fees, and Corrections

Description	Amount
Service Charge	1 65
Total Deductions	$ *1.65*

ADJUSTED CHECKBOOK BALANCE --$ *145.04*

5   6   4   8   10   9

6. She subtracts the total checks outstanding from the previous subtotal for the adjusted bank balance, $145.04.

7. Tina checks her arithmetic in her checkbook register to catch any error she might have made adding or subtracting an entry. And yes, she finds that she made a mistake when she entered Check 115. She subtracted $.10 too much in computing the balance. She will have to add the $.10 back in to correct her error. She enters $.10 in two places.

8. Correcting her $.10 mistake gives her a subtotal of $146.69.

9. Tina enters the service charge for this month, $1.65, in two places.

10. She subtracts the service charge from the previous subtotal for an adjusted checkbook balance of $145.04. And as you can see, it agrees with the balance shown on her bank statement. Tina has reconciled her bank statement with her checkbook register.

Now Tina must update her checkbook. She finds her new balance by subtracting the service charge from her old balance. And she adds $.10 to her balance to correct her mistake in the entry for Check 115.

DO YOU KNOW

what the unusual-looking numbers on your check refer to? Actually, they're a way to route checks. Banks receive thousands of checks every day and must sort through them in order to record the information in the depositors' accounts. Banks sort checks using MICR machines that read numbers printed in magnetic ink characters along the bottom of every check.

Look at the check below. On the lower left side of the check, two groups of numbers are printed in magnetic ink characters. The first group of eight characters indicates both the region of the country, called the Federal Reserve area, and the bank on which the check was drawn. The second group of characters shows the depositor's account number.

The fraction on the upper right side of the check is the American Bankers Association (ABA) number. The ABA number identifies the city or state number of the bank, the bank number, and the Federal Reserve number for the area.

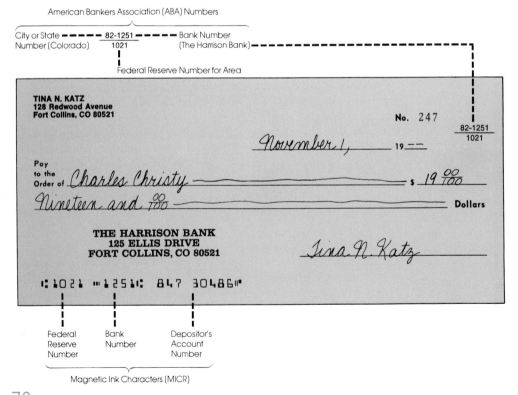

American Bankers Association (ABA) Numbers

City or State ▪ ▪ ▪ ▪ 82-1251 ▪ ▪ ▪ ▪ Bank Number
Number (Colorado)   1021   (The Harrison Bank)

Federal Reserve Number for Area

TINA N. KATZ
128 Redwood Avenue
Fort Collins, CO 80521

No. 247

82-1251
1021

November 1, _____ 19 --

Pay
to the
Order of Charles Christy _____ $ 19 00/100

Nineteen and 00/100 _____ Dollars

THE HARRISON BANK
125 ELLIS DRIVE
FORT COLLINS, CO 80521

Tina N. Katz

⑆1021⑆ ⑈1251⑈ 847 30486⑈

Federal   Bank   Depositor's
Reserve   Number   Account
Number   Number

Magnetic Ink Characters (MICR)

Suppose Tina forgot to record a check in her register. Or suppose she wrote in the wrong amount. She would include the correction on her reconciliation form. She would also adjust her checkbook. Below are the steps she would follow.

BALANCE SHOWN IN CHECKBOOK	$ *184.20*

Plus: Corrections

Description	Amount
Error, Register #121	10 00

Total Additions	$ *10.00*

SUBTOTAL $ *194.20*

Less: Charges, Fees, and Corrections

Description	Amount
Service Charge	1 65
Error, Register #124	9 00
Error, Register #130	8 50

Total Deductions	$ *19.15*

ADJUSTED CHECKBOOK BALANCE $ *175.05*

- If Tina wrote Check 121 to the market for $25, but recorded $35, she would write the difference of $10 ($35 − $25 = $10) in the Plus: Corrections box. She would add the $10 to any other corrections in the box and then find the total. Finally, she would correct her checkbook by adding $10 to the balance.
- If Tina wrote Check 124 for $21 to her mother, but recorded it as $12 in her checkbook, she would write the difference of $9 ($21 − $12 = $9) in the Less: Charges, Fees, and Corrections box. Then she would add the amount to the service charge and find the total. She would make the correction in her checkbook by subtracting this total from the balance.
- If Tina forgot to record Check 130 for $8.50 to Lee's Pharmacy, she would write the amount of $8.50 in the Less: Charges, Fees, and Corrections box. She would treat this correction as in the step above.

Sooner or later everyone has a problem balancing his or her checkbook. Suppose you can't reconcile your bank statement with your checkbook register. You've made sure that all canceled checks were subtracted in your register. You've subtracted your outstanding checks from the bank statement balance, and you've added your deposits in transit. You've made sure that the math in your register is correct. What do you do now?

Your best bet is to go to your bank. You should take your checkbook, monthly statement, canceled checks, and deposit slips with you. It's a good idea to go within ten days of receiving your statement. A bank employee can help you solve your problem but can do it most easily when the problem is handled as soon as possible.

Exercises for Section Three

For the following exercises you may draw your own forms or you may use the forms in the activity guide.

1. Keith Manfred received a bank statement for the period ending April 30. Use the information below to prepare a reconciliation form for Keith.

Bank statement balance:	$204.05
Checkbook balance:	$123.45
Checks outstanding:	Check 231–$44.25, Check 233–$7.05, Check 234–$31.20
Service charge:	$1.90

2. John Lightfoot's checkbook balance was $172.68 at the end of March. His March bank statement shows a $348.51 balance and a $3.25 service charge. John compared his check register with his canceled checks. He saw that he hadn't recorded Check 263 for $38.90 and Check 276 for $16.42. He also had the following outstanding checks: Check 261–$164.12, Check 274–$15.50, Check 279–$54.78. Prepare a reconciliation form for John.

3. Use the information below to reconcile Marian Thurston's February bank statement with her checkbook.

Bank statement balance:	$276.28
Checkbook balance:	$118.36
Checks outstanding:	Check 172–$25.35, Check 179–$84.66, Check 183–$6.19, Check 194–$46.27
Service charge:	$2.55

After examining her check register, Marian realized that she had forgotten to record her $2 service charge from January. Show this adjustment when you reconcile her February balances.

4. On April 30, Penny Meehan's check register shows a balance of $144.83. Her April bank statement balance is $362.24. These are the outstanding checks: Check 62 for $27.93, Check 67 for $58.45, Check 75 for $14.84, Check 77 for $36.56, and Check 80 for $77.78. Penny's April service charge is $4.15. Penny recorded Check 65 as $46.55 when she should have written $40.55. Show this adjustment on Penny's reconciliation form.

5. When Kerry McClain compared her canceled checks with her check register, she found two checks outstanding: Check 324 for $83.97 and Check 332 for $157.25. Her checkbook has a balance of $298.20. Kerry's bank statement does not show a deposit of $274.40, which she mailed to the bank on April 28. Refer to Kerry's bank statement to help you reconcile her balances.

KERRY MCCLAIN
351 GREENBRIER TERRACE
FORT COLLINS, CO 80521

ACCOUNT NUMBER 66-61571

PERIOD ENDING APRIL 30, 19--

Checks	Checks	Deposits	Date	Balance
			APRIL 1	249.60
34.45			2	215.15
		269.80	4	484.95
18.50			8	466.45
27.56	75.61		12	363.28
		22.10	16	385.38
155.00			17	230.38
		272.90	19	503.28
41.95	63.19		22	398.14
2.25	9.55			
8.95			25	377.39
		24.30	26	401.69
63.74			29	337.95
2.00 SC			29	335.95
72.93			30	263.02

Beginning Balance	Total Amount of Deposits	Total Amount of Checks Paid	Total Charges	Ending Balance
249.60	589.10	573.68	2.00	263.02

	Number of Deposits Made	Number of Checks Paid	Number of Other Charges	
	4	12	1	

REVIEW FOR CHAPTER 4
USING A CHECKING ACCOUNT

1. Herb Sol's minimum checking account balance for the month of March was $264.63. The fee on a minimum balance of below $299 is $.50. During March Herb wrote 13 checks which were paid by the bank. A charge of $.15 is made for each check paid. What was the amount of Herb's service charge for March?

2. The beginning balance in Iris Lopez's check register is $276.45. What would the balances be after each of the following items is recorded?
   a. A check—$39.20.
   b. A check—$58.58.
   c. A deposit—$57.44.
   d. A check—$8.95.

3. Given below are several of Doug McDaniels' check register entries and the resulting balances. Work through Doug's computations, correcting any errors you find. What is the corrected balance?

Entry No.	Amount	Balance
Check 304	$ 32.50	$430.43
Check 305	141.23	289.20
Check 306	78.46	210.74
Deposit	325.50	527.24
Check 307	9.98	516.26
Check 308	160.00	356.26
Check 309	72.66	283.59
Deposit	37.12	320.71
Check 310	26.59	294.12

4. Ann Parker's final check register balance is $192.56. Her September bank statement balance is $190.61. Ann has found that the balances differ only by the amount of the service charge. What was the amount of Ann's service charge for September?

5. During the month, Ron Hayes wrote checks for the following amounts: $6.48, $31.50, $17.95, $86.22, $43.76, $155, $4.37, $64.65, $29.41, $26.83, $54.15. Ron's bank statement indicates that the following amounts have been deducted from his checking account: $31.50, $155, $4.37, $86.22, $54.15, $43.76, $64.65. How many checks are still outstanding? What is the total of the check amounts still outstanding?

6. The last bank statement that Kelley Morgan received showed a final balance of $319.47 and a service charge of $2.55. According

to Kelley's check register, her account balance was $328.29. Reconcile Kelley's balance by preparing a reconciliation form. Make the following adjustments on the form: Check 263 for $21.48 outstanding, Check 251 for $18.75 not recorded in the check register, and Check 256 for $43.90 entered in her register as $34.90. Date the form May 31. For this exercise and Exercises 8 to 10, you may draw your own forms or use the ones in the activity guide.

7. Terry Wiggins has a special checking account at the First National Bank. His checks and deposits from February 28 to March 8 are shown in the register below. Review Terry's computations. What errors did he make? What should his corrected balance be?

CHECK NO.	DATE	CHECK ISSUED TO	AMOUNT OF CHECK	√	FEE	AMOUNT OF DEPOSIT	BALANCE
		BALANCE BROUGHT FORWARD →					303 45
87	2/28	Holly Drug Store	9 60				9 60
		vitamins					293 85
88	3/3	Valley Gas Company	13 81				13 81
		February bill					280 04
89	3/3	Trans-Motor Gas Corporation	27 42				27 42
		credit card statement					262 62
90	3/3	Mid-State Electric Company	18 30				18 30
		February bill					244 32
	3/5	Semimonthly paycheck				308 76	308 76
							553 08
	3/5	Refund on lamp returned				21 55	21 55
		(Cargo East Inc.)					575 63
92	3/6	Ryan Apartments	152 50				152 50
		March rent					423 13
93	3/6	Wanda Perez	3 50				3 50
		baby-sitting					419 63
94	3/6	Joe's Supermarket	48 22				48 22
		groceries					371 41
95	3/8	Harlow Men's Shop	11 75				11 75
		shirt					359 66

8. Starting with Terry's March 8 balance, complete the register computations for the items listed below and on page 85. (Set up your work as you did when you completed Tina Katz's check register on page 72.)

Check 96, March 9, to Walton's Garage, for car repairs—$34.50.

Check 97, March 10, to 32nd Street Cleaners, for jacket cleaned—$4.75.

FIRST NATIONAL BANK

40 Chelsea Street
Jacksonville, FL 32204

Terry Wiggins
3 Elmwood Drive
Jacksonville, FL 32204

ACCOUNT NUMBER 36-09834

PERIOD ENDING March 31, 19--

Checks	Checks	Deposits	Date	Balance
			March 1	303.45
9.60			2	293.85
		308.76	5	602.61
		21.55	5	624.16
50.00			6	574.16
48.22			9	525.94
152.50			10	373.44
3.50	11.75		12	358.19
34.50			13	323.69
4.75	18.30		17	300.64
27.42	13.18		18	260.04
15.80	32.95	308.76	20	520.05
1.30 SC			27	518.75

Beginning Balance	Total Amount of Deposits	Total Amount of Checks Paid	Total Charges	Ending Balance
303.45	639.07	422.47	1.30	518.75

Number of Deposits Made	Number of Checks Paid	Number of Other Charges
3	13	1

Codes: CC Certified Check   OD Overdrawn
DM Debit Memorandum   RI Returned Item
EC Error Correction   SC Service Charge

Please examine this statement upon receipt and report at once if you find any difference. If no error is reported in ten days, the account will be considered correct. All items are subject to final payment.

Check 98, March 15, to Mayfield Department Store, for two shirts—$15.80.

Check 99, March 17, to Joe's Deli, for groceries—$32.95.

Check 100, March 17, to Wanda Perez, for baby-sitting—$3.75.

Deposit, March 20, of semimonthly paycheck—$308.76.

Check 101, March 21, to *Sun and Sports* Magazine, for one-year subscription—$6.

Check 102, March 23, to Mayfield Department Store, for raincoat—$41.29.

Check 103, March 27, to Surety Insurance Co., for semiannual car insurance premium—$47.50.

Check 104, March 30, to Travel Posters, for one poster—$.95.

9. Shown on page 84 is Terry's bank statement for the period ending March 31, 19—. Prepare a reconciliation form to reconcile the bank statement balance with the ending balance in Terry's check register.

10. When Anne Burnett compared her canceled checks for May with the amounts in her check register, she realized she had incorrectly written Check 308 for $98.50 as $48.50, Check 326 for $92.35 as $72.35, and Check 320 for $20.82 as $28.82. Anne's final checkbook balance before making the corrections was $194.52. She had no checks outstanding for the month. Her May bank statement shows a final balance of $130.62 and a service charge of $1.90. Prepare Anne Burnett's reconciliation form for May.

DO YOU KNOW

about special banking services that you may need to use occasionally? Popularly known as "money substitutes," these services include cashier's checks, certified checks, and traveler's checks.

Cashier's checks are officially guaranteed checks issued against the bank's own account. Cashier's checks are a safe way to transfer large amounts of money from one place to another.

Certified checks are regular personal checks which a bank certifies with a special stamp. This guarantees the payee that the check is good.

Traveler's checks can be bought from banks in denominations of $10, $20, $50, $100, and larger amounts. Traveler's checks can be cashed throughout the world and are a safe way to carry money when traveling. If you lose traveler's checks, you can get your money back if you have a listing of the serial numbers of the checks.

CHAPTER 5

Borrowing Money From a Bank

Consumers today borrow more money than ever before. They are willing to pay money in order to get money to buy what they want. What are some of the things for which consumers borrow?

Mike Williamson is a telephone lineman earning a net income of $745 a month. He and his wife Margie plan to buy a house and new furniture. But Mike's earnings aren't enough for them to pay cash for these purchases, and their savings are limited.

The Williamsons realized they would have to borrow money. So they shopped around to find several places that offer cash loans. These include:

1. Banks or savings and loan companies.
2. Credit unions.
3. Credit card loans.
4. Small finance companies.
5. Loans from family or friends.

The Williamsons discovered that each place charged different interest rates. *Interest* is money that is paid for the use of someone else's money. The amount of the interest is added to the amount of the loan itself to determine the amount that must be repaid. The interest rates depend on the kind of loan and the amount of time it will take to repay it.

Mike and Margie decided to do business with a bank. In this chapter, we will learn about different kinds of bank loans. Chapters 6 and 7 will deal with loans from other sources.

Section One
The Cost of Consumer Credit

It costs money to borrow money. You pay a fee for money that's lent to you. The fee is the interest, and it is a percentage of the amount you borrow.

Credit: the acquiring of money, goods, or services on an agreement to pay at a later date.

Even though you pay to borrow, it is a privilege to borrow because you are obtaining credit. *Credit* is the acquiring of money, goods, or services on an agreement to pay at a later date. Having credit means that the people who loan you the money know that you will pay it back later as agreed. If you have the use of credit, you are trusted by the people you do business with.

How much will Mike and Margie pay for credit on a loan of $1,200 that they will pay back in 12 monthly payments of $108 each?

Amount repaid for loan	$108 \times 12 = \$1,296$
Cost of credit	$\$1,296 - \$1,200 = \$96$

Here is how to compute the same loan of $1,200 paid back in two years, with monthly payments of $58.

Amount repaid for loan	$\$58 \times 24 = \$1,392$
Cost of credit	$\$1,392 - \$1,200 = \$192$

The Williamsons realized they would have to change their budget allowances each month to allow for the loan payments. They decided to seek an agreement with the bank to pay off their loan in two years. This would make budgeting easier.

Mike filled out an application for a loan. The bank then made an investigation called a *credit check*. A credit agency looked into Mike's employment record, including his present salary, his record of paying past debts, his checking and saving accounts, and his charge accounts. They reported that Mike is a reliable person in the use of credit. Mike and Margie got their loan.

Exercises

What will be the cost of credit for each of the following loans?

Amount of Loan	Number of Payments	Amount of Each Payment	Amount Repaid for Loan	Cost of Credit
1. $2,400	24	$108.00	$ 2,592	$ 192
2. 950	12	86.30	_____	_____
3. 3,700	36	113.57	_____	_____
4. 575	6	103.98	_____	_____
5. 2,650	24	120.91	_____	_____
6. 1,625	18	97.95	_____	_____
7. 5,500	36	166.53	_____	_____
8. 7,450	30	273.17	_____	_____
9. 1,375	12	126.62	_____	_____
10. 4,200	24	191.80	_____	_____

Types of Loans

Single-payment loan: loan that is paid back in one sum on a fixed date or on demand of the lender.

There are two basic types of loans, the single-payment loan and the installment loan. A *single-payment loan* is paid back in one sum on a fixed date or on demand of the lender. It is paid back all at once, with interest charges added.

Installment loan: loan that is paid back in fixed amounts at set times—usually monthly.

An *installment loan* is paid back in fixed, partial amounts, called *installments*, at set times until it is repaid. Payments are usually made on the same day of each month. The *due date*, the day that the last installment must be paid, of installment loans varies. Short-term loans may be paid off in periods ranging from 1 to 36 months. A long-term loan may be paid off over a 20- to 30-year period.

The interest cost is computed on the total amount of the loan. There are different interest rates for different types of installment loans. It's important to shop for credit, just as you would for any other purchase. Buy your credit on the best available terms.

Simple Interest

Simple interest: interest paid on the total amount of the loan when the term of the loan ends.

Sarah Perkins had a family emergency. She needed $1,200 to cover expenses. Sarah decided it would be wiser and less costly to take out a single-payment loan at 6-percent simple interest. *Simple interest* is paid on the total amount of the loan when the term of the loan ends. To find out how much interest Sarah would pay for her loan, she needs to know three things.

1. The *principal,* or the amount borrowed.
2. The interest *rate.*
3. The *time* for which the money is borrowed.

The simple-interest formula below helped Sarah compute the amount of interest she would pay.

Simple-interest
formula:
$I = P \times R \times T$.

$$\text{Interest} = \text{Principal} \times \text{Rate} \times \text{Time}$$
$$or$$
$$I = P \times R \times T$$

How much interest did Sarah pay for her $1,200 loan? It was totally repaid in one year at a rate of 6 percent a year.

$I = P \times R \times T$

$P = \$1,200$

$R = 6\%$ *or* $.06$ (Remember to change the percent to a decimal.)

$T = 1$ year

$I = \$1,200 \times .06 \times 1$

$= \$72$

If Sarah took out her loan for 6 months, T would equal .5. This is because 6 months is equal to $\frac{1}{2}$, or .5, of a year ($\frac{6}{12} = \frac{1}{2}$). If Sarah took out her loan for 4 months, T would equal .333 ($\frac{4}{12} = \frac{1}{3} = .333$). If Sarah took out her loan for 3 months, what would T equal?

Exercises

Compute the simple interest that the following borrowers will pay on their loans. (If necessary, round off to the nearest cent.)

Borrower	Principal	Rate	Term of Loan	Interest Charge
1. C. Miller	$2,400	8.5%	1 yr	$ 204
2. R. Feldman	7,500	10.5%	1 yr	_____
3. L. Ordoff	2,600	9.0%	6 mo	_____
4. B. Rowe	4,750	9.5%	1 yr	_____
5. G. Dubinsky	1,800	8.5%	9 mo	_____
6. J. Watson	4,000	9.25%	6 mo	_____
7. B. D'Amato	500	8.5%	3 mo	_____
8. J. Delgado	4,700	9.0%	6 mo	_____
9. R. Cooper	2,650	9.5%	24 mo	_____
10. L. McBain	5,300	10.25%	18 mo	_____

Exercises for Section One

1. Vicki Ross is paying $59.04 each month for the $650 she borrowed from the bank.

   a. What total amount will she pay for her 12-month loan?

   b. What is her cost of credit?

2. Betsy and Tim King borrowed from the bank in order to buy a boat which cost $4,150. They will pay $126.35 each month for 36 months.
   a. What total amount will they pay the bank by the end of the 36-month period?
   b. What amount of interest will they pay for the use of the $4,150?
3. In order to pay her business college tuition in full, Sylvia Short borrowed $1,875 from the bank. She agreed to repay it in one payment plus 8.25 percent interest at the end of a year. What will be Sylvia's interest charge?
4. Bob Switzer borrowed $2,140 from the bank in order to purchase a new furnace. The interest rate on his single-payment, 1.5-year loan is 9.3 percent. What amount of interest will Bob pay for his $2,140 loan?
5. The principal of Jeff Foley's single-payment, 2-year loan is $2,250. The annual interest rate is 9.5 percent.
   a. What will be the amount of Jeff's 2-year interest charge?
   b. What is the total amount which Jeff will pay the bank at the end of the loan period?

When most people buy a car, they need to borrow money to finance it.

Section Two
Finding Interest Rates

At different banks, single-payment loans are offered at different terms. Look at the examples below.

Loan 1: $1,000 repaid in a single payment at the end of 3 months with $60 interest.

Loan 2: $500 repaid in a single payment at the end of 4 months with $30 interest.

Which loan is cheaper? To answer the question, find the rate of interest paid for one month on each loan. Use the simple-interest formula to find the rate.

$$I = P \times R \times T, \quad or \quad R = \frac{I}{P \times T}$$

LOAN 1:

$$R = \frac{60}{1,000 \times 3} = \frac{60}{3,000} = .02 \ or \ 2\%$$

The rate of interest for one month is 2 percent.

LOAN 2:

$$R = \frac{30}{500 \times 4} = \frac{30}{2,000} = .015 \ or \ 1.5\%$$

The rate of interest for one month is 1.5 percent.

Loan 2 is cheaper because the rate of interest is less than that of Loan 1.

To find the annual rates of interest for Loans 1 and 2, change the number of months to a decimal and allow the same rate formula. For example, the 3-month term of Loan 1 equals $\frac{3}{12}$ or $\frac{1}{4}$ (.25) year.

LOAN 1:

$$R = \frac{I}{P \times T} = \frac{60}{1,000 \times .25} = \frac{60}{250} = .24 \ or \ 24\%$$

Notice that the annual rate of interest for the loan is exactly 12 times the monthly rate (2% × 12 = 24%).

Exercises

Compute the monthly rate of interest and the annual rate of interest to be paid on loans obtained by the people listed on the next page. (Round off the monthly interest rate to the nearest tenth of a percent.)

Borrower	Principal	Term of Loan in Months	Interest	Monthly Interest Rate	Annual Interest Rate
1. T. Rogers	$ 350	6	$ 42.00	2%	24%
2. K. Baum	1,500	4	110.00		
3. L. Elder	2,500	3	225.00		
4. O. Matsu	4,300	4	380.00		
5. J. Keil	1,600	6	140.00		
6. B. Haas	3,400	3	204.00		
7. S. Bracco	6,000	6	780.00		
8. W. Shulsky	700	4	78.00		
9. C. McClintock	2,600	3	117.00		
10. R. Diaz	850	6	117.50		

Add-on Interest

Patty Chu wants to get a $1,200 installment loan. She will pay an interest charge of $72. She will repay the total of the principal and interest, $1,272, in 12 equal monthly payments of $106 each. With each payment, $100 goes toward the principal and $6 goes toward the interest charge.

Add-on interest: interest that is added to the principal.

This type of interest is called *add-on interest* because the interest is added to the principal when Patty gets the loan. (Another type of loan is one with discount interest, which we'll examine later.) She will pay toward the principal and interest each time she makes a payment on the loan.

Principal	$1,200
Time of loan	12 months
Monthly principal payment	$1,200 ÷ 12 = $100
Interest	$72
Monthly interest payment	$72 ÷ 12 = $6
Total monthly payment	$100 + $6 = $106

Actual annual interest rate: true cost of loan shown in terms of percent.

Six percent is the stated interest rate that yields the $72 credit charge on Patty's loan. However, the *actual annual interest rate* of Patty's loan is not the same as the stated interest rate. Instead, it is almost double the 6-percent amount. This is because Patty will end up paying 6 percent on the full amount of the loan at the same time she is paying back the loan in installments. Suppose Patty has paid back half the $1,200 loan. Does she now pay interest on only the $600 she now owes? No, she still pays 6-percent interest based on $1,200.

Let's look at Patty's payments on the principal for a moment. They are 12 monthly payments of $100 each. After Patty makes her first payment, she owes $1,100 on the principal ($1,200 − $100 = $1,100). But when she makes her second payment, the credit charge is not based on 6 percent of $1,100. It is still based on 6 percent of the original $1,200.

A friend at the bank does some simple computing to estimate the actual annual interest rate of Patty's loan. He first finds out what is the average amount that Patty owes the bank between the time she borrows the principal and the time she finishes paying it back. This is done by averaging $1,200 with the amount of the last payment, $100.

First amount owed	$1,200
Last amount owed	$100
Average monthly principal	$\dfrac{\$1,200 + \$100}{2} = \dfrac{\$1,300}{2} = \$650$

On the average, Patty owes the bank $650 during the 1-year term of her loan. Her friend now shows her that, for this amount, the $72 credit charge is actually more than the stated 6 percent. He uses the simple-interest formula. P stands for average monthly principal.

$$R = \frac{I}{P \times T} = \frac{\$72}{\$650 \times 1} = .1107 \; or \; .111$$

$$= 11.1\% \text{ actual annual interest rate}$$

As you can see, the actual interest rate is estimated at close to 12 percent, or twice the stated interest rate.

Exercises

1. For each of these add-on interest loans, compute the monthly principal payment, the monthly interest payment, and the total monthly payment. (If necessary, round off to the nearest cent.)

Principal	Interest	Term of Loan in Months	Monthly Principal Payment	Monthly Interest Payment	Total Monthly Payment
a. $2,500	$175.00	10	$ 250	$ 17.50	$ 267.50
b. 750	60.00	12			
c. 900	76.50	12			
d. 1,500	270.00	24			
e. 2,000	210.00	18			
f. 650	29.25	6			

2. For each of these add-on interest loans, compute the monthly principal payment, the monthly average principal, and (to the nearest tenth of a percent) the actual annual interest rate.

Principal	Interest	Term of Loan in Months	Monthly Principal Payment	Average Monthly Principal	Annual Interest Rate
a. $ 600	$ 48.00	12	$ 50	$\dfrac{\$600 + \$50}{2} = \$325$	14.8%
b. 3,000	510.00	24			
c. 450	42.75	9			

Discount Interest

Discount interest: interest that is subtracted from the principal.

Proceeds: amount of a loan you receive after the discount interest is deducted.

With discount interest, the credit charge is deducted from the principal of the loan at the time you get the money. Suppose you borrow $600 at a 7-percent stated discount rate. This means you pay a credit charge of $42. However, the $42 will be deducted in advance. You will receive only $558 ($600 − $42 = $558). This sum is called the *proceeds*. You must, of course, repay $600.

We saw that the stated add-on interest rate was not the same as the actual annual interest rate. The same is true with the stated discount rate. But you can estimate the actual annual interest rate. Let's do it for a loan of $600 to be paid back in 12 monthly payments of $50. The stated interest rate is 7 percent.

STEP 1:
Using this method, we treat the loan as a 1-month loan. This means that we must total the principal owed for each month. (The interest is paid all at once in the first month, but it applies to the amounts owed for the entire term of the loan.)

	Principal	Monthly Principal Payment	Interest
Month 1	$ 558	$ 8	$42
Month 2	550	50	0
Month 3	500	50	0
Month 4	450	50	0
Month 5	400	50	0
Month 6	350	50	0
Month 7	300	50	0
Month 8	250	50	0
Month 9	200	50	0
Month 10	150	50	0
Month 11	100	50	0
Month 12	50	50	0
TOTAL	$3,858		

The total principal is $3,858. Think of it as $3,858 borrowed for one month with an interest charge of $42.

STEP 2:
Use the simple-interest formula to find the actual annual interest rate.

Rate per month
  (rounded off to the
  nearest tenth of
  a percent)

$$R = \frac{I}{P \times T}$$

$$= \frac{42}{\$3,858 \times 1}$$

Rate per year $\quad\quad = .0108 \ or \ .011$

Actual annual interest rate per year $\quad = 12 \times .011$

$$= .132 \ or \ 13.2\%$$

Notice that the actual annual interest rate for a discount loan of $600 from which $42, or 7 percent, is discounted, will be slightly higher than for a $600 loan with a 7-percent add-on rate. Both loans are payable over a 12-month period. Compare them.

Truth-in-Lending Law

In the past, borrowing money could be very confusing because it was difficult to compare interest charges and rates. But in 1968 the federal government passed the Consumer Credit Protection Act. This is better known as the Truth-in-Lending Law. Now, when consumers borrow money, they must be told the exact cost of credit. The total finance charge and the actual annual interest rate must be printed clearly so that consumers know the exact terms of their loan. Today it is easier to compare interest charges and rates.

Exercises for Section Two

1. For each of the following discount interest loans, compute the total interest to be paid for the loan. Also find the proceeds.

Principal	Annual Interest Rate	Term of Loan in Months	Interest	Proceeds
a. $2,500	7.0%	12	$ 175.00	$2,325.00
b. 750	8.0%	12		
c. 900	8.5%	12		
d. 1,500	9.0%	24		
e. 2,000	7.0%	18		
f. 650	9.0%	6		
g. 500	9.5%	12		

2. David Benet will pay $56.25 in interest for his single payment, 6-month, $450 loan.
   a. Compute David's monthly interest rate.
   b. Compute his annual interest rate. (Round off your answers to the nearest tenth of a percent.)
3. The interest Carol Bing is paying for her $1,300 add-on interest loan is $175.50. She will repay the borrowed money in 18 equal payments. What is the amount of each of Carol's monthly payments? (Round off to the nearest cent.)
4. The principal owed on Carol Bing's loan for the first month was $1,300. The principal owed on her last payment (the 18th) will be $72.22. What is the monthly average principal that Carol will owe?
5. The annual interest rate charged for Eric Santo's $950 discount interest loan is 9 percent. Eric will repay his loan over a 2-year period. How much will he pay in interest? What were the proceeds of Eric's loan?
6. Estimate the annual interest rate on a discount interest loan of $1,200 to be paid back in 12 monthly installments of $100. The discount is $84. (Round off to the nearest tenth of a percent.)

Section Three
The Interest Year and Interest Tables

Banker's year: year treated as 360 days long for the purpose of computing interest.

Interest is sometimes computed on a 360-day year known as a *banker's year.* Originally, the 360-day year was used because it made computations easier. Now banks use computers to simplify computations. Some banks use a 365-day year. Others continue to use the 360-day year. Why is this done? The two examples below and on the next page will show you.

You can see the difference in interest charges based on a 360-day year and on a 365-day year. Suppose that $800 was lent to a borrower at 9.5-percent annual interest rate payable in 40 days. (Remember that 9.5 percent is the same as .095.)

Example A: 360-day year

STEP 1: *Compute the annual interest charge.*

Annual interest charge $I = P \times R$
$$= \$800 \times .095 = \$76$$

STEP 2: *Compute the daily interest charge.*

Daily interest charge $\$76 \div 360 = \$.2111$, *or* $\$.211$
(rounded off to a tenth of a cent)

STEP 3: *Compute the short-term interest charge.*

Daily interest charge $.211

Term of loan   40 days

Short-term interest charge $.211 × 40 = $8.44

Example B: 365-day year

STEP 1: *Compute annual interest charge.*

(Same as Example A)

STEP 2: *Compute the daily interest charge.*

Daily interest charge $76 ÷ 365 = $.2082 or $.208
(rounded off to the
nearest tenth of
a cent)

STEP 3: *Compute the short-term interest charge.*

Daily interest charge $.208

Term of loan   40 days

Short-term interest charge $.208 × 40 = $8.32

As you can see, the 360-day year brings the bank a higher interest payment. To save money on a loan, you may wish to borrow from a bank that does not compute its interest rates using a banker's year.

Exercises

1. For the following loans, find the daily interest charge for a 360-day year and a 365-day year. (Round off to the nearest tenth of a cent.)

Annual Interest	Daily Interest, 360-Day Year	Daily Interest, 365-Day Year
a. $182	$ .506	$ .499
b. 96		
c. 155		
d. 320		
e. 400		

2. Compute the annual interest charge that would be charged for the loans on the next page. Then compute the short-term charges based on a 360-day year and a 365-day year. Then determine the additional amount paid at the 360-day rate. (Round off the *daily* interest charge to the nearest tenth of a cent. *But,* round off the short-term charges—for 360 days and for 365 days—to the nearest cent.)

Principal	Annual Interest Rate	Annual Interest	Term of Loan in Days	360-Day Interest	365-Day Interest	Extra Paid for 360-Day Rate
a. $2,600	8.5%	$ 221	90	$ 55.26	$ 54.45	$ .81
b. 3,700	9.0%	_____	60	_____	_____	_____
c. 6,400	9.5%	_____	182	_____	_____	_____
d. 1,850	7.5%	_____	45	_____	_____	_____
e. 4,500	9.0%	_____	96	_____	_____	_____

Using an Annual Interest Rate Table

Jane Wilson works at Central Savings and Loan. Central Savings, like most lending organizations, uses federally approved tables to find the annual interest rate. Jane wants to find out the annual interest rate on a $1,300 loan. The loan will be paid back in 24 monthly payments of $63.38 each. Jane follows the steps below.

STEP 1: *Find the total interest charge.*

Number of payments   24
Amount of each payment $63.38
Total amount of payments 24 × $63.38 = $1,521.12
Total interest charge $1,521 − $1,300.00 = $221.12

STEP 2: *Compute the interest cost per $100 borrowed.*

Number of $100s borrowed   1,300 ÷ 100 = 13
Interest cost per $100 borrowed $221.12 ÷ 13 = $17.009
                                               or $17.01

STEP 3: *Use the table shown below.* Read down the Number of Payments column to 24. Read across this row to $16.94, the amount closest to $17.01. Then find the figure at the top of this column. It is 15.50 percent, the annual interest rate.

Number of Payments	Annual Interest Rate							
	15.00%	15.25%	15.50%	15.75%	16.00%	16.25%	16.50%	16.75%
12	8.31	8.45	8.59	8.74	8.88	9.02	9.16	9.30
24	16.37	16.65	16.94	17.22	17.51	17.80	18.09	18.37
30	20.54	20.90	21.26	21.62	21.99	22.35	22.72	23.08

Exercises for Section Three

1. For each of the following loans, compute the total amount of payments, the total interest charge, the number of $100s borrowed, and the interest cost per $100 borrowed (round off to the nearest cent.) Then, using the Annual Interest Rate table on page 98, determine the annual interest rate for each loan.

Principal of Loan	Number of Payments	Monthly Payments	Total Amount of Payments	Total Interest Charge	Number of $100s Borrowed	Interest Cost per $100 Borrowed	Annual Interest Rate
a. $ 530	12	$ 48.14	$ 577.68	$ 47.68	5.3	$ 9.00	16.25%
b. 2,200	12	198.61					
c. 5,400	30	218.25					
d. 2,500	24	122.92					
e. 4,200	24	205.63					
f. 650	12	59.04					
g. 8,000	30	327.50					
h. 1,100	12	100.03					
i. 3,600	30	146.25					
j. 1,900	24	92.31					

2. Brian Whitley has taken out a 90-day, $1,400, single-payment loan. The annual interest rate is 9 percent, based on a banker's year of 360 days. Compute the following.
   a. The annual interest charge.
   b. The daily interest charge Brian will pay.
   c. His total 90-day interest charge.

3. Linda Svensen has borrowed $2,700 from her bank at an annual interest rate of 9.5 percent. She will repay the principal plus interest at the end of 120 days. If Linda's interest had been based on a 360-day year, she would pay $85.56. However, the interest is based on a 365-day year.
   a. Compute Linda's 120-day interest charge. (Round off the daily charge to the nearest cent.)
   b. Compute the amount she will save because her interest is based on a 365-day year.

4. Kathy Cantrell will repay the $1,750 she borrowed in 24 payments of $86.77. What total interest charge will she pay for her loan?

5. John Greenberg is paying off his $1,400 loan with 12 payments at an interest charge of $128.50. Use the Annual Interest Rate table on page 98 to determine the rate he is paying.

Section Four
Promissory Notes

Promissory note: promise signed by a borrower to repay the loan by a certain time.

When Sarah Perkins went to National Bank to get a $1,200 loan for a family emergency, she got a single-payment loan at 6-percent interest, payable in a year. She was asked to sign a *promissory note.* This note is a promise to repay the total sum by a certain period of time. It clearly states when and where the money is to be repaid. When Sarah signed the note, the bank inserted the following information.

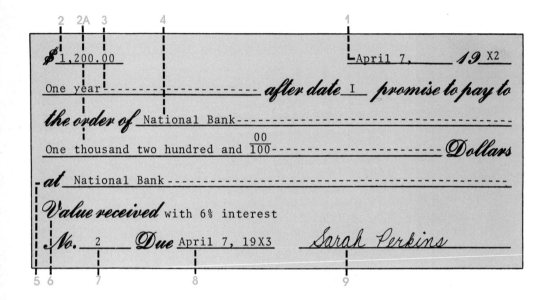

1. The *date* of the note is April 7, 19X2. This is the day Sarah signed the note.
2. The *principal* of the note is one thousand two hundred dollars. It is the amount of money borrowed. Notice that the principal is given in both figures (2) and words (2A).
3. The *time* is one year. This is the length of time from the date Sarah signed the note to the date it is due.
4. The *payee* is National Bank. This is the bank (sometimes it's a business firm or a person) to whom the money will be paid.
5. The *location* is the place where the money is to be paid. Sarah will pay her note at National Bank.
6. The *interest rate* is 6 percent. Sarah promises to pay "value received" (the principal of $1,200) plus 6-percent interest.
7. The *number* is assigned by Sarah. She uses the number for her own records.

8. The *due date* or the *maturity date* of the note is April 7, 19X3. This is the date on which the money must be paid.
9. The *maker* of the note is Sarah Perkins. She is the person borrowing the money and promising to repay.

Finding the Due Date

Promissory notes are often made out for 30, 60, 90, or 120 days. Timetables are often used to find the due date. Here is how to use the table to find the due date of a note, for example, with a term of 60 days from April 7.

TIMETABLE												
Day of Month	Jan.	Feb.	Mar.	Apr.	May	Jun.	Jul.	Aug.	Sep.	Oct.	Nov.	Dec.
1	1	32	60	91	121	152	182	213	244	274	305	335
2	2	33	61	92	122	153	183	214	245	275	306	336
3	3	34	62	93	123	154	184	215	246	276	307	337
4	4	35	63	94	124	155	185	216	247	277	308	338
5	5	36	64	95	125	156	186	217	248	278	309	339
6	6	37	65	96	126	157	187	218	249	279	310	340
7	7	38	66	97	127	158	188	219	250	280	311	341
8	8	39	67	98	128	159	189	220	251	281	312	342
9	9	40	68	99	129	160	190	221	252	282	313	343
10	10	41	69	100	130	161	191	222	253	283	314	344
11	11	42	70	101	131	162	192	223	254	284	315	345
12	12	43	71	102	132	163	193	224	255	285	316	346
13	13	44	72	103	133	164	194	225	256	286	317	347
14	14	45	73	104	134	165	195	226	257	287	318	348
15	15	46	74	105	135	166	196	227	258	288	319	349
16	16	47	75	106	136	167	197	228	259	289	320	350
17	17	48	76	107	137	168	198	229	260	290	321	351
18	18	49	77	108	138	169	199	230	261	291	322	352
19	19	50	78	109	139	170	200	231	262	292	323	353
20	20	51	79	110	140	171	201	232	263	293	324	354
21	21	52	80	111	141	172	202	233	264	294	325	355
22	22	53	81	112	142	173	203	234	265	295	326	356
23	23	54	82	113	143	174	204	235	266	296	327	357
24	24	55	83	114	144	175	205	236	267	297	328	358
25	25	56	84	115	145	176	206	237	268	298	329	359
26	26	57	85	116	146	177	207	238	269	299	330	360
27	27	58	86	117	147	178	208	239	270	300	331	361
28	28	59	87	118	148	179	209	240	271	301	332	362
29	29		88	119	149	180	210	241	272	302	333	363
30	30		89	120	150	181	211	242	273	303	334	364
31	31		90		151		212	243		304		365

1. Follow down the Day of Month column to the 7th day.
2. Move across that line to the April column. Notice that the 7th day of April is the 97th day of the year.

3. Add the number of days in which the note is due to 97 days (60 + 97 = 157).

4. Locate the answer, 157, in the table. The 157th day of the year is June 6. Thus the due date is June 6.

Exercises for Section Four

Use the timetable on page 101 to find the due dates for the following promissory notes.

Maker	Date	Term in Days	Due Date
1. J. Seigman	Feb. 14	90	May 15
2. S. Angelli	Aug. 23	120	_____
3. J. Drew	May 7	85	_____
4. A. Hobbes	Jan. 15	184	_____
5. L. Allan	Oct. 8	57	_____
6. R. Helmer	Dec. 26	65	_____
7. L. Alvarez	Mar. 25	60	_____
8. P. Harris	Nov. 2	54	_____
9. T. McNeal	July 11	146	_____
10. J. DeMarco	April 19	45	_____

11. On March 3, Jack Gerard, as maker, signed a promissory note with a face value of $2,600. Jack promised to pay Hans Croft the $2,600 plus interest at 9 percent in 90 days. Interest was computed on a 365-day year. Jack agreed to pay Mr. Croft at his home at 145 Maple Avenue in Lincoln, Nebraska. The note number is 14.

a. When is the note due?

b. What amount of interest did Jack promise to pay? (See page 97 for a review of computing interest for a short-term loan based on a 365-day year.)

c. Using the illustration on page 100 as your guide, prepare Jack Gerard's promissory note. (For this exercise and the next, you may wish to draw a promissory note or use the one in your activity guide.)

12. Tammy Carr, as maker, has signed a $480 promissory note dated October 7. The principal of the loan plus 8-percent interest is payable in 72 days. Tammy's note is payable to the order of First National Bank, Campville, Michigan. The note number is 1.

a. What is the maturity date of Tammy's note?

b. What amount of interest must she pay, based on the 360-day banker's year? (See pages 96 and 97 for a review of computing interest for a short-term loan based on a 360-day year.)

c. Using the illustration on page 100 as a guide, prepare Tammy's promissory note.

Section Five
Secured Loans

Secured loan: loan for which borrowers are required to offer collateral.

Many banks make *secured loans*. These loans require borrowers to offer, or "put up," collateral. *Collateral* is something that's worth at least as much money as the amount borrowed. Examples are stocks and bonds, property, or a savings account passbook. If a borrower doesn't repay the money, the lender has the right to sell whatever collateral is offered.

Collateral: something worth at least as much money as the amount borrowed.

One type of secured loan is a passbook loan. Jane Lourie secured a loan with $600 in her savings account. She can deposit money in or withdraw it from her account, but she must keep a balance of at least $600. The bank continues to pay interest on the total amount on deposit.

Passbook loans are often made without a set due date. Instead, they are payable "on demand" and are called demand loans. A *demand loan* or demand note must be paid whenever the lender asks for repayment. But until then the borrower may repay the loan at any time. Borrowers who do not know how long they will need the money may find this arrangement attractive.

Demand loan: loan that must be paid whenever the lender asks for repayment.

Jane Lourie took out a passbook loan for $600 on April 1 at 6 percent annual interest on the outstanding balance. She received bills for interest due on the loan for the next three quarters. She repaid the loan with interest at the end of three quarters. What was the interest charge for the loan? (Remember that three quarters of a year equals the decimal .75, two quarters equals .5, and one quarter equals .25.)

$$I = P \times R \times T$$

Interest due on loan $600 \times .06 \times .75 = 27

Jane, meanwhile, earned $22.50 interest on her savings account during the time she had the loan. What was the difference between the interest paid on the loan and the interest earned on her savings account?

Whatever kind of bank loan you decide you need, it's important to shop around and compare credit terms. In doing so, don't forget your budget. Be sure that you can safely pay out additional money each month for the payments on a loan. And continue to save, even if it's only a small amount each month. With these things in mind, you'll be a wise user of credit.

Exercises for Section Five

1. Each of the following people used a savings account balance as security for a loan.
   a. Compute the interest charge for each loan. (If necessary, round off to the nearest cent.)
   b. Compute the difference between the interest charged for the loan and the interest earned from the savings account.

Borrower	Principal	Annual Interest Rate	Term of Loan	Interest Charge	Savings Interest Earned	Difference
a. K. Rubio	$ 250	7%	1 qtr	$ 4.38	$ 3.13	$ 1.25
b. L. Purdy	430	8%	2 qtr	_____	10.75	_____
c. J. York	175	7.5%	1 qtr	_____	2.19	_____
d. M. Madrid	1,350	6.5%	1 yr	_____	67.50	_____
e. S. Wagner	500	7%	3 qtr	_____	18.75	_____
f. B. Scott	2,100	7.5%	1 yr	_____	105.00	_____
g. D. Ryan	85	7%	1 qtr	_____	1.06	_____
h. G. Chu	700	8%	3 qtr	_____	26.25	_____
i. K. Grier	550	7.5%	2 qtr	_____	13.75	_____
j. V. Todd	300	8.5%	2 qtr	_____	7.50	_____

2. The interest rate on an unsecured loan at Ray Cohen's bank is 9.5 percent. For a secured loan, the rate is 8 percent. Compute the following amounts for Ray, who wants to borrow $3,500 for 1 year.
   a. The total interest if the loan is unsecured.
   b. The total interest if the loan is secured.
   c. The amount of savings if he takes out a secured loan.

3. Alice Doyle is using her car as security for a 2-year, $2,800 loan. What amount of interest will Alice pay at a 7.5-percent annual rate?

4. Renee LaSalle earned $31.42 in interest on her savings account balance of $625. She has used her savings account as security for a $625 loan. Interest on her loan is 7.5 percent. Compute the following amounts for Renee.
   a. The interest owed on her loan. (Round off to the nearest cent.)
   b. The amount of difference in interest earned and interest owed.

5. Marian Blume earned $35.69 interest on her savings account balance during 3 quarters. During this time she had a $940 loan secured by this account.

a. At an 8-percent rate, what amount of interest did Marian owe for her loan during the 3 quarters?

b. How much more did she owe in interest than she received for her savings?

6. Brad Wiley borrowed $260, using his savings account as security for the loan. The loan rate was 7.5 percent. During the 6-month loan period, he earned $6.54 on the $260 in his savings account. How much more did he pay in interest expense than he earned in interest income?

REVIEW FOR CHAPTER 5
BORROWING MONEY FROM A BANK

1. Sandra Lane has promised to repay a $2,800 loan in equal monthly installments over a 3-year period. She is charged an annual interest rate of 9.5 percent.

   a. What is the total amount of interest that Sandra will pay?

   b. What will be the amount of each of her monthly payments? (Round off to the nearest cent.)

2. The monthly payment that Ben Conti makes on his $2,000, add-on interest loan is $97.08. He will make this monthly payment for 2 years. How much will Ben pay in interest? What (to the nearest cent) is the average monthly principal? What (to the nearest tenth of a percent) is the actual annual interest rate?

3. Barbara Henderson is going to borrow $4,700 at a 10.5-percent annual interest rate. Rounding off to the nearest cent, what would be the amount of each of her monthly payments if she repays the loan over a 2-year period? Over a 3-year period?

4. Louie Brown has borrowed $1,350 at an annual rate of 10.5 percent for a 120-day loan period. What is his interest charge for 120 days based on a 365-day year? (Round off to the nearest cent.)

5. Kit Washington's $7,400, 1-year loan was discounted at an annual rate of 8.5 percent. It is a single-payment loan.

   a. What amount of interest was deducted from the principal of Kit's note?

   b. What amount of proceeds did Kit receive?

   c. What was the actual annual interest rate? (Round off to the nearest tenth of a percent.)

6. What are the due dates of the following notes? (Use the table on page 101, if you wish.)

   a. Anne Master's 90-day note, dated July 14?

   b. Jud O'Brien's 120-day note, dated March 30?

7. Tom Key has borrowed $5,325 for 96 days at a 9-percent interest rate.
   a. What is his annual interest charge?
   b. Based on a 365-day year, determine Tom's interest charge for the 96 days. (Round off the daily rate to the nearest tenth of a cent.)
   c. How much less is Tom's interest charge than it would have been on a 360-day basis? (Round off the daily rate to the nearest tenth of a cent.)

8. The interest charged on Ellen Jolly's single-payment, $740 loan is $59.20. Ellen had the loan for 4 months (.333 of a year). Compute Ellen's monthly interest rate and annual interest rate.

9. The total interest charge on Joe Dunn's 2-year, $2,300 loan is $419.75. The principal owed on his first payment is $2,300. The principal owed on the final payment is $95.83.
   a. Determine Joe's average monthly principal. (Round off to the nearest cent.)
   b. Estimate the annual interest rate he is paying. (Round off to the nearest tenth of a percent.)

10. Use the table on page 98 to find the annual interest rate for Manuel Gomez's loan. Manuel borrowed $3,400. He will pay it back in 30 monthly payments with an interest charge of $735.35. (Remember to round off the interest cost per $100 borrowed to the nearest cent.)

Other Sources of Cash Credit

Banks are not the only places where you can get a loan. James Rivers—just hired as a driver at Ace Trucking Company—discovered this last month. He wanted to borrow money to pay for a new washing machine that was on sale. James and his wife Rosa didn't have the cash to pay for the machine. James went to a few banks to see about getting a loan. However, since he'd worked for only a short time at Ace Trucking, banks thought he might be a poor credit risk. So he had to look elsewhere for a loan.

James knew that some of his co-workers belonged to a credit union. A *credit union* is a banking organization formed by people who usually belong to the same group, such as a company. Members deposit money in the credit union. The credit union lends money at low interest rates to members who need short-term loans. Several of the Ace Trucking Company employees formed a credit union a few years ago. As a company worker, James could join. This was one place where he could borrow money.

James also knew of another way to get the loan he wanted. He could use a credit card to borrow money. This is called getting a *cash advance*. He decided to look into this method of borrowing, too.

Near Ace Trucking there is a small loan company called People's Loan Company. James's friend Alberto had gone there once for a loan. Alberto didn't have a steady job at the time, but he got his loan just by signing a promissory note to pay off the loan in a few months. James decided to look into People's Loan Company to see what they were charging for credit.

James had heard of a man who lent money to people who had trouble getting loans. But as much as he wanted the washing machine, he was not about to borrow money from this man. The interest was actually illegal; it ranged from 1,000 to 2,000 percent a year! It could only mean trouble—serious trouble—paying for money at these rates.

As a last resort, James could ask his Uncle Ralph for a loan. But did he want to discuss his financial needs with his uncle? And wouldn't agreeing on an interest rate be awkward?

James now had a list of other cash credit sources besides banks. His plan was to find the best credit terms for the $350 loan he needed. How was James going to do this? He would compare the interest rates charged by the different lending organizations.

Best way to shop for credit: compare actual annual interest rates.

Remember, the best way to do your credit shopping is to compare actual annual interest rates. As you remember from Chapter 5, this rate is different from the stated interest rate. The actual annual interest rate includes the basic finance charge as well as any additional fees. Other fees that might be included are credit investigation fees, service charges, or credit insurance premiums. (Most lending organizations want their customers to carry credit insurance. If the borrower should die before the loan is paid up, the insurance company would then be responsible for repaying the loan.)

James set out to compare the dollar cost of borrowing $350 from several lending organizations by using the actual annual interest rate for each. He hoped to find a loan that wouldn't cost too much.

Section One
Credit Union Loans

The employees' credit union at James's company is run by and for credit union members. Its operations are inspected regularly by government officials and must follow government regulations. Members have to work for the company. They can deposit amounts from their gross pay in their credit union accounts. These savings deposits buy shares in the credit union, usually valued at $5 a share.

Members earn interest on each share they own. This interest is

Dividend:
interest earned on money deposited in a credit union; a percentage of each share.

known as a *dividend*. It is a percentage of the share. To compute the amount of the dividend, multiply the value of the share by the percent of the dividend. Remember to change the percent to a decimal. For example, Ellen Pagano owns 30 shares worth $5 each. For that year, a dividend of 5 percent was declared. Here is how Ellen computed her earnings.

Dividend a share = Value of share × Percent of dividend

Dividend a share $5 × .05 = $.25

Total earnings   30 × $.25 = $7.50

All credit unions, whether formed by members of local clubs, church groups, companies, or labor unions, are in business to help their members. So they do not seek a profit from lending as banks do. That's why their interest rates are lower than bank rates.

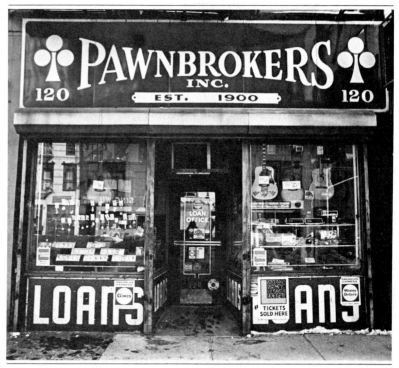

When James Rivers was looking for a source of a loan, he thought of going to a pawnshop. He could take his stereo set as collateral, and the manager would let James borrow a fraction of the value of the set. But James would have to leave the stereo set at the shop for as long as he had the loan. And the interest rate would be higher than if he used other sources. James decided against using a pawnshop.

Linda Monti, the manager of the credit union, told James that he could join by opening an account with a small deposit. Then he could apply for the loan he needs. The stated interest rate for a personal loan is .75 percent (.0075) a month on the unpaid balance.

Here is how James figured out what a $350 loan would cost if he repaid it over the next seven months. He would pay $50 toward the principal each month. He would also pay an interest charge of .75 percent each month on the unpaid balance.

To compute the interest charge for one month, James began with the entire amount owed, $350.

Interest (I = P × R × T) $350 × .0075 × 1 = $2.625

James continued to compute the interest charge for each month by subtracting the monthly payment toward the principal from the balance owed. Thus, his interest charge would be based only on what he owed after each monthly payment.

Series of Payments	Unpaid Balance	Payment Toward Principal	Interest on Unpaid Balance
First month	$350	$50	$2.625
Second month	300	50	2.25
Third month	250	50	1.875
Fourth month	200	50	1.50
Fifth month	150	50	1.125
Sixth month	100	50	.75
Seventh month	50	50	.375
		$350	$10.50

Total payment toward principal $350
Total interest charge $10.50
Total payment $350 + $10.50 = $360.50

To find the total credit cost for the loan, James added the interest charges. (If necessary, he would have rounded off the total interest charge to the nearest cent.) The total interest charge is $10.50. What actual annual interest rate is James paying? For this kind of a loan, it is quite simple. Just multiply the monthly rate by 12 (12 × .0075 = .09 or 9%).

You will arrive at about the same answer if you use the method of computing the actual annual interest rate as shown on page 93 in Chapter 5. Here is a quick review of that method. Remember that the time of the loan is 7 months or $\frac{7}{12}$ year. Here is how to express $\frac{7}{12}$ year in decimal form: 7 ÷ 12 = .583.

$$\text{Average monthly principal } \frac{\$350 + \$50}{2} = \frac{\$400}{2} = \$200$$

$$R = \frac{I}{P \times T} = \frac{\$10.50}{\$200 \times .583} = \frac{\$10.50}{\$116.60} = .09 \text{ or } 9\%$$

Make a note of the total credit cost and the actual annual interest rate. You will need to refer to them again at the end of this chapter.

Exercises for Section One

A 6-percent dividend was declared on each $5 share in the Civic Credit Union. Find the dividend a share and the total earnings for each member.

Member	Number of Shares Owned	Dividend a Share	Total Earnings
1. J. Walker	30	$ .30	$ 9.00
2. M. Spencer	35		
3. S. Repetti	50		
4. K. Lipman	79		
5. V. Garbar	100		

Each Teachers' Credit Union loan below was from a different city. Each was repaid with payments of $50 toward the principal each month plus interest on the unpaid balance. Find the total interest charged and the actual annual interest rate for each loan. (To help you with your computations, the term of the loan is also expressed in decimal form. Round off the total interest charged to the nearest cent.)

Principal	Monthly Interest Rate	Term of Loan	Total Interest	Actual Annual Interest Rate
6. $100	.01%	2 mo (.167)	$ 1.50	12%
7. 200	.75%	4 mo (.333)		
8. 250	.00.4%	5 mo (.417)		
9. 300	.00.5%	6 mo (.5)		
10. 400	.00.25%	8 mo (.667)		

Shares in the Community Group Credit Union (see Exercises 11 to 15) are worth $5 and pay a dividend of 5.5 percent. Members may borrow up to $500 at .5 percent interest a month.

11. Frances Keller owns 38 shares in the Community Group Credit Union. What dividend will she earn a share? What will her total earnings be?

12. Harvey Lyman borrowed $300 from the Community Group Credit Union for 4 months. If he paid $75 a month toward the principal plus interest on the unpaid balance, how much interest was he charged the first month? The second month? The third month? The fourth month? How much total interest was he charged? (Round off the total interest to the nearest cent.)

13. Joyce Burton borrowed $450 from the Community Group Credit Union. She repaid the loan with 9 monthly payments of $50 toward the principal plus interest on the unpaid balance. What total interest was she charged? What total amount (principal plus interest) did she pay?

14. Calvin Boyd can get a loan from the Community Group Credit Union, or his wife Suzie can get the loan from her credit union at work. Suzie's credit union offers an actual annual interest rate of 7.5 percent. From which credit union should they borrow? Why?

15. Tanya Myers owns 100 shares in the Community Group Credit Union. She borrowed $500 from the credit union and repaid the loan in 5 monthly payments of $100 toward the principal plus interest on the unpaid balance. Which was more, her total dividend earnings or her total interest payment? How much more?

Section Two
Cash Advance on a Credit Card

Some credit cards allow you to borrow cash as well as to make purchases. A credit card loan is usually simple to get if you hold a credit card such as Master Charge, Visa (BankAmericard), or American Express. You should have no trouble getting a credit card loan if your credit rating is good and if you have a steady source of income. Rates on this kind of loan are much like those on other bank loans. But, if you don't make your payments on time, you will be charged a late fee (often 5 percent of the late payment).

James found that he can use his bank credit card to get a cash loan of up to $500. He has only to fill out a form and discuss it with a bank officer. The bank will bill James monthly. In most states, borrowers pay a monthly interest charge of 1.5 percent on the unpaid balance. (In other states, the interest rates may be slightly lower.)

Suppose James takes a $350 cash advance on his bank credit card. What are the total interest charges for a 7-month period if the bank bills him a monthly 1.5 percent interest charge on the unpaid balance? James would be billed monthly for $50 payments toward the principal. What is the actual annual interest rate? (Make a note of the interest charges and the actual annual interest rate. You will need to refer to them again at the end of this chapter.)

Series of Payments	Unpaid Balance	Payment Toward Principal	Interest on Unpaid Balance
First month	$350	$ 50	$ 5.25
Second month	300	50	4.50
Third month	250	50	3.75
Fourth month	200	50	3.00
Fifth month	150	50	2.25
Sixth month	100	50	1.50
Seventh month	50	50	.75
		$350	$21.00

Total payment toward principal $350

Total interest charge $21

Total payment $350 + $21 = $371

DO YOU KNOW

how to find the credit plan that's best for you? If you find that each of the following ten statements is true, then you will be able to select a consumer credit plan that makes sense for you.

1. The creditor has fair and reliable standards.
2. Security requirements for credit are reasonable.
3. The total cost of credit is the same as (or less than) other sources of credit.
4. Monthly credit payments are not excessive.
5. The terms of the credit agreement are written clearly.
6. Credit can be gotten easily and fast.
7. Credit deals are treated confidentially.
8. Budget-planning help is available, if needed.
9. Charges for late payments are reasonable, and refunds are made on prepaid credit charges.
10. Insurance, if sold with credit plans, provides sufficient protection at a fair cost.

Exercises for Section Two

Sarah Morrison got a cash advance of $750 on her credit card. She repaid the loan in 10 monthly payments of $75 toward the principal plus 1.25 percent interest on the unpaid balance. Complete these exercises to find the interest on the unpaid balance for each month. (Do not round off to the nearest cent.)

Series of Payments	Unpaid Balance	Payment Toward Principal	Interest on Unpaid Balance
1. First month	$ 750	$ 75	$ 9.3750
2. Second month			
3. Third month			
4. Fourth month			
5. Fifth month			
6. Sixth month			
7. Seventh month			
8. Eighth month			
9. Ninth month			
10. Tenth month			

Use Exercises 1 to 10 to solve these problems.

11. How much total interest did Sarah pay? (Round off your answer to the nearest cent.)

12. What total amount did Sarah repay over the 10-month period? (Round off your answer to the nearest cent. Use this answer in Exercise 15).

13. What actual annual interest rate did Sarah pay?

14. Suppose Sarah Morrison was late sending in her seventh payment. What was her total payment that month if the late fee is 5 percent of the late payment? (Round off your answer to the nearest cent.)

15. Sarah could have used another credit card that charged 1.4 percent on the unpaid balance. How much did she save by using the credit card that she did use?

Section Three
Finance Companies

Finance companies are another source of loans. A finance company may be the only place you can get a loan if the bank considers you to be a poor credit risk. You can get a loan at a finance company

Co-signer:
person who
signs a note
along with the
borrower,
promising to
pay if the
borrower does
not.

merely by signing a promise to pay. Customers who have no regular source of income must have someone, such as a friend, to sign the note with them. Then, if the loan is not repaid, the *co-signer* of the note is responsible for the unpaid balance.

Since finance companies take greater risks with their customers, their interest rates are higher. The credit charges can be two or three times higher than what banks charge. These charges are, however, controlled by state laws.

You can borrow only small amounts of money, though, usually up to $1,000. For that reason, finance companies are often called small loan companies.

James found that People's Loan Company charges a monthly interest rate of 2.75 percent on unpaid balances. This rate includes the cost of credit insurance. James found the actual annual interest rate by taking the monthly rate and multiplying by 12.

Actual annual interest rate $.0275 \times 12 = .33$ *or* 33%

Suppose James takes out a $350 loan at a monthly interest rate of 2.75 percent. What will be the credit cost if he pays back $50 a month toward the principal for 7 months? What is the actual annual interest rate? (Make a note of your answers. You will need them at the end of this chapter.)

Series of Payments	Unpaid Balance	Payment Toward Principal	Interest on Unpaid Balance
First month	$350	$ 50	$ 9.625
Second month	300	50	8.25
Third month	250	50	6.875
Fourth month	200	50	5.50
Fifth month	150	50	4.125
Sixth month	100	50	2.75
Seventh month	50	50	1.375
		$350	$38.500 *or* $38.50

Total payment toward principal $350
Total interest charge $38.50
Total payment $350 + $38.50 = $388.50

Many finance companies charge different interest rates depending on the amount of the unpaid balance. One such company is E-Z Loan Company. James studied their rates, which are shown at the top of the next page.

Unpaid Balance	Interest Rate
First $100 or less	3% a month
Next $200 ($100.01 to $300)	2.5% a month
Next $600 ($300.01 to $900)	2% a month

If James takes out his loan at E-Z Loan Company, his interest charge will be computed as shown below. What will be the credit cost? What is the actual annual interest rate? (Remember, you will need your answers at the end of this chapter.)

Unpaid Balance	Payment Toward Principal	Amt. Owed at 2%	Int. at 2%	Amt. Owed at 2.5%	Int. at 2.5%	Amt. Owed at 3%	Int. at 3%	Total Int.
$350	$50	$50	$1	$200	$5.00	$100	$3.00	$ 9.00
300	50			200	5.00	100	3.00	8.00
250	50			150	3.75	100	3.00	6.75
200	50			100	2.50	100	3.00	5.50
150	50			50	1.25	100	3.00	4.25
100	50					100	3.00	3.00
50	50					50	1.50	1.50
	$350							$38.00

Total payment toward principal $350
Total interest charge $38
Total payment $350 + $38 = $388

To check your work, first find the total amount owed at each interest rate. For example, $1 is owed at the 2-percent rate, and $17.50 at the 2.5-percent rate. How much is owed at 3 percent? Add these amounts. Your answer should be the same as that in the Total Interest Column ($38). If not, recheck your work.

Exercises
Karen Langer borrowed $750 from AAA Loan Company. The company charged these rates.

Unpaid Balance	Monthly Interest Rate
First $300 or less	3%
Next $300 ($300.01 to $600)	2.5%
$600.01 and more	2%

She repaid the loan in 10 monthly payments of $75 toward the principal plus interest. Complete the exercises to find her total interest payment. (Do not round off your answers to the nearest cent.)

Check your work. What is the amount of interest owed at the 2-percent rate? 2.5 percent? 3 percent? Add these amounts. Are they the same as your answer to Exercise 11? If not, recheck your work.

Series of Payments	Unpaid Balance	Amt. Owed at 2%	Int. at 2%	Amt. Owed at 2.5%	Int. at 2.5%	Amt. Owed at 3%	Int. at 3%	Total Int.
1. First month	$ 750	$ 150	$ 3	$ 300	$ 7.50	$ 300	$ 9	$ 19.50
2. Second month	___	___	___	___	___	___	___	___
3. Third month	___	___	___	___	___	___	___	___
4. Fourth month	___	___	___	___	___	___	___	___
5. Fifth month	___	___	___	___	___	___	___	___
6. Sixth month	___	___	___	___	___	___	___	___
7. Seventh month	___	___	___	___	___	___	___	___
8. Eighth month	___	___	___	___	___	___	___	___
9. Ninth month	___	___	___	___	___	___	___	___
10. Tenth month	___	___	___	___	___	___	___	___
11. Total			___		___		___	___

Loans from Family and Friends

Finally, James and Rosa discussed the possibility of asking James's Uncle Ralph for a $350 loan. At first, Rosa thought it was a good idea. They could take longer to pay back the money. James did want to pay interest on the loan if they decided to borrow from Uncle Ralph. But he and Rosa couldn't agree on a rate of interest. The more James thought about it the more he realized that to borrow money from someone in the family might change a good relationship. Can you think of some reasons for this? James and Rosa finally decided that borrowing the money from Uncle Ralph was not the best solution.

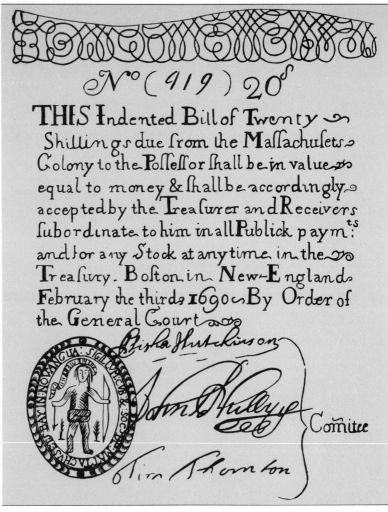

The first example of paper money in America is this bill from the year 1690.
Compare it with the paper money of today.

Choosing the Best Loan

Which loan do you think James and Rosa should take? Look at the notes you have made of the interest charges and the actual annual interest rates for the following loan sources.

1. The credit union.
2. A cash advance on a credit card.
3. People's Loan Company.
4. E-Z Loan Company.

Which has the lowest interest charge? The lowest actual annual interest rate? Which would be the best choice for James and Rosa? Why?

Borrowing money and paying for its use is a way of life for many people. Banks and other sources have made lending a big business. Alert consumers shop for credit just as they would for any other item. Only by shopping for credit will you know exactly what you'll pay for the use of borrowed money. Comparing terms of credit, including the actual annual interest rate and the amount of time to repay the loan, will give you an accurate idea of the cost of credit. After all, everyone wants to find a source for credit that's not going to cost a lot.

Exercises for Section Three

Margot and Tom Harrison need to borrow $400 to improve their home. They plan to repay the loan in 4 monthly payments of $100 toward the principal plus interest on the unpaid balance. Complete these exercises about the sources they investigated. (If necessary, round off the total interest charge to the nearest cent.)

Source of Loan	Monthly Interest Rate on Unpaid Balance	Total Interest	Total Principal Plus Interest	Actual Annual Interest Rate
1. Cannon Loan Co.	1.75%	$ 17.50	$ 417.50	21%
2. People's Loan Co.	2.75%	_____	_____	_____
3. E-Z Loan Co.	3% on first $100 or less / 2.5% on next $200 ($100.01 to $300) / 2% on $300.01 and more	_____	_____	
4. Midtown Loan Co.	2.5%	_____	_____	_____
5. City Loan Co.	3% on first $200 or less / 2.5% on next $200 ($200.01 to $400) / 2% on $400.01 and more	_____	_____	
6. Uncle Hank	.5%	_____	_____	_____
7. Aunt Marianna	1%	_____	_____	_____

Use your answers to Exercises 1 to 7 to solve these problems.

8. How much would they save by borrowing from Cannon Loan Company rather than the E-Z Loan Company?
9. How much would they save by borrowing from People's Loan Company rather than from City Loan Company?
10. How much would they save by borrowing from Midtown Loan Company rather than from People's Loan Company? E-Z Loan Company? City Loan Company?
11. How much would they save by borrowing from Uncle Hank rather than from Aunt Marianna?
12. Rank the sources they investigated from best to worst according to actual annual interest rates.

REVIEW FOR CHAPTER 6
OTHER SOURCES OF CASH CREDIT

The Neighborhood Block Association Credit Union (NBACU) pays a 6.5-percent dividend on its shares valued at $5. It charges 1.25 percent a month on the unpaid balance on loans of $1,000 or less. (Note: In the following 10 exercises, round off the total interest charge to the nearest cent whenever necessary.)

1. How much money does the Marx family earn in dividends if Mr. Marx owns 53 shares in the NBACU, Mrs. Marx owns 55 shares, their daughter owns 12 shares, and their son owns 15 shares?
2. The Patterson family borrowed $600 for a vacation from the NBACU. They repaid the loan in 10 monthly payments of $60 toward the principal plus interest on the unpaid balance.
   a. How much interest did they pay the first month? The fifth month? The tenth month?
   b. What was the total cost of the loan? The total amount repaid?
   c. What was the actual annual interest rate for the loan?
3. The Sapio family borrowed $600 for ski equipment from the NBACU. They repaid the loan in 6 monthly payments of $100 toward the principal plus interest on the unpaid balance. How much less interest did they pay than the Patterson family in Exercise 2?

Holders of the Red and Blue credit card are charged 1.5 percent a month on the unpaid balance for cash advances. Holders of the

Green and Yellow credit card are charged 1.3 percent a month on the unpaid balance for cash advances.

4. What actual annual interest rate is charged on loans from the Red and Blue credit card? The Green and Yellow credit card?

5. Should Lance Mitchell use his Red and Blue credit card or his Green and Yellow credit card to get a cash advance of $280 if he intends to pay off the loan in 5 monthly payments of $56 each toward the principal plus interest on the unpaid balance? How much will he save by using one credit card rather than the other one?

For each loan source in Exercises 6 to 10, compute (a) the total amount of interest paid and (b) the actual annual interest rate on a loan of $240 repaid in 4 monthly payments of $60 toward the principal plus interest on the unpaid balance. Then solve this problem. Which of the loan sources in Exercises 6 to 10 would you recommend first? Second? Third? Fourth? Fifth? (Round off the actual annual interest rate to the nearest tenth of a percent, if necessary.)

6. The Police Officers Credit Union charges .9 percent monthly on the unpaid balance.

7. The Bankers Club credit card charges 1.75 percent monthly on the unpaid balance.

8. Friendly Loan Association charges 2.4 percent monthly on the unpaid balance.

9. Main Street Loan Company charges these rates on the unpaid balance.

> 2.5% monthly on first $50 or less
> 2% monthly on next $50 ($50.01 to $100)
> 1.5% monthly on $100.01 or more

10. Cousin Charlie charges 2 percent monthly on the unpaid balance.

CHAPTER

Buy Now, Pay Later

Consumers use telephones, gas, and electricity, for which they are billed each month. Many charge their clothing expenses at department stores and use credit cards to buy gasoline. They visit doctors and dentists and pay for the visits at the end of the month.

These are just some of the ways that consumers can buy now and pay later for the things they want and need. Instead of paying immediately with cash, they use credit. This credit is just as much a loan as money borrowed from a bank is. The difference is that the loan comes in the form of goods and services.

Is credit buying a wise consumer choice? Most people find that buying on credit is a convenience. Those who buy on credit don't have to carry large amounts of cash when they shop. They can keep better budgets since they receive monthly bills listing their purchases. And, of course, they can use the goods while they're paying for them. During emergencies when income is low, credit may be more than a convenience. It may be necessary to pay for food and other vital needs.

What are some of the pitfalls of buying on credit? Some people can't resist the slick advertising for many goods and services they don't need. They begin to think they do need them. They use credit to buy expensive items and then go into debt trying to pay for them. People can be misled into buying items they can't afford because the terms appear so easy. They frequently fail to consider the cost of credit. Those who overlook the fact that credit costs money can end up paying more money for a purchase than is necessary. Consumers should compare the costs of various credit arrangements just as they compare the cost of different products.

As a consumer, you always have a choice. One important choice is selecting the best and least expensive way to pay for the goods and services that you need. Credit, if used wisely, can be a real advantage.

In this chapter, you will learn about some forms of buying on credit, such as paying for a car on time and using charge accounts and credit cards. You will also become more aware of the *real* costs of credit.

Section One
Buying on the Installment Plan

Installment plan: way to buy expensive items on credit by making a series of partial payments.

The credit you get from the seller of an expensive item, such as an automobile or an appliance, is called *installment plan* credit. On the installment plan, you must make a *down payment*, which is a partial cash payment. Then you pay an agreed amount of money at regular intervals until the item is paid for. Paying this way is also known as buying "on time."

Down payment: partial cash payment made before receiving an installment plan purchase.

Janet Sheehan, a young accountant, needs a car to visit the different companies that pay her to handle their financial records. She has decided to buy a used car, and, like most car buyers, she plans to buy the car on time.

Janet has found a car she likes for $3,600, and she has been shopping for the best deal in financing her car. First, she got the facts on what her local dealer offered. The dealer asked for a down payment of at least 25 percent of the total cash price.

If Janet decides to use the dealer's installment plan and makes a 25-percent down payment on the $3,600 cost of the car, how much will her down payment be? What will be the amount of the loan?

Cost of car	$3,600
25-percent down payment	$3,600 \times .25 = \$900$
Amount of loan	$3,600 - \$900 = \$2,700$

Exercises

Each person listed below is going to buy something on the install-ment plan. Compute for each buyer (a) the amount of the down payment and (b) the amount of the loan.

Buyer	Credit Purchase	Cash Price	Down Payment Rate	Down Payment	Loan Amount
1. A. Jones	Fur coat	$ 904	9%	$ 81.36	$ 822.64
2. D. Lathem	Motorboat	3,737	23%	_____	_____
3. H. Brill	Furniture	1,776	30%	_____	_____
4. T. Rosti	Piano	1,327	15%	_____	_____
5. S. Wing	Carpet	2,346	20%	_____	_____
6. K. Miller	Washer-dryer	658	7%	_____	_____
7. T. Rowe	Lawn mower	163	9%	_____	_____
8. M. Case	Sewing machine	237	12%	_____	_____
9. R. Nunzio	Freezer	329	30%	_____	_____
10. C. Johnson	Automobile	4,250	25%	_____	_____

Finance Charges

Finance charge: total credit cost of a loan— interest, fees, and so on.

Janet asked the dealer about the finance charges, or the cost of paying for her car on the dealer's installment plan. The *finance charge* is the difference between the cash price of an item and the price the buyer pays on the installment plan. The finance charge includes all credit costs—interest, credit investigation fees, service charges, credit insurance premiums, and so on—which are added to the principal. Although Janet needs the car as soon as possible, she insists on understanding the financing terms before she accepts the dealer's offer. First, Janet asks what the total finance charge would be if she paid for the car over a 3-year period. (Janet knows that the finance charge would be less if she repaid the loan over 24 or 12 months. However, she can only afford to pay a limited amount of money each month.)

To find the total finance charge, the dealer consulted a payment table. According to the table, Janet must pay $95.25 a month for 36 months. What will the finance charge be if Janet makes a down payment of 25 percent on the $3,600 car and then pays $95.25 a month over a 3-year period? In other words, how much more than the list price of $3,600 will Janet be paying?

Cash down payment	$900
Total monthly installments	$95.25 × 36 = $3,429
Price on installment plan	$3,429 + $900 = $4,329
Total finance charge	$4,329 − $3,600 = $729

The dealer asked Janet to sign a contract agreeing to monthly payments to be paid over a 3-year period. Janet understands that she will not own the car until she has paid the total cost, including the finance charges. Janet also has other questions about the dealer's terms. Can she have a refund on the finance charges if she is able to repay the loan sooner than she planned? What are the penalties for late payment? Is credit life insurance included in the deal? If so, what is the cost? She has much to consider before making a decision. More importantly, she wants to compare the financing offered by the dealer with financing available at the local bank.

Janet found that the local bank offered her an installment loan at a lower finance charge. If Janet agrees to pay 25 percent of the cash price of the car as a down payment, she can pay the bank $93 in equal monthly installments. She can pay back the loan over 3 years. How much is the finance charge on the bank's cash installment loan? How does it compare to the loan offered by the auto dealer?

Janet has a good credit rating with the bank. Even so, her loan

Most restaurants today accept credit cards.

Security:
something
pledged to
assure the
lender of
repayment.

Repossess: to
take back if the
installment
payments are
not met.

will be granted only if she pledges the car as *security*, or collateral. This means that if Janet cannot repay her loan, the bank can *repossess*, or take back, the car.

As you remember, the Truth-in-Lending Law requires both car dealers and banks to tell the consumer the total finance charges. This amount includes fees and charges required for car purchases except for taxes and for license and registration fees. The dealer or bank must give the customer all conditions of the loan in writing, usually in the form of a contract. Be sure you get a copy of such a contract if you decide to buy a car on time.

DO YOU KNOW

there can be dangers in borrowing money? Consumers take unnecessary financial risks if they sign loan contracts or agreements without fully understanding the terms or clauses. It's a good idea to get legal advice before signing anything as important as an installment loan contract. Watch out for the following traps.

Holder in due course is an example of a danger. Some dealers or retail sellers sell an item or service on credit and then immediately sell the installment contract to a finance company. The consumer may have a complaint about the purchase, but the finance company can demand payment without handling the consumer's complaint. Suppose you buy a vacuum cleaner on an installment plan. The machine breaks, and when you bring it back to the store, you find that the seller has gone out of business. But your loan has been sold to another lender. The new holder of your loan still insists on monthly payments but refuses to deal with your problem. If you don't pay, you can be sued.

This practice is illegal in some states, but there are still some dealers who use these methods to make money. However, the 1976 Federal Trade Commission ruling has given consumers the right to do something about these unfair practices. For example, this ruling allows consumers to sue creditors if they feel they've been cheated.

Repossession is another risk in buying on installment. Repossession is taking back something on loan because the buyer has failed to make payments. You may have heard of someone who bought a car on time from a dealer, made monthly payments with finance charges, paid all fees and insurance, and then missed one payment. In the meantime, the dealer had sold the contract to a lending company. Along came a representative of the finance company, who drove the car away. The lending company had repossessed the car. The buyer lost all that money and interest.

This type of repossession may be on the way out. A recent U. S. Supreme Court ruling states that no item may be repossessed unless the buyer is told that the matter is in court. The buyer can appear in court to argue the case. Unfortunately, there are still many dealers who continue these practices.

Balloon payments can be a real financial problem if the terms of an installment plan are not clear. The balloon payment is the last payment on a loan. It is larger than any other monthly payment. Sometimes it is actually larger than the loan itself. In installment plans with balloon payments, monthly payments are kept deliberately low until the final payment. For example, you might borrow $600 and pay $10 in 24 equal monthly installments. Then, the last payment might be $680. This payment alone is more than you borrowed. In addition, you have already paid $240 ($10 × 24 = $240) in interest. Thus your total payments on the loan are $920 ($240 + $680 = $920). If you cannot meet the last payment, your purchase may be repossessed. This type of loan is illegal in some states.

Exercises for Section One

1. Each person listed below bought an item on an installment plan. For each buyer, compute (a) the price of the item on the installment plan and (b) the total finance charge to be paid.

Buyer	Cash Price	Cash Down Payment	Number of Monthly Payments	Amount of Monthly Payment	Installment Price	Total Finance Charge
a. K. Johns	$ 935	$ 46	12	$ 82.97	$ 1,041.64	$ 106.64
b. C. Moore	472	19	9	53.73		
c. H. Chin	1,384	35	18	87.31		
d. M. Harte	869	87	12	72.99		
e. R. Rio	376	55	6	61.12		
f. D. Allen	2,780	556	18	147.65		
g. L. Rice	5,390	1,185	36	158.86		
h. O. Hober	765	54	12	66.95		
i. T. Smith	378	95	7	43.97		
j. E. Lynski	1,740	261	15	114.62		

2. Wendy and Carl Sands made a 15-percent down payment on a set of patio furniture. The cash price was $268.84. How much was the down payment?

3. Gary McSwain is paying for his stereo set with 18 monthly payments of $72.01 each. If the cash price is $982, how much is Gary paying as a finance charge?

4. Lester Mack can pay for his new car in 36 payments of $164.10 or in 24 payments of $223.13. Lester chooses to pay in 36 payments. How much more will he be paying than if he had chosen the 24-month plan?

5. The Wilsons are paying for their new refrigerator with 12 monthly payments of $31.24 each. What amount would they have saved if they had chosen to pay $40.19 for 9 months?

6. Diane Simpson made a 15-percent down payment on a pair of skis and boots. The cash price was $264.70. Diane will pay $30.09 for 8 months. What finance charge is she paying on her credit purchase? (Round off to the nearest cent, if necessary.)

Section Two
Charge Accounts

Drew Perkins has a job as a computer operations trainee. When he goes to work, he wants to look his best. So he wants to buy some new clothes. Drew has opened a charge account at Chase's, a local department store. A charge account is another way to buy now and pay later. In many ways, a charge account is like an installment plan.

In order to open a charge account, Drew had to fill out an application form like the one on page 129. The store approved Drew's application and issued him a charge card with his name and account number.

Types of Charge Account Plans

Regular charge account: requires that the monthly bill be paid in full at once.

Chase's Department Store offers two different charge account plans. With one plan, Drew would have to pay the entire bill at once. He would pay only for the actual cost of the items. There would be no finance charge. If Drew chose this payment plan, he would be using the store's *regular charge account*.

Revolving charge account: allows the bill to be paid in small payments over a period of several months.

The other method of payment Drew could use is known as a *revolving charge account*. With this plan, Chase's states the largest amount of money a customer may owe the store at any one time. Each month the customer must pay a stated amount of the balance, called the *minimum payment*. Interest is charged on the unpaid balance. As long as the minimum payment is paid, the customer can continue to charge purchases to the account.

NAME				
1. Applicant's Name — First, M.I., Last: Drew B. Perkins	2. Date of Birth: 10/21/–	3. Spouse's Name—First, M.I.		
4. Social Security Number: 346-20-6511	5. Marital Status: ☒ Single ☐ Married	☐ Widowed ☐ Separated ☐ Divorced	6. Telephone Number: 309-1224	☒ Own ☐ Close-by

ADDRESS			
7. Address — Number & Street: 2670 Bonn Drive	8. ☐ Own ☒ Rent ☐ With Parents	9. ☐ Furnished ☒ Unfurnished	
10. City — State: Midland, Michigan	11. Zip Code: 48640	12. How Long? $4\frac{1}{2}$ Yrs.	
13. Previous Address: 6210 East Way, Akron, Ohio 44327		14. How Long? 13 Yrs.	

EMPLOYMENT			
15. Applicant's Employer: DOE Systems	16. Position: trainee–computer oper.	17. How Long? 1 Yrs.	
18. Business Address — Street, City, State, Zip: 23446 Hamilton Street, Midland, Michigan 48640	19. Tel. No. & Ext.: 381-6035	20. Salary: $804 ☐ Wk. ☒ Mo. ☐ Yr.	
21. Previous Employer — Name & Address: Harper Brothers, 84 Mason Road, Akron, Ohio		22. How Long? $3\frac{1}{2}$ Yrs.	
23. Spouse's Employer — Name & Address	24. Position	25. How Long? Yrs.	

REFERENCES			
26. Nearest Relative not living in same household — Name & Address: Lena Perkins, 6210 East Way, Akron, Ohio 44327			
27. Bank — Name, Address: Second National Bank, Midland, Michigan		Account No.: 392-1677	
28. Automobile: 19— Yr. Ford Make	29. Financed by — Name, Address: Doxie Motor Company, Midland, MI	☐ Paid in Full ☒ Open Balance	

DEPARTMENT STORE, BANK CREDIT CARDS & OTHER CREDIT REFERENCES—Important—Give Account Numbers

Reference	Account No./Location	Reference	Account No./Location
30. Highland Store	23-156/Akron, Ohio	31.	
32.		33.	

34. Date: December 3, 19–	35. Applicant's Signature: Drew B. Perkins

Computing Finance Charges

Drew chose the revolving account and has been using it regularly. Drew recently visited the men's department at Chase's and charged several things. He bought a suit, two shirts, a pair of boots, and a down-filled jacket, which was on sale. The following month Drew received his account statement, shown on page 130. Look at the fine print on the bottom of the statement. It explains the way Drew is required to pay for the merchandise he charged.

Drew can charge up to $1,000 worth of merchandise, send the minimum payment that is shown on his statement, and pay a finance charge on the unpaid balance. The finance charge is 1.5 percent a month on the first $500 of the unpaid balance and 1 percent a month on any unpaid balance over $500.

Notice that Drew's statement shows a balance of $43.10 from a previous purchase. It also shows a payment of $10 which he paid toward his account last month. The total of Drew's current purchases is $186.85. What is his new balance?

SEND BILLING INQUIRIES TO: CHASE'S P.O. BOX 16, MIDLAND, MICHIGAN 48640

DATE	STORE	REFERENCE NUMBER	DEPT. NO.	MERCHANDISE AND TRANSACTION DESCRIPTION	AMOUNT OF PURCHASES	PAYMENTS AND CREDITS
OCT 10	8	3894728	12	MEN'S SHOP	186.85	10.00

You are not required to pay the amount of any item you properly reported as disputed, pending our compliance with applicable billing error law.

✱ **NOTICE: See reverse side for important information**

Any **FINANCE CHARGE** is determined by applying Periodic Rates of **1 ½ %** per month to the first **$500** of the Previous Balance and **1%** on such balance in excess of **$500** (Minimum **FINANCE CHARGE 50¢**), corresponding to **ANNUAL PERCENTAGE RATES** of **18%** and **12%** respectively. New Balance may be paid in full at any time. To avoid **FINANCE CHARGE** on next statement, full payment of New Balance must be received by due date shown.

PREVIOUS BALANCE	+ FINANCE CHARGE +	PLUS: TOTAL PURCHASES −	LESS: TOTAL PAYMENTS AND CREDITS =	NEW BALANCE	CLOSING DATE	MINIMUM PAYMENT AMOUNT	DUE DATE
43.10	.65	186.85	10.00	220.60	OCT 20, 19–	25.00	NOV 12

Balance subject to finance charge (previous balance)	$43.10
Rate of finance charge	1.5% *or* .015
Finance charge	$43.10 × .015 = $.6465 *or* $.65
New balance (previous balance plus finance charge plus current purchase minus total payments)	$43.10 + $.65 + $186.85 − $10 = $220.60

If Drew had charged more than $500, his finance charge would be computed in a different way. He would pay 1.5 percent on the balance up to $500 and 1 percent on any part of the balance above $500.

Here is how a finance charge would be computed for a bill with a previous balance of $681.

1.5% finance charge on first $500	$500 × .015 = $7.50
Additional balance over $500	$681 − $500 = $181
1% finance charge on additional balance	$181 × .01 = $1.81
Total finance charge	$7.50 + $1.81 = $9.31
New balance	$681 + $9.31 = $690.31

Exercises

Use the charge account plan described on pages 129 and 130 to find the finance charge (if necessary, round off to the nearest cent), and the new balance.

Previous Balance	Finance Charge	Current Purchases	Total Payments	New Balance
1. $ 75.00	$ 1.13	$703	$ 10	$ 769.13
2. 0	_____	43	0	_____
3. 0	_____	194	0	_____
4. 45.00	_____	71	10	_____
5. 168.08	_____	408	115	_____
6. 0	_____	95	0	_____
7. 272.10	_____	0	25	_____
8. 97.45	_____	312	25	_____
9. 101.00	_____	64	85	_____
10. 209.81	_____	431	20	_____

Finding Minimum Payments

Drew's statement gives the minimum payment due in the bottom right corner. Note that the minimum payment due for the month is $25. How did the store arrive at that figure? Every department store or large retail store that sells merchandise on credit has a schedule of payments. An example of a schedule of payments is shown below.

SCHEDULE OF PAYMENTS

Balance	Minimum Monthly Payment	Balance	Minimum Monthly Payment
$ 20 to 50.99	$10	$501 to 550.99	$42
51 to 100.99	12	551 to 600.99	45
101 to 150.99	15	601 to 650.99	47
151 to 200.99	20	651 to 700.99	50
201 to 250.99	25	701 to 750.99	52
251 to 300.99	30	751 to 800.99	55
301 to 350.99	32	801 to 850.99	57
351 to 400.99	35	851 to 900.99	60
401 to 450.99	37	901 to 950.99	62
451 to 500.99	40	951 to 1,000.00	67

Drew's new balance for the month is $220.60. Look at the schedule of payments on page 131. In the Balance column, find the range of figures in which Drew's balance falls. The balance falls between $201 and $250.99. The minimum payment that Drew should send the store is $25.

Of course, Drew can choose to pay more than this minimum payment. If he wishes, he can even pay off the entire balance. Suppose, however, that Drew pays $30 and then waits until the following month to pay more of his bill. He will discover that the 1.5-percent finance charge is computed on a balance that already includes a finance charge of 1.5 percent. In a way, that's a penalty for making small payments.

Exercises for Section Two

1. Use the schedule of payments on page 131 to find the minimum payment for each of the charge account customers below.

Customer	Balance of Account	Minimum Payment
a. R. Lopez	$ 86.40	$ 12
b. C. Alexander	124.90	_____
c. A. Gross	30.00	_____
d. F. Radler	211.13	_____
e. F. Wells	49.61	_____
f. H. Williams	550.83	_____
g. B. Fong	452.60	_____
h. D. Nadar	39.44	_____
i. R. Prince	28.00	_____
j. S. Sloan	958.88	_____

2. Dora Riley has a revolving charge account at Chase's Department Store. Her new balance is $101.86. Since she has other bills to pay, Dora is making only the minimum payment due of $15. If she makes no other purchases, what will her account balance be next month? (In Exercises 2–6, round off to the nearest cent.)

3. Sally Novito made the minimum payment of $37 on her $421.70 revolving charge account balance at Chase's. The next month Sally made the minimum payment of $35 on her new balance. That same month she purchased some items worth $93.46. What will be the new balance on Sally's next statement if she makes no more purchases?

4. Charles Dean's revolving charge account statement from Chase's

shows a new balance of $937.42. What would Charles be billed on next month's statement if he pays only the minimum payment due this month?

5. Charles Dean has decided to reduce his $937.42 revolving charge account balance by paying $225 each month. What amount will Charles be billed next month if he does make a $225 payment? What would the finance charge be? Remember that Chase's computes finance charges in the following way: 1.5 percent on the first $500; 1 percent on any amount of the balance above $500.

6. Lynn Haynes's revolving charge account balance at Chase's was $49.62 last month. During this month, she made the minimum payment of $10. Lynn has made additional purchases in the amounts of $81.21, $1.95, and $21.80. What will be her new balance? By what amount will her next statement balance be greater than her last month's balance?

Section Three
Credit Cards

It's been said that we live in an age of plastic credit. Indeed, consumers in the United States have more than 500 million credit cards. Those small plastic identification cards enable cardholders to charge almost anything from college tuition to cat food. All the holder of the credit card has to do is sign the receipt.

A consumer uses a company's credit card to charge merchandise or services of that company and is billed once a month. Some businesses charge a fee for the card, as well as interest—usually 1.5 percent a month—for late payment. But other businesses, such as oil companies, do issue credit cards to customers without a fee.

Diner's Club and American Express are credit companies in the travel and entertainment field. These giant companies charge fees of up to $20 a year for their cards. Holders of Diner's Club and American Express credit cards can charge purchases of merchandise or services from thousands of businesses all over the world. The cardholders receive monthly bills, and they must pay the entire balance upon receipt. There is no finance charge, but the issuers request a late fee from customers who are very late in paying their bill.

Visa (BankAmericard) and Master Charge are the best-known bank credit cards. These cards are usually issued free, and customers can use them to charge merchandise and services at a variety of stores and businesses that take part in the credit card plan. Cardholders can also get an installment cash loan up to a certain amount approved by the bank. Customers are billed monthly. Those who pay the balance due within 25 days of the day of billing avoid a finance charge. There is a monthly finance charge of 1.5 percent on a balance not paid within 25 days.

What does the merchant, store, or business owner pay for participating in a credit card plan? Those who accept credit cards for goods and services are charged up to a 7-percent fee by the credit card issuers for handling credit purchases.

Whether you prefer basketball or hockey, the theater or a concert, tickets for most entertainment events can be charged to a credit card.

Janet Sheehan, for example, invites a client to lunch and charges the bill for $15.50 on her credit card. How much of the $15.50 bill will the restaurant receive from the card issuer if the restaurant pays a 5-percent fee to the credit card company?

Bill	$15.50
5% credit fee	$.05 \times \$15.50 = \$.7750$ *or* $\$.78$
Amount restaurant receives	$\$15.50 - \$.78 = \$14.72$

Some businesses do not accept credit cards because of the fee they would have to pay. Other businesses find that accepting credit cards increases their business enough to make the fee worthwhile.

Many people use credit cards to make their budgeting easier. The cardholder receives a monthly bill on which each item charged is listed separately. In addition, the cardholder can write just one check for all of the purchases. Credit cards are convenient, and if cardholders treat credit cards like cash and keep them in a secure place, credit cards are also safe.

Credit cards are cash substitutes. They are a convenient form of credit that the wise consumer will not use to overspend. Each purchase charged with a credit card should be viewed as if it were a cash purchase. In addition, it's important to budget money each month to repay balances due in time to avoid high finance charges.

DO YOU KNOW

how to use credit wisely? Because credit costs money it's smart to follow the hints listed below.
- Check how much credit you are able to carry without going into debt.
- Get everything in writing that's related to your credit deal.
- Ask yourself honestly if you would buy the same item if you had to pay cash.
- Read your credit contract carefully and understand it before you sign.
- Keep payment receipts in a safe place.
- Pay off one credit plan before you sign up for another.
- Be certain that your monthly payments are about equal and that no large final payment is due.

Avoid any credit plan if any of these warning signals are missing. And continue to save regularly as you pay off your credit plan.

Exercises for Section Three

1. Each of the cardholders shown below will be billed for the total amount of their purchases. The merchants, however, may not receive the full price of their sale. Complete the exercise by computing the credit fee for each purchase and the amount the merchant will actually receive for the purchase. (If necessary, round off to the nearest cent in Exercises 1 to 6.)

Card-Holder	Amount of Purchase	Rate Charged by Issuer	Credit Fee	Amount Merchant Receives
a. A. Shay	$ 49.85	4.5%	$ 2.24	$ 47.61
b. F. Clark	347.90	6%		
c. I. Alonzo	84.62	7%		
d. N. Roose	546.71	5.5%		
e. R. Brenn	293.64	3%		
f. B. Green	7.52	6%		
g. W. Moon	18.76	3.5%		
h. P. Knight	438.50	7%		
i. H. Jarvis	73.45	6.5%		
j. M. Upton	751.37	4%		

2. Alice Kay used her bank credit card to pay $13.75 for fuel for her car. The card issuer charges merchants at the rate of 4.5 percent. What amount did the gas station receive for Alice's purchase? (Round off your answer to the nearest cent.)

3. Hal Wood used his entertainment credit card to take three people out to dinner. The dinner bill was $41.38. The credit card issuer charges the restaurant at the rate of 6 percent. What amount did the restaurant receive for Hal's dinner?

4. Tom Waters charged purchases totaling $183.57 to his bank credit card. His account already had a $78.50 unpaid balance. On his next bill, Tom was charged the 1.5 percent monthly rate on his total balance.
   a. What amount did the credit card issuer receive as a monthly finance charge from Tom?
   b. What amount, at a 6-percent rate, did the credit card issuer receive from the merchant's $183.57 sale?

5. During their vacation, Mary and Greg Jefferson stayed in motels and ate meals at restaurants. They used a bank credit card on most occasions rather than cash or checks. At the end of the month the Jeffersons received a statement for $932.67. They also received an oil company credit card statement for $162.46. No finance charges were added to either statement. What was the

total of the Jeffersons' payment if they paid both credit card balances in full?

6. The minimum payment indicated on the Jeffersons' bank credit card balance of $932.67 is $62. The minimum payment on the oil company credit card balance of $162.46 is $20. Suppose the Jeffersons had made only the minimum payment on each account. What amounts would they be billed on the next month's statements if they made no additional purchases? The finance charges for both credit cards are made at a rate of 1.5 percent of the balance due.

REVIEW FOR CHAPTER 7
BUY NOW, PAY LATER

Round off to the nearest cent when necessary.

1. Don and Molly Watson both have jobs, and they enjoy good credit ratings. They purchased household furnishings costing $3,478. They made a 15-percent down payment for the purchases. They also made a 20-percent down payment for landscaping that cost $1,265. What down payment have the Watsons made for the total of their purchases?

2. For household furnishings, the Watsons will pay $152.74 a month for 2 years. For landscaping, they will pay $93.61 a month for 1 year.
   a. During the first year, what will be the monthly total of these 2 payments?
   b. What total amount will the Watsons pay for household furnishings? (Remember to add the down payment.)
   c. What total amount will the Watsons pay for landscaping? (Remember to add the down payment.)

3. Leo Haig purchased tires from Race Automotive for $268. He will pay for them with 5 monthly installments of $56.28. What finance charge is Leo paying?

4. Ella Wyatt uses her Chase's Department Store revolving charge account to buy a variety of items: clothes, gifts, household goods. Her previous balance from last month is $238. She paid her minimum payment of $25 and made no other purchases during this month. At the 1.5-percent monthly rate, what would be Ella's new balance?

5. Margaret and Melvin Ashley had an unpaid balance of $34.85 on their Chase's revolving charge account. They paid $20 towards their balance. They made purchases this month totaling $892.54. What will be their next monthly finance

charge at the rate of 1.5-percent interest on the first $500 of the balance and 1 percent on the amount above $500?

6. Sheila Martin is paying $703.50 for a stereo set using her Chase's revolving charge account. She expects to pay $100 a month. The first month there will be no finance charge. After her $100 payment, what will be the finance charge for the second month? (Use the finance charges described in Exercise 5.) What will be the total balance for the second month?

7. Suppose Sheila made only a minimum payment of $52 on her $703.50 purchase. What would be the finance charge on the second month's billing? (Use the finance charges described in Exercise 5.) What would Sheila's total balance be for that month?

8. Jack Bailey made a $38.94 purchase using his Chase's revolving charge account. He made the minimum payment of $10 each month until the amount was paid. At the 1.5-percent monthly rate on the unpaid balance, what amount of interest did Jack pay? (The minimum finance charge according to Chase's agreement is $.50.)

9. Repairs on Cecil Albert's car cost $384.60. Cecil used his bank credit card to pay for the repairs. The garage owner was charged a 5-percent handling fee by the credit card issuer. What amount did the garage owner receive for the repair job?

10. Roger Rubio purchased a set of luggage for $74. He was going to pay for it with his bank credit card. The merchant's fee for Roger's credit card was 5.5 percent of the purchase. The merchant offered to reduce Roger's purchase price by 3 percent if Roger would pay cash. Roger accepted.
   a. How much did the merchant receive for the luggage?
   b. How much less would the merchant have received if Roger had used his credit card?

PART WRAP-UP

Consumer Challenge

Gloria Platter is waiting in the checkout line at the supermarket. Her bill is $21.48, but she only has $18.75 in her wallet. She would like to pay by check. Yesterday her checkbook balance was $105.80. Earlier this morning Gloria wrote checks for $81.22 and $14.00. However, she forgot to record the last check and isn't quite sure if her checking account will cover this purchase. She doesn't know what to do.

To make a wise decision, Gloria must be certain of her current checkbook balance. Do the following computations, and answer the questions. Explain your answers.

1. What is Gloria's current checkbook balance? (Assume a service charge of $.15 a check.) Will her balance cover the check?
2. What are the options open to Gloria? What do you think she should do?
3. Suppose Gloria had just been to the bank and deposited $110 to her account. What would be her new balance? How would this affect her decision? Suppose Gloria had just mailed in a deposit of $110 to her account. How would this affect her decision?
4. What are some ways Gloria could have avoided being placed in such an awkward situation?

For You To Solve

1. Hazel Brown wanted a low-cost checking account. She discovered that Citizens State Bank offers free checking with no required minimum balance and no monthly service charge. The bank did, however, have the following miscellaneous charges.
   a. 200 personalized and numbered checks—$2.50
   b. Stop payment order—$3
   c. Overdrawn account charge—$5
   d. Traveler's checks per $100—$1
   e. Safe deposit box rental (depending on size)—$5 to $10
   f. Money orders—$.40 up to $500; $.60 above $500
   g. Certified check—$2.50
   h. Cashier's check—$2.50

Hazel opened a checking account with an initial deposit of $300. During the first year, she did the following.

- Made 53 deposits.
- Wrote 220 personalized checks.
- Requested that the bank stop payment on 2 checks.
- Was overdrawn once.
- Purchased $500 in traveler's checks.
- Rented the smallest sized safe deposit box.
- Purchased 4 money orders, each under $500.
- Sent 1 certified check.
- Mailed 2 cashier's checks.

How much did Hazel spend for banking services the first year after she opened her checking account?

2. Carl Pimm opened a charge account at the local department store. If the monthly ending balance is paid within 30 days of the billing date, he is not required to pay the rate of 1.5 percent a month normally charged. During the month of May, Carl made purchases costing $6.75, $8.98, $12.24, $14.75, and $11.89. He received his bill on June 2. (June 1 is the billing date shown on the bill.) Do the necessary computations to answer the following questions. (Round off to the nearest cent.)

   a. How much was the total bill for the month ending May 31?
   b. On what date would Carl have to pay this bill in order to avoid paying a finance charge?
   c. Carl neglected to pay the bill until July 10. How much did he then owe the store?
   d. How much did he pay in interest each day for this oversight?

3. Carl also has a credit card at Lenox Square Department Store. The store computes a 1.5-percent monthly finance charge on the amount owed on the billing date of the previous bill. (No interest is charged the first 30 days.) Carl made purchases the first month of $60, $80, and $40. He made no payments on the account the first month. The second month he paid $80 on the account. Answer the following questions about his account.

   a. What was the total of his purchases at the end of the first month?
   b. What was the finance charge on his first month's purchases?
   c. What was the ending balance of his account at the end of the second month, including the finance charge?

4. Anne Smith began having some problems with a charge account. The store's computerized billing system broke down, and she received her monthly bill too late to pay her monthly balance within the 30-day no-interest period. In addition, one payment for $40 was not listed, and she was not given credit for a defective lamp costing $36. Her previous end-of-month balance was $220. Answer the questions below to compute the adjustments Anne must make to arrive at her correct bill.

   a. What should be the balance of her current month's bill? (Don't include any finance charges.)

   b. She was charged 1.5 percent on the previous end-of-month's balance because of the late billing. How much extra in finance charges was she billed for?

   c. By how much will she ask the store to adjust her bill because of the late billing and the failure to accurately credit her account?

Living Expenses

Performance Goals

When you finish work on this part, you should be able to:

- ☐ Compute approximate weekly food costs for families of different sizes and incomes.
- ☐ Compute unit prices.
- ☐ Select the better buy among food items by estimating prices, by using unit pricing, by computing price per serving, and by comparing costs of different preparation methods.
- ☐ Compute the amount saved and the rate of discount when buying items on sale.
- ☐ List aliquot parts of $1 as fractions, decimals, and percents.
- ☐ Compute rents to be paid on given leases.
- ☐ Compute total costs of moving.
- ☐ Determine monthly mortgage payments by using a mortgage loan schedule.
- ☐ Demonstrate how the term of a mortgage loan affects the amount of interest to be paid.
- ☐ Identify the amount of a monthly mortgage payment paid toward interest and the amount paid toward the principal.
- ☐ Compute closing costs in buying a home.
- ☐ Compute property taxes.
- ☐ Convert watthours into kilowatthours.
- ☐ Compute electric, gas, and water bills by using the appropriate rate schedules.
- ☐ List electric, gas, and water meter readings.
- ☐ Compute the costs of local and long-distance telephone calls (including initial and overtime charges).

CHAPTER

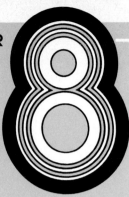

Going Shopping

Taxes take a big chunk from hard-earned paychecks. Services such as electricity cost more than ever. And the battle with inflation seems never-ending. What can we do when faced with rising costs? For one thing, we can try to stretch our dollars by shopping wisely.

There are two obvious weapons each consumer can use to cut costs when shopping for food and other goods.

1. *Substitution.* Buy items whose prices have not gone up, instead of popular and more expensive items.
2. *Elimination.* Don't buy goods that you don't really need.

These steps are only a beginning in the effort to get low-cost, quality goods in a rising price market. In this chapter, you will discover ways to cut costs by buying with skill and using money-saving techniques.

Section One
Shopping for Food

Food is one of the biggest items in most consumers' budgets. Unlike other expensive items that are not bought very often, food is bought several times a week. So the food budget can be adjusted readily to correct costly shopping errors.

Why are food bills sometimes higher than necessary? One reason is that many nonfood items are bought in food stores. But they can usually be bought for less elsewhere.

Let's look at the Fanoli family for an example. Mrs. Fanoli usually goes to the supermarket for her husband and two teenagers. She is asked to buy many things that are not even food items. Frank, a high school senior, always needs batteries for his transistor radio. Mr. Fanoli likes to have a stock of houseware products—everything from spot remover to glue—for his various hobbies. Mrs. Fanoli herself finds it a timesaver to buy the family's toothpaste, paper products, soaps, and so on, while shopping for food. Many of these items can be bought cheaper in discount stores.

One day Mrs. Fanoli bought the following nonfood items.

Product	Price	Product	Price
Soap powder	$ .79	Aluminum foil	$1.49
Paper towels	.55	Cookie cutters	1.81
Furniture wax	1.05	Magazines	1.75
Hand lotion	.59	Toothpaste	1.10
Hair spray	1.39	Pet food	3.30

Mrs. Fanoli's total bill at the supermarket that day was $39.92. How much did she spend on nonfood items? How much did she actually spend on food? What percent of Mrs. Fanoli's bill at the supermarket was for nonfood items? (To find the percent, simply divide the amount spent on nonfood items by the total amount of the bill. Then round off to the nearest percent.) It is estimated that 20 percent of all money spent in supermarkets goes for nonfood items. Did Mrs. Fanoli spend more or less than 20 percent?

Exercises

1. What percent of the Winston family's total grocery bill was spent for nonfood items on these shopping days? (Round off to the nearest percent.)

Date	Total Bill	Total of Nonfood Items	Percent for Nonfood Items
a. Sept. 2	$41.67	$7.32	18 %
b. Sept. 9	45.03	9.19	
c. Sept. 15	38.55	5.91	
d. Sept. 21	35.81	7.17	
e. Sept. 30	52.12	8.83	

2. Complete these exercises to find what percent of each shopper's total grocery bill was spent on nonfood items. (Round off to the nearest percent.)

Shopper	Total of Food Items	Total of Nonfood Items	Total Bill	Percent for Nonfood Items
a. A. Martino	$27.75	$ 6.39	$ 34.14	19 %
b. K. Griffin	40.19	10.03	————	————
c. C. Vota	6.32	.25	————	————
d. M. Chang	12.19	3.87	————	————
e. G. Collins	33.94	7.72	————	————

Budgeting for Food

Food spending depends on:
1. The number and ages of the people in the household.
2. The household income.
3. Where the household is located.

How much should you spend on food? There is no dollars-and-cents answer to this question. The amount a household spends for food depends upon the size of the household, income, the ages of its members, and location. The types of food and the importance of food as compared to other needs will also affect food budgeting.

Recent surveys by the U.S. Department of Agriculture have turned up a disturbing fact. The more people earn, the more they spend for food. But people who spend more for food do not necessarily have more nutritious diets. Why? Changing eating habits, the craze for snack foods, and the hundreds of fast-food stores may be some of the reasons. The popularity of more expensive, but often less nutritious, convenience foods may also be a reason.

The following table is adapted from a U.S. Bureau of Labor Statistics publication. Approximate weekly food costs for 1974 are shown for four-person families which include two teenagers and which have different incomes.

Annual Family Income	Weekly Food Cost	Annual Food Cost	Percent of Annual Income for Food
$ 9,198	$53.13	$2,763	30%
14,333	68.23	3,548	24.8%
20,777	85.63	4,453	21.4%

Given the first family's total annual income and their weekly food costs, here is how the 30-percent figure is arrived at.

Annual income	$9,198
Food cost a week	$53.13
Food cost a year (rounded off to nearest dollar)	52 × $53.13 = $2,762.76 *or* $2,763
Percent of annual income spent for food (rounded off to nearest tenth of a percent)	2,763 ÷ 9,198 = .300 *or* 30%

Note that the higher each family's income, the greater the amount of money spent for food. However, the percent they spend is lower.

People shopping for fresh fruits and vegetables can go to a specialty food store (above), a supermarket, or even a farmer's market. What are the advantages of each type of store? What other types of specialty food stores can you think of?

Exercises

1. These figures, adapted from the U.S. Bureau of Labor Statistics, show the yearly income and weekly food cost for different families in 1975. Find each family's yearly food cost and the percent of their annual income spent for food. (Round off food cost a year to the nearest dollar, and percent of annual income spent for food to the nearest tenth of a percent.)

Annual Family Income	Weekly Food Cost	Annual Food Cost	Percent of Annual Income for Food
a. $ 9,588	$56.76	$ 2,952	30.8 %
b. 15,318	73.60	_____	_____
c. 22,294	92.67	_____	_____

2. For each of the families below, find their approximate food cost a year. Then find the percent of their annual incomes spent for food. (Round off yearly food cost to the nearest dollar and percent of income to the nearest tenth of a percent.)

Family	Annual Income	Weekly Food Cost	Annual Food Cost	Percent of Annual Income for Food
a. Thompson	$ 4,250	$32.00	$ 1,664	39.2 %
b. Dietz	6,500	33.50	_____	_____
c. Diaz	8,400	38.00	_____	_____
d. Grant	10,750	50.25	_____	_____
e. Katz	12,000	53.00	_____	_____
f. Anders	14,550	61.00	_____	_____

Comparing Food Prices by Unit Price

Thrifty shoppers buy the kinds and amounts of food that their families will use with a minimum of waste. To make the most of their food dollar, they also compare food prices.

Unit price: the cost per unit of measure.

One way to compare food, and many nonfood, prices is to compute the unit prices. The *unit price* is the cost per unit of measure, for example, the cost of a pound, an ounce, an item, and so on. Before you can use unit prices to compare costs, though, you should be familiar with the measures used on containers of food and many nonfood items.

Measures Used on Containers. The law requires that the net weight or net volume of every box, can, bag, or bottle be written on its

*Volume:
capacity,
the ability
to contain.*

label. A bottle or can of liquid must show the *net volume*, or volume of the contents. The container for any other item must show the *net weight*, or weight of the contents. Most containers show net weight in ounces and net volume in fluid ounces.

Liquid measure is used to find the net volume of items such as syrup, fruit juice, and cooking oil. In the U.S. Customary system of liquid measure, 16 fluid ounces is equal to 1 pint. Other units of liquid measure are the quart and the gallon. The system used to measure the net weight of items such as sugar, cereal, and spaghetti is called *avoirdupois* (av-er-de-**poiz**) *weight*. In avoirdupois weight, 16 ounces is equal to 1 pound.

*The *avoirdupois*
system is used
to measure dry
products. Liquid
measures are
used for fluids.*

Thus, ounce, pound, pint, quart, and gallon are the measures that commonly appear on food labels. The relationships between these units of measure are shown below.

Avoirdupois Weight
1 pound (lb) = 16 ounces (oz)

Liquid Measure
1 gallon (gal) = 4 quarts (qt) = 128 fluid ounces (fl oz)
1 quart (qt) = 2 pints (pt) = 32 fluid ounces (fl oz)
1 pint (pt) = 16 fluid ounces (fl oz)

Many container labels also show net volume and net weight in metric units. You can read about metric measures on pages 151 to 153 and in the metric section in the back of the book.

To help you compare costs, you can use the price-an-ounce method of unit pricing. This method can be used for products measured by avoirdupois weight as well as for those measured by liquid measure, since both systems use ounces. You must be sure, however, that the items you are comparing use the same system of measurement, since a fluid ounce does not equal an avoirdupois ounce.

To use the price-an-ounce method, first change the measure of the items to ounces. (This is already done on most labels.) Then divide the number of ounces into the price of each item. This gives you the price of each ounce.

For example, a package of breakfast cereal costs $.69 for the 1-pound 2-ounce size. What is the cost an ounce of this cereal to the nearest tenth of a cent?

Ounces in a pound	16 oz
Additional ounces	2 oz
Total ounces in package	16 + 2 = 18 oz
Price for 18 ounces	$.69
Price an ounce	$.69 ÷ 18 = $.0383 *or* $.038

that prices for fresh vegetables and fruits are influenced by season and supply? Prices of these foods, canned or frozen, vary widely by item, brand, type of processing, and seasoning.

To save money, always be ready to:

1. Buy less expensive fruits and vegetables.
2. Check different forms of a food (fresh, frozen, canned, dried) to see which is the best buy.
3. Limit purchases of perishable food.
4. Take advantage of foods in season.
5. Watch for specials on canned and frozen products.
6. Try lower-priced brands.

Exercises

For each of these packaged cereals, find the price an ounce. (Round off to the nearest tenth of a cent.)

Type of Cereal	Weight of Package	Total Price	Price an Ounce
1. Crispies	13 oz	$ .71	$ .055
2. Nut flakes	1 lb 2 oz	.73	___
3. Corn flakes	18 oz	.55	___
4. Shredded wheat	13 oz	.75	___
5. Bran	20 oz	.87	___
6. Toasted oats	1 lb 2 oz	.51	___
7. Cracklers	16 oz	.86	___
8. Wheat flakes	1 lb 2 oz	.69	___
9. Natural cereal	1 lb 8 oz	1.29	___
10. Natural cereal with dates	1.5 lb	1.49	___

To help you compare food costs of products whose volumes are given in liquid measure, use the same method as that used above. For example, what is the price an ounce, to the nearest tenth of a cent, of a 1-quart 14-ounce can of unsweetened grapefruit juice costing $.69?

Fl oz in a quart	32
Additional fl oz	14 fl oz
Total fl oz in can	32 + 14 = 46 fl oz
Price for 46 fl oz	$.69
Price a fl oz	$.69 ÷ 46 = $.015

For each of these products, find the volume in ounces and the price an ounce. (Round off to the nearest tenth of a cent.)

Product	Volume	Volume in Fl Oz	Total Price	Price a Fl Oz
1. Vegetable oil	1 pt	16	$ .83	$ .052
2. Vinegar	1 qt		.49	
3. Dishwashing liquid	1 pt 6 fl oz		1.09	
4. Milk	1.5 gal		1.88	
5. Steak sauce	.5 pt		.69	
6. Ketchup	1.5 pt		1.13	
7. Soda	2 qt		1.12	
8. Spaghetti sauce	15.5 fl oz		.79	
9. Orange juice	.5 gal		1.05	
10. Liquid cleanser	1.5 qt		1.55	

The Metric System. As you have learned, ounces, quarts, pints, and so on, are part of the U.S. Customary system of measurement. On most products in the supermarket today, you will find other terms of measurement as well. These measurements are part of the International System of Units (SI). This system of measurement is used throughout the world. For our purposes, we will refer to it as the *metric system.* Now that the United States is moving toward using the metric system, many package labels include both kinds of measures. (For more information on the metric system, turn to pages 358 to 362 of this book.) Some frequently used metric measures are listed below.

Some *metric measures:* gram, kilogram, liter.

Avoirdupois Weight
1 gram (g) = .035 ounces
1,000 grams (g) = 1 kilogram (kg)
1 kilogram (kg) = 2.2 pounds

Liquid Measure
1 liter (L) = 1.06 quarts

As you can see, a liter is slightly larger than a quart, and a kilogram is slightly larger than 2 pounds.

To use unit pricing for goods measured on the metric system, follow the same method you used for goods measured on the U.S.

Customary system. For example, a sack of flour weighing 2 kilograms sells for $1.09. What is the price a kilogram to the nearest tenth of a cent?

Number of kilograms	2
Price for flour	$1.09
Price a kilogram	$1.09 ÷ 2 = $.545

Exercises

For each seasoning, find the price a gram. (If necessary, round off to the nearest hundredth of a cent.)

Seasoning	Weight	Price	Price a Gram
1. Sage	21 g	$.43	$ .0205
2. Oregano	14 g	.65	_____
3. Curry powder	42 g	.23	_____
4. Black pepper	49 g	.58	_____
5. Mustard	42 g	.39	_____
6. Basil	14 g	.59	_____
7. Cinnamon	32 g	.55	_____
8. Marjoram	9 g	.15	_____
9. Celery seeds	57 g	.65	_____
10. Nutmeg	39 g	.53	_____

Packages of Different Sizes. Most consumers would not pay more than a dollar for a package of breakfast cereal. They would, and do, pay that price by the ounce or gram unit for smaller packages— often without realizing it.

One way to avoid being fooled this way is to compute the unit price. Unit pricing is very helpful in comparing costs of different-sized packages selling at different prices.

For example, one market sells a 504-gram package of brand X corn flakes for $.81. How does this compare with a 364-gram package of brand Y corn flakes being sold at $.63?

Brand X   504 grams (1 box) for $.81
Brand Y   364 grams (1 box) for $.63

STEP 1: *Find the price a gram of the smaller package.*

Grams in brand Y corn flakes	364
Price for brand Y corn flakes	$.63
Price a gram of brand Y (rounded off to the nearest hundredth of a cent)	$.63 ÷ 364 = $.0017

STEP 2: *Compute the cost of the larger package at the same unit price as the smaller package.*

Grams in brand X 504
Price for brand X at .0017 × 504 = $.856 *or* $.86
unit price for brand Y
(rounded off to the
nearest cent.)

STEP 3: *Compare with the price of 504 grams of brand X.*

Price for 1 box brand X $.81
Price difference $.86 − $.81 = $.05

If both packages were 504 grams, brand Y would cost $.05 more than brand X. Thus, brand X is the better buy.

Decisions! Decisions! Even when buying cereal in a market, shoppers face numerous choices. Bran, wheat, oats, or corn? Toasted, puffed, frosted, or plain? Twelve, fourteen, or sixteen ounces? And, of course, price also is important to consider.

Of course, most shoppers wouldn't do these computations in a supermarket unless they had a calculator. For this reason, many states have passed a unit pricing law. According to this law, stores must post the unit price right under the product being sold. Most consumers find the posting of unit prices helpful in selecting the better buy.

When more than one item is included in the selling price. Another time that unit pricing helps shoppers is when more than one jar or can is included in the selling price. For example, frozen apple juice sells in 6-ounce cans and 12-ounce cans. The 6-ounce cans sell at 5 cans for $1.09. The 12-ounce cans sell at 3 cans for $1.35. Which is the better buy?

STEP 1: *Find the unit price an ounce of the small cans.*

Ounces in five 6-ounce cans	$5 \times 6\,oz = 30\,oz$
Price for 30 ounces	$1.09
Unit price an ounce	$1.09 \div 30 = $.0363 or $.036
(rounded off to the	
nearest tenth of a cent.)	

STEP 2: *Compute the cost of the large cans at the same unit price as the small cans.*

Ounces in three 12-ounce cans	$3 \times 12\,oz = 36\,oz$
Price for 36 ounces at unit	$36 \times $.036 = $1.296 or $1.30
price for small cans	
(rounded off to the	
nearest cent.)	

STEP 3: *Compare the prices given for the small and large cans.*

Price difference $1.35 − $1.30 = $.05

If both products totaled 36 ounces, the small cans would sell for less. The small cans are, therefore, the better buy.

Exercises
Complete the exercises on the next page. Which product in each pair is the better buy? (When computing price a gram, round off the unit price to the nearest hundredth of a cent. With all other measurements, round off the unit price to the nearest tenth of a cent. To answer the second column, round off to the nearest cent.)

Item and Price	Unit Price for Small Size	Cost of Large Size at Unit Price for Small Size	Price Difference
1. Soda	.017		
a. 1 qt–$.55	$ a fl oz	$ 1.09	$ .01
b. .5 gal–$1.10			
2. Detergent			
a. 35 fl oz–$.90	———	———	———
b. 50 fl oz–$1.20			
3. Evaporated milk			
a. 16-oz pkg–$.99	———	———	———
b. 24-oz pkg–$1.28			
4. Cereal			
a. 340-g box–$.45	———	———	———
b. 400-g box–$.73			
5. Crackers			
a. 8-oz box–$.65	———	———	———
b. 9-oz box–$.79			
6. Dog food			
a. 15-oz can–6 for $1.75	———	———	———
b. 29-oz can–2 for $1			
7. Tomatoes			
a. 8-oz can–2 for $.49	———	———	———
b. 15.5-oz can–2 for $.99			
8. Peas			
a. 12-oz can–4 for $1	———	———	———
b. 1-lb bag–3 for $1.19			
9. Spinach			
a. 10-oz bag–3 for $1.29	———	———	———
b. 1-lb bag–2 for $1.35			
10. Chow mein noodles			
a. 115-g box–2 for $.97	———	———	———
b. 170-g box–2 for $1.49			

Using estimates. Mrs. Fanoli often finds sales when she gets to the supermarket. She wants to know quickly if the savings arc worthwhile. Doing the computing in her head, she estimates the difference in price. She rounds the prices off, compares them, and finds the possible savings on bargain items. For example, an 8-ounce jar of pickles sells at 2 for $.41, and a 16-ounce jar sells at 2 for $.59. Which size is the better buy? (Remember that four 8-ounce jars weigh the same as two 16-ounce jars.)

Estimated price of four 8-ounce jars	$2 \times \$.41$ *or* $2 \times \$.40 = \$.80$
Estimated price of two 16-ounce jars	$\$.59$ *or* $\$.60$
Estimated difference	$\$.80 - \$.60 = \$.20$

Thus, 32 ounces of the 16-ounce jars costs about $.20 less than 32 ounces of the 8-ounce jars. Mrs. Fanoli will save about $.20 if she buys the larger jars.

If Mrs. Fanoli wants to buy only one 16-ounce jar how much will she pay? $\$.59 \div 2 = \$.295$. Since the price doesn't end in a whole cent, the store will round it off to the higher price of $.30.

DO YOU KNOW

seven tips for saving on food costs? Some ways to save on food costs were mentioned earlier in this chapter. Here are still others:

1. Sometimes prepackaged items such as meat or fruit are not marked with their correct weight. Most supermarkets have scales that customers can use to weigh items. Use the scales to check the weight of what you buy.
2. Use less expensive foods when they are part of a casserole.
3. Check labels carefully for expiration dates.
4. Money-saving coupons are often printed in newspapers and magazines. Use these coupons whenever possible.
5. Never shop when you are hungry. (You may buy out the store!)
6. Buy store brands when possible. These are goods sold only under the name of a particular chain or store. Often they are cheaper than the popular "name" brands.
7. Use unit pricing when possible. This can help you avoid buying a large, "economy" size that may be more expensive than smaller packages. Size alone cannot always be used as a guide.

Exercises

Complete these exercises. By estimating, decide which product in each pair is probably the better buy. Then compute the unit price of each product. Were you right? (Round off to the nearest tenth of a cent.)

Product	Estimated Better Buy		Unit Price
1. Cheese	b	**a.**	$.118 an oz
a. .75-lb wedge—$1.41		**b.**	.108 an oz
b. 8-oz pkg—$.86			
2. Potato chips		**a.**	
a. 106-g pkg—2 for $.79	———	**b.**	
b. 151-g pkg—$.63			
3. Potato sticks		**a.**	
a. 5-oz pkg—8 for $.75	———	**b.**	
b. 4 oz pkg—$.53			
4. Tea bags		**a.**	
a. 48 for $.87	———	**b.**	
b. 100 for $1.76			
5. Evaporated milk		**a.**	
a. 157-ml can—2 for $.48	———	**b.**	
b. 384-ml can—$.39			

Price a Serving

You have learned how to compare food values by unit price. Another way to compare is by the serving. A 1-pound box of instant mashed potatoes costing $.99 contains 24 servings. To find the price a serving, do the following computation. (Round off to the nearest cent.)

Price for package	$.99
Number of servings	24
Price a serving	$.99 ÷ 24 = $.041 *or* $.04

Price-a-serving comparisons are especially useful in buying meat. The number of servings in a pound of meat can vary widely from one cut to another depending on how much bone and fat the meat contains. A pound of boneless meat usually makes from three to four servings, but a pound of bony meat may make only one serving. So price a serving is usually a much better guideline than price a pound for finding bargains in meat.

For example, 1.5 pounds of ground beef costs $2.20. This is enough for 1 meal for a family of 4. A 4-pound pork loin roast costs

$4.20. The roast can serve a family of 4 for 2 meals. Which is the better buy? Find the price a serving of each type of meat, and compare the price difference. (Round off to the nearest cent.)

Price for ground beef for 4	$2.20
Price a serving	$2.20 ÷ 4 = $.55
Price for pork loin roast	
for 2 meals for 4	$4.20
Price for pork loin for 4	$4.20 ÷ 2 = $2.10
Price a serving	$2.10 ÷ 4 = $.525 *or* $.53
Price difference	$.55 − $.53 = $.02

Since the difference is so slight, the shopper could select either meat, depending on the family's preference.

Exercises

Find the total cost and the price a serving of each product. (Round off to the nearest cent.) Then for each group of products, find the better buy.

Product	Price	Approx. Number of Servings	Total Cost	Price a Serving
1. a. 12-lb ham	$1.19 a lb	24	$ 14.28	a. $ .60
b. 20-lb turkey	$ .69 a lb	36	13.80	b. .38
c. 5-lb roast	$1.69 a lb	13	8.45	c. .65
2. a. 3.5-lb chicken	$ .49 a lb	6	_____	a. _____
b. Pkg. frankfurters	$1.39	5	_____	b. _____
c. 2 lb Canadian bacon	$1.49 a lb	8	_____	c. _____
d. 1.5-lb chuck steak	$1.59 a lb	3	_____	d. _____
3. a. 10 lb potatoes	$1.09 a 5-lb bag	32	_____	a. _____
b. Natural cereal	$ .99 a box	15	_____	b. _____
c. 2 lb rice	$ .47 a lb	16	_____	c. _____

Preparation Differences

In choosing between fresh versus convenience foods, consider:
1. Time and effort.
2. Cost.
3. Taste.

Price is not the only thing people consider when they buy food. Most people also consider the time and effort needed to prepare different foods. Many consumers have to budget time as well as money. They may find that convenience foods, or ready-made foods, are the answer.

The cost of convenience foods often adds to food budgets. The added cost may be worthwhile if a convenience food saves you time and effort. Remember, too, that a convenience food doesn't always cost more than the same dish fixed from scratch. When you must choose between preparing food at home and buying it ready-made, compare the price a serving for the convenience food with that of the dish made at home.

For example, Mrs. Fanoli wants to serve peas with pearl onions. She can buy fresh peas for $.33 and onions for $.09. This will make about 6 one-half cup servings. A package of frozen peas with pearl onions costs $.59. This package serves 4. Which is the better buy?

STEP 1: *Find the price a serving of each dish. (Round off to the nearest cent.)*

Price a serving for frozen
   peas and onions $\$.59 \div 4 = \$.147$ *or* $\$.15$
Price for fresh peas and
   onions $\$.33 + \$.09 = \$.42$
Price a serving when homemade $\$.42 \div 6 = \$.07$

STEP 2: *Compare the price of 4 servings of frozen peas and onions with 4 servings of fresh peas and onions.*

4 servings of frozen peas and onions $\$.59$
4 servings of fresh peas and onions $4 \times \$.07 = \$.28$
Price difference $\$.59 - \$.28 = \$.31$

Mrs. Fanoli saves $\$.31$ by cooking fresh peas and onions. And she gets two more servings than she would with frozen peas and onions.

Mrs. Fanoli is planning to serve french fried potatoes. Her family prefers french fries made from scratch. But homemade french fries take more work. They also use a lot of oil for frying.

Mrs. Fanoli compared the costs of fresh and frozen french fries. As is sometimes true, the fresh potatoes actually cost more to make than the frozen potatoes. Look at the results of Mrs. Fanoli's comparison below.

2-pound bag of frozen french fries $\$.75$
2 pounds of fresh potatoes at $\$.19$
   a pound $2 \times \$.19 = \$.38$
1 quart of vegetable oil $\$.89$
Cost of homemade french fries $\$.38 + \$.89 = \$1.27$
Price difference $\$1.27 - \$.75 = \$.52$

Remember that time, cost, and taste all play a part in deciding on fresh foods versus convenience foods. In this case, Mrs. Fanoli can save both time and money by buying the frozen food product. Which product would you buy?

Exercises for Section One

Find the cost of 4 servings for each ingredient and the total price a serving of each dish on the next page. (Round off to the nearest cent.) Which is the better buy?

Dish and Ingredients for 4	Cost of 4 Servings	Price a Serving
1. Beans and franks		
a. Two 8-oz cans beans—2 for $.49	**a.** $ .49	**a.** $ .47
1 pkg hot dogs—$1.38	1.38	
b. Two 16-oz cans beans and franks—$.89 a can	**b.** 1.78	**b.** $ .45
2. Pizza		
a. 2 boxes pizza mix—$.98 a box	**a.** _____	**a.** _____
1 pkg sliced peppe-roni—$.98	_____	
b. 3 small frozen peppe-roni pizzas—2 for $1.75	**b.** _____	**b.** _____
c. 1 large pepperoni pizza from pizza parlor—$3.55	**c.** _____	**c.** _____
3. Applesauce		
a. 1.5 lb apples—$.39 a lb	**a.** _____	**a.** _____
.25 lb sugar—5 lb for $1.03	_____	
b. Two 1-lb jars apple-sauce—$.39 a jar	**b.** _____	**b.** _____
4. Corn		
a. 4 ears corn—3 for $.59	**a.** _____	**a.** _____
$\frac{1}{2}$ stick butter —$1.40 for 4 sticks	_____	
b. Two 8-oz cans but-tered corn—$.39 a can	**b.** _____	**b.** _____
5. Baked stuffed potatoes		
a. 2 lb potatoes—5 lb for $1.19	**a.** _____	**a.** _____
$\frac{1}{2}$ stick butter —$1.40 for 4 sticks	_____	
$\frac{1}{2}$ cup sour cream—$.45 a cup	_____	
b. 4 frozen stuffed pota-toes—2 for $.59	**b.** _____	**b.** _____
6. Spaghetti with sauce		
a. 1 lb spaghetti—$.53	**a.** _____	**a.** _____
1 lb beef—$1.19	_____	
Three 8-oz cans to-mato sauce—2 for $.49	_____	

b. Three 10-oz cans spaghetti with meat
sauce—$.87 a can

b. _____   **b.** _____

7. George Alt bought the following items for a picnic.

ground beef—$1.09   mayonnaise—$.87
hamburger buns—$.59   cups—$.99
catsup—$.47   paper plates—$1.15
potato chips—$.79   plastic forks—$.39
lettuce—$.45   pickles—$.79

a. What was his total bill?
b. How much did he spend for food?
c. How much did the nonfood items cost?
d. What percent of his total bill was for nonfood items? (Round
off to the nearest percent.)

8. Mr. McDuffy earns $9,750 each year. Mrs. McDuffy works
part-time and earns $98.50 a week. Their son Craig delivers
papers Monday through Friday and earns $1.55 a day.
a. What is the McDuffy family's gross annual income?
b. If their weekly food cost is $62.75, what is their annual food
cost? What percent of their annual income is spent for food?
(Round off to the nearest percent.)

9. Mr. King can buy potato sticks in a can at $.77 for 198 grams, or
in bags at $.71 for 6 bags. Each bag weighs 21.25 grams.
a. What is the price a gram of the potato sticks in a can? In
bags? (Round off to the nearest hundredth of a cent.)
b. Which is the better buy? Why?

10. Food Country Supermarket sells its brand of soap in three sizes.

3.5 oz personal size at 4 bars for $.59
4.5 oz bath size at 2 bars for $.43
9 oz large size at 2 bars for $.79

a. What is the price an ounce of the personal size? Bath size?
Large size? (Round off to the nearest tenth of a cent.)
b. Which size is the best buy? Why?

11. Marta Burns is making arrangements for a banquet at her club.
She needs food for 25 people in all. She has ordered a 10-pound
ham at $1.19 a pound, 5 heads of lettuce at $.59 a head, 7
pounds of potatoes at 5 pounds for $1.29, 5 dozen rolls at $.69 a
dozen, and 2 gallons of ice cream at $1.29 a quart.
a. What is the cost a serving of the ham? Lettuce? Potatoes?
Rolls? Ice cream? (Round off to the nearest cent.)
b. What did each person's dinner cost?

Section Two
Saving at Sales

What's the mystery of a sale? Why do people spend money at a sale that they never planned to spend? Why do they buy things they never left home to buy? Because "they were on sale." Part of any mystery is not knowing all the facts. This is true of sales, too. Before consumers buy something on sale, they should solve the mystery by knowing certain facts about the sale item.

When you consider buying a sale item, be sure to know the following facts.

1. The regular price of the item.
2. The sale price.
3. The amount saved.
4. The rate of discount.

Often a merchant gives only two of these four figures. This gap in sales information is where the mystery comes in. For example, look at the ad below. Are any of the facts left out? If so, which ones?

Computing the Amount Saved

Before you decide if the shirts below are good sale items, you should find out exactly how the sale price differs from the regular price. In other words, find the amount of savings. Find the sale price and regular price of one item so you can compare prices.

1 shirt, regular price	$2.49
1 shirt, sale price	$4.81 ÷ 2 = $2.405 *or* $2.41
Savings on 1 shirt	$2.49 − $2.41 = $.08

Now you have solved the mystery. You find that the savings is only $.08 a shirt or $.16 on the purchase of two shirts. That's not much of a bargain!

Here is how to find the savings if the regular price of an item is given along with the rate of discount. To find the savings on a $7.99 book sold at a 20-percent discount, multiply the price by the rate ($7.99 × .20 = $1.598 *or* $1.60 savings).

Computing Discount Rates

Rate of discount: fraction or percent of the regular price that the savings is.

If you know the regular price of an item and the savings, you can find the rate of discount. The *rate of discount* is the fraction or the percent of the regular price that the savings is. The rate of discount is stated as a percent (10%, 25%, and so on) or as a fraction ($\frac{1}{10}$, $\frac{1}{4}$, and so on). It is found by dividing the amount saved by the regular price. Here is how to compute the rate of discount on a record, regularly selling for $8.99, which offers a $4 savings.

Regular price	$8.99
Amount saved	$4
Rate of discount	4 ÷ 8.99 = .444 *or* 44%
(Rounded off to the nearest percent)	

Exercises

Compute the amount saved and the rate of discount (round off to the nearest percent) for each of the sale items shown below.

Sale Item	Regular Price	Sale Price	Amount Saved	Rate of Discount
1. Lined jacket	$ 14.97	$12.72	$ 2.25	15 %
2. Clock radio	39.99	35.19		
3. Tennis racket	20.99	18.89		
4. Leather boots	64.97	58.77		
5. Cardigan sweater	15.99	12.79		
6. Pocket calculator	15.95	10.45		
7. Blue jeans	14.59	11.19		
8. CB radio	44.77	37.67		
9. Tennis bag	13.99	10.49		
10. Golf clubs	119.99	95.49		

Aliquot Parts in Advertisements

Sales go on all the time. But as you learned at the start of this section, sales ads are often not complete. Many times they don't give all the information consumers need to decide if they are really saving money. Ads for sales usually use figures that make the products appear to be a good bargain.

A common way to advertise sales is to use certain fractions called aliquot parts. An *aliquot part* is any number that can be the divisor of another number without a remainder. For example, $\frac{1}{5}$ is an aliquot part of $1; it is contained 5 times in $1 without a remainder. You know that $\frac{1}{5}$ expresses the same thing as 20 percent. They are both considered aliquot parts of $1. Now think of $5 as the regular price of an item that is on sale for $\frac{1}{5}$ off. The amount of the discount and the sales price are easily arrived at. First multiply the discount rate by the regular price to find the amount of the discount.

Discount $\qquad \frac{1}{5} \times \$5 = \$1$

Then subtract the discount amount from the regular price to find the sale price.

Sale price $\qquad \$5 - \$1 = \$4$

Some ads use fractions, such as $\frac{1}{2}, \frac{1}{3}, \frac{2}{3}$, and so on, to show how much sale items are marked down. Others use percents, such as 50%, 25%, $33\frac{1}{3}$%. These are all aliquot parts of $1. The table below shows the aliquot parts of $1 that are used most often.

TABLE OF ALIQUOT PARTS

Fraction	Decimal	Percent	Fraction	Decimal	Percent
$\frac{1}{2}$ =	.50	= 50%	$\frac{4}{5}$ =	.80	= 80%
$\frac{1}{3}$ =	$.33\frac{1}{3}$	= $33\frac{1}{3}$%	$\frac{1}{6}$ =	$.16\frac{2}{3}$	= $16\frac{2}{3}$%
$\frac{2}{3}$ =	$.66\frac{2}{3}$	= $66\frac{2}{3}$%	$\frac{5}{6}$ =	$.83\frac{1}{3}$	= $83\frac{1}{3}$%
$\frac{1}{4}$ =	.25	= 25%	$\frac{1}{8}$ =	$.12\frac{1}{2}$	= $12\frac{1}{2}$%
$\frac{3}{4}$ =	.75	= 75%	$\frac{3}{8}$ =	$.37\frac{1}{2}$	= $37\frac{1}{2}$%
$\frac{1}{5}$ =	.20	= 20%	$\frac{5}{8}$ =	$.62\frac{1}{2}$	= $62\frac{1}{2}$%
$\frac{2}{5}$ =	.40	= 40%	$\frac{7}{8}$ =	$.87\frac{1}{2}$	= $87\frac{1}{2}$%
$\frac{3}{5}$ =	.60	= 60%			

Exercises

Complete the problems below by filling in the missing fraction, percent, or decimal.

1. $\frac{1}{5} = \underline{\ 20\%\ } = .20$
2. $25\% = .25 = \underline{\hspace{1cm}}$
3. $\frac{2}{3} = \underline{\hspace{1cm}} = .66\frac{2}{3}$
4. $\frac{3}{8} = 37\frac{1}{2}\% = \underline{\hspace{1cm}}$
5. $\underline{\hspace{1cm}} = 80\% = .80$
6. $\underline{\hspace{1cm}} = 87\frac{1}{2}\% = .87\frac{1}{2}$
7. $\frac{3}{4} = \underline{\hspace{1cm}} = .75$
8. $\frac{1}{2} = 50\% = \underline{\hspace{1cm}}$
9. $\frac{1}{8} = \underline{\hspace{1cm}} = .12\frac{1}{2}$
10. $\frac{1}{3} = 33\frac{1}{3}\% = \underline{\hspace{1cm}}$

We often have to decide quickly about whether a sale item is worth buying. As you can see in the table on page 165, each aliquot part of $1 can be shown as a fraction, a decimal, or a percent. Usually only one of these aliquot parts is used in an ad. Often it's the one that seems like the bigger discount. For example, consumers might see 20 percent off as a greater savings than $\frac{1}{5}$ off, even though both have the same value.

Two ads are shown below for the same sale. Can you tell which ad offers the better discount? By now you know they're both the same.

Chromatone—$\frac{1}{5}$ off 17-inch color TV portable Regularly priced at **$375**	20% off **Chromatone** 17-inch color TV portable Regularly priced at **$375**

How can you best compute the sale price of the television set? Since $\frac{1}{5}$ and .20 are equal, you can use whichever one you find easier.

Example A:

Regular price	$375
Fractional equivalent of discount rate	$\frac{1}{5}$
Discount	$375 \times \frac{1}{5} = \$75$
Sale price	$375 - \$75 = \$300$

Example B:

Regular price	$375
Discount rate	20%
Discount	$375 \times .20 = \$75$
Sale price	$375 - \$75 = \$300$

Part 3 LIVING EXPENSES

Suppose you wish to know what percent the sale price is of the regular price.

Regular price	$375
Sale price	$300
Percent of regular price	$300 \div 375 = .80$ *or* 80%

Another way to find out is to subtract the discount rate expressed as a percent from 100%: $100\% - 20\% = 80\%$.

Consumer Beware

As a consumer, you should read sale ads carefully and check all sale items for defects before you buy them. Be sure you get what you pay for. Compare prices and buy selectively. It is your right as a consumer to be protected from dishonest business practices, including sale gimmicks.

Many sales offer real bargains. If you are well informed and careful, you can save a good deal of money at sales.

DO YOU KNOW

where to go with a consumer complaint? Suppose you buy a new item, find it to be damaged, and then try to get it repaired or replaced. Sometimes you can get quick action by going directly to the seller of the item. If you don't, write or telephone the manufacturer's Customer Relations Department. Or send a letter to the company's president. Addresses of major companies are usually found in *Moody's Industrial Manual* in your local library. Mail a copy of your letter to your local Better Business Bureau or Chamber of Commerce. Many states and major cities have a Consumer Affairs Bureau that deals with consumer frauds and problems.

Some national organizations located in Washington, D.C., follow up on consumer complaints. A few of the better-known organizations are listed here.

1. *Bureau of Consumer Protection*, Federal Trade Commission, for consumer frauds, misleading advertising, and unfair trade practices.
2. *Office of Consumer Affairs* for all kinds of consumer problems.
3. *Consumers Union* for consumer lawsuits.
4. *Council of Better Business Bureaus* for information on your local bureau.

Exercises for Section Two

For each sale item, find the discount and the sale price. Then express the discount rate as a percent, and find what percent the sale price is of the original price.

Sale Item	Regular Price	Discount Rate as Fraction	Discount	Sale Price	Discount Rate as Percent	Percent of Original Price
1. Water skis	$ 88.00	$\frac{1}{4}$ off	$ 22.00	$ 66.00	25 %	75 %
2. Tennis racket	39.99	$\frac{1}{3}$ off				
3. Stereo speakers	165.00	$\frac{1}{3}$ off				
4. Tape player	88.88	$\frac{1}{4}$ off				
5. Desk chair	78.00	$\frac{1}{6}$ off				
6. Desk lamp	35.50	$\frac{1}{5}$ off				
7. Vanity mirror	37.60	$\frac{1}{8}$ off				
8. Oil painting	110.00	$\frac{2}{5}$ off				
9. Car radio	40.80	$\frac{3}{8}$ off				
10. Portable radio	17.40	$\frac{1}{10}$ off				

When necessary, round off the discount rate to the nearest percent and the price to the nearest cent.

11. Food Center is having a sale on grape soda. The regular price is $.79 a liter. The sale price is $.69 a liter.

   a. What is the amount saved?

   b. What is the rate of discount?

12. A package of three 90-minute cassettes was on sale for $5.16. Ann Farber figured that the regular price of each cassette had been reduced by $.72.

   a. What is the sale price of 1 cassette?

   b. What is the regular price of 1 cassette?

   c. What is the discount rate based on the savings on 1 cassette?

13. One newspaper ad offers a $6.98 record album at 40 percent off. Another ad offers the same album at $\frac{1}{3}$ off. What is the difference between the higher and lower advertised prices? (Hint: When computing your answer, use the fraction, not the decimal.)

14. Jack Gross would like to buy a camera lens that regularly sells for $88.75. He heard it advertised on the radio for $\frac{1}{4}$ off. He rushed to the camera shop to find them sold out of that brand. But a similar $82.50 lens was selling for $73.95. What was the discount rate on the similar lens? Which lens offered a better discount rate?

15. A dishonest merchant wants to make it appear that he is selling lamps at 16 percent off. What will he state as the original price of a lamp that usually sells for $35 in order to get $35 for the lamp on sale?

REVIEW FOR CHAPTER 8
GOING SHOPPING

In Exercises 1, 2, and 3, use unit pricing to determine which product is the better buy. (Round off the unit price of the popcorn to the nearest hundredth of a cent. Round off all other items to the nearest tenth of a cent.)

1. Ravioli
   a. 7.5-ounce can—$.39
   b. 14-ounce can—$.57

2. Party punch
   a. Two 46-fl oz cans—$.89
   b. 64-fl oz can—$.59

3. Popcorn
   a. 225-gram bag—$.25
   b. 280-gram bag—$.33

4. For a picnic for 6 people, Angelo Guarez bought the items below. What is the price a serving for each item? (Round off to the nearest cent.)
   a. 2 packages of hot dogs—$.99 each
   b. 2 packages of hot dog buns—$.39 each
   c. 2 containers of coleslaw—$.65 each
   d. 2 packages of potato chips—$.49 each
   e. Large bottle of soda—$1.09

In Exercises 5 to 10, round off the discount rate to the nearest percent.

5. Sally Perez has decided to buy an electric ice cream maker on sale for $31.89. The sale price is $6.40 off the regular price.
   a. What is the regular price of the ice cream maker?
   b. What is the rate of discount?

6. Elaine Marks bought a $6.98 record album and a $7.98 8-track tape at 15 percent off. She bought a $29.95 cassette recorder and four $2.20 cassette tapes at $\frac{1}{5}$ off.
   a. What was her savings?
   b. What was her total bill?

7. Jack Pease priced instant cameras at Camera World. The model that he wanted was selling for $33.95, reduced from $38.95.

   a. What was the savings?

   b. What was the rate of discount?

8. A flower shop is selling 3 spider plants for $4.86. The regular price of each plant has been reduced by $.22.

   a. What would 3 spider plants regularly cost?

   b. What is the rate of discount?

9. Which discount rate is a better deal? How much better?

   a. $\frac{1}{3}$ or 35% off?

   b. $\frac{1}{4}$ or $\frac{1}{5}$ off?

   c. 35% or $\frac{3}{8}$ off?

10. Heather Fleming can subscribe to a weekly magazine and get 34 weeks for $12. If she buys it at the newsstand, the price is $1 a copy.

    a. What is the regular price of 34 issues? The subscription price?

    b. What is the amount saved by subscribing for 34 weeks? The discount rate of a subscription?

Renting or Buying?

Like food, housing is a necessity of life. We all need a roof over our heads. And the odds are that some day soon you'll decide to buy or to rent a home.

There are several advantages to owning your own home. It is an investment. You pay for your house while you live there, just as you would pay for a long-term credit purchase. Owning your home offers security for you and your family. The monthly principal will not increase over the 20 or more years that you are paying off your home loan. And after you've paid your loan, the house is yours. There are certain tax advantages for homeowners. And homeowners are considered a better credit risk. In addition, since your home is your own property, you may use it as it suits your needs and tastes.

There are also some disadvantages to being a homeowner. You need a sizable amount of cash to make a down payment. Down payments are usually 10 to 30 percent of the home's cost. You must take care of all taxes, repairs, and upkeep for as long as you live in your home. Every month you must meet regular payments on your home loan.

Renting, on the other hand, involves fewer chores. Your landlord is responsible for taxes, insurance, and repairs. Renting also involves fewer financial risks. If your income goes down, you can leave a rented apartment or house without heavy losses. Renting a home does not tie you down to one spot. It gives you time to decide whether you want to live in a certain area.

But there are also disadvantages to renting a home. As rents go up, you will pay more and more money for that roof over your head. All you will have to show for it is a lot of rent receipts. Your monthly payments will not go toward buying the home. And since you are living on someone else's property, you are not free to make changes you might make in your own home.

In choosing whether to rent or buy a home, you will need to consider what your housing needs are at different times of your life. For example, if you are a single person from 18 to 25 years old, you will probably rent. Renting will help you keep your costs to a minimum. Are you over 25? Are you married? Then you are more likely to rent a larger apartment or a small house.

During the next ten years, you may have children. Also, your family income may be higher. So you might buy a small house. Later you may have an even higher income and want to invest in a larger house. When you have retired or your children have left home, you may have a lower income and need less room. You may then decide to rent a smaller, more convenient place and to sell the house.

Section One
Renting and Leases

George and Lois Baker feel cramped in their one-room apartment. They have decided to rent a larger apartment. They found a two-bedroom apartment by checking the real estate section of their local paper.

Lease: legal agreement between owner and renter.

Tenant: one who rents a house or apartment.

Landlord: owner of property that is rented to another.

Before the Bakers can move in, they must sign a lease. A *lease* is a legal agreement between an owner and a renter that states the terms under which property is rented. The Bakers are called *tenants.* The owner of the apartment they rent will be their *landlord.* Under the terms of their lease, the Bakers will rent the apartment for $210 a month for two years. Some apartment and house leases run for one year. Other leases, such as in public housing financed by the government, allow the tenant or the landlord to cancel the lease with only one month's notice.

The Bakers have read their lease carefully. The lease includes the following items.

1. Description and location of the property.
2. Terms of the lease with the exact beginning and ending dates.

3. Amount of rent and when it is to be paid.
4. Limits on the number of people living in the apartment and ban, if any, on pets.

5. *Security deposit.* This is usually a fee equal to one month's rent. It is often required by the landlord to protect against property damage or tenants' failure to pay rent.
6. Repairs. The duties of the landlord and those of the tenants in cases of certain types of damage to property.
7. Tenant's right to *sublet* (lease to someone else) before the end of the lease.

8. Which utilities and services, such as water, gas, and electricity, may be included in the rent.
9. Landlord's right of entry. The conditions under which the landlord can enter the apartment. For example, the landlord can enter to show the property to new renters one month before the end of the lease.
10. Renewal or cancellation of the lease. The steps a tenant should take to renew or cancel.
11. In a case of public housing, certain facts about a tenant's income.

The Bakers will have a 2-year lease and will rent their apartment for $210 a month. What is the total rent they will pay over the 2-year period?

Monthly rent	$210
Number of months in 2-year period	$2 \times 12 = 24$
Total rent for 2-year period	$210 \times 24 = \$5,040$

Exercises

Compute the term of each lease in months and the total amount of rent to be paid.

Amount of Monthly Rent	Time of Lease in Years	Time of Lease in Months	Total Rent Paid
1. $195.00	1.5	18	$ 3,510
2. 215.00	1		
3. 90.70	3		
4. 305.25	2		
5. 179.60	1.5		
6. 333.34	2		
7. 89.50	2		
8. 269.44	2.5		
9. 608.08	3		
10. 201.45	2.5		

Costs of Moving

When Lois and George move from their small apartment to their new one, they'll need more cash than just their first month's rent. Their lease requires one month's rent as security. The Bakers must also pay charges for electricity and telephone service. They will also hire movers to take their large pieces of furniture. These expenses are part of any move, so it's important to set aside enough cash for them if you move.

The Bakers computed the amount they'd need the first month. Their moving costs were $110.65, their utility deposits were $15.75, and their telephone hookup fee was $18.75. Remember that they also need to pay their first month's rent, plus security.

Moving costs	$110.65
Utility deposits	15.75
Telephone hookup	18.75
First month's rent	210.00
One month's security	210.00
Total cost	$565.15

Exercises for Section One

Find the total amount that each of these moves cost.

Moving Costs	Utility Deposit	Phone Hookup	First Month's Rent	Security Deposit	Total Cost
1. 6 hr at $28 an hr	0	$13.40	$205.00	1 mo rent	$ 591.40
2. $179	$11.25	15.50	187.50	2 mo rent	_____
3. $66	7.65	9.90	116.00	$100	_____
4. 8 hr at $32 an hr	15.40	19.85	340.00	1 mo rent	_____
5. $35	5.85	0	95.00	0	_____
6. $883	16.60	21.25	295.00	2 mo rent	_____
7. 10 hr at $29.50 an hr	0	17.20	310.00	$200	_____
8. $237.50 plus 10% tip for movers	0	14.40	Free concession	1 mo rent ($212)	_____
9. 6.5 hr at $24 an hr	17.70	12.35	243.30	$150	_____
10. $192.75	16.45	13.30	227.70	2 mo rent	_____

11. Linda Horton has just signed a 2-year lease for an apartment. The monthly rent is $179.50. What is the total rent to be paid over the 2-year period?

12. Wallace Jennings has found two apartments he likes. One has a monthly rent of $139.20 and utilities are included. The other has a monthly rent of $119 and the cost of utilities is estimated at $24.25 a month. What will be the cost of each apartment with utilities over a 1-year period? 2-year period? 3-year period?

13. The McQuistons pay a monthly rent of $235.70 for their apartment. In addition, they rent a summer bungalow for $65 a week for 12 weeks each summer. How much rent do they pay for a 3-year period?

14. When the Carlsons moved, they contracted for a van and 3 movers at $27.80 an hour plus 1 extra hour of travel time for the movers to get back. The move took 6.5 hours, not counting the travel time. The Carlsons' initial moving costs also included $12.30 for a utility deposit, $16.65 for telephone hookup, $245.30 for the first month's rent, and $200 for a security deposit. What were their total moving expenses?

When you move into a new apartment or house, don't forget about costs for furniture and decorations. Whether you're starting from scratch or just filling in a few pieces, furniture will be an important expense in your budget.

15. When the Wheatleys moved, they chose a mover who charged a flat rate of $205. They decided to give the movers a 10-percent tip because of the careful treatment of their furniture. The Wheatleys moved into a $279-a-month apartment where utilities are included. The telephone company charged $9.80 to install the first phone and $4.35 for the two extension phones installed. The landlord required 2 months' rent as security. What were the Wheatleys' total moving expenses?

Section Two
Buying and Mortgages

Friends of the Bakers, Edna and Jonas Slezak, are buying a home in the suburbs. They have two children and need more room. The Slezaks weren't sure how much they should pay for a house, so they used the one-fourth rule to help them decide.

The "one-fourth rule" is a guideline used by some agencies of the federal government that deal with housing and loans. The rule says: "Housing expenses should be about one-fourth of your gross income." (Housing expenses include insurance and all utilities except telephone.) For example, if the Slezaks' total gross income is $12,000, will they have enough to cover monthly housing costs of $250? Use the one-fourth rule.

Gross income	$12,000
Percent set aside for housing expenses	25% *or* .25
Yearly housing expenses	$12,000 × .25 = $3,000
Monthly expenses	$3,000 ÷ 12 = $250

The Slezaks *can* afford about $250 a month for housing expenses, according to this rule.

There are other rules followed by other experts, too. But all of these rules are subject to change. The Slezaks could spend more or less on a house than the rules suggest depending on their answers to the following questions.

1. Are they expecting their income to rise, stay the same, or possibly end?
2. Do they already owe a good deal of money?
3. Are they prepared for emergency expenses?
4. Are they willing to give up other things in order to own their home?

DO YOU KNOW

that a home is not always a house? Of course, we've all learned about tepees and igloos, which are still in use today. Many people own something other than a typical one-family house. Cooperatives, condominiums, and mobile homes are three modern alternatives in housing.

If you choose a *cooperative*, or *co-op*, apartment, you buy stock in a corporation that owns the apartment house. You pay a monthly fee to cover your share of the building's operating costs.

With a *condominium* you hold individual title. You actually own the unit you occupy.

Or you may want a *mobile home*. If you invest in a mobile home, you will have a compact, newly built home that you can move to a rented space, usually among other mobile homes. Most mobile homes can be hauled and give the freedom to move around that some people want.

Of course, cooperatives, condominiums, and mobile homes all have advantages and disadvantages. Careful study is needed before you decide to buy.

Exercises

Compute the yearly and monthly amounts that each person or family pays for housing. (If necessary, round off to the nearest cent.)

Person or Family	Gross Income	Percent for Housing	Yearly Housing Expenses	Monthly Housing Expenses
1. G. Chesson	$ 7,800	28%	$ 2,184	$ 182
2. S. Grossman	9,200	23%		
3. Glazier	11,000	25%		
4. Hill	11,750	21%		
5. J. Hein	12,000	29%		
6. Kamm	13,200	24%		
7. Pike	13,900	20%		
8. S. Smithe	14,000	22%		
9. Trimmer	14,675	26%		
10. Walker	15,500	27%		

Computing Mortgage Payments

The Slezaks, like most young couples, had to find a way to finance their home. The real estate agent told them about available home loans from local lenders such as banks. They were told which banks were offering the best credit terms. The Slezaks found that the amount of money they could borrow to pay for a home depended on the following things.

1. Their credit rating and the total amount of other debts.

2. Their income.

3. The value of the house they were buying.

Mortgage: legal agreement that if the borrower does not meet home loan payments, the lender becomes owner of the property.

When the Slezaks are approved for a home loan they will sign a mortgage. A *mortgage* is a legal agreement that if the borrower does not meet the home loan payments, the lender then becomes the owner of the property.

Payments on home loans are made in monthly installments and may extend over a period of 15 to 30 years. The amount of the monthly payments is determined by the amount of money borrowed, the length of time taken to pay the loan back (called the *term* of the loan), and the interest rate.

Often, when you sign a mortgage, you are required to make a down payment. The down payment is usually about 10 to 30 percent of the price of the house. Of course, the more you can afford to put down on your house, the less money you need to borrow.

The Slezaks will make a down payment of $5,000 on their $25,000 home. They will take out a mortgage for the balance of the price, $20,000. They can get a mortgage loan for the balance at 8-percent interest. They will pay the loan back in monthly payments over 20 years. Their monthly payments repay the principal, the $20,000 borrowed, and the interest.

MORTGAGE LOAN SCHEDULE
(MONTHLY COST PER $1,000)

Years	7%	7.5%	8%	8.5%	9%	9.5%	10%	11%
15	8.99	9.27	9.56	9.85	10.14	10.44	10.75	11.37
20	7.75	8.06	8.36	8.68	9.00	9.32	9.65	10.32
25	7.07	7.39	7.72	8.05	8.39	8.74	9.09	9.80
30	6.65	6.99	7.34	7.69	8.05	8.41	8.78	9.52

To determine the Slezaks' monthly payments, the bank uses the mortgage loan schedule shown above. Here is how the Slezaks' monthly payments are computed. Locate 20 in the Years column. Go across the 20 row to the 8% column. The amount where the row meets the 8% column is $8.36. This is the monthly payment for each $1,000 the Slezaks borrow. Determine how many $1,000s are in the $20,000 they are borrowing. Then multiply that number by $8.36.

Number of $1,000s in $20,000	$20,000 \div 1,000 = 20$
Monthly payment on $1,000 at 8%	$8.36
Monthly payments on $20,000 at 8%	$20 \times \$8.36 = \$167.20$

Exercises

Compute the monthly payments on each of these mortgages. Use the mortgage loan schedule on page 178. (If necessary, round off the monthly payment to the nearest cent.)

Mortgage	Interest Rate	Term of Mortgage	Monthly Payment on $1,000	Monthly Payment
1. $22,000	9%	25 yr	$ 8.39	$ 184.58
2. 22,000	9%	30 yr		
3. 29,000	9.5%	20 yr		
4. 29,000	10%	20 yr		
5. 30,500	8.5%	15 yr		
6. 32,500	8.5%	15 yr		

Each of these houses has a 25-year mortgage at 9 percent. Compute the down payment, the amount of the mortgage, and the monthly payments for each house. Use the mortgage loan schedule on page 178. (If necessary, round off the monthly payment to the nearest cent.)

Cost of House	Percent of Down Payment	Down Payment	Amount of Mortgage	Monthly Payment
7. $26,000	10%	$ 2,600	$ 23,400	$ 196.33
8. 28,200	15%			
9. 30,000	12%			
10. 32,500	11%			

What is the Interest on Mortgage Payments?

As you have learned, part of the monthly payment is interest on the loan. The amount you pay each month that goes toward interest decreases as you take longer to repay the mortgage loan. But actually, you will pay more interest on a long-term loan.

To get an idea of how this works, let's compare the cost of a $1,000 loan at 7 percent to be repaid in 15 years to the cost of the same loan to be repaid in 20 years. This example will show you how the term of a loan affects the interest. Use the mortgage loan schedule on page 178.

STEP 1:

Monthly payment on $1,000 loan at 7 percent for 15 years	$8.99
Number of months in 15 years	$15 \times 12 = 180$
Amount repaid in 15 years	$180 \times \$8.99 =$ $1,618.20

STEP 2:

Monthly payment on $1,000 loan at 7 percent for 20 years	$7.75
Number of months in 20 years	$20 \times 12 = 240$
Amount repaid in 20 years	$240 \times \$7.75 =$ $1,860.00

STEP 3:

Difference in payments on 15-year loan and 20-year loan	$1,860.00 − $1,618.20 = $241.80

Since the amount of money borrowed is the same in each case, the difference is in the interest paid. The 20-year loan costs $241.80 more in interest than the 15-year loan.

Exercises
Suppose $10,000 is borrowed at 7.5 percent for each given period. Complete these exercises to find the total amount paid for each loan. Use the mortgage loan schedule on page 178. Remember that the mortgage loan schedule tells the monthly payment per $1,000.

Number of Years	Number of Months	Monthly Payment per $1,000	Total Monthly Payment	Total Amount Repaid on Loan
1. 15	180	$ 9.27	$ 92.70	$ 16,686
2. 20				
3. 25				
4. 30				

5. What is the difference in the total amount repaid on a $10,000 loan at 7.5 percent for 15 years and the same loan for 20 years? For 25 years? For 30 years?

Suppose $20,000 is borrowed at 9 percent for each given time period. Complete these exercises to find the total amount repaid on each loan. Follow the method you used with Exercises 1 to 4.

Number of Years	Number of Months	Monthly Payment per $1,000	Total Monthly Payment	Total Amount Repaid on Loan
6. 15	_____	$ _____	$ _____	$ _____
7. 20	_____	_____	_____	_____
8. 25	_____	_____	_____	_____
9. 30	_____	_____	_____	_____

10. What is the difference in the total amount repaid on a $20,000 loan at 9 percent for 15 years and the same loan for 20 years? For 25 years? For 30 years?

Monthly payments on a home mortgage loan remain the same for however long it takes to pay off the loan. Most of the early payments go toward paying interest. Later, the payments go toward paying off the principal. Interest on a home mortgage loan is always based on the unpaid balance.

For example, the Slezaks' monthly payment on a $20,000 home loan at 8-percent interest is $167.20. How much of this first monthly payment is for interest? Use the simple interest formula $(I = P \times R \times T)$ to find out.

Principal	$20,000
Rate	8% or .08
Time	1 month *or* $\frac{1}{12}$ year
Interest	$20,000 \times .08 \times \frac{1}{12}$ = $133.333 *or* $133.33

The monthly payment of $167.20 includes interest. If the $133.33 interest is subtracted from $167.20, the difference is the amount that goes toward reducing the principal.

Monthly payment	$167.20
Interest	$133.33
Amount paid toward principal	$167.20 − $133.33 = $33.87

The amount of $33.87 is subtracted from $20,000 to find the new balance of the Slezaks' loan. Then the interest for the second month is computed on the new balance. How much interest will the Slezaks pay for the second month?

New balance of loan	$20,000 − $33.87 = $19,966.13
Interest (I = P × R × T)	
First find P × R	$19,966.13 × .08 = $1,597.2904
	or $1,597.29
Multiply P × R by T	$1,597.29 × $\frac{1}{12}$ = $133.1075
	or $133.11

The $133.11 interest is subtracted from the monthly payment of $167.20 to find the amount that reduces the principal of the loan.

Amount paid toward principal	$167.20 − $133.11 = $34.09
New balance of loan	$19,966.13 − $34.09 = $19,932.04

These figures can be arranged in a table, as shown here.

ORIGINAL LOAN: $20,000 (8%)

Payment Number	Monthly Payment	Interest	Amount Paid Toward Principal	Balance of Loan
1	$167.20	$133.33	$33.87	$19,966.13
2	167.20	133.11	34.09	19,932.04

Exercises

Prepare a table for the first 10 payments toward a $10,000 loan at 9 percent for 15 years. Use the same headings shown in the table above. Begin with these answers for the first payment: Monthly Payment, $101.40; Interest, $75; Amount Paid Toward Principal, $26.40; Balance of Loan, $9,973.60. (Round off the interest to the nearest cent.)

Other Costs of Buying

Point: fee added to the basic mortgage cost. A point is 1 percent.

Some states set a legal maximum interest rate for home loans. But many lending institutions, banks included, add a fee to their basic mortgage charges. These fees are called points. A *point* is another name for 1 percent.

The Slezaks' local bank charges them 2 points on their $20,000 mortgage. They will have to pay the point fee when they receive the loan. The point fee for the use of the loan is computed using the simple interest formula.

Mortgage	$20,000
Rate of 2-point fee	2% *or* .02
Time (this fee is paid only once)	1
Charge for receiving mortgage	$20,000 × .02 × 1 = $400

Closing costs: costs involved in making the purchase of property legal and final.

Some closing costs:
Title search.
Lawyer's fee.
Title insurance.
Appraisal.
Property survey.

In addition to the point fee, the Slezaks must pay other costs known as *closing costs*. One closing cost is for the title search. The *title search* is like a history of the property. It must show that no one else has a claim on the property. Without this proof, the Slezaks cannot get a mortgage loan. The *deed* describes the property in detail. It also transfers ownership of the property to the buyer. The Slezaks' closing costs will include their lawyer's fee. The lawyer charges for checking the contract, the title search, and the deed.

In addition to these costs, the Slezaks must pay for *title insurance*. This insurance protects the bank against any risk or hidden property claim not turned up in the title search. The Slezaks must also pay the property taxes for the rest of the year. If the current owner has paid the taxes through the end of the year, the Slezaks will pay the owner their share of those taxes. The Slezaks will also pay for an *appraisal,* an estimate of the value of their property. And they must pay for home insurance. The home insurance is based on 80 percent of their home's value.

The Slezaks thought they had a complete list of closing costs. But there was a question about the boundaries of their property, so a surveyor was called in. A *surveyor* is a person who inspects land records and the field measurements based on these records. The surveyor measured the Slezaks' property accurately, and the information was entered in the town land records. Of course, the surveyor charged a fee for this work.

Let's look at the closing costs the Slezaks must pay on the day they take possession of their home.

Legal fees	6 hours at $50 an hour = 6 × $50 = $300
Title search	$225
Title insurance	
Rate	$5.25 per $1,000 of mortgage
Mortgage	$20,000
Number of $1,000s in $20,000	20,000 ÷ 1,000 = 20
Title insurance	20 × $5.25 = $105

Quarterly property taxes	$164.06
Appraisal and other bank charges	3 days at $80 a day = 3 × $80 = $240
Home insurance	
Rate	$6 per $1,000 on 80 percent of value of property
Value of property	$25,000
80 percent of the value	.80 × $25,000 = $20,000
Number of $1,000s in $20,000	20
Home insurance	20 × $6 = $120
Surveyor's fee	1.5 days at $60 a day = 1.5 × $60 = $90
2-point fee	$400
Total fees and expenses	$300 + $225 + $105 +$164.06 + $240 + $120 + $90 + $400 = $1,644.06

In addition to the closing costs and the cash down payment, the Slezaks will also have to pay some of the same charges as the Bakers. For example, both families must pay moving costs, utility deposits, and phone hookup charges.

Exercises

1. The Manolds bought a $30,000 townhouse in the city. They made a 10-percent down payment and borrowed the rest from a bank at 8 percent for 20 years.

   a. What was the amount of the down payment?
   b. What was the amount of their mortgage?
   c. What is 80 percent of the value of their property?

2. Some of the additional expenses that the Manolds must pay are listed below. Find the cost of each expense, and then compute the total amount.

   a. Bank fee—1.5 points.
   b. Legal fees—5 hours at $45 an hour.
   c. Title insurance—$4.75 per $1,000 of mortgage.
   d. Home insurance—$3.50 per $1,000 on 80 percent of property value.
   e. Surveyor's fee—1.5 days at $50 a day.
   f. Semiannual property taxes—$393.75.
   g. Other bank fees—$52.10.

h. Moving expenses—7 hours at $28 an hour.

i. Utilities deposits—$21.19.

j. Telephone hookup—$17.90.

k. Total costs.

Property Taxes

Property assessment: estimate of a property's value.

Most local governments and some state governments tax property. Here is how the amount is computed. A government official *assesses*, or estimates, the value of your property. You pay a certain percent of the assessed value. The percentage you pay is computed using the tax rate set by the local government.

For example, the Slezaks' property tax is stated at the rate of $3.50 per $100 of the assessed value. The assessed value is 75 percent of the actual value. What is the tax on the Slezaks' $25,000 home?

Actual value of property	$25,000
Assessed value—75 percent of actual value	$25,000 × .75 = $18,750
Tax rate	$3.50 per $100
Number of $100s in $18,750	$18,750 ÷ 100 = 187.5
Tax	187.5 × $3.50 = $656.25

Exercises

Compute the assessed value and the tax for each piece of property. (If necessary, round off to the nearest cent.)

	Actual Value	Assessment Rate	Assessed Value	Tax Rate per $100	Property Tax
1.	$15,200	45% of actual value	$ 6,840	$2.50	$ 171
2.	17,000	50% of actual value		2.90	
3.	18,500	55% of actual value		3.00	
4.	19,750	60% of actual value		3.10	
5.	20,000	62% of actual value		2.85	
6.	22,250	64% of actual value		3.25	
7.	25,000	67% of actual value		3.50	
8.	28,600	70% of actual value		4.10	
9.	35,000	72.5% of actual value		3.75	
10.	43,200	75% of actual value		4.00	

Although there is no American coin that represents a mill, many local communities quote their tax rate on property in terms of mills.

Mill: one-thousandth of $1. One mill equals $.001.

A *mill* is one-thousandth of $1, or $.001. Here is how to compute the tax on a house assessed for $25,000 in a city where the tax rate is 37.5 mills.

Tax rate per $1 in mills	37.5 mills
1 mill	$.001
Tax rate per $1	37.5 × $.001 = $.0375
Number of $1s in $25,000	25,000 ÷ 1 = 25,000
Tax	$.0375 × 25,000 = $937.50

Exercises

Compute the tax rate per $1 and the property tax for each of these property owners.

Property Owner	Assessed Value	Tax Rate per $1	Tax Rate per $1	Property Tax
1. B. Volk	$15,300	27.5 mills	$ .0275	$ 420.75
2. J. Reese	17,000	30.5 mills		
3. Q. Mavis	19,750	30 mills		
4. V. Wiener	21,000	32.6 mills		
5. M. Victor	22,500	33 mills		
6. R. Berry	25,000	34.5 mills		
7. J. James	30,000	35 mills		
8. L. Brace	35,000	35.5 mills		
9. D. Fisher	40,000	36 mills		
10. C. Hunter	43,500	36.5 mills		

What Property Taxes Pay For

Most homeowners pay property taxes. The taxes are used to support public schools, parks, fire departments, police departments, and so on.

In the Slezaks' community, 37.5 percent of their annual property tax is budgeted for schools. Remember that the Slezaks pay property taxes of $656.25 a year. How much of the Slezaks' tax money goes for schools?

Total property tax	$656.25
Percent budgeted for schools	37.5% *or* .375
Amount of tax budgeted for schools (rounded off to the nearest cent)	$656.25 × .375 = $246.093 *or* $246.09

Many colleges today are partly supported by tax funds.

Choosing a home is one of the biggest decisions a consumer makes. Whether we decide to rent an apartment or buy a house, we all want a place that we'd like to come home to. So when you are deciding about your home, take your time. There are few things more important than a home.

Exercises for Section Two

These agencies receive portions of the Slezaks' local property taxes of $656.25 a year. Compute the amount each agency receives. Then check to see that the percents total 100 percent and that the total tax amount is about $656.25. (If necessary, round off to the nearest cent. Because of rounding off, the final answer will not be exactly $656.25.)

Agency	Percent of Property Taxes	Amount Received
1. Schools		
a. Local	28.80%	$ 189.00
b. State	1.26%	_____
c. Community college	7.44%	_____
2. Libraries	5.00%	_____
3. County-wide aid	15.37%	_____
4. City parks and recreation	12.58%	_____
5. Water agency	5.90%	_____
6. Police	7.41%	_____
7. Fire protection	5.66%	_____
8. Sanitation	4.23%	_____
9. Roads and traffic	3.19%	_____
10. Flood control and soil conservation	3.16%	_____
11. Totals	_____ %	_____

Solve these problems. (When necessary, round off to the nearest cent.)

12. The Gabor family has a gross income of $13,000. They follow the one-fourth rule for their housing expenses. How much can they afford a year for housing? A month?

13. The Chromowskis just bought a $36,000 house. They made a down payment of 15 percent and financed the rest with a 25-year mortgage at 10 percent. (Use the mortgage loan schedule on page 178 for this exercise and for Exercises 14 and 15.)

    a. What amount was the down payment?

    b. What was the amount of the mortgage?

c. What is their monthly mortgage payment? Yearly mortgage payment?

d. What total amount did they pay over the 25-year period?

14. Juan Gonzales financed the property for his business with a $15,000 mortgage for 20 years at 9 percent. What amount did he pay in interest, and what amount did he pay toward the principal on his first four payments? What was the balance of the loan after each of the first four payments?

15. The Juno family bought a $40,000 brownstone house. They made a down payment of 25 percent and financed the rest at 8 percent for 20 years. Find the amount of these house-related expenses.

a. Bank fee—2.5 points.

b. Title insurance—$4.50 per $1,000 of mortgage.

c. Property taxes—$4.10 per $100 of assessed value. (Assessed value in their city is 70 percent of actual value.)

d. First monthly house payment.

16. Helene Goldman bought a house assessed for $16,000 in a town where the tax rate is 35.5 mills per $1 of assessed value.

a. How much are her taxes?

b. If 32 percent of her property taxes goes for schools, what amount do the schools receive?

c. If 9.5 percent of her property taxes goes for police protection, how much does this department get?

REVIEW FOR CHAPTER 9
RENTING OR BUYING?

1. Mary Ellen and her roommate rented an apartment from March 1, 19X7, through December 31, 19X9. They each paid $132.50 a month for rent. How much total rent did they pay over the entire lease?

2. Carl and his two roommates are each paying $127 rent for their apartment. If they renew their lease for 1 year, they will get a 10-percent increase in rent. If they renew for 2 years, they will get a 7-percent increase.

a. What would the new monthly rent payment be if they renew for 1 year? For 2 years?

b. What total rent would they pay for 1 year? For 2 years?

3. The Edgartons moved from a one-room apartment to a two-bedroom apartment in the same complex. They rented a dolly at $3 an hour for 7 hours so that they could move their posses-

sions themselves. They had already made security deposits for their smaller apartment. However, they had to pay an additional $3.75 for their utility security deposit and $105 for their rent security deposit. It cost them $9.50 to have the telephone reinstalled. Their first new rent payment was $264. What is the total of these moving costs?

4. Justin Laker figures that he can pay 28 percent of his gross annual income of $9,800 for housing. How much can he afford to pay a *month* for housing? (Round off to the nearest cent.)

5. When the Hamners bought their $29,000 home, they made a 20-percent down payment and financed the rest at 7.5 percent for 20 years. (Use the mortgage loan schedule on page 178 for this exercise and for Exercises 6 and 7.)

   a. What was the amount of the down payment? Of the mortgage?

   b. What was their monthly mortgage payment? Yearly mortgage payment? (Round off to the nearest cent.)

6. The Crockers financed their home with a $23,000 mortgage at 7.5 percent for 25 years. The Fullers had the same mortgage, but for 20 years. What is the difference in the total amounts paid by the Crockers and the Fullers?

7. The Samsons financed their new summer home with a $20,000 mortgage at 9 percent for 25 years. What was their interest payment, the amount paid toward decreasing their loan, and the balance on the loan on the first payment? The third payment? (If necessary, round off to the nearest cent.)

8. The Shamhart family bought a $16,000 vacation house. They made a 15-percent down payment and borrowed the rest from the bank at 8 percent for 15 years. They paid $3 per $1,000 of the mortgage for title insurance. They paid $2.60 per $1,000 on 80 percent of their property value for home insurance. What total amount did the Shamharts pay for insurance?

9. The town assesses the Shamharts' property at 65 percent of actual value. The tax rate is $2.40 per $100 of assessed value.

   a. How much property tax do the Shamharts pay?

   b. How much of their property tax will the fire department receive if 6.3 percent of all property taxes goes for fire protection? (Round off to the nearest cent.)

10. The Bartons' property was assessed at 60 percent of its actual value of $41,800. The tax rate was 21.5 mills per $1 of assessed value. How much property tax did the Bartons pay?

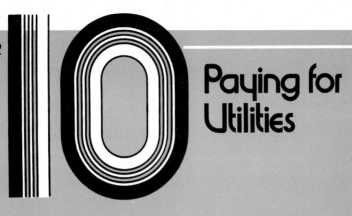

CHAPTER

Paying for Utilities

OUR UTILITY BILLS ARE TOO HIGH! WE MUST CUT DOWN!

OKAY, IF YOU SAY SO!

NANCY! WHERE ARE MY EGGS?

I PUT THEM IN THE SUN TO COOK AND THEY AREN'T DONE YET!

You can live in a house, a cabin, or a mobile home. You can be single or married, have children or not have children. One thing is certain. It's difficult to live anywhere without electricity, telephone, gas, and water. These conveniences are often called *utilities*.

You will find useful information in this chapter to help you understand how you are charged for utilities. You will also discover a number of ways to save on the cost of these increasingly expensive items.

Section One
Electricity

Consumers need electricity. Many things in your home run on electricity. You can light, heat, and cool your home with electricity, and you can store and cook your food with it. In addition, most appliances—from steam iron to vacuum cleaner—run on electricity.

With today's energy shortage, declining fuel supplies create high prices. Thus, it's important for all of us to save, or *conserve*, energy. By conserving energy, you can help prevent worse shortages and lower your own energy bills at the same time.

Electricity is measured in watts. *Watts* (W) measure the total energy flowing in an electric circuit at any moment. For example, a 100-watt light bulb uses 100 watts of electricity every moment it is turned on.

Watts do not measure how much electricity is used over a period of time. The total amount of electricity used for any period is measured in *watthours* (Wh). To find the watthours that an appliance uses in a certain period of time, multiply the watts used at any moment by the number of hours the appliance is used. For example, find the watthours a 100-watt light bulb uses if it's on for 10 hours.

Watthours: units of measure for amount of electricity used over a period of time.

Number of watts	100
Hours used	10
Watthours used	100 × 10 = 1,000

You could pay for the electricity you use by watthours, but you don't. Instead you pay by kilowatthours. As you learned in Chapter 8, *kilo* means "thousand" in the metric system of measures. So a kilowatthour (kWh) equals 1,000 watthours. Your electric meter registers 1,000 watthours as 1 kilowatthour. To change watthours to kilowatthours, just divide the number of watthours by 1,000. For example: 4,500 watthours ÷ 1,000 = 4.5 kilowatthours.

Kilowatthour: 1,000 watthours.

Exercises

Each exercise gives the number of watts in a light bulb and the length of time it was burned. Find the number of watthours and the number of kilowatthours used in each case. (Round off to the nearest whole kilowatthour.)

Number of Watts	Amount of Time Used	Number of Watthours	Number of Kilowatthours
1. 100	60 hr	6,000	6
2. 200	30 hr		
3. 75	20 hr		
4. 60	30 hr		
5. 300	12 hr		

Rate Schedules

The cost of electricity varies. It depends on what part of the country you live in and on how much it costs the utility company to supply electric current to your home. You are charged according to the number of kilowatthours you use each month.

Part 3 LIVING EXPENSES

In one region of the country, the rate schedule below is in effect. Note that consumers do not pay a flat rate for each kilowatthour used. Instead, the more they use, the less they pay for each kilowatthour. Note, too, that there is a minimum monthly service charge, or *meter charge*, and a fuel cost adjustment (see below).

KILOWATTHOUR RATE SCHEDULE

CUSTOMER METER CHARGE
Minimum monthly charge $1.50

ENERGY CHARGE

First 60 kWh	$ .060 a kWh
Next 90 kWh	.045 a kWh
Next 150 kWh	.027 a kWh
Next 600 kWh	.021 a kWh
Over 900 kWh	.018 a kWh

FUEL COST ADJUSTMENT
To be applied to total monthly kWh $.009 a kWh.

What is the cost (without the fuel cost adjustment) to a customer in this region who uses 1,072 kilowatthours of electricity in a month? To compute the customer's bill, use the rate schedule above, and do the computation as shown below. The middle column is for computing the costs; the right column is for showing the number of kilowatthours used at different prices. (For our purposes, costs are rounded off to the nearest cent when necessary.)

		kWh used
Minimum charge	$ 1.50	
		1,072
Cost for first 60 kWh	60 × $.060 = $ 3.60	− 60
		1,012
Cost for next 90 kWh	90 × $.045 = 4.05	− 90
		922
Cost for next 150 kWh	150 × $.027 = 4.05	− 150
		772
Cost for next 600 kWh	600 × $.021 = 12.60	− 600
		172
Cost for next kWh	172 × $.018 = 3.10	
Subtotal electric bill	$28.90	

*Fuel cost
adjustment:*
extra charge for
use of energy.

As national energy supplies become scarce, the companies that supply your electricity pay more for the fuel they use. Often this increase in cost is passed on to the consumer as an extra charge called a *fuel cost adjustment*. Rather than change their rates each

Fuel factor rate: amount used to find extra charge customers pay toward fuel costs.

time fuel costs increase, most utility companies just increase their fuel factor rate. The *fuel factor rate* is an amount that the company multiplies by a customer's total kilowatthours used to find the customer's fuel cost adjustment.

For example, the fuel factor rate on the bill we just discussed is $.009. How would you find this customer's fuel cost adjustment and the total amount of the bill?

Total kilowatthours used	1,072
Fuel factor rate	$.009
Fuel cost adjustment	1,072 × $.009 = $9.648
(rounded off to nearest cent)	or $9.65
Subtotal electric bill	$28.90
Fuel cost adjustment	$9.65
Total amount of bill	$28.90 + $9.65 = $38.55

Exercises

Use the kilowatthour rate schedule on page 193 to complete these exercises, and find the total monthly electric bill in each case. (If necessary, round off each answer to the nearest cent.)

Kilowatt-hours Used	Meter Charge	Cost at $.060 Rate	Cost at $.045 Rate	Cost at $.027 Rate	Cost at $.021 Rate	Cost at $.018 Rate	Fuel Cost Adjt.	Total Bill
1. 257	$ 1.50	$ 3.60	$ 4.05	$ 2.89	$ 0	$ 0	$ 2.31	$ 14.35
2. 142								
3. 84								
4. 140								
5. 225								
6. 280								
7. 730								
8. 870								
9. 962								
10. 1,274								

Reading an Electric Meter

The kilowatthours you use are registered on an electric meter. An employee of the utility company records the kilowatthours you use each month by reading meters such as the one on the next page. Each meter has several dials, and each dial reads in the reverse direction from the dial following it. Here is how to read the meter. Look first at the dial farthest to the left. The hand is between the

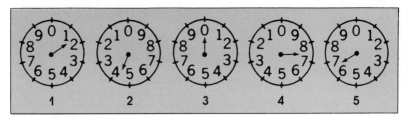

| 1 | 2 | 3 | 4 | 5 |

Always record the smaller number if the meter hand points between two numbers.

numerals 1 and 2. Write down the *smaller* number. On the second dial, the hand is between 4 and 5. Again, write down the smaller number. Of course, if the hand points exactly at a number, you write down that number. Read and record the other dials. When you finish, your meter reading should be 14076.

The meter reading of 14076 means that 14,076 kilowatthours of electricity have been used since the meter was installed or since it began measuring all over again at 00000 kilowatthours. To find out how many of those kilowatthours were used during the past month, subtract the previous month's reading from the current reading.

For example, the two meter readings on a customer's electricity bill are 14076 and 13418. The meter reading of 13418 is from the previous month. To find how many kilowatthours were used in the past month, subtract the smaller reading from the larger reading.

Meter reading for previous month	13418
Meter reading for present month	14076
Total kilowatthours used for the month	$14{,}076 - 13{,}418 = 658$

DO YOU KNOW

how to save on electricity bills? Here are some tips.

1. Turn off lights, radios, and TVs when they're not in use.
2. Defrost your refrigerator before too much ice forms. Set the control switch to "economy" whenever possible.
3. Be sure your house is well insulated to keep in the cool air during the summer and the warm air during the winter.
4. In hot weather, use fans instead of air conditioners whenever you can.
5. If you need an air conditioner, buy one that is efficient. Maintain your air conditioner according to the manufacturer's instructions.
6. Avoid buying small electrical appliances that you don't really need.

Exercises for Section One

What meter reading does the utility company record in each case?
Note: Always use the markings on the circle rim as a guide.

1.   51872

2.

3.

Find the number of kilowatthours used by each family in May.
Then use the rate schedule shown here to find their monthly
electric bill. (Don't forget the fuel adjustment charge. And, if
necessary, round off to the nearest cent.)

KILOWATTHOUR RATE SCHEDULE	
CUSTOMER METER CHARGE	
Minimum monthly charge	$1.75
ENERGY CHARGE	
First 70 kWh	.070 a kWh
Next 80 kWh	.055 a kWh
Next 160 kWh	.036 a kWh
Next 500 kWh	.028 a kWh
Over 810 kWh	.019 a kWh
FUEL COST ADJUSTMENT	
To be applied to total monthly kWh	$.012 a kWh

Family	Reading at Beginning of May	Reading at End of May	Number of Kilowatthours Used	Cost of Electricity in May
4. Ross	70631	71001	370 kWh	$ 22.93
5. Koski	52714	52844	_____	_____
6. Bello	19088	19348	_____	_____
7. Schwartz	68275	68800	_____	_____
8. Ville	68392	69592	_____	_____

9. Diagrams of Paul Armaze's electric meters are given below.

Beginning of September

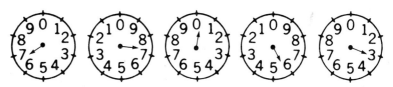

End of September

What meter readings would the employee of the utility company record?

How many kilowatthours of electricity did Paul use?

10. What is Paul's electric bill for September? Use the kilowatthour rate schedule in Exercises 4 to 8 and follow the same rounding off procedure.

Section Two
Your Telephone

For most consumers, living in an apartment or house without a telephone would be unthinkable. Telephone companies have a variety of plans to provide service to as many people as possible.

Types of phone service:
1. Party lines.
2. Budget.
3. Regular private lines.

Customers can choose among party lines, budget plans, and regular private lines. With a two- or four-person party line, the phone number is shared by a number of households. In one state with the budget plan, customers pay a monthly service charge of only $4.45. They then pay for each outgoing call at the rate of $.082 or $.06, depending on the time the call is made.

Many customers choose a regular private line. For them, the privacy and convenience are worth the extra cost. In one state, the regular plan includes a monthly charge of $7.42 plus 50 message units. A *message unit* is a unit of measure of telephone usage; it is not the same as one call. (Message units are discussed in more detail later.) With the regular plan, there is an additional charge for any calls over 50 message units a month. Customers who choose to have an extra phone or extension, or to have an unlisted phone

Message unit: unit of measure of telephone usage.

number, also pay an extra monthly charge. The cost of a phone call depends on the following things: the distance you call, the amount of time you talk, the time and day you call, and whether the operator helps you place the call.

Costs of Different Calls

Message Unit. In one region, there is a large city and two nearby counties. This city and the two counties make up a "message unit calling system." The system is divided into 36 zones. Customers living in Zone 1 are charged only 1 message unit to call anyone in the same zone. The charge is the same no matter how long the call is. But calling from Zone 1 to Zone 12, for example, customers are charged 2 message units for the first 3 minutes, and then 1 message unit for each additional 2 minutes or fraction of 2 minutes.

Phone-call costs are made up of the initial charge and the overtime charge.

Table 1 below shows how the message unit charges are figured. Locate Zone 1 under *Find Your Zone Here*. Move your finger to the right to Zone 12. Notice that 2 message units are charged for a call to this zone. This is the *initial charge*.

TABLE 1: INITIAL CHARGES BY MESSAGE UNIT

Find your	Find the zone you're calling here:																											
zone here:	1	2	3	4	5	6	7	8	9	10	11	12	13	14	15	N1	N2	N3	N4	N5	N6	N7	N8	N9	W1	W2	W3	W4
1	1	1	1	1	2	1	1	1	1	1	2	2	2	2	2	3	3	3	4	4	4	5	5	5	3	3	3	4
2	1	1	1	1	1	1	2	1	1	1	2	2	2	2	3	3	3	3	4	4	4	5	5	5	2	2	2	3
3	1	1	1	1	1	1	2	1	1	2	2	2	3	3	3	3	3	3	3	4	4	4	4	5	2	2	2	3

Table 2 shows the *overtime charges*. Locate the 2 message units line. Move to the right along this row, and you'll see that the initial period is 3 minutes. If you talk longer than 3 minutes, there is a charge of 1 message unit for each additional 2 minutes or fraction.

TABLE 2: OVERTIME CHARGES

If your initial message unit charge is:	Your initial period is:	If you talk longer than the initial period, the overtime charge is:
1 message unit	Unlimited	None
2 message units	3 min	1 message unit for each additional 2 min or fraction
3, 4, or 5 message units	3 min	1 message unit for each additional 1 min or fraction
6 message units	3 min	2 message units for each additional 1 min or fraction

For example, Mary Brinks lives in Zone 1. Yesterday morning she called Tom Ahern in Zone 12. They talked for 14 minutes. How much did the call cost at the rate of $.082 a message unit?

Cost of message unit	$.082
Length of call	14 min
Number of message units in initial period of 3 minutes	2
Initial charge	$2 \times \$.082 = \$.164$
Number of minutes in overtime period	$14 - 3 = 11$
Number of message units in overtime period	$11 \div 2 = 5.5$ *or* 6
Overtime charge	$6 \times \$.082 = \$.492$
Total cost of call (final answer is rounded off to nearest cent)	$\$.164 + \$.492 = \$.656$ *or* $.66

Exercises

Marv Gordon lives in Zone 2, and he made the calls listed below. He is charged for calls at a rate of $.082 a message unit. Compute the cost of each call. (Round off the total cost of each call to the nearest cent.)

Zone Called	Length of Call	Initial Charge	Overtime Charge	Total Cost
1. N4	5 min	$ .328	$ .164	$ .49
2. 8	7 min			
3. W4	2 min			
4. 14	21 min			
5. N9	18 min			
6. 15	6 min			
7. 7	8 min			
8. N1	11 min			
9. N2	4 min			
10. N8	23 min			

Types of long-distance calls:
1. Station-to-station.
2. Person-to-person.

Long Distance. Telephone costs add up when you call long distance—that is, outside of your message unit calling system. Your message unit calling system, or area, is often shown in the front of your telephone directory. Many directories also include a schedule of rates to help customers figure the price of long-distance calls. An example of a rate schedule is shown on page 201.

There are two main types of long-distance calls: station-to-station and person-to-person. *Station-to-station* means the call is paid for how to save on phone bills?

1. Dial long-distance calls yourself. It's cheaper.
2. When possible, make your calls at off hours or on weekends.
3. Time your calls; keep conversation to a minimum.
4. Organize your calls if you call long-distance and several family members want to talk.
5. Choose your extension phones with care. Fancy phones cost more.
6. Use the toll-free numbers provided by many organizations.
7. If your phone is out of order, report the length of time. You may be due for a credit.

no matter who receives it. With *person-to-person* calls, the call is paid for only if a certain person receives the call.

Types of station-to-station calls:
1. Direct distance dialed.
2. Operator-assisted.

There are two types of station-to-station calls. A *direct distance dialed* call is a call you dial yourself. An *operator-assisted* call is a call the operator helps you to place. For example, you would make an operator-assisted call if you wanted to reverse the charges of a phone call.

Let's look at the different costs for a long-distance call to Atlanta, Georgia. In the Station-to-Station section, find the Direct Distance Dialed columns, then the Full Weekday Rate column. Note that a customer who dials a number directly to Atlanta during a weekday pays $.50 for the first minute and $.34 for each additional minute. Now look at the next two columns. As you can see, calling in the evening, late at night, and on weekends is cheaper. Continue across on the same line to the Operator-Assisted columns. Note that the charge for an operator-assisted call to the same city made at any day or hour is $2.05 for the first 3 minutes. The overtime charges depend on the day and time of day that the call is made.

The most expensive call to Atlanta is person-to-person. In the Person-to-Person columns you find that the charge is $3.15 for the first 3 minutes. The overtime charge on a person-to-person call also depends on when the call is made.

Here is how to use the rate schedule on page 201. Jonathan Lux lives where that long-distance rate schedule is in effect. On Tuesday he dialed a call to Luisa Alvarez in Philadelphia at 9:30 a.m., and they talked for 15 minutes. What was the cost of his call? First, look in the Station-to-Station section for the Direct Distance Dialed columns. Then find Philadelphia in the list of cities.

Long-distance rates to other states <small>(excluding Alaska and Hawaii)</small>

CALLS TO:	STATION-TO-STATION								PERSON-TO-PERSON			
	DIRECT DISTANCE DIALED (Paid by calling party)				OPERATOR-ASSISTED					OVERTIME		
						OVERTIME						
	FULL WEEKDAY RATE Mon.-Fri. 8 AM-5 PM	35% EVENING DISCOUNT Sun.-Fri. 5 PM-11 PM	60% NIGHT & WEEKEND DISCOUNT Every Night 11 PM–8 AM All Day and Night on Sat. to 5 PM Sun.	ALL DAYS & HOURS	WEEKDAYS 8 AM-5 PM	35% EVENING DISCOUNT Sun.-Fri. 5 PM-11 PM	60% NIGHT & WEEKEND DISCOUNT. Every Night 11 PM–8 AM; All Day and Night on Sat. to 5 PM Sun.	ALL DAYS & HOURS	WEEKDAYS 8 AM-5 PM	35% EVENING DISCOUNT. Sun.-Fri. 5 PM-11 PM	60% NIGHT & WEEKEND DISCOUNT Every Night 11 PM–8 AM; All Day and. Night on Sat. to 5 PM Sun.
	Init. 1 Min.	Ea. Add. Min.	Init. 1 Min.	Ea. Add. Min.	Init. 1 Min.	Ea. Add. Min.	Init. 3 Mins.	Ea. Add. Min.	Ea. Add. Min.	Ea. Add. Min.	Init. 3 Mins.	Ea. Add. Min.	Ea. Add. Min.	Ea. Add. Min.

CALLS TO:	Full Init.	Full Add.	35% Init.	35% Add.	60% Init.	60% Add.	All Days Init. 3 Mins.	Wkdy Add.	35% Add.	60% Add.	All Days Init. 3 Mins.	Wkdy Add.	35% Add.	60% Add.
Atlanta, Ga.	.50	.34	.33	.22	.20	.14	2.05	.34	.22	.14	3.15	.34	.22	.14
Atlantic City, N.J.	.43	.28	.28	.18	.17	.11	1.75	.28	.18	.11	2.75	.28	.18	.11
Boston, Mass.	.44	.29	.29	.19	.18	.12	1.85	.29	.19	.12	2.85	.29	.19	.12
Chicago, Ill.	.50	.34	.33	.22	.20	.14	2.05	.34	.22	.14	3.15	.34	.22	.14
Cleveland, Ohio	.48	.33	.31	.21	.19	.13	2.00	.33	.21	.13	3.05	.33	.21	.13
Denver, Colo.	.52	.36	.34	.23	.21	.14	2.15	.36	.23	.14	3.30	.36	.23	.14
Detroit, Mich.	.50	.34	.33	.22	.20	.14	2.05	.34	.22	.14	3.15	.34	.22	.14
Hartford, Conn.	.43	.28	.28	.18	.17	.11	1.75	.28	.18	.11	2.75	.28	.18	.11
Houston, Tex.	.52	.36	.34	.23	.21	.14	2.15	.36	.23	.14	3.30	.36	.23	.14
Los Angeles, Cal.	.54	.38	.35	.25	.22	.15	2.25	.38	.25	.15	3.55	.38	.25	.15
Miami, Fla.	.52	.36	.34	.23	.21	.14	2.15	.36	.23	.14	3.30	.36	.23	.14
Milwaukee, Wisc.	.50	.34	.33	.22	.20	.14	2.05	.34	.22	.14	3.15	.34	.22	.14
New Orleans, La.	.52	.36	.34	.23	.34	.14	2.15	.36	.23	.14	3.30	.36	.23	.14
Philadelphia, Pa.	.43	.28	.28	.18	.17	.11	1.75	.28	.18	.11	2.75	.28	.18	.11
Portland, Maine	.46	.31	.30	.20	.18	.12	1.95	.31	.20	.12	2.95	.31	.20	.12
St. Louis, Mo.	.50	.34	.33	.22	.20	.14	2.05	.34	.22	.14	3.15	.34	.22	.14
Seattle, Wash.	.54	.38	.35	.25	.22	.15	2.25	.38	.25	.15	3.55	.38	.25	.15
Washington, D.C.	.46	.31	.30	.20	.18	.12	1.95	.31	.20	.12	2.95	.31	.20	.12
Wilmington, Del.	.43	.28	.28	.18	.17	.11	1.75	.28	.18	.11	2.75	.28	.18	.11

Total minutes of call	15
Initial charge	$.43
Number of additional minutes	$15 - 1 = 14$
Cost of each additional minute	$.28
Cost of additional minutes	$14 \times \$.28 = \$3.92$
Total cost of call	$\$.43 + \$3.92 = \$4.35$

Suppose Jonathan had asked the operator to place his call person-to-person to Luisa Alvarez and then reached Luisa. What would have been the cost of his call? Look at the Person-to-Person section.

Total minutes of call	15
Cost of first 3 minutes	$2.75
Number of additional minutes	$15 - 3 = 12$
Cost of each additional minute	$.28
Overtime charge	$12 \times \$.28 = \$3.36$
Total cost of call	$\$2.75 + \$3.36 = \$6.11$

Your phone bill is full of information about your service and how to use it. Study it and discover ways to save money. It will pay off.

Exercises for Section Two

Suppose each of these long-distance calls is made to Detroit, Michigan. The rate schedule on page 201 is in effect. Complete the exercises to find the total cost of each call.

Type of Call	Time Call is Placed	Length of Call	Initial Charge	Charge for Additional Minutes	Total Cost
1. Direct	Monday 10:30 a.m.	8 min	$ .50	$ 2.38	$ 2.88
2. Direct	Wednesday 5:30 p.m.	8 min	_____	_____	_____
3. Direct	Saturday 11:00 a.m.	8 min	_____	_____	_____
4. Operator-assisted	Tuesday 2:00 p.m.	8 min	_____	_____	_____
5. Operator-assisted	Friday 5:15 p.m.	8 min	_____	_____	_____
6. Operator-assisted	Saturday 1:40 p.m.	8 min	_____	_____	_____
7. Person-to-person	Wednesday 4:20 p.m.	8 min	_____	_____	_____
8. Person-to-person	Thursday 6:14 p.m.	8 min	_____	_____	_____
9. Person-to-person	Sunday 1:27 p.m.	8 min	_____	_____	_____
10. Direct	Sunday 6:02 p.m.	25 min	_____	_____	_____

Use the rate schedule on page 201 to solve the following problems.

11. Marcie Blair called Houston, Texas, at 7:30 on Sunday evening. She dialed the call herself and talked for 9 minutes. What was the cost of the call?

12. Henry Gross called Atlantic City, New Jersey, at 2:45 p.m. He had the operator reverse the charges. The call lasted 14 minutes. What was the cost of the call on a Friday?

13. Allison Skinner made a person-to-person, long-distance call to her friend in Seattle, Washington. She placed the call on Thursday night at 9:14 p.m., and they talked until 9:36 p.m. What was the cost of the call?

14. What is the difference in price between a 19-minute, operator-assisted, long-distance call to Los Angeles, California, made on a weekday at 4:00 p.m. and:

a. The same call made on a weekday at 6:30 p.m.?

b. The same call made on a weeknight at 11:30 p.m.?

c. The same call made on Sunday at 4:00 p.m.?

15. What is the difference in price between a 14-minute long-distance call dialed direct to Denver, Colorado, at 6:21 p.m. on Thursday and:

a. The same call requiring the assistance of an operator?

b. The same call placed person-to-person?

Section Three
Gas and Water

Natural Gas

Natural gas is one of the cleanest fuels and, until the late 1970s, was an inexpensive source of energy. A number of apartment dwellers and homeowners use gas for cooking and heating.

How does the gas get to consumers' homes? Utility companies pump it out of huge storage tanks or trucks into homes. Then it passes through gas meters which register the amount of gas used.

Gas is measured in cubic feet and sold by units of 100 cubic feet. Gas meters are read much like electric meters. To find how much gas is registered on the meter below, you first read the dial at the left. The hand is on 7 and is read as 70,000 cubic feet. On the middle dial, the hand is between 4 and 5 and is read as 4,000 cubic feet. (Always read the smaller number as you did with the electric meter.) The right dial registers between 3 and 4. This is read as 300 cubic feet. The reading becomes 74,300 cubic feet. (Since customers are charged by units of 100 cubic feet, the meter is read as 743 hundreds of cubic feet.) The previous month's reading is subtracted from this month's reading to determine how many hundreds of cubic feet were used during the month.

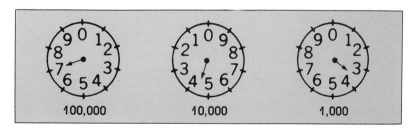

The schedule below gives one company's rates for natural gas.

MIDWESTERN NATURAL GAS COMPANY RATE SCHEDULE	
First 2 hundred cubic feet	$1.26 (minimum charge)
Next 8 hundred cubic feet	.264 per hundred cubic feet
Next 18 hundred cubic feet	.228 per hundred cubic feet
Next 22 hundred cubic feet	.174 per hundred cubic feet
Over 50 hundred cubic feet	.126 per hundred cubic feet

For example, a Midwestern Natural Gas Company customer's gas meter was read on September 15 as 838. On October 16, it showed a reading of 952. The customer used 114 hundred cubic feet of gas ($952 - 838 = 114$). What was the customer's gas bill for this period? Use the rate schedule above. (Note that for our purposes the costs are rounded off to the nearest cent, when necessary.)

Hundreds of cu ft used

			114
Cost of first 2 hundred cu ft	(Minimum charge)	$ 1.26	−2
			112
Cost of next 8 hundred cu ft	8 × $.264 = $2.112 *or* $ 2.11		−8
			104
Cost of next 18 hundred cu ft	18 × $.228 = $4.104 *or* 4.10		−18
			86
Cost of next 22 hundred cu ft	22 × $.174 = $3.828 *or* 3.83		−22
			64
Cost of next 64 hundred cu ft	64 × $.126 = $8.064 *or* 8.06		
Total gas bill		$19.36	

Exercises

Use the rate schedule on this page to complete these exercises. (When necessary, round off each answer to the nearest cent.)

Hundreds of Cu Ft Used	Minimum Charge	Cost at $.264 Rate	Cost at $.228 Rate	Cost at $.174 Rate	Cost at $.126 Rate	Total Cost
1. 12	$ 1.26	$ 2.11	$ .46	$ 0	$ 0	$ 3.83
2. 8						
3. 21						
4. 46						
5. 64						
6. 125						

What is the number of hundreds of cubic feet shown in each meter?

7.

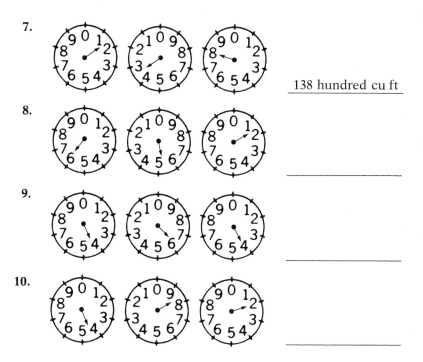

138 hundred cu ft

8.

9.

10.

Water Supply

Water is a true necessity of life. But, like gas and oil, water is not as easy to come by as it used to be. Most homeowners are billed for the water they use unless they have their own well. Bills are usually paid quarterly.

Water is often measured and paid for by the cubic foot. The amount of water a household uses registers on a meter like this.

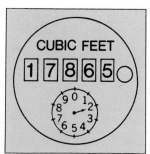

The number of cubic feet used is shown both on the dial and in the small squares. For an exact reading, read the numbers in the squares. The total on the meter above is read as 178,650 cubic feet.

(Although the exact total is 178,652, the final 2 is dropped from the reading because it is too small to use easily in computations.) This is the amount of cubic feet of water used since the meter was installed. In some areas, water is sold by the gallon. Meters in those areas register the use of water by gallons rather than by cubic feet.

Below are the water rates for one area, Union Township. Notice that rates are quoted in units of hundreds of cubic feet, as they were for gas.

UNION TOWNSHIP
QUARTERLY SCHEDULE OF WATER RATES

First 3 hundred cubic feet	$2.10 (minimum charge)
Next 17 hundred cubic feet	.30 per hundred cubic feet
Next 10 hundred cubic feet	.25 per hundred cubic feet
Next 250 hundred cubic feet	.10 per hundred cubic feet
Over 280 hundred cubic feet	.07 per hundred cubic feet

For example, using these rates, what would a customer's water bill be for 4,320 cubic feet consumed during one quarter? To simplify your computations, first find the number of hundreds of cubic feet used: $4,320 \div 100 = 43.2$.

		Hundreds of cu ft used
		43.20
Cost of first 3 hundred cu ft	(Minimum charge) $2.10	-3.00
		40.20
Cost of next 17 hundred cu ft	$17 \times \$.30 = \$5.10$	-17.00
		23.20
Cost of next 10 hundred cu ft	$10 \times \$.25 = \$2.50$	-10.00
		13.20
Cost of next 13.2 hundred cu ft	$13.2 \times \$.10 = \underline{\$1.32}$	
Total water bill	$\$11.02$	

If it had been necessary, any answers would have been rounded off to the nearest cent.

As you can see, the cost of your home includes more than your rent or mortgage payments. You must also consider the cost of utilities. These services cost more each year, and consumers everywhere are looking for ways to cut these climbing costs. You can cut your expenses if you know how you consume and pay for energy and water and how you are charged for telephone calls. Plan ahead. As these services become more expensive, using them wisely becomes an even more important part of managing your budget.

Exercises for Section Three

Use the rate schedule for Union Township to complete these exercises, and find the total quarterly water bill in each case. (When necessary, round off the cost to the nearest cent.)

Number of Cu Ft Used	Minimum Charge	Cost at $.30 Rate	Cost at $.25 Rate	Cost at $.10 Rate	Cost at $.07 Rate	Total Cost
1. 2,510	$ 2.10	$ 5.10	$ 1.28	$ 0	$ 0	$ 8.48
2. 975	____	____	____	____	____	____
3. 255	____	____	____	____	____	____
4. 5,600	____	____	____	____	____	____
5. 30,000	____	____	____	____	____	____

Compute the quarterly water consumption for each of these households. Then use the rate schedule for Union Township to compute their total water bill. (When necessary, round off your answer to the nearest cent.)

Household	Reading at Beginning of Quarter	Reading at End of Quarter	Number of Cu Ft of Water Used	Total Cost
6. Heiple	003920	004200	280 cu ft	$ 2.10
7. Hughes	044550	046200	____	____
8. Doyles	075400	077910	____	____
9. Thomas	253670	259340	____	____
10. Grand	664540	699640	____	____

Diagrams of Judy Taylor's gas meters and rate schedule for natural gas are given below. Use them for Exercises 11 to 13.

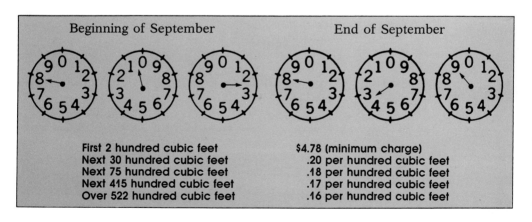

Beginning of September   End of September

First 2 hundred cubic feet $4.78 (minimum charge)
Next 30 hundred cubic feet   .20 per hundred cubic feet
Next 75 hundred cubic feet   .18 per hundred cubic feet
Next 415 hundred cubic feet   .17 per hundred cubic feet
Over 522 hundred cubic feet   .16 per hundred cubic feet

11. How many hundreds of cubic feet of gas did she use?
12. What was Judy's gas bill for September?
13. What was Judy's gas bill for December if she used 10,700 cubic feet of gas that month?

REVIEW FOR CHAPTER 10
PAYING FOR UTILITIES

1. How many kilowatthours of electricity are consumed by a 300-watt bulb that burns for 9 hours? For 54 hours? (Round off to the nearest whole kilowatthour.)
2. How many kilowatthours of electricity are consumed by a 150-watt bulb that burns for 30 minutes? For 48 hours? (Round off to the nearest whole kilowatthour.)
3. What is the Abbotts' electricity bill for January if they use 953 kilowatthours of electricity that month? Use the rate schedule below. (If necessary, round off your answers to the nearest cent.)

KILOWATTHOUR RATE SCHEDULE

CUSTOMER METER CHARGE
Minimum monthly charge $1.50

ENERGY CHARGE

First 60 kWh	$ .060 a kWh
Next 90 kWh	.045 a kWh
Next 150 kWh	.027 a kWh
Next 600 kWh	.021 a kWh
Over 900 kWh	.018 a kWh

FUEL COST ADJUSTMENT
To be applied to total monthly kWh $.009 a kWh.

4. Joyce Grant's electric meter reading for last month was 15927. A diagram of her meter reading for this month is given below. What is the new reading?

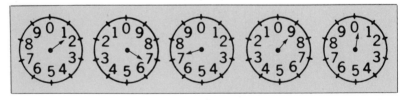

5. How many kilowatthours of electricity did Joyce use?
6. What is Joyce's electric bill for the month? Use the rate schedule used in Exercise 3. (Round off your answers to the nearest cent.)

Solve Exercises 7 and 8 using the rate schedule on page 201.

7. Which costs more—a person-to-person call to Detroit, Michigan, on Tuesday from 11:30 p.m. to 11:41 p.m. or a station-to-station call to Los Angeles, California, on Wednesday from 10:41 a.m. to 10:58 a.m.? How much more? The call to Los Angeles is direct distance dialed.

8. Which costs more—an operator-assisted call to Houston, Texas, on Thursday from 11:15 p.m. to 11:31 p.m. or a person-to-person call to Boston, Massachusetts, on Friday from 8:25 a.m. to 8:33 a.m.? How much more?

9. The gas meter for the Westbrook household showed that 341 hundreds of cubic feet of gas had been used in a month. What was their gas bill for that month? Use the rate schedule on this page. (When necessary, round off each answer to the nearest cent.)

MIDWESTERN NATURAL GAS COMPANY
RATE SCHEDULE

First 2 hundred cubic feet	$1.26 (minimum charge)
Next 8 hundred cubic feet	.264 per hundred cubic feet
Next 18 hundred cubic feet	.228 per hundred cubic feet
Next 22 hundred cubic feet	.174 per hundred cubic feet
Over 50 hundred cubic feet	.126 per hundred cubic feet

10. The water meter for the Fitch family read 186740 at the beginning of the quarter and 189980 at the end of the quarter.
    a. How many cubic feet of water did the Fitches use that quarter?
    b. What was their water bill for that quarter? Use the rate schedule below.

QUARTERLY SCHEDULE OF WATER RATES

First 3 hundred cubic feet	$2.10 (minimum charge)
Next 17 hundred cubic feet	.30 per hundred cubic feet
Next 10 hundred cubic feet	.25 per hundred cubic feet
Next 250 hundred cubic feet	.10 per hundred cubic feet
Over 280 hundred cubic feet	.07 per hundred cubic feet

PART WRAP-UP

Consumer Challenge

Phyllis and Merv Kramer went looking for an apartment in a large city. After a week of looking, they found an apartment they liked at $325 a month. Utilities in that area would add about $40 a month to their expense. The Kramers didn't want to pay that much, so they continued their search. Another apartment they liked rented at $285 a month (utilities included). But they weren't so sure about the management. When the Kramers asked about the length of the lease, the managers said, "Don't worry about the lease; you don't have to sign any lease."

The Kramers finally went to a real estate agent who would charge a fee of one month's rent. The real estate agent found them an apartment costing $310 a month (not including utilities). The Kramers like all three apartments equally and aren't sure which one they should take.

In order to make an informed decision, the Kramers need to perform certain computations. Do the following computations, and answer the questions. Explain your answers.

1. Including utilities, how much will the first apartment cost the Kramers over a 2-year period? The second apartment? The third apartment? (Remember to include the cost of the agent's fee.)
2. What are the advantages of renting the first apartment? The disadvantages?
3. What are the advantages of renting the second apartment? The disadvantages?
4. What are the advantages of renting the third apartment? The disadvantages?
5. Which apartment do you think the Kramers should take?
6. What impression did you get of the people who showed the Kramers the second apartment? Why is a lease important from a tenant's point of view?
7. What are some other things (besides money) to consider when deciding upon an apartment?

For You To Solve

1. Nan and Joe Roberts try to buy goods when there are special sales. Calculate their savings on the following purchases.

Month	Sale Items	Discount Price
January	Winter clothes for Nan	$150 less $\frac{1}{3}$
	Winter clothes for Joe	$185 less 40%
	Christmas decorations	$30 less 50%
	Bedding	$50 less 40%
February	Winter shoes for Joe	$40 less 25%
	Raincoat for Joe	$36 less $\frac{1}{3}$
	Housewares	$80 less 35%
March	Garden supplies	$36 less 25%
	Television set	$180 less 40%
	Records	$30 less 50%
	Bicycle for Nan	$75 less 30%

Answer the following questions. (Round off your answers to the nearest tenth of a percent when necessary. Use the fraction $\frac{1}{3}$ rather than the decimal .33$\frac{1}{3}$.)

  a. How much did the Robertses spend in January? In February? In March?
  b. How much did they save each month by buying items on sale?
  c. What was the total rate of discount for each month?
  d. How much did they spend during the three months?
  e. How much did they save during the three months?
  f. What was the total rate of discount on their purchases for the three months?

2. In the Uptown Towers, a tenant renewing a lease for 1 year gets an 11% increase in rent. If a tenant renews for 2 years, the increase is 9 percent. Find the new monthly rent payments and the total amount of rent paid for the term of the new lease for the tenants below.

Tenant	Old Monthly Rent	Term of New Lease	New Monthly Rent	Total Rent Paid
a. M. Horowitz	$210	1 yr	_____	_____
b. L. Beame	210	2 yr	_____	_____
c. H. Husker	255	1 yr	_____	_____
d. F. Schmidt	255	2 yr	_____	_____

Transportation

Performance Goals

When you finish work on this part, you should be able to:

- ☐ Compute the total cost of a car, including options.
- ☐ Select a fair price to pay for a new car by using the sticker price and the dealer's cost.
- ☐ Compute fees for license plates and registration, and sales tax when buying a new car.
- ☐ Compute amounts of car loans.
- ☐ Determine amounts paid by an insurance company under different types of liability and collision coverage.
- ☐ Determine amounts paid by an insurance company under comprehensive and no-fault coverage.
- ☐ Compute depreciation, gas, and oil costs.
- ☐ Compute costs of renting and leasing cars.
- ☐ Demonstrate ability to read train timetables and airline schedules.
- ☐ Compute train fares using different fare plans.
- ☐ List amounts saved when commuters buy commutation tickets.
- ☐ Determine time in different zones of the United States by using a time zone map.

The Consumer Buys a Car

Everyone is on the move today. Bicycles, motorcycles, dune buggies, and campers are carrying people to work, to vacation spots, and across the country. But most people who own their means of transportation still rely on cars to get them where they're going. Many city dwellers may not need cars, but many other people have no choice but to own a car. They live on farms, in the suburbs, or up in the mountains where public transportation is poor.

Most consumers today want to buy lighter, smaller, more fuel-efficient cars. The right car for you—a sedan, sports car, station wagon, hardtop, or hatchback—depends on the features you need and on the price you can afford. These basic styles can be found in most of the four common sizes shown below.

1. *Subcompact,* the smallest and least powerful. Inexpensive to operate.
2. *Compact,* larger than subcompacts, but still inexpensive to operate.
3. *Intermediate,* more powerful and costlier to keep up.
4. *Standard,* the largest and most powerful. Most expensive to operate.

Section One
Buying a New Car

Gas mileage: number of miles that a car goes on a gallon of gas.

As area manager for a chain of fast-food restaurants, David Chan needs a car to drive several thousand miles a month. He has decided to buy a new car. He has budgeted $4,200 for a compact, two-door hardtop that gives good gas mileage. *Gas mileage* is the number of miles a car goes on a gallon of gas.

Options and Other Charges

Optional equipment: extra features, or options, a car buyer can select.

David knows that *optional equipment*, or options, will raise the price of his compact. For example, the air conditioner he wants for hot summer driving will cost $425. Automatic transmission costs $215, and an AM radio costs $60.

In addition, there is a transportation charge of $60 and a dealer's preparation charge of $50. If the cost of the basic car is $3,325, how much will David's new car cost with the options and the other charges?

Cost of car	$3,325
Cost of options	$425 + $215 + $60 = $700
Other charges	$60 + $50 = $110
Total cost of car	$3,325 + $700 + $110 = $4,135

Exercises

Suppose the price for a basic intermediate car is $4,100. The transportation charge is $65, and the dealer's preparation fee is $45. Complete these exercises to find the total cost of an intermediate car with each set of options.

Options	Total Cost of Options	Total Cost of Car
1. Automatic transmission—$225; Power steering—$110; Power brakes—$60.	$ 395	$ 4,605
2. AM radio—$75; Stereo tape deck—$280; 2 rear speakers—$25 each.	————	————
3. Sun roof—$1,000; Air conditioning—$500; Automatic transmission—$225; Power windows—$90; Power seats—$75.	————	————
4. Whitewall tires—$45; Rear-window defogger—$45; Clock—$30.	————	————
5. Automatic transmission—$225; Vinyl roof—$100; Whitewall tires—$45; Power steering—$110; Clock—$30.	————	————

Sticker Prices and Dealer Prices

Walk into any car showroom, and you will see a sticker pasted somewhere on the window of each car. The sticker gives the price of the car. It also lists the prices of the options and other charges. Under federal law, dealers must tell the consumer the price that the manufacturer suggests for a car. This is known as the *sticker price*. It's the highest price a dealer can charge. However, unless they are in great demand, cars usually sell for less than the sticker price.

Sticker price: manufacturer's suggested price. Also called list *price.*

David wants to find out how much of a discount one dealer will offer on the purchase of a new compact. First he has to know the dealer's cost. He can compute the dealer's cost from the sticker price. For example, here are the figures from the sticker on the compact.

Manufacturer's suggested price	$3,325
Transportation charge	60
Dealer's preparation charge	50
Options:	
Air conditioner	425
Automatic transmission	215
AM radio	60
Total sticker price	$4,135

To find the dealer's cost, David follows the steps below.

1. He takes the basic cost of the car on the sticker price and multiplies it by 85 percent. This is the approximate price the dealer paid for the car. (Dealers pay about 85 percent of the sticker price for subcompacts and compacts. They pay about 81 percent of the sticker price for intermediate cars and 77 percent for standard cars.)

Sticker price	$3,325
Dealer cost (basic car)	.85 × $3,325 = $2,826.25

2. He multiplies the optional equipment cost by 80 percent. Dealers pay about 80 percent of the sticker price of options no matter what size the car is.

Cost of options	$425 + $215 + $60 = $700
Dealer cost (options)	$700 × .80 = $560

3. David adds the dealer's cost for the basic car, the options, and other charges. (The transportation and preparation charges are about the same as what the dealer pays.)

Dealer cost of car	$2,826.25
Dealer cost of options	$560.00
Transportation charge	$60
Preparation charge	$50
Total dealer cost of car	$2,826.25 + $560 + $60 + $50 = $3,496.25

The final amount ($3,496.25) is approximately what the car cost the dealer. David's bargaining range with the dealer is the difference between the sticker price and the dealer cost.

Total sticker price	$4,135
Total dealer cost	$3,496.25
Bargaining range	$4,135 − $3,496.25 = $638.75

Since a dealer needs to make a profit and allow for the costs of doing business, the car buyer should usually add between $200 and $300 to the dealer cost to find a fair price for a car. David added $250 to $3,496.25. He thinks that about $3,746.25 would be a good price to pay for his compact. Of course, David will have to negotiate with the dealer about the price.

Exercises for Section One

Suppose the suggested price for a subcompact car is $3,490. The transportation charge is $65, and the dealer's preparation charge is $50. Complete these exercises to find the bargaining range for a subcompact with the given options. Then, using $300 for dealer profit, decide on a fair price to pay for the car.

Cost of Options	Approx. Dealer Total Car Costs	Total Sticker Price	Bargaining Range	Fair Price
1. $ 395	$ 3,397.50	$ 4,000	$ 602.50	$ 3,697.50
2. 405	_____	_____	_____	_____
3. 1,890	_____	_____	_____	_____
4. 270	_____	_____	_____	_____
5. 510	_____	_____	_____	_____

Debbie Appel wants to buy a new intermediate car. The manufacturer's suggested price for the car is $3,920. In addition, Debbie wants a vinyl roof costing $100, an automatic transmission costing $225, power steering costing $110, power brakes for $60, and an AM radio for $75. The transportation charge is $55, and the dealer's preparation charge is $45.

6. What is the total price for all the options that Debbie wants?
7. What is the total sticker price for the car she wants?
8. What is the dealer's approximate cost for the car? For the options? For the complete purchase? (Remember to add the transportation charge and the dealer's preparation fee.)
9. What is the difference between the sticker price of the car and the dealer's complete purchase?
10. What would be a fair price for Debbie to pay for the car that would allow the dealer to make a $275 profit?

Section Two
Other Costs in Buying Your Car

When you buy a car, you must follow the motor vehicle regulations of your state. These regulations usually include the purchase of license plates and the registration of a car. *Registration* of a car is the recording of car ownership at the motor vehicle office. Fees are charged for license plates and for registration. Inspection fees and state sales taxes are usually paid at the time a car is purchased. Some states also require that you pay an ownership fee.

Registration: recording of car ownership at a motor vehicle office.

License Plates and Registration Fees

Fees for license plates and registration vary from state to state. They are usually computed on a combination of the age, weight, and value of a car. The motor vehicle office in David's town uses the table shown below. The fees for David Chan's new compact, which weighs 3,190 pounds, total $26.66. The way to compute the amount of fees is shown at the top of page 219.

LICENSE PLATES AND REGISTRATION FEES

Weight	Rate
Up to 2,000 pounds	$10 (minimum charge)
Over 2,000 pounds	$10 plus $1.40 for each 100 pounds over 2,000 pounds

Weight of David's car	3,190 pounds
Minimum charge	$10
Additional pounds	$3,190 - 2,000 = 1,190$
Number of 100 pounds in 1,190 pounds (to the nearest tenth)	$1,190 \div 100 = 11.9$
Cost of additional pounds	$11.9 \times \$1.40 = \$16.66$
Fees for license plates and registration	$\$10.00 + \$16.66 = \$26.66$

Auto-Use Tax. You pay an auto-use tax each time you renew your registration, usually as part of the registration fee. If David Chan's city charged a $15 auto-use tax, how much would his license plates and registration fee be?

Registration and license plates fee	$26.66
Auto-use tax	$15
Total fee cost	$\$26.66 + \$15 = \$41.66$

DO YOU KNOW

that a used car often provides good service for less cost than a new one? Cars are built to last 100,000 miles or more with careful maintenance. So consider buying a used car. Here is a brief checklist of things to look for when you buy a used car.

1. Consult *Consumer Reports* and the National Automobile Dealers Association *Official Used Car Guide*. These list current prices. They rate used cars according to performance, such as the number of miles you can expect from a gallon of gas.
2. Know your car dealer. Find out if the dealer is a member of a car dealer's association. Check with your friends about a local dealer's reputation.
3. Test-drive the car. Or, better yet, get a mechanic to inspect it in a variety of traffic conditions. Have the mechanic inspect important parts of the car, such as the engine, transmission, and brakes. Get an estimate on repairs.
4. Look for trouble spots, such as a dented muffler or worn tires. Check the battery. Make sure a jack and spare tire are in the trunk and are usable.

Exercises

Use the rate schedule on page 218 to find the fee for license plates and registration of cars weighing the given amounts. Then compute the total fee by adding an auto-use tax of $17.50. (If necessary, round off the number of 100 pounds to the nearest tenth.)

Weight	Minimum Charge	Charge for Weight Over 2,000 lb	License Plates and Registration	Total Fee
1. 2,500 lb	$ 10	$ 7	$ 17	$ 34.50
2. 2,750 lb				
3. 2,990 lb				
4. 3,100 lb				
5. 3,210 lb				
6. 3,390 lb				
7. 3,500 lb				
8. 3,650 lb				
9. 3,810 lb				
10. 3,900 lb				

Inspection Fees

Most states require safety inspections of all motor vehicles at least once a year. A fee, usually about $3, is charged for the inspection in most states. Lights, tires, and brakes are some of the items checked. Once your car has passed the inspection, the inspection official will put a sticker on your windshield. You may have to pay the fee for your first inspection when you receive your new car.

Sales Tax

David Chan lives in a state where the sales tax on a new or used car is 7 percent. If he pays the dealer $3,746.25 for his new compact, how much is the sales tax?

Cost of car	$3,746.25
7-percent sales tax	$3,746.25 × .07 = $262.237
	or $262.24

Exercises for Section Two

Compute the sales tax for each car listed on the top of page 221. (If necessary, round off to the nearest cent.)

220

Car Model	Cost of Car	Tax Rate	Sales Tax
1. Subcompact	$ 2,820.00	4%	$ 112.80
2. Compact	3,185.00	4.5%	_____
3. Intermediate	5,160.00	5%	_____
4. Standard	8,220.00	5.5%	_____
5. Sports car	6,479.30	6%	_____

The people named below live in a state where the sales tax on cars is 6 percent, the inspection fee is $3.50, the auto-use tax is $16. The following license plate and registration fees apply: Up to 1,500 pounds, $8 (minimum charge); over 1,500 pounds, $8 plus $1.25 for each 100 pounds over 1,500 pounds. (Round off to the nearest cent.)

6. Henry Kaliski just bought a $3,950 compact car weighing 2,900 pounds. How much is his total cost for all four fees?

7. Lilian Kaliski just bought a $4,300 intermediate car weighing 3,470 pounds. What will be her total cost for all four fees?

8. Jay Peterson just bought a $2,800 subcompact car weighing 2,560 pounds. What is his total cost for all four fees?

9. Katherine Peterson just bought a $3,250 sports car weighing 2,750 pounds. What is her total cost for all four fees?

10. How much do the Kaliskis pay together for sales taxes? For inspection? For auto-use tax? For license plates and registration? Answer the same questions for the Petersons.

Section Three
Paying for Your Car

Very few consumers have enough money to pay cash for a new car. Most finance their car purchases through credit plans. There are three basic sources of credit for car loans: car dealers, commercial banks, and credit unions. Dealer plans are convenient, but they are usually more expensive than loans from banks or credit unions. Finance companies are also a loan source, but they charge the highest interest rates of all.

Best sources for car loans:
1. Car dealers.
2. Commercial banks.
3. Credit unions.

As a condition for granting a loan, the bank or dealer may require that your car be held as collateral for the loan. As you learned in Chapter 5, a loan made with this condition is a secured loan.

Down Payment

Now that David Chan has decided to buy a new compact, how will he pay for it? Luckily, he belongs to a credit union and can take advantage of its low rates. The compact costs $3,746.25. He plans to make a down payment of $746.25 to be paid in cash to the dealer. How much will his loan be? Simply subtract: $3,746.25 − $746.25 = $3,000.

What percent is the down payment of the total cost? (Round off the answer to the nearest tenth of a percent.)

Down payment	$746.25
Cost of car	$3,746.25
Percent of total cost	746.25 ÷ 3,746.25 = .1991
	or 19.9%

Finance Charges

David needs $3,000 to finance his car. He wants to repay the loan in 24 monthly payments. To find the amount of each monthly payment, the credit union where he works looked at a monthly payment table. According to the table, the amount of his monthly payment will be $143.22. That figure includes insurance for the term of the loan. If David pays $143.22 a month for 24 months, how much will his loan cost him?

Total amount paid in 24 months	$143.22 × 24 = $3,437.28
Amount of loan	$3,000
Cost of loan	$3,437.28 − $3,000 = $437.28

Exercises for Section Three

For each car cost given, find the percent of the total cost that the down payment is, and find the amount of the loan. (Round off to the nearest tenth of a percent.)

Total Cost of Car	Amount of Down Payment	Percent of Total Cost	Amount of Loan
1. $2,400	$ 650	27.1%	$ 1,750
2. 3,100	500	_____	_____
3. 3,620	620	_____	_____
4. 4,217	757	_____	_____
5. 5,390	1,390	_____	_____

Gwen Carrie bought a new subcompact car for $3,128.50. She made a down payment of $628.50.

6. What percent of the total price did Gwen put down? (Round off to the nearest tenth of a percent.)

7. How much did Gwen have to borrow?

8. Gwen borrowed the amount in Exercise 7 from a bank for 12 months. The amount of her monthly payment was $285.83. What total did Gwen pay in principal and interest for the loan?

9. What amount did the loan cost Gwen?

10. Larry Grollier bought a car costing $5,105. He made a down payment of $1,105. What percent of the total cost is the down payment? (Round off to the nearest tenth of a percent.) What is the amount of the loan?

Section Four
Auto Insurance

Most states require you to have car insurance before you can register your car. And with good reason: there's a 55-percent chance that every car owner will be involved in some kind of car

Parking fees are one of the hidden costs involved in car ownership. Suppose there are no parking spaces available and you leave your car in a garage for three hours on a holiday night. Use the rates shown above to find out how much parking can add to your evening's expenses.

accident during any three-year period. And you have a 75-percent chance of being involved in an accident in any five-year period.

Few people can afford the risk of being sued as a result of a car accident. Suppose the victim of an accident sued you for $300,000. For most drivers, this would mean bankruptcy. There are several kinds of insurance designed to protect the car owner.

Liability Insurance

Liability insurance: pays another person for injury or damage caused by the insured person.

David Chan lives in a state that requires all drivers to carry liability insurance. With *liability insurance,* your insurance company promises to pay the other person any amount up to a limit stated in the policy. The payment is for any bodily injury or property damage in an accident that you have caused to happen.

Liability coverage is expressed in multiples of $10,000. For example, David Chan bought liability insurance that pays a maximum of $50,000 for injuries to one person. It pays a maximum of $100,000 if more than one person is injured. His insurance also pays up to $5,000 for damages to property. This coverage is expressed as 50/100/5. Larger or smaller amounts of liability coverage can be bought, such as 100/300/25 or 10/20/5.

David is forty-two and has insured his new car for liability. David's son, Robert, owns a three-year-old compact. Robert was amazed that the liability insurance for his older car costs more than the same amount of liability insurance for his father's new car.

The amounts Robert and David pay for bodily-injury and property-damage coverage are shown in the table below. How much does each one pay for liability insurance?

Kind of Coverage	Limits	Robert, Age 19	David, Age 42
Bodily-injury liability	$ 50,000 a person $100,000 an accident	$456	$178
Property damage	$5,000 an accident	$256	$ 99

Collision Insurance

Collision insurance: pays insured person for injury or damage caused by himself or herself.

Suppose you have an accident and it's your fault. The property damage insurance in liability coverage pays only for damage to other people's property. You must pay the cost of repairs to your own car unless you have collision insurance.

With *collision insurance,* your insurance company will pay for damages up to a reasonable limit, usually the cash value of your

224   Part 4   TRANSPORTATION

Deductible:
amount that
insured must
pay toward
damages before
insurance
payments begin.

car. You can buy a policy with a $50 or $100 deductible. This means that you'll pay only a certain amount, such as the first $50 or $100, for car repairs. The insurance pays for damages over that amount. The amount you pay is the *deductible*. The higher the deductible, the lower the premium you will have to pay. Below is a rate table for collision insurance.

Kind of Coverage	Limits	Robert, Age 19	David, Age 42
Collision	$100 deductible	$72	$54

Charles Nates was involved in an accident that was his fault. The damages to his car were estimated at $678. Damages to the other car were estimated at $959. Which kind of insurance covered the repair of Charles's car? Which covered the repair of the other car? If Charles has the same liability and collision coverage as Robert Chan, how much did the accident cost the insurance company?

Cost of Charles's car repairs	$678
Deductible	$100
Insurance company costs	$678 − $100 = $578
Cost of other car repairs	$959
Property-damage maximum	$5,000
Insurance company costs	$959
Total insurance company costs	$578 + $959 = $1,537

Exercises

Each exercise gives the name of the driver involved in an accident and the type of insurance this person has. Find the insurance company cost in each case.

Driver	Liability Coverage	Collision Coverage	Amount of Damage	Insur. Co. Cost
1. A. Kelly	10/20/5	$50 deductible	$431 to another person's car.	$ 431
2. R. Max	10/20/5	$50 deductible	$329 to driver's car.	____
3. M. Ashley	50/100/5	$100 deductible	$629 to another person's car, $95 to driver's car.	____
4. E. Brook	50/100/5	$100 deductible	$455 to driver's car.	____

Comprehensive Insurance

Comprehensive insurance: pays for car damages not caused by a collision.

Comprehensive insurance pays for most car damages not covered by collision insurance. This includes damage caused by fire, theft, earthquake, floods, vandalism, explosions, lightning, storms, and collisions with animals or birds. For any of these types of damage, the insurance company will pay amounts up to the value of each of the Chans' cars. Look at the table below.

Kind of Coverage	Limits	Robert, Age 19	David, Age 42
Comprehensive physical damage	Cash value	$110	$51

Here's how comprehensive insurance works. Last week several items were stolen from Robert Chan's locked car. A tape deck valued at $78, a leather bag valued at $32, and a sweater valued at $15. Robert's claim was $125 ($78 + $32 + $15 = $125).

No-Fault Insurance

No-fault insurance: protects the insured person no matter who is at fault. Also called *personal injury insurance.*

Many states require drivers to have no-fault insurance. *No-fault insurance* protects you no matter who is at fault. (In some places, this is referred to as *personal injury insurance.*) If you have an accident, you make a claim to your own insurance company. Benefits vary according to state laws. No-fault pays for your medical costs, wage losses, and other expenses related to the accident.

Look at the table below. Notice that for both of the Chans there is a $200 deductible. If you, the insured driver, have an accident and are injured, you must pay the first $200 of medical expenses. (In many cases, a driver's medical plan covers the deductible.) No-fault insurance will pay the balance of any other medical costs.

Kind of Coverage	Limits	Robert, Age 19	David, Age 42
No-fault of up to $36,000	$200 deductible	$37	$22

David's no-fault insurance pays 80 percent of monthly wages up to $1,000 a month, with a maximum of $36,000 for loss of earnings. The policy includes a deductible of $200.

For example, if David Chan has an accident and his medical expenses are $875, how much will the insurance pay him?

Medical expenses	$875
Deductible	$200
Insurance company costs	$875 − $200 = $675

If it took David 6 weeks to recover from a fractured hip, how much could he collect in wage losses from his insurance company? David earns $325 a week. His employer will pay his salary for the first 2 weeks.

Total recovery time	6 wk
Wages for 2 weeks	$325 × 2 = $650
Period of insurance benefits	6 wk − 2 wk = 4 wk
Wages for 4 weeks	$325 × 4 = $1,300
80 percent of wages for 4 weeks	$1,300 × .80 = $1,040
Maximum wages paid each month by insurance company	$1,000
Insurance company costs	$1,000

Exercises for Section Four

Each person has comprehensive insurance covering the cash value of the given damages. Find the amount each person received from the insurance company.

Person	Damages	Insur. Co. Cost
1. J. Beane	Ripped vinyl roof—$100, 2 stolen hubcaps—$15 each	$ 130
2. H. Wynne	Broken window—$35, Stolen camera—$225, Stolen brief case—$22.50	_____
3. P. Adams	Forced trunk—$55.50, Stolen spare tire—$40.28, Stolen auto repair kit—$25.79	_____
4. M. Gura	Cracked windshield—$123.60, Ruined paint job—$85.45, Scratched roof—$150.47	_____
5. V. Bowe	Flood damage to engine—$110.10, Flood damage to interior—$79.56, Ruined paint job—$85.45, Ripped vinyl roof—$35.08	_____

Each of these people is covered under a no-fault plan that has a $100 deductible for medical expenses and pays 75 percent of monthly wages up to $900 a month with a maximum of $25,000 for loss of earnings. Complete these exercises to find the total cost to the insurance company for each accident. (Assume that each person listed here has already been paid by his or her employer for 2 weeks' worth of wages. When necessary, round off your answer to the nearest cent.)

Person	Medical Expenses	Medical Expenses Paid by Insur. Co.	Work Loss	Wages Lost	Wage Loss Paid by Insur. Co.	Insur. Co. Cost
6. F. Alviar	$ 380.00	$ 280.00	7 days— $37 a day	$ 259.00	$ 194.25	$ 474.25
7. M. Canon	1,257.00	————	16 wk— $255 a wk	————	————	————
8. L. Hank	937.18	————	5 wk— $303.18 a wk	————	————	————
9. U. Tripp	56.18	————	2 days— $33.55 a day	————	————	————

10. How much are Robert Chan's total annual liability (including property damage), collision, comprehensive, and no-fault insurance premiums? How much are David's annual car insurance premiums? Use the rate tables on pages 224–226 to solve this exercise. How much higher are Robert's annual premiums than David's?

11. Jeff Moss has 50/100/25 liability coverage and $250-deductible collision coverage. How much will his insurance company pay for a three-car accident that he caused if the damage to the other two cars was $1,093.12 and $842.41, the damage to his car was $1,490.27, and injury to a person in another car was $532.77?

12. Hilda Tracy has $100-deductible comprehensive insurance costing $38.10 semiannually. A tree fell on her car, breaking the $135 windshield and putting a $65 dent in the hood. How much will the insurance company pay? Is the amount she receives from the insurance company more or less than her annual premium? How much?

Section Five
Costs of a Car After Purchase

How much does your car cost to own and operate? There are two kinds of ownership costs, fixed and variable. *Fixed costs* stay the same whether you drive 50,000 miles a year, 10,000 miles, or less. Examples of fixed costs are depreciation, insurance, credit, and garage and parking. *Variable costs* depend on the number of miles you drive your car. You can control variable costs by the way you operate and care for your car. Examples of variable costs are gas, oil, and maintenance. In this section we will discuss some of the fixed and variable costs car owners must pay.

Fixed Costs

Depreciation. The difference between what you pay for a new car and the price it sells for later is depreciation. It is the loss of value due to age. David Chan's new compact sold for $3,746.25. During the first year, his car will depreciate by 30 percent. What will its value be at the end of the first year?

Cost of car new	$3,746.25
30-percent depreciation	$3,746.25 × .30 = $1,123.875
	or $1,123.88
Value of car after first year	$3,746.25 − $1,123.88 = $2,622.37

Variable Costs

Gas. A new compact, such as David Chan's, gets good gasoline mileage. In city driving, David averages 19 miles a gallon. On the highway, he averages 25 miles a gallon. Recently David took a trip of 130 miles. If he drove mostly on highways and averaged 25 miles a gallon, how much gas did he need for the trip? How much did the gas cost if it sold at $.61 a gallon?

Number of miles a gallon	25
Total miles driven	130
Number of gallons of gas used	130 ÷ 25 = 5.2
Cost of gallon of gas	$.61
Cost of 5.2 gallons	$.61 × 5.2 = $3.172
	or $3.17

Oil. David's car is new and doesn't consume much oil. However, he uses about 2 quarts each month. If one quart sells for $1.10, what would his monthly oil bill be?

Quart of oil	$1.10
Quarts needed monthly	2
Monthly cost of oil	$1.10 × 2 = $2.20

Maintenance and Repairs. Today's car has about 15,000 parts. What does this mean to car owners? It means regular maintenance. Wise operating practices are needed to protect your investment. Car manuals spell out how to keep mechanical problems from becoming major, costly items. They tell you how often to have the car greased and the engine tuned-up. Read your manual closely and follow its advice.

Buying and owning a car is a very important consumer decision. Investing hard-earned income to buy a car requires wise budgeting. Begin with your net income and develop a sound spending plan. See if you can really afford a car. No one wants to become "car poor"—too much car for too little income.

Exercises for Section Five

Compute the number of gallons of gas used on each trip. (Round off to the nearest tenth of a gallon.) Then find the cost of gas and oil for each trip. Assume that gas sells for $.62 a gallon, and oil for $1.15 a quart. (When necessary, round off to the nearest cent.)

Miles Driven	Miles a Gallon of Gas	Gallons of Gas Used	Cost of Gas for Trip	Quarts of Oil Used	Cost of Oil for Trip
1. 320	19	16.8	$ 10.42	$\frac{1}{4}$	$ .29
2. 580	22	_____	_____	$\frac{1}{2}$	_____
3. 714	25.5	_____	_____	$\frac{3}{4}$	_____
4. 935	27	_____	_____	1	_____
5. 1,063	29.3	_____	_____	$1\frac{1}{2}$	_____

For Exercises 6 to 10, gas was bought by the liter, and distance was measured in kilometers. Compute the number of liters of gas used on each trip. (Round off to the nearest tenth of a liter.) Then find the cost of gas for each trip if gasoline sells for $.144 per liter. (Round off to the nearest cent.)

Kilometers Driven	Kilometers a Liter of Gas	Liters of Gas Used	Cost of Gas for Trip
6. 250	7	_35.7_	$ _5.14_
7. 820	5	_____	_____
8. 2,920	5.5	_____	_____
9. 504	6	_____	_____
10. 1,160	7.2	_____	_____

11. Bill McDevitt paid $4,805 for his new car. He sold it a year later for $3,925. What was the amount of depreciation? The cost a month of depreciation? (Round off to the nearest cent.)

12. Kelly Hill paid $5,810 for her car when it was new. She sold it a year later for $4,510. What was the amount of depreciation? The percent of depreciation? (Round off to the nearest tenth of a percent.) The cost a month of depreciation? (Round off to the nearest cent.)

13. Paul Hallowman traveled 28,063 miles last year, and his car averaged 17.5 miles a gallon. If he bought gas at $.639 a gallon, how much did he spend for gas that year?

14. Marie Lanz traveled 300 kilometers last week. Her car averages 6 kilometers for each liter of gas. How many liters of gas did her car use? What was the cost of gas if it sells for $.168 per liter?

15. Mark Snow traveled 12,495 miles last year, and his car averaged 21 miles a gallon. If he bought gas for $.59 a gallon, how much did he spend on gas for the year? What was his cost a month for gas? (Round off to the nearest cent.) His cost a mile? (Round off to the nearest tenth of a cent.)

REVIEW FOR CHAPTER 11
THE CONSUMER BUYS A CAR

1. Carlos Black was looking at the compact car described below. What is the selling price of the car with all the options?

Manufacturer's suggested retail price	$4,300
Transportation charge	55
Dealer's preparation charge	50
Options:	
Automatic transmission	225
Sun roof	950
Whitewall tires	45
AM radio	75
Rear speaker	25

2. How much did Carlos' car, including options, cost the dealer? What would be a fair price to offer the dealer, allowing the dealer to make a $400 profit?

3. The car's weight is 3,600 pounds. What is the license plate and registration fee for the car if the rate is $9.50 for the first 2,500 pounds, plus $1.05 for each 100 pounds over 2,500 pounds?

4. Sylvia Mayo bought a car for $3,435.55. She made a down payment of $535.55 and made monthly payments of $93.58 for 3 years. How much more did she pay for the car in interest charges?

5. Sylvia has 20/100/5 liability coverage and $250-deductible collision insurance. If she had a bad accident and her new car was totally wrecked, how much would her insurance company pay? (In this exercise and the following three exercises, round off to the nearest cent whenever necessary.)

6. Sylvia has $100-deductible comprehensive insurance. If her new car was destroyed by a flood, how much would her insurance company pay?

7. Sylvia's car depreciated 27 percent the first year. What is the amount of depreciation that year? The cost of depreciation a month?

8. How much total sales tax would Sylvia pay if state tax in her area is 5 percent and city tax is 3 percent? (Add the two taxes together before you begin your computations.)

9. Charlie Busby drove his car 18,000 miles the first year he owned it. His car averaged 19 miles a gallon. If he used gas at $.63 a gallon, how much did he spend for gas that year? (Round off your answers to the nearest tenth of a gallon and to the nearest cent.)

10. Charlie Busby drove his car 21,100 miles the second year he owned it. That year the car averaged 22 miles a gallon. If he used gas at $.64 a gallon, how much did he spend for gas that year? (Round off your answer to the nearest cent.)

Using Public Transportation

A car is an expensive convenience. High insurance rates, repair charges, and the cost of fuel add many dollars to already tight budgets. Car owners in cities also have to put up with high garage rents and parking nuisances. Using public transportation is one way to avoid the added costs and difficulties that go along with owning a car. Buses, subways, and taxis are cheaper and often easier to use than your own car. And for long-distance travel, trains and planes are fast and economical.

Some people, such as vacationers or business travelers, need cars only occasionally. For those people, renting or leasing a car is more practical than buying one.

In this chapter, you'll look at some of the ways of traveling without owning a car. Then you can decide which way is best for you.

Section One
Renting or Leasing a Car

You must be at least 21 years old and a licensed driver to rent a car. Rates vary with rental companies and with the kinds of cars available. Charges sometimes include insurance coverage. Less frequently, gas and oil are included. When you rent a car, check to see what is included.

A company in one major city advertises the following car rental rates.

CAR RENTAL RATE SCHEDULE

Car Model	Hour	Day	Week	Mileage Charge
Subcompact	$3.50	$13.95	$ 69.70	$.14 a mile
Compact	3.75	14.95	74.70	.17 a mile
Standard	5.00	19.95	99.70	.20 a mile
Station wagon	5.25	20.95	104.70	.22 a mile
Luxury sedan	5.50	21.95	109.70	.25 a mile

Minimum charge: one day plus mileage.
Gas not included.

Yvonne Banks rented a subcompact car for 10 days. She drove the car 1,375 miles. (Note that there is a mileage charge of $.14 a mile for subcompacts.) She spent $26.70 for gas. And though insurance is included in the charges, there is a $250 deductible. Yvonne could eliminate the deductible by paying a $2-a-day insurance option. She chose to do so.

What was Yvonne's total rental cost, including gas? Use the rate table above. Here is how to use this table to compute a car rental charge.

Weekly rental charge	$69.70
Daily rental rate	$13.95
Number of days at daily rate	$10 - 7 = 3$
Total charge for 3 days	$3 \times \$13.95 = \$41.85$
Mileage charge	$1,375 \times \$.14 = \$192.50$
Insurance option	$\$2 \times 10 = \$20$
Gas	$26.70
Total car rental cost	$\$69.70 + \$41.85 + \$192.50$ $+ \$20.00 + \$26.70 = \$350.75$

Exercises
The exercises on page 235 describe Mr. Grossman's car rental expenses on business trips to the same city. Use the rate schedule shown above to find the total car rental charge in each case.

Car Model	Rental Period	Miles Driven	Gas and Oil Costs	Insurance Costs	Total Rental Costs
1. Compact	2 days	84	$2.55	0	$ 46.73
2. Standard	3 days	115	3.25	0	_____
3. Subcompact	3 hr	10	0	0	_____
4. Station wagon	1 wk	246	4.10	$2.75 a day	_____
5. Luxury sedan	9 days	512	10.35	$3 a day	_____
6. Standard	3 days, 1 hr	92	3.00	0	_____
7. Station wagon	4 days, 3 hr	177	4.00	$2.75 a day or part	_____
8. Subcompact	1 wk, 2 hr	734	16.20	$2 a day or part	_____
9. Compact	9 days, 3 hr	1,085	18.35	$2.25 a day or part	_____
10. Standard	8 days, 2 hr	831	14.60	$2.50 a day or part	_____

DO YOU KNOW

how to get the best deal on a car rental? Companies charge different rates for car rentals. Since rates can vary, it's a good idea to know how to find the least expensive arrangement. Here are some tips.

1. Estimate how many miles you might drive the car.
2. Approximate how long you will need the car. If it is for less than a week, a daily rate is probably less expensive. If it is for a longer period, then the weekly or monthly rate will usually be a better deal.
3. Decide what is more important, the comfort of a large car or the economy of a compact.
4. Find out about special rates, such as weekend and "see the country" specials.
5. Ask about drop-off charges. Drop-off charges may apply if you rent the car in one city and then leave it in another city. If there is a drop-off charge, it could be minimal or quite high.
6. Inspect the car for dents or scratches before you rent it. Have any damage noted on the contract so you won't be charged for it later.

Leasing

Leasing is another way to have the use of a car without owning one. When you lease a car, you sign a contract to pay a certain amount each month for the time you use the car. Maintenance, repairs, and insurance are included in the monthly rate.

Below is a schedule of monthly leasing rates from a company in another large city. All rates include 3,000 miles a month and all maintenance. In addition to the monthly rate, the customer pays only for the gas used and miles driven over 3,000 miles a month. As you can see from the schedule, leasing a car is more long-term than renting.

LEASING RATES BY THE MONTH

Car Model	One Month	Two Months	Three Months	Four Months	Five Months	Six Months	Over 3,000 Miles a Month
Compact	$395	$395	$375	$350	$325	$300	$.10 a mile
Intermediate	420	420	400	375	350	325	.10 a mile
Sedan	465	465	440	415	390	365	.10 a mile
Station wagon	505	505	480	455	430	405	.15 a mile
Van	490	490	465	435	405	375	.15 a mile
Luxury sedan	575	575	550	515	480	445	.15 a mile
Camper	655	655	625	585	545	505	.25 a mile

If a person leases a sedan for 6 months and drives it 7,000 miles, what will be the total cost of leasing the car?

6-month leasing rate	$365 a month
Cost of leasing for 6 months	6 × $365 = $2,190

Explain why there is no charge for mileage. If this car had been driven 23,305 miles, however, there would be a mileage charge.

Here is how to figure the mileage charge.

Mileage included in cost	3,000 miles a month
Mileage included in a 6-month period	3,000 miles × 6 = 18,000 miles
Additional miles driven	23,305 − 18,000 = 5,305
Charge for additional miles driven	5,305 × $.10 = $530.50

Exercises for Section One

For Exercises 1 to 5, 8, 9, and 10 find the leasing charge, find the mileage charge, and find the total cost of leasing the car. Use the leasing rate schedule shown on page 236.

Car Model	Length of Lease	Leasing Charge	Miles Driven	Mileage Charge	Total Leasing Cost
1. Station wagon	5 mo	$ 2,150	15,060 mi	$ 9	$ 2,159
2. Intermediate	3 mo	_____	8,572 mi	_____	_____
3. Van	1 mo	_____	7,230 mi	_____	_____
4. Compact	2 mo	_____	4,598 mi	_____	_____
5. Camper	4 mo	_____	13,250 mi	_____	_____

Use the rental rate schedule on page 234 to solve Exercises 6 and 7 and the leasing rate schedule on page 236 to solve Exercises 8 to 10.

6. When Chris Wolf rented a compact car, the mileage meter read 12796.5. When he returned the car after 4 days, it read 12946.5. How many miles had he driven? If he spent a total of $4.06 for gas and $2.25 a day for insurance, what was the total car rental cost?

7. The Kelly family rented a standard car for the 18 days they were on vacation. They traveled 220 miles a day, spent $10 a day on gas, and paid insurance premiums of $2.50 a day. What was their total car rental bill?

8. Mary Jane Sutton leased a station wagon for 2 months so that she could participate in craft shows. She drove 6,170 miles altogether and spent $130 a month on gas. How much was the total cost with gas and mileage?

9. The Wilsons leased an intermediate car for the 3 months they had a summer house. They drove 1,500 miles during the 3 months and spent $39.80 on gas. What was the total cost of leasing?

10. Jim Frazier needs a compact car for 1 month while his car is being repaired. He expects to drive about 1,200 miles that month, pay $30.50 for gas, and pay $2 a day for insurance (if he rents). What is the difference in cost between renting a car for a month of 30 days and leasing it? (Use the rental rate schedule on page 234.) What is the wisest course for him to follow?

Section Two
Riding the Train

You can travel on a train for 1 hour to go to work. Or you can ride a train across the country for $3\frac{1}{2}$ days on a vacation. Although trains are not as fast as planes, they are a relaxed way to travel. Trains are also fuel savers. They can carry many more passengers on a gallon of fuel than a compact car can.

Reading a Train Timetable

Joan Poulos lives in New York, but her parents live in Boston. One weekend she decided to visit them. She picked up a train schedule at the station and checked the time of departure for several trains leaving New York for Boston. The schedule below shows this information.

New York - New Haven - Boston

Train Number	Frequency	NEW YORK NY (Pennsylvania Station)	Rye NY	Stamford CT	Bridgeport	NEW HAVEN	PROVIDENCE RI	Route 128 MA	BOSTON (Back Bay Sta.)	BOSTON MA (South Sta.)
		Dp	Dp	Dp	Dp	Ar / Dp	Dp	Dp	Ar	Ar
66	Daily	3 10a	3 50a	4 03a	4 28a	4 45a 5 05a	7 25a	8 03a	8 20a	8 25a
180	Sa Only	8 10a	8 48a	9 00a	—	9 42a 9 52a	11 54a	12 27p	12 45p	12 50p
168	Daily	9 10a	9 48a	10 00a	10 25a	10 45a 10 55a	12 57p	1 29p	2 00p	2 07p
170	Daily	11 10a	11 48a	—	—	12 40p 12 50p	2 43p	3 15p	3 45p	3 52p
172	Daily	1 05p	1 43p	1 55p	2 20p	2 40p 2 50p	4 54p	5 24p	5 56p	6 06p
152	Su thru Fr		2 25p	2 51p	3 23p	3 45p 4 00p	6 05p			
174	Daily	3 10p	—	4 00p	4 25p	4 45p 4 55p	6 48p	7 18p	7 50p	7 57p
150	Mo thru Fr	4 10p	—	—	—	5 38p 5 53p	7 41p	8 23p	8 43p	8 50p
184	Su Only	4 10p	—	5 00p	—	5 40p 5 50p	7 45p	8 20p	8 37p	8 42p
144	Daily	4 45p	—	5 34p	5 58p	6 20p				
176	Daily	5 10p	—	—	—	6 42p 6 52p	8 47p	9 19p	9 49p	9 56p
162	Daily	6 30p	—	—	—	8 00p 8 10p	10 10p	10 50p	11 12p	11 19p
178	Daily	7 57p	—	8 42p	—	9 25p 9 35p	11 28p	12 10a	12 30a	12 37a
60	Daily	10 10p	10 48p	11 00p	11 25p	11 45p				

Joan couldn't leave until 5 p.m. on Friday. She looked at the New York column to find a train departing about this time. Starting at the top of the table, Joan worked her way down to 5:10 p.m. Note that p.m. is written as *p*, while a.m. is written as *a*. By reading to the left, she saw that this time is for Train 176. The schedule shows that this train runs daily. To find what time it arrives (Ar) in Boston, Joan read across the table on the same line. The last column, BOSTON MA (South Station), was the destination she wanted. The schedule shows that Train 176 arrives in Boston at the South Station at 9:56 p.m.

To find the number of hours it takes Train 176 to travel from New York to Boston, Joan subtracted the departure (Dp) time in New York, 5:10 p.m., from the arrival time in Boston, 9:56 p.m. It is a good idea to convert the time to hours and minutes before subtracting. For example, read 5:10 p.m. as 5 hours and 10 minutes.

Time leaving New York	5:10 p.m. *or* 5 hours and 10 minutes
Time arriving in Boston	9:56 p.m. *or* 9 hours and 56 minutes
Traveling time	9 hours and 56 minutes −5 hours and 10 minutes
	4 hours and 46 minutes

Exercises

For each trip below, departure place and the desired departure time are given. Which train should be taken in each case? Use the train schedule on page 238 to find the train number, the departure time, the arrival time, and the length of the trip for each exercise.

Departure Place	Desired Departure Time	Desti- nation	Train Number	Departure Time	Arrival Time	Length of Trip
1. New Haven	5:45 p.m. Monday	Boston (B.B. Sta.)	150	5:53 p.m.	8:43 p.m.	2 hr 50 min
2. New York	8:00 a.m. Saturday	New Haven				
3. Bridgeport	10:15 a.m. Tuesday	New Haven				
4. Rye	1:30 p.m. Wednesday	Boston (So. Sta.)				
5. Stamford	5:00 p.m. Sunday	New Haven				

Train Fares

Joan's trip from New York to Boston and back cost $35 by coach. A trip to a place and back is referred to as a *round trip. Coach* is the usual and simplest way to travel by train (or plane). Passengers, however, can also go in a *club car,* where they have a reserved seat. If Joan had decided to go in a club car, her ticket would have cost $25.25 one way. Traveling in a club car is more expensive than traveling by coach, but it is more comfortable.

How much more would it have cost Joan to travel in a club car? The schedule below shows the one-way fares in coach and club car.

	In Coach	In Club Car (Seat Charge Included)
ONE - WAY FARES (Double for round-trip) (Fares subject to change)		
BETWEEN		
New York (Penn. Sta.) and		
New Haven	$ 8.00	$12.75
Old Saybrook	9.00	14.25
New London	10.00	15.50
Westerly	11.00	17.00
Kingston	12.50	18.50
Providence	15.50	21.50
Hartford	9.25	14.50
Springfield	10.50	16.50
Boston/Route 128	17.50	25.25
Stamford and		
Old Saybrook	6.50	11.25
New London	8.25	13.00
Providence	12.50	18.25
Hartford	6.75	11.75
Springfield	8.75	13.75
Boston/Route 128	16.00	22.00
New Haven and		
New London	4.75	9.50
Providence	9.50	14.50
Springfield	5.00	10.00
Boston/Route 128	12.50	18.50
New London and		
Providence	5.00	10.00
Boston/Route 128	9.00	14.00
Providence and		
Route 128	3.25	7.75
Boston	4.00	8.50
Boston/Route 128 and		
Kingston	6.25	11.00
Westerly	7.75	12.50
New London	9.00	14.00
Old Saybrook	10.00	15.50
New Haven	12.50	18.50
Bridgeport	14.00	20.00
Stamford	16.00	22.00
Rye	16.50	23.00
New York (Penn. Sta.)	17.50	25.25

Find the place of departure, New York. It is in the first box. Now read down the list in the first box until you come to Boston. Read across this line for coach and club-car fares.

One-way club-car fare	$25.25
Round-trip club-car fare	$25.25 $\times$ 2 = $50.50
One-way coach fare	$17.50
Round-trip coach fare	$17.50 $\times$ 2 = $35.
Difference in fare costs	$50.50 $-$ $35 = $15.50

Part 4 TRANSPORTATION

To save money, Joan chose to travel by coach. To save more money, she could have traveled during less popular hours. If she were able to leave on Thursday and return on Monday morning, she could get a special fare with a 25-percent discount. How much would her discount be? (That is, the amount she would *save* by traveling at a less popular hour.) How much would her special fare be?

Round-trip coach fare	$35
Discount	25%
Amount of discount	$35 × .25 = $8.75
Special fare	$35 − $8.75 = $26.25

Exercises

Use the fare schedule on page 240 to complete these exercises, and find the difference between the fare in the club car and the fare in coach. (Remember to double the one-way fares for round trip.)

Departure Place	Destination	Type of Ticket	Coach Fare	Club-Car Fare	Difference
1. New Haven	Providence	round-trip	$ 19	$ 29	$ 10
2. New York	Kingston	one-way	____	____	____
3. New York	Hartford	round-trip	____	____	____
4. Boston	Bridgeport	one-way	____	____	____
5. Stamford	Old Saybrook	round-trip	____	____	____

Assume the following trips are made during off hours and a 20-percent discount on fares is in effect. Complete these exercises to find the special fare.

Departure Place	Destination	Type of Ticket	Coach Fare	Amt. of Discount	Special Fare
6. Stamford	Hartford	one-way	$ 6.75	$ 1.35	$ 5.40
7. Stamford	Boston	round-trip	____	____	____
8. New York	Springfield	round-trip	____	____	____

Commutation Tickets

Commuter: person who journeys daily from a suburban home to a city job.

Trish Patterson lives in Stamford, a Connecticut town about an hour from New York, where she works. She is a *commuter*, a person who journeys daily from a suburban home to a city job. Commuters, like Trish, can get special commutation tickets and save quite a bit of money each month. These tickets are usually bought for 1 month or for 10 rides. Commuters who buy a commutation ticket may make as many trips as they want during the month. Those who buy 10-ride tickets may take 10 one-way trips within the month. Either kind of commutation ticket offers commuters a savings over regular one-way or round-trip tickets.

Look at the sample fares on page 243. Find Stamford in the left column by reading down the schedule. Now run your finger across the line to find how much Trish pays for her monthly commutation ticket from Stamford to New York. This is listed under the Monthly Commutation column.

Do you know the least expensive (and sometimes only) way to travel between many cities and small towns? It's scheduled bus service. Although buses might take longer than other means of public transportation, they are comfortable and economical.

If Trish commutes to work an average of 22 days each month, how much does she save by buying a monthly commutation ticket rather than one-way tickets?

Sample Fares from New York

Ask your ticket agent about *all* the various fares available.

between GRAND CENTRAL TERMINAL and	Regular One Way	Off-Peak One Way	Monthly Commu- tation	Ten Ride	Senior Citizen & Handicapped One Way
Mt. Vernon Pelham New Rochelle	2.25	1.70	45.00	20.25	1.10
Larchmont Mamaroneck Harrison	2.65	2.00	51.50	23.85	1.30
Rye Port Chester	2.90	2.20	56.00	26.10	1.45
Greenwich Cos Cob Riverside Old Greenwich	3.15	2.35	61.00	28.35	1.55
Stamford	3.40	2.55	64.00	30.60	1.70
Glenbrook Springdale	3.60	2.70	67.50	32.40	1.80
Talmadge Hill	3.65	2.75	70.00	32.85	1.80
New Canaan	3.75	2.80	73.00	33.75	1.85
Noroton Heights	3.60	2.70	67.50	32.40	1.80
Darien Rowayton	3.65	2.75	70.00	32.85	1.80
South Norwalk	3.75	2.80	73.00	33.75	1.85
East Norwalk Westport	3.90	2.95	76.00	35.10	1.95
Green's Farms Southport Fairfield	4.25	3.20	80.50	38.25	2.10
Bridgeport	4.50	3.40	87.00	40.50	2.25
Stratford Milford	5.00	3.75	92.50	45.00	2.50
New Haven	5.40	4.05	99.00	48.60	2.70

Cost of monthly commutation ticket	$64
Cost of one-way trip	$3.40
Number of one-way trips in 1 day	2
Number of one-way trips in 22 days	$22 \times 2 = 44$
Cost of 44 one-way trips	$44 \times \$3.40 = \$149.60$
Savings	$\$149.60 - \$64 = \$85.60$

Exercises for Section Two

Use the fare schedule on this page to complete these exercises, and find the amount each commuter saves by buying a monthly commutation ticket to New York.

Commuter's Town	Round Trips a Month	Monthly Cost at Regular Fare	Monthly Commutation Fare	Monthly Savings
1. New Rochelle	16	$ 72	$ 45	$ 27
2. Harrison	19	____	____	____
3. Greenwich	20	____	____	____
4. New Canaan	21	____	____	____

The people taking these trips do not travel enough to make the monthly commutation ticket worthwhile. Instead, they use a combination of the 10-ride fare and the regular fare, or only the regular fare. Use the fare schedule on page 243 to find the amount each commuter would pay at the 10-ride rate and the regular rate, and find the total cost for the month.

Commuter's Town	Round Trips a Month	Monthly Cost of 10-Ride Fare	Monthly Cost of Regular Fare	Total Monthly Cost
5. Pelham	8	$ 20.25	$ 13.50	$ 33.75
6. Rye	7	____	____	____
7. Glenbrook	6	____	____	____
8. Darien	5	____	____	____

9. Horace Caliper is planning a trip to Boston for a long weekend. He can leave New York's Pennsylvania Station after 5:30 p.m. on Thursday. (Use the train schedule on page 238.)

   a. Which train should he take?

   b. What time will it depart? What time will it arrive in Boston at Back Bay Station?

   c. How long does the trip take?

10. How much does a regular, round-trip coach fare cost between Pennsylvania Station in New York and Hartford? What is the club-car fare? (Use the fare table on page 240.)

11. If the fare for round trips between New York's Pennsylvania Station and Springfield are discounted 25 percent during off hours, what is the cost of a round trip in the coach? In the club car? (Use the fare table on page 240.)

12. Which costs less, to commute for 20 days between New York's Grand Central Terminal and Port Chester using the off-hour rates, or the monthly commutation rate? What is the difference in price? (Use the fare table on page 243.)

Section Three
Flying in a Plane

When should you fly? If you do not have much time or must travel a great distance, you should probably go by plane. Major airlines offer a variety of travel discounts for travelers who meet certain requirements. Always check with the airline or a good travel agent for up-to-the-minute information.

Airline Schedules

Airlines publish booklets that list the cities from which they fly and the different flights and costs. These schedules also show the times of departure and arrival, whether there are meals served, the kinds of planes, and how often planes fly from one city to another.

Below is part of a major airline's schedule, showing flight service from New York to Los Angeles and from New York to Louisville. Also shown is an explanation of the various codes and symbols used. Look at the New York to Los Angeles schedule.

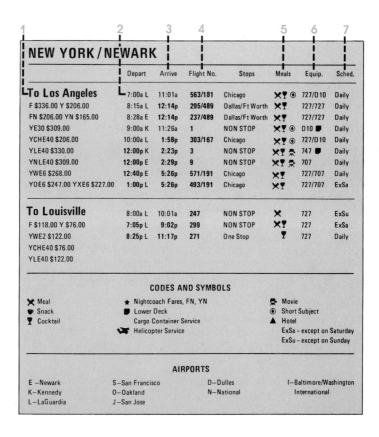

	Depart	Arrive	Flight No.	Stops	Meals	Equip.	Sched.
NEW YORK / NEWARK							
To Los Angeles	7:00a L	11:01a	**563/181**	Chicago	✕♥ ◉	727/D10	Daily
F $336.00 Y $206.00	8:15a L	12:14p	**295/489**	Dallas/Ft Worth	✕♥	727/727	Daily
FN $206.00 YN $165.00	8:28a E	12:14p	**237/489**	Dallas/Ft Worth	✕♥	727/727	Daily
YE30 $309.00	9:00a K	11:26a	**1**	NON STOP	✕♥ ◉	D10 ◼	Daily
YCHE40 $206.00	10:00a L	1:58p	**303/167**	Chicago	✕♥ ◉	727/D10	Daily
YLE40 $330.00	12:00p K	2:23p	**3**	NON STOP	✕♥ ⛻	747 ◼	Daily
YNLE40 $309.00	12:00p E	2:29p	**9**	NON STOP	✕♥ ⛻	707	Daily
YWE6 $268.00	12:40p E	5:26p	**571/191**	Chicago	✕♥	727/707	Daily
YOE6 $247.00 YXE6 $227.00	1:00p L	5:26p	**493/191**	Chicago	✕♥	727/707	ExSa
To Louisville	8:00a L	10:01a	**247**	NON STOP	✕	727	ExSu
F $118.00 Y $76.00	7:05p L	9:02p	**299**	NON STOP	✕♥	727	ExSa
YWE2 $122.00	8:25p L	11:17p	**271**	One Stop	♥	727	Daily
YCHE40 $76.00							
YLE40 $122.00							

CODES AND SYMBOLS

✕ Meal	★ Nightcoach Fares, FN, YN	⛻ Movie
♥ Snack	◼ Lower Deck	◉ Short Subject
♥ Cocktail	Cargo Container Service	▲ Hotel
	Helicopter Service	ExSa – except on Saturday
		ExSu – except on Sunday

AIRPORTS

E –Newark	S–San Francisco	D–Dulles	I–Baltimore/Washington
K–Kennedy	O–Oakland	N–National	International
L–LaGuardia	J–San Jose		

1. Under the To Los Angeles head, a number of codes refer to all the available flight plans for this trip. For example, the F code is for first class, the most expensive and comfortable plan. The price is $336 for a one-way ticket to Los Angeles. The Y code is for coach. Most passengers travel by coach. The seats are closer together, and meals are simpler than in first class. The price of a one-way coach fare on the same flight is $206.

2. The column to the right shows that the first flight departs at 7:00a L. This means it leaves at 7 a.m. from LaGuardia Airport. (See the explanation of airport codes.)

3. The third column shows that the plane arrives in Los Angeles at 11:01 a.m.

4. The fourth column shows the flight number 563/181. Passengers flying to Los Angeles take Flight 563 to Chicago. Then they pick up Flight 181 to Los Angeles. (As you look down the column you can see that some flights are nonstop and so have only one flight number.)

5. In this column, symbols tell the kinds of meals and other flight features available.

6. In the Equipment (Equip.) column, the types of planes used in this particular flight are shown. A 727 aircraft will fly to Chicago, and then a DC-10 will fly to Los Angeles.

7. The Schedule (Sched.) column shows that this flight is scheduled for every day of the week.

Exercises

Use the New York to Los Angeles schedule to answer these questions about Flight 9.

1. From which airport does it leave?
2. What time does it leave?
3. What time does it arrive in Los Angeles?
4. Does it make a stop along the way? If so, where?
5. What kind of aircraft is used?
6. What kind of food and beverage service is offered?
7. Is a movie shown during the flight?
8. On what days is the flight scheduled?

Time Zones

United States time zones:
Eastern
Central
Mountain
Pacific

When you travel across the country, you cross several *time zones*. The United States is divided into four zones from east to west. They are Eastern, Central, Mountain, and Pacific. Crossing from one zone to another, you either lose or gain an hour in time.

For example, if you travel west from New York to Chicago, you should turn your watch *back* 1 hour. Traveling east from Chicago to New York, you should set your watch *ahead* by 1 hour.

The map below shows the four time zones in the United States. Notice that when it's 11:00 in New York, it is only 8:00 in Los Angeles.

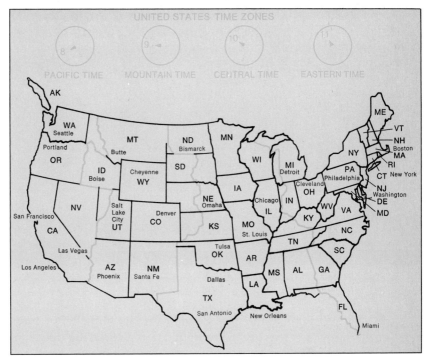

Suppose you fly from New York to Los Angeles. You leave at 12 p.m. and land at 2:23 p.m. But the flight is over 5 hours long. The map shows that while traveling to Los Angeles you cross three time zones. With each crossing of a time zone, you "lose an hour." If you don't reset your watch, it will read 5:23 instead of 2:23 when you arrive. This is because Los Angeles is located in the Pacific time zone, where the time is 3 hours behind New York's Eastern time zone. ($5:23 - 3:00 = 2:23$).

You will be in flight from 12 p.m. EST (Eastern Standard Time) until 5:23 p.m. EST. The hour of noon is sometimes referred to as *zero hour* and written as 00 hours. Exactly how long is the flight?

EST departure from New York	12 p.m. *or* 00 hours
EST arrival in Los Angeles	5:23 p.m. *or* 5 hours and 23 minutes
Time in flight	5 hours and 23 minutes − 00 hours = 5 hours and 23 minutes

Welcome to our no-frills Flight 409.

Exercises for Section Three

Look at the time given in the city in the left column. What time is it in the city in the right column? (Use the time zone map on page 247.)

City and Time	City and Time
1. Boston, Mass. 1:20 p.m.	Las Vegas, Nev. 10:20 a.m.
2. Boise, Idaho 12:00 noon	New York, N.Y. _____
3. Denver, Colo. 11:15 a.m.	Detroit, Mich. _____
4. Dallas, Tex. 9:30 p.m.	Chicago, Ill. _____
5. Seattle, Wash. 12:00 midnight	Omaha, Nebr. _____
6. St. Louis, Mo. 6:30 a.m.	Denver, Colo. _____
7. Butte, Mont. 4:17 p.m.	Portland, Oreg. _____

Find the length of each flight. (Use the time zone map on page 247.)

Departure	Arrival	Length of Flight
8. Chicago, Ill.	San Francisco, Calif.	
1:12 p.m.	2:57 p.m.	___ hr ___ min
9. New York, N.Y.	Chicago, Ill.	
7:30 a.m.	8:35 a.m.	___ hr ___ min
10. Las Vegas, Nev.	Philadelphia, Penn.	
6:30 p.m.	2:00 a.m.	___ hr ___ min

Use the New York to St. Louis, Mo., flight schedule given below for Exercises 11 and 12.

NEW YORK / NEWARK							
	Depart	Arrive	Flight No.	Stops	Meals	Equip.	Sched.
To St. Louis	7:55a L	9:24a	125	NON-STOP	✕	727	ExSaSu
F $147.00 Y $92.00	9:50a K	11:18a	151	NON-STOP	●	707	Sa
YE30 $147.00	10:00a L	12:54p	303/231	Chicago	●❚	727/727	Daily
YWE2 $147.00	10:00a E	12:54p	291/231	Chicago	●❚ ◉	D10/727	Daily
YCHE40 $92.00	12:10p L	1:29p	121	NON-STOP	✕❚	727	Daily
YLE40 $147.00	12:40p E	3:56p	571/343	Chicago	✕❚	727/727	Daily
	1:30p L	3:43p	385	One-Stop	●❚	727	Daily
	5:55p L	7:20p	473	NON-STOP	✕❚	727	ExSa
	7:00p L	10:01p	259/567	Chicago	✕❚	727/727	Daily
	7:15p E	10:01p	45/567	Chicago	✕❚	707/727	Daily

11. Which flights leave from LaGuardia Airport? From Kennedy Airport? From Newark Airport? (Give the flight numbers.)

12. What information about Flight 291/231 does the schedule give?

13. What time is it in St. Louis, Mo., when it is 7:55 a.m. in New York, N.Y.? When it is 12 noon in Chicago, Ill.? When it is 2:32 p.m. in San Francisco, Calif.?

14. Flight 385 leaves New York's LaGuardia airport at 1:30 p.m. and arrives in St. Louis, Mo., at 3:43 p.m. How long does the flight take?

REVIEW FOR CHAPTER 12
USING PUBLIC TRANSPORTATION

1. Marie Lopez rented a luxury sedan from 8:30 a.m. on Wednesday until 10:30 a.m. the next day. When she got the car, the mileage registered 10563.8. When she returned the car, it registered 10737.8. (Use the table on page 234 to answer the following questions.)

   a. For how long did she rent the car?

   b. How much did the rental company charge for the basic car?

   c. How far did she drive?

   d. How much did the rental company charge for mileage?

   e. The car gets 15 miles to a gallon of gas, and gas cost $.65 a gallon. How much did she spend for gas?

   f. How much did she spend for insurance at $3 a day or part of a day?

   g. What was her total car rental bill?

2. Alexander Levin leased a van for 4 months. He drove 775 miles

each week he had it. (Use the table on page 236 to answer the following questions. Round off your answers to the nearest cent and nearest tenth of a mile when necessary.)

    a. How much was he charged for the van? For mileage?

    b. How much did he spend on gas if the van got 17 miles to the gallon and he bought gas at $.61 a gallon?

    c. What were his total costs for the 4-month period?

3. Which takes longer to get to Boston's Back Bay Station from New York, Train 66 or Train 178? How much longer? (Use the schedule on page 238.)

4. Kim Lourie lives in Connecticut and travels regularly from New York's Pennsylvania Station to Westerly. Which costs more, traveling in the club car at off hours with a 25-percent discount or traveling in coach during rush hours? How much more? (Use the fare table on page 240.)

5. Mr. Pullen is a senior citizen who commutes between New York's Grand Central Terminal and Stamford for 20 days each month. Which is cheaper for him, the senior citizen's fare or the monthly commutation fare? How much cheaper? (Use the fare table on page 243.)

6. When it is 4:30 p.m. in Omaha, Nebr., what time is it in Boston, Mass.? In Portland, Oreg.? (Use the time zone map on page 247.)

7. Answer these questions about Flight 633 from Washington, D.C.

WASHINGTON, D.C.

	Depart	Arrive	Flight No.	Stops	Meals	Equip.	Sched.
To Salt Lake City	7:00a N	11:01a	563	One Stop	✕❢	727	Daily
F $277.00 Y $170.00	8:45a N	1:54p	141	Two Stop	✕❢	727	Daily
YE30 $272.00	10:00a D	1:54p	291/141	Chicago	✕❢ ◉	D10/727	Daily
YCHE40 $170.00	10:00a N	1:54p	303/141	Chicago	✕❢	727/727	Daily
YLE40 $272.00	12:40p D	5:59p	571/633	Chicago	✕❢	727/727	Daily
	2:00p N	5:59p	633	One Stop	✕❢	727	Daily
	3:00p N	8:04p	431/137	Chicago	✕❢	727/727	Daily
	3:45p D	8:04p	423/137	Chicago	✕❢	707/727	Daily
	4:00p N	8:04p	315/137	Chicago	✕❢	727/727	ExSa

    a. What time does it depart? Arrive in Salt Lake City?

    b. From which airport does it leave? (See page 245 for codes.)

    c. What kind of food service is available?

    d. What kind of aircraft is used?

    e. What days is the flight scheduled?

    f. Must a passenger change planes during the trip?

8. How long does Flight 291/141 take?

Consumer Challenge

Geri Weston and John Robertson plan to marry when they finish college in three months. They will have 10 days for a honeymoon in Orlando, Florida. They considered the time they could spend traveling and the total time they would have in Orlando. They compared the costs of traveling by bus, train, car, and plane. They knew they had to add in the costs of meals and lodging. Geri and John also thought about traveling convenience, how important comfort and relaxation were to them. John and Geri made the chart below to help them decide the best way to travel.

Travel for Two, Round Trip	Time, One Way	Meals for Two, One Way	Room, One Way
Bus—$198	28 to 30 hr	8	None (sleep 1 night on bus)
Train—$214	19 hr 40 min	6	None (sleep 1 night on train)
Plane—$317	2 hr 20 min	0	None
Geri's car— 4,392 miles at $.125 a mile	24 hr 50 min	14	2 nights in motel

To make a wise decision, Geri and John must perform certain computations. Do the following computations for Geri and John and answer the questions that follow. Explain your answers.

1. How much will each method of transportation amount to? (Assume an average cost of $7 a meal during the trip and $30 a night for lodging for the two when traveling by car.)
2. Which travel method is the most expensive? The most economical? The longest? The shortest?
3. What are the advantages and disadvantages of each method?
4. Geri and John will have to pay for food and lodging once they reach Florida. Assume an average cost of $8.65 a meal and $32 a night in lodging for the two. How will these factors affect their total expenses for each method of transportation?
5. Suppose both Geri and John enjoy exploring and taking drives to new places. How would that influence their choice?
6. Suppose Geri's car has been breaking down frequently. How would that influence their decision?
7. Which way would you prefer to travel? How big a role does money, comfort, and personal taste play in your decision?

For You to Solve

1. Robert James was in the market for a new intermediate car. He read an advertisement by a car dealer who was willing to sell any car on the lot for $150 above dealer cost. The car Robert liked best had a sticker price of $5,600. It also had the following options: air conditioner at $450, an automatic transmission at $250, an AM-FM radio at $110, a CB radio at $150, and protective floor mats at $60. Compute the following amounts. Then determine how much Robert would pay for the car.

   a. Dealer cost of car at 81 percent of sticker price.

   b. Optional equipment at 80 percent of sticker price.

   c. Transportation cost of car at $90.

   d. Preparation charges on car at $60.

   e. Sales tax at 7 percent.

2. Robert decided to buy the car. Before he could drive it, he had to register it, take out insurance, pay an auto-use tax, and pay an inspection fee. Based upon the following information, what are the additional costs that Robert will have to pay before he can drive his new car?

   a. The amount of the registration fee is $.50 per 100 pounds of weight. The car weighs 4,900 pounds.

   b. The auto-use tax is $20.

   c. The insurance policy costs $360.

   d. The inspection fee is $6.

3. Robert James drives his car an average of 1,500 miles a month. He estimates the annual depreciation on the car will be 28 percent the first year. His car averages 16 miles to a gallon of gasoline. Gasoline costs about $.69 a gallon. His car manual says the car will use a quart of oil every 500 miles. Every 3,000 miles he plans to have the car lubricated, the oil changed, and a new oil filter installed. Oil costs $.75 a quart, the oil filter costs $3.50, and the lubrication costs $2.50. When a new oil filter is added, it takes 5 quarts of oil. Calculate the annual cost of operating the car using information, where necessary, from Exercises 1, 2, and 3. (If necessary, round off your answers to the nearest cent, with the exception of question k, which you should round off to the nearest tenth of a cent.)

   a. How much is the depreciation on the car the first year?

   b. How many miles will the car be driven in a year?

   c. How many gallons of gasoline will be used in a year?

   d. What is the annual cost for gasoline?

e. How many quarts of oil will Robert's car use in a year?

f. How much will oil cost a year?

g. How many oil filters will be used in a year?

h. How much will oil filters cost a year?

i. How much will it cost to grease and lubricate the car each year?

j. How much will it cost to operate the car for one year? (Remember to include insurance, registration fee, auto-use tax, inspection fee and depreciation.)

k. How much per mile will it cost Robert to operate the car?

4. Leslie Newton is a traveling sales representative who is based in New York City. She was sent to California for 3 weeks in September. Her plan was to fly from New York to Los Angeles, rent a car for 3 weeks, and then return home by plane. She examined the plane schedules and decided to fly out at 8:15 a.m. Monday morning using the regular coach fare. She purchased a round-trip ticket. On arriving at Los Angeles, she rented a station wagon for three weeks. During the three weeks she drove 2,100 miles. Insurance was covered in the car rental fee. Using the airline table on page 245, the car rental table on page 234, and the time zone chart on page 247, answer the following questions.

a. What time did she arrive at Los Angeles?

b. How many hours were spent in flying from New York to Los Angeles?

c. What was the round-trip coach fare? (Add an 8-percent tax to the round-trip total.)

d. If her motel rooms averaged $26 a day, how much did she spend for lodging in California? (Assume 21 nights.)

e. If her meals averaged $22 a day, how much did she spend for meals in California? (Assume 22 days.)

f. How much did the rental of the station wagon cost if it was driven 2,100 miles in a 3-week period?

g. What was the total cost of Leslie's business trip?

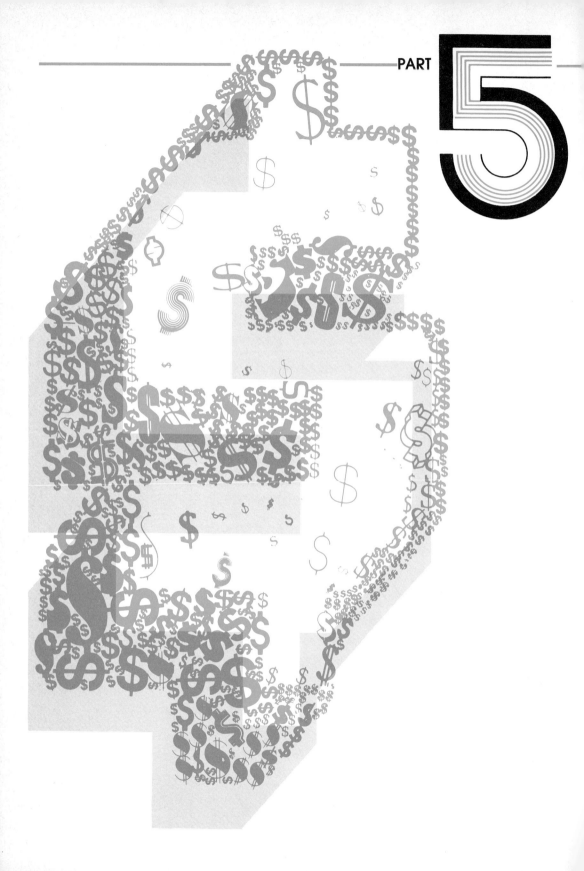

Managing Money

Performance Goals

When you finish work on this part, you should be able to:

- ☐ Determine the time it should take to save a desired amount of income, given different savings goals and plans.
- ☐ Compute total annual savings, including regular savings from income and savings from other sources.
- ☐ Compute simple interest on an annual, semiannual, quarterly, and daily basis.
- ☐ Compute compound interest for annual, semiannual, and quarterly time periods by using a compound interest table.
- ☐ Compute total costs, including market price and broker's commission, of buying round lots and odd lots of stock.
- ☐ Demonstrate ability to read stock and bond trading tables.
- ☐ Compute dividends on preferred and common stocks.
- ☐ Compute profits or losses on stock transactions.
- ☐ Compute rates of return on stocks and bonds.
- ☐ Compute life insurance costs for different types of coverage.
- ☐ Compute life insurance premiums paid on a periodic basis.
- ☐ Compute amounts of property damage to be paid by the insured and by the insurance company when property is insured to full value or to 80 percent of value.
- ☐ Compute amount of medical expenses to be paid by the insured and by the insurance company.
- ☐ Compute the amounts of federal income tax owed by taxpayers who qualify for Forms 1040A and 1040.
- ☐ Determine whether taxpayers must pay more or get a refund from the Internal Revenue Service.
- ☐ Compute the amount of state income tax owed by taxpayers.

CHAPTER 13

Saving Money

What do ants, squirrels, pack rats, jackdaws, bears, and people have in common? They all do banking of sorts. They all store things away for one reason or another—habit, greed, or need.

People save all kinds of things. And one of the most important things people save is money. Many people put money aside for vacations, for down payments on a house or car, for education, even for a baby. And without some kind of savings, emergencies such as accidents or loss of a job can become a real drain on budgets. But people with savings plans can often meet such problems without hardship.

Saving money does *not* mean putting it into a jar or under the mattress. One of the safest and smartest places to keep your money is in a savings account in a bank. Bank savings accounts are protected, and, what's more, banks pay you interest for the use of the money that you deposit in a savings account.

Consumers looking for the best savings plans often need to do some comparison shopping. They may find some banks trying to get new customers by giving away free gifts when they open a savings account. But these gifts are often gimmicks. The interest rate may not be as high at a bank that offers free gifts as it is at a bank that doesn't. Shoppers will also find that most banks have a variety of savings plans. Some accounts pay higher interest if a depositor leaves the money in the account for a specified period of time. If the money is withdrawn early, however, the depositor pays a penalty. Besides a variety of savings plans, many banks offer other services to depositors. Some have safe deposit boxes, for example. Some offer free traveler's checks. You must consider all these things and more when you choose a bank for your savings.

Frank and Millie Baxter, a young couple living in a small city, decided to open a savings account. In selecting the best bank for their account, the Baxters looked for the following things.

1. A number of different savings plans to choose from.
2. A high rate of interest. Also, interest computed at least quarterly.
3. No restrictions on withdrawing their money if they needed cash in a hurry.
4. Convenient location and hours.
5. Certainty that their deposits would be insured.

Section One
How Much Money to Save

The Baxters weren't sure what amount they should aim for in their savings account. The bank manager advised them that for emergencies they should save at least 2 months' gross salaries. Frank works as a foreman in a large auto factory a few miles out of the city. He earns a gross salary of $12,600 a year. Millie is starting a job as an assistant bookkeeper in a department store and expects to gross $660 a month. About how much money should the Baxters aim to keep in their savings account if they follow the manager's advice?

Millie's monthly income	$660
Frank's monthly income	$12,600 ÷ 12 = $1,050
Total monthly income	$1,050 + $660 = $1,710
2 months' income	$1,710 × 2 = $3,420

If the Baxters save 5 percent of their gross income each month, how much will they save in a year?

Monthly gross income	$1,710
Monthly 5-percent savings	$1,710 × .05 = $85.50
Yearly savings	$85.50 × 12 = $1,026

By looking at the figure for the Baxters' yearly savings, you can get an idea of how long it will take them to save $3,420. It will take about 3 years (3 × $1,026 = $3,078). Or, to be more exact, it will take 3.3 years (3,420 ÷ 1,026 = 3.3).

Exercises

Complete these exercises to find the amount each person or family saves a year and the number of years it will take to save 2 months' gross salary. (Round off income saved to the nearest dollar and time to the nearest tenth of a year. Assume that 2 months is 8 weeks and—for computing annual income—that 1 year is 52 weeks.)

Employee and Gross Income Each Payday	2 Months' Gross Income	Annual Income	Percent of Annual Income Saved	Amount of Annual Income Saved	Time Needed to Save 2 Months' Gross Income
1. R. French—$135 a wk	$ 1,080	$ 7,020	4%	$ 281	3.8 yr
2. S. Chase—$157.50 a wk	_____	_____	4%	_____	_____
3. P. Davis—$210.35 a wk	_____	_____	5%	_____	_____
4. M. Feder—$780 a mo	_____	_____	4%	_____	_____
5. K. Gould—$1,146 a mo	_____	_____	5%	_____	_____

Increasing Savings

After six months, Frank and Millie wanted to spend some of their savings on a visit to Frank's mother, who lives 1,800 miles away. They realized, though, that they wouldn't have much left in their savings account if they took the trip. They looked for ways to increase their savings. Millie started to put aside all her loose change at the end of each day. In an average week, she saved about $10.50. Once a week, she deposited this money into their savings account.

Frank estimated the cost of his eating lunch at a restaurant three times a week. It was $12.50. He decided to eat at the plant's cafeteria and save that money. He also gave up cigarettes, saving about $5.50 a week.

How much will the Baxters save in a month if they put aside this extra money as they have planned? (Assume that there are four weeks in a month.)

Millie's extra weekly savings	$10.50		
Millie's monthly savings	$10.50 × 4 = $42		
Frank's extra weekly savings	$12.50		
Frank's monthly savings	$12.50 × 4 = $50		
Yearly cigarette savings	$300		
Monthly cigarette savings	$300 ÷ 12 = $25		
Total extra monthly savings	$42 + $50 + $25 = $117		

What will be the total of the Baxters' savings in a year if they save on these extras and also put 5 percent of their combined income in a savings account?

Yearly 5-percent savings on income	$1,026
Extra yearly savings	$117 × 12 = $1,404
Total yearly savings	$1,026 + $1,404 = $2,430

Exercises for Section One

In these exercises, each person or family saves 6 percent of their annual gross income plus some extra amount. Find the amounts saved in each case. (If necessary, round off your answers to the nearest cent.)

Gross Income	Annual Gross Income Saved	Extra Savings	Annual Extra Savings	Total Annual Savings
1. J. Opel— $160 a wk	$ 499.20	Birthday gifts of $10, $12.50, and $25	$ 47.50	$ 546.70
2. P. Purvis— $214 a wk	_____	$4.75 a wk by saving change	_____	_____
3. E. Quinn— $313.42 a wk	_____	$2 a wk by saving change, $12.40 gift	_____	_____
4. C. Rizer— $845 a mo	_____	$1.10 a day on bag lunch for 10 days a mo	_____	_____
5. L. Spayer— $1,270 a mo	_____	$303 a mo for overtime	_____	_____

6. How many months will it take Sarah Forrest to save $2,106 if she saves $648 a year?

7. Farley Mann earns $220 a week gross. What is 2 months' gross income for Farley? (Assume 4 weeks in a month.) For how many years will he have to save before he puts 2 months' gross salary into savings if he saves 6 percent a year?

8. For the first 4 months of last year, Alfred Noto saved 3 percent of his monthly salary. For the remaining months of last year, he saved 6 percent of his monthly salary. If he makes $931 a month how much did he save for the year?

9. Lynn Sullivan earns $1,105 a month gross. She saves 7 percent of this amount. She also saves an average of $3.75 a week by putting aside her loose change. How much will Lynn save in a year?

10. Each year, Carl and Rose Kogen save 5.5 percent of Rose's annual gross income of $9,240. They save 4 percent of Carl's annual gross income of $8,000, plus the $65-a-month car allowance that he receives. What is their total annual savings?

Section Two
Earning Simple Interest

Banks put depositors' money into investments such as bonds and mortgage loans. These investments earn money for the bank. In turn, banks pay depositors interest for the use of their money.
    As you know, the rate of interest is stated as a percent. The rate is used to compute the amount of interest paid on a savings account. Interest is paid at regular times during the year, such as annually, semiannually, or quarterly. Some banks even pay interest monthly or daily.

Annual Interest Periods

You've seen bank advertisements that claim you can earn certain high percentages in annual interest on your savings account. If this rate of interest is paid once a year, the simple interest formula is used to compute the interest.

$$\text{Interest} = \text{Principal} \times \text{Rate} \times \text{Time}$$

or

$$I = P \times R \times T$$

Suppose the annual interest rate is 5 percent at one bank. How much is the interest on a savings account of $2,800 at the end of one year?

Annual interest rate	5% *or* .05
Annual interest payment	$2,800 \times .05 \times 1 = $140

Exercises

As a review, compute the amount of simple interest that would be earned on each savings account in a year.

Amount in Savings	Interest Rate	Annual Simple Interest
1. $3,112	4.5%	$ 140.04
2. 900	4%	
3. 1,200	4.5%	
4. 1,650	5%	
5. 2,435	5.2%	

Semiannual and Quarterly Interest Periods

Principal: amount of money on deposit in a savings account.

If a person makes deposits or withdrawals, the *principal*, or amount on deposit, will vary. Banks that pay interest semiannually and quarterly often follow these guidelines.

1. Money deposited on or before the tenth day of each interest period earns interest from the first day of the period.
2. Money withdrawn during the last three business days of the interest period is credited with interest to the end of the period.

To compute semiannual interest payments, use the simple interest formula. But because interest is paid every 6 months, the time period will change. In the formula, T will be written as a fractional part of a year, or $\frac{6}{12}$, which is reduced to $\frac{1}{2}$, or changed to .5.

Quarterly interest payments are paid 4 times a year (every 3 months), and the time is written as $\frac{3}{12}$, which is reduced to $\frac{1}{4}$, or changed to .25.

For example, a customer has $1,200 in a savings account. What is the semiannual interest payment if the annual interest rate is $4\frac{3}{4}$ percent? For our purposes, in this and other examples, we will assume that no deposits or withdrawals are made.

$$I = P \times R \times T$$

Annual interest rate $4\frac{3}{4}\%$ *or* .0475
Semiannual interest payment $1,200 \times .0475 \times .5 = \$28.50$

If the same account earned quarterly interest, how much interest would be due at the end of a quarter?

$$I = P \times R \times T$$

Quarterly interest payment $1,200 \times .0475 \times .25 = \$14.25$

Exercises

Compute the amount of interest the bank pays semiannually on each savings account. (Round off to the nearest cent when necessary.)

	Principal	Interest Rate	Semiannual Interest
1.	$2,604	5%	$ 65.10
2.	800	4%	_____
3.	1,300	4.2%	_____
4.	1,960	5.5%	_____
5.	3,285	5%	_____

Compute the amount of interest the bank pays quarterly on each savings account. (Round off to the nearest cent when necessary.)

	Principal	Interest Rate	Quarterly Interest
6. $	600	4%	$ 6
7.	1,400	5.2%	_____
8.	1,830	4.5%	_____
9.	2,265	5%	_____
10.	10,308	5.25%	_____

One way to meet college costs is to begin saving early.

Part 5   MANAGING MONEY

Many banks use computers to determine daily interest from the day customers deposit money in their accounts until the day they withdraw the money. Computers are programmed to figure the amount of daily interest earned even if the amount on deposit changes because of deposits or withdrawals.

The simple interest formula can be used to compute daily interest. For T, just divide the number of days that the money is on deposit by 365. Suppose you have money on deposit for 45 days. T would be written as $\frac{45}{365}$.

Here's how to find the interest on $1,300 on deposit at 5-percent interest for 45 days. First, it's important to understand that $\frac{45}{365}$ can be simplified. This will make the answer easier to compute. If you divide both 45 and 365 by 5, you get the fraction $\frac{9}{73}$.

$$\frac{45 \div 5}{365 \div 5} = \frac{9}{73}$$

Try working out the following example yourself.

$$I = P \times R \times T$$

Deposit period $\qquad \frac{45}{365}$ or $\frac{9}{73}$

Daily interest total $\quad \$1,300 \times .05 \times \frac{9}{73} = \$\frac{585}{73}$

$$= \$8.013 \ or \ \$8.01$$

Exercises for Section Two

For each given fraction, find a simpler fraction.

Fraction	Simpler Fraction	Fraction	Simpler Fraction
1. $\frac{30}{365}$	$\frac{6}{73}$	6. $\frac{80}{365}$	_____
2. $\frac{25}{365}$	_____	7. $\frac{75}{365}$	_____
3. $\frac{60}{365}$	_____	8. $\frac{90}{365}$	_____
4. $\frac{35}{365}$	_____	9. $\frac{225}{365}$	_____
5. $\frac{120}{365}$	_____	10. $\frac{305}{365}$	_____

Compute the amount of simple interest the bank pays on the principal in each savings account listed on the next page for the given number of days. (Round off your answer to the nearest cent.)

Principal	Interest Rate	Time in Days	Daily Interest Total
11. $ 800	4%	60	$ 5.26
12. 1,200	5%	80	_____
13. 1,540	4.2%	25	_____
14. 2,250	4.5%	75	_____
15. 3,146	5%	30	_____
16. 10,420	5.25%	90	_____

Solve these problems. (If necessary, round off your answer to the nearest cent.)

17. How much simple interest does a bank pay on $1,500 at 5 percent for 1 year? For 6 months? For 3 months? For 20 days?

18. How much simple interest does a bank pay on $2,000 at 5.5 percent annually? Semiannually? Quarterly? Daily?

19. How much simple interest does a bank pay on $3,540 at 5.75-percent for 5 years? For 1 year? For $\frac{1}{2}$ year? For $\frac{1}{4}$ year? For 50 days?

Section Three
Earning Compound Interest

Compound interest: interest earned on the sum of the principal and earned interest.

Most banks offer interest on savings accounts that is compounded quarterly. *Compound interest* means that the interest you earn is added to your principal and, in turn, draws interest. You earn interest on your interest as well as on your deposits.

Suppose the Baxters deposit $1,500 in a savings account in which interest is compounded semiannually at 6 percent. If no other deposits or withdrawals are made, what will their balance be at the end of 2 years? (Remember that there are 4 semiannual interest periods in 2 years.)

STEP 1: *Find the interest rate for one interest period.*

Interest periods in 1 year   2
Yearly interest rate   6%
Interest rate for 1 interest period   6% ÷ 2 = 3% *or* .03

STEP 2: *Find the interest for the first interest period.*
(T equals one interest period in this case.)

Interest for first period $1,500 × .03 × 1 = $45

STEP 3: *Add the interest from the first period to the principal.*

New principal $1,500 + $45 = $1,545

STEP 4: *Continue computing interest and adding it to the principal.*

Interest for second period $1,545 × .03 × 1 = $46.35
New principal $1,545 + $46.35 = $1,591.35

Note that compound interest is not earned for amounts under $1. Drop any amounts under $1 when you are computing interest. Therefore, interest for the next period would be computed on a new principal of $1,591.

Interest for third period $1,591 × .03 × 1 = $47.73
New principal $1,591.35 + $47.73 = $1,639.08
                                                              or $1,639

Interest for fourth period $1,639 × .03 × 1 = $49.17
Final principal $1,639.08 + $49.17 = $1,688.25

Exercises

Compute the interest and new principal at each interest period on a savings account of $2,000 at 6 percent compounded quarterly for 2 years. Do not compute interest on amounts less than $1. (Round off your answers to the nearest cent, if necessary.)

Interest Period	Interest	New Principal
1. First	$ 30	$ 2,030
2. Second		
3. Third		
4. Fourth		
5. Fifth		
6. Sixth		
7. Seventh		
8. Eighth		

Compute the interest and new principal on a savings account of $2,000 at 6 percent compounded annually for 2 years.

Interest Period	Interest	New Principal
9. First	$	$
10. Second		

Millie Baxter discovered that her grandfather had deposited $200 for her in a savings account 20 years ago at 3.5-percent interest compounded annually. The money has been earning interest for 20 years. Every year the interest has been added to the deposit, and new interest has been computed on these new balances. Millie would have a lot of work to do to compute how much the account is worth now.

Banks today use computers, but in the past, they used tables such as the one below to compute compound interest. This table can give you an idea of how compound interest is computed.

COMPOUND INTEREST TABLE
Value of $1

Number of Periods	1.5%	2%	2.5%	3%	3.5%	4%	5%	6%	7%	8%	9%	10%
1	1.0150	1.0200	1.0250	1.0300	1.0350	1.0400	1.0500	1.0600	1.0700	1.0800	1.0900	1.1000
2	1.0302	1.0404	1.0506	1.0609	1.0712	1.0816	1.1025	1.1236	1.1449	1.1664	1.1881	1.2100
3	1.0457	1.0612	1.0769	1.0927	1.1087	1.1248	1.1576	1.1910	1.2250	1.2597	1.2950	1.3310
4	1.0614	1.0824	1.1038	1.1255	1.1475	1.1699	1.2155	1.2625	1.3108	1.3605	1.4116	1.4641
5	1.0773	1.1041	1.1314	1.1593	1.1877	1.2167	1.2763	1.3382	1.4026	1.4693	1.5386	1.6105
6	1.0934	1.1262	1.1597	1.1941	1.2293	1.2653	1.3401	1.4186	1.5007	1.5869	1.6771	1.7716
7	1.1098	1.1487	1.1887	1.2299	1.2723	1.3159	1.4071	1.5036	1.6058	1.7138	1.8280	1.9487
8	1.1265	1.1717	1.2184	1.2668	1.3168	1.3686	1.4775	1.5938	1.7182	1.8059	1.9926	2.1436
9	1.1434	1.1951	1.2489	1.3048	1.3629	1.4233	1.5513	1.6895	1.8385	1.9990	2.1719	2.3579
10	1.1605	1.2190	1.2801	1.3439	1.4106	1.4802	1.6289	1.7908	1.9672	2.1589	2.3674	2.5937
11	1.1779	1.2434	1.3121	1.3842	1.4600	1.5395	1.7103	1.8983	2.1049	2.3316	2.5804	2.8531
12	1.1956	1.2682	1.3449	1.4258	1.5111	1.6010	1.7959	2.0122	2.2522	2.5182	2.8127	3.1384
13	1.2136	1.2936	1.3785	1.4685	1.5640	1.6651	1.8856	2.1329	2.4098	2.7196	3.0658	3.4523
14	1.2318	1.3195	1.4130	1.5126	1.6187	1.7317	1.9799	2.2609	2.5785	2.9372	3.3417	3.7975
15	1.2502	1.3459	1.4483	1.5580	1.6753	1.8009	2.0789	2.3966	2.7590	3.1722	3.6425	4.1772
16	1.2690	1.3728	1.4845	1.6047	1.7340	1.8730	2.1829	2.5404	2.9522	3.4259	3.9703	4.5950
17	1.2880	1.4002	1.5216	1.6528	1.7947	1.9479	2.2920	2.6928	3.1588	3.7000	4.3276	5.0545
18	1.3073	1.4282	1.5597	1.7024	1.8575	2.0258	2.4066	2.8543	3.3799	3.9960	4.7171	5.5599
19	1.3270	1.4568	1.5987	1.7535	1.9225	2.1068	2.5270	3.0256	3.6165	4.3157	5.1417	6.1159
20	1.3469	1.4859	1.6386	1.8061	1.9898	2.1911	2.6533	3.2071	3.8697	4.6610	5.6044	6.7275
21	1.3671	1.5157	1.6796	1.8603	2.0594	2.2788	2.7860	3.3996	4.1406	5.0338	6.1088	7.4003
22	1.3876	1.5460	1.7216	1.9161	2.1315	2.3699	2.9253	3.6035	4.4304	5.4365	6.6586	8.1403
23	1.4084	1.5769	1.7646	1.9736	2.2061	2.4647	3.0715	3.8198	4.7405	5.8715	7.2579	8.9543
24	1.4295	1.6084	1.8087	2.0328	2.2833	2.5633	3.2251	4.0489	5.0724	6.3412	7.9111	9.9497
25	1.4509	1.6407	1.8539	2.0938	2.3673	2.6658	3.3864	4.2919	5.4274	6.8485	8.6231	10.8347

The table tells you the value of a $1 deposit when interest is compounded at various rates and for different interest periods. For example, $1 deposited 20 years ago at 3.5-percent interest compounded annually would amount today to $1.9898. Here's how to use the table to get this information. Run your finger down the Number of Periods column until you come to the number 20. (Since the interest is compounded once a year, there are 20 interest periods.) Move across that line to the 3.5% column. This column gives the value of $1 on deposit for different interest periods at the 3.5-percent interest rate.

To how much would $200 grow after 20 years at 3.5-percent

interest compounded annually? Multiply 200 and $1.9898 to find the new principal.

New principal $1.9898 × 200 = $397.96

Exercises

Interest on these savings accounts is compounded annually. Use the table on page 266 to find the value of $1 and the new principal of each account for the given time. (If necessary, round off your answers to the nearest cent.)

Principal	Interest Rate	Time in Years	Value of $1 Deposit	New Principal
1. $ 2,000	6%	2	$ 1.1236	$ 2,247.20
2. 800	4%	3		
3. 1,100	5%	6		
4. 1,500	3.5%	10		
5. 2,250	3%	15		
6. 2,540	3.5%	11		
7. 2,990	4%	8		
8. 10,300	5%	9		
9. 10,450	6%	3		
10. 15,981	4%	12		

Semiannual and Quarterly Periods. Note that the compound interest table is set up by interest period, not by year. Thus, this table can also be used if interest is compounded semiannually or quarterly.

For example, here is how to compute the value of $200 at 6-percent interest compounded semiannually for 3 years. First, find the number of semiannual periods in 3 years (2 periods a year × 3 years = 6 periods). Now find the rate for each interest period. For interest compounded semiannually, use half the annual interest rate (6% ÷ 2 = 3%).

Now that you know the number of periods and the interest rate for each period, refer to the compound interest table. Find 6, the number of periods. Then look across the row to find the interest rate of 3 percent. The amount in that column is $1.1941. To find what $200 would grow to, multiply: $1.1941 × 200 = $238.82.

You may wish to find the amount of interest compounded quarterly on $200 over a 3-year period. There are 12 interest periods in this case (4 interest periods × 3 years = 12 interest periods). You would use one-fourth of the annual interest rate (6% ÷ 4 = 1.5%). Using the table, we see that $1 would grow to $1.1956. Now multiply $1.1956 by 200, the number of dollars. The answer is $239.12.

Exercises

Interest on these savings accounts is compounded semiannually. Use the table on page 266 to complete these exercises. Find the value of $1 and the new principal for the time given. (If necessary, round off your answer to the nearest cent.)

Principal	Annual Interest Rate	Time in Years	Semi-annual Interest Rate	Number of Interest Periods	Value of $1 Deposit	New Principal
1. $ 2,100	5%	4	2.5%	8	$ 1.2184	$ 2,558.64
2. 700	4%	2				
3. 1,200	6%	5				
4. 2,350	3%	12				
5. 10,400	6%	3				

Interest on each given account is compounded quarterly. Use the table on page 266 to complete these exercises. Find the value of $1 and the new principal for the time given. (If necessary, round off your answer to the nearest cent.)

Principal	Annual Interest Rate	Time in Years	Quarterly Interest Rate	Number of Interest Periods	Value of $1 Deposit	New Principal
6. $ 900	6%	2	1.5%	8	$ 1.1265	$ 1,013.85
7. 1,000	8%	3				
8. 1,500	10%	4				
9. 2,340	6%	5				
10. 10,450	8%	6				

Watching Savings Grow

No savings account is too small. If you put aside just $5 each week, you'll be surprised at the results. Look at the table on page 269. It shows how different amounts, if deposited in a savings account at 5.25-percent interest compounded quarterly, can grow.

For example, how much will deposits of $5 a week be worth if they are left on deposit for 10 years at 5.25-percent interest compounded quarterly?

Look down the Time in Years column to the line marked 10 years. Move across this line to the $5 Weekly column. Notice that the savings of $5 a week can grow to $3,412.26 in 10 years.

Time in Years	$1 Weekly	$2 Weekly	$3 Weekly	$5 Weekly	$10 Weekly	$20 Weekly
.5	26.35	52.66	79.04	131.68	263.38	526.77
1	53.40	106.72	160.16	266.84	533.71	1,067.47
2	109.66	219.15	328.89	547.96	1,096.00	2,192.09
3	168.93	337.60	506.66	844.14	1,688.40	3,376.93
4	231.38	462.40	693.95	1,156.17	2,312.51	4,625.20
5	297.16	593.87	891.26	1,484.91	2,970.05	5,940.32
10	682.87	1,364.69	2,048.09	3,412.26	6,825.04	13,650.60
15	1,183.50	2,365.19	3,549.59	5,913.88	11,828.66	23,658.23
20	1,833.30	3,663.79	5,498.49	9,160.87	18,323.15	36,647.70

If you put $5 in a box each week, how much would you have at the end of 10 years? In other words, what is the difference between putting the money in the bank and putting it in a box?

Weekly savings	$5
Weeks in a year	52
Savings in a year	$5 × 52 = $260
Savings in 10 years	$260 × 10 = $2,600
Savings with 5.25-percent interest compounded quarterly	$3,412.26
Difference in savings	$3,412.26 − $2,600 = $812.26

That's quite a difference!

Consumers can always find ways to save money. It may be difficult at times, especially when inflation hits. But savings provide security for "rainy days." It's wise to put a certain amount of money aside each week or month. Watch it grow in no time. It's a good feeling to know that the cash in your savings account is earning money for you every day.

Exercises for Section Three

Use the table on this page to complete these exercises. Find the difference between the total amount saved in a bank at 5.25-percent interest compounded quarterly and the same amount put aside without interest.

Weekly Amount Saved	Time in Years	Total Bank Savings	Total Nonbank Savings	Difference in Bank and Nonbank Savings
1. $ 1	5	$ 297.16	$ 260	$ 37.16
2. 1	10			
3. 3	1			
4. 3	5			
5. 3	10			
6. 3	20			
7. 5	15			
8. 10	15			
9. 20	15			
10. 20	20			

11. Sylvia Gladwin invested $10,000 in a savings account at 6-percent interest compounded quarterly for $1\frac{1}{2}$ years. (Remember that interest is not computed on amounts less than $1.)

   a. For how many interest periods did she invest the money?

   b. What interest rate did she get for 1 period?

   c. What was her interest and new principal at the end of the first period? The third period? The sixth period? (If necessary, round off your answer to the nearest cent).

12. How much interest does Stacey Rogers earn for 1 year on $1,000 with 4-percent interest compounded annually? Semiannually? Quarterly?

13. Barney Kolen invested $7,500 at 5-percent interest compounded annually for 6 years. Use the table on page 266 to find out how much his investment was worth after 6 years. How much interest did he earn?

14. Lucille Mogos invested $5,400 at 6-percent interest compounded semiannually for 4 years. Harold Okan invested the same amount for 4 years at 6-percent interest compounded quarterly. Use the table on page 266 to determine who earned more interest. How much more?

15. Maurice Pilzer belongs to a payroll savings plan in which he saves $10 weekly at 5.25-percent interest compounded quarterly. Use the table on page 269 to find out how much his savings will be worth in 5 years if he makes no withdrawals. How much interest did he earn in 5 years?

REVIEW FOR CHAPTER 13
SAVING MONEY

1. Jerry Hall's banker suggests that Jerry keep $1\frac{1}{2}$ months' gross salary in a savings account for emergencies. Jerry makes $224 a week gross and saves 7 percent of it. How many years will it take Jerry to save the recommended amount? (Hint: To find Jerry's monthly earnings, multiply his weekly salary by 52 and then divide the total by 12. Round off your answers to the nearest cent and to the nearest tenth of a year.)

2. Lynn Feyer saves 4 percent of her gross income of $10,340. She also saves $2 in change a week. Is her total savings more or less than 5 percent of her gross income? How much more or less?

3. How much simple interest does a bank pay on $3,215 deposited at 5.25 percent for 1 year? (Round off your answer to the nearest tenth of a year.)

4. Carl Shells has a savings account deposit of $3,400 in a bank which pays 5-percent simple interest. How much annual interest does he earn? Semiannual interest? Quarterly interest?

5. How much simple interest is earned on $3,300 at 5 percent for 20 days?

In the following exercises, round off your answers to the nearest cent.

6. Mozelle Remer invested $6,000 in a savings account for 2 years at 5-percent interest compounded semiannually. Give the interest and new principal at each interest period.

Use the tables on pages 266 (Exercises 7 through 9) and 269 (Exercise 10) to find the amount of interest earned in each case.

7. $3,400 invested at 8-percent interest compounded annually for 6 years.

8. $3,400 invested at 8-percent interest compounded semiannually for 6 years.

9. $3,400 invested at 8-percent interest compounded quarterly for 6 years.

10. $15 a week invested at 5.25-percent interest compounded quarterly for 4 years. (Hint: Use the columns labeled $5 Weekly and $10 Weekly.)

Investing Money

Many people dream of starting their own business. José Torres, Lucy Small, and Robbie James actually did just that. The three are recent high school graduates who specialize in auto mechanics. José suggested that they open their own auto repair shop. Good idea, Lucy and Robbie agreed. But where would the money come from?

The young mechanics had $1,500 among them. They needed an additional $4,500 to start the shop. They decided to raise the money by asking friends to invest money in their new business. *Investing* in a business is putting money into a business in hopes of earning more money in return.

José, Lucy, and Robbie hired a lawyer and took the legal steps necessary for their business, called the TSJ Company, to issue stock. *Stock* represents part ownership in a business. When stock is issued, the worth of a business is divided into equal portions. Each portion is called a *share* of stock. Anyone who owns shares of a business's stock is a *stockholder*, or *shareholder*. Each stockholder is a part owner of the business.

The TSJ Company issued 300 shares of stock valued at $20 a share. This means that for every $20 that a stockholder invested in the TSJ Company, the stockholder got 1 share of stock. José, Lucy, and Robbie became their company's first stockholders.

José invested $600, Lucy invested $500, and Robbie invested $400. There were five other investors who contributed $900 each. The total value of shares issued equals the value of the company, $6,000.

Many people, such as TSJ Company's stockholders, invest in stocks to earn money. If the business they invest in is profitable, the investors make money. But if it isn't, the investors lose money. There *is* a risk in investing. In this chapter, we will see how people earn or lose money in investments.

Section One
Investing in Stocks

Stockbroker: skilled employee of a brokerage firm who advises customers on stocks. Also called a *broker*.

Trade: to buy or sell stocks.

When investors buy or sell stocks, they usually do it through stockbrokers. *Stockbrokers* (also called *brokers*) are skilled employees of companies called brokerage firms, which advise customers on stocks.

When stockbrokers *trade* (buy or sell) stocks for customers, they are paid a commission. The size of the commission depends on the amount of the sale or purchase and is stated as a percent of that amount. A straight dollar amount may also be included in the commission.

There is no one way of figuring brokers' commissions. Different companies use different methods. Below is part of a table of commissions used by one brokerage firm. For our purposes, we will use this table as an example.

Dollar Value of Sale or Purchase	Broker's Commission*
Less than $100	7.5% of price for 100 shares
$100 to and including $800	2.4% of price for 100 shares + $7.50
Above $800 to and including $2,500	1.5% of price for 100 shares + $15.00
Above $2,500 to and including $5,000	1.1% of price for 100 shares + $26.00

*Commission based on 100 shares. Shares bought in multiples of 100 shares are determined by commission for 100 shares multiplied by the multiple. If less than 100 shares are traded, the same commission is charged as for 100 shares, and in addition, there is an extra charge of $.125 a share.

Bill Adams bought 300 shares of United Company stock selling at $25 a share. What is the stockbroker's commission? Use the commission table on page 273.

STEP 1: *Find the commission on 100 shares.*
Do the computation within the parentheses before you add the money amount.

Market value of 100 shares	$100 \times \$25 = \$2,500$
Broker's commission on 100 shares	$(1.5\% \times \$2,500) + \$15$ $= \$37.50 + \$15 = \$52.50$

STEP 2: *Find the commission on the multiple of 100 shares.*
This means you must first find the number of 100s in the total number of shares.

Total shares traded	300
Multiple of 100 shares	$300 \div 100 = 3$
Broker's commission on 300 shares	$3 \times \$52.50 = \$157.50$

Bill Adams's total expense in buying this stock was equal to the market value of the stock plus the broker's commission. What was the total cost to Bill?

Market value of stock	$300 \times \$25 = \$7,500$
Broker's commission	$157.50
Total cost	$\$7,500 + \$157.50 = \$7,657.50$

Round lot: unit of shares, usually 100, used in trading stocks.

Most stocks are bought in lots of 100 shares. These are called *round lots.* Any other amounts, such as an order for 65 shares of stock, are known as *odd lots.*

Odd lot: unit of shares, usually less than 100, used in trading stock.

Suppose Bill Adams bought 65 shares of United Company stock selling at $25 a share. The same commission is charged for an odd lot of stock as for 100 shares, and there is an additional charge of $.125 for each share in the odd lot.

Market value of 100 shares	$2,500
Broker's commission on 100 shares	$52.50
Additional odd lot charge	$65 \times \$.125 = \$8.125$ *or* $8.13
Broker's total commission	$\$52.50 + \$8.13 = \$60.63$

Here's how to find the total cost for 65 shares of stock.

Market value of 65 shares of stock	$65 \times \$25 = \$1,625$
Broker's total commission	$60.63
Total cost	$1,625 + \$60.63 = \$1,685.63$

Exercises

Complete these exercises to find the total cost of buying each stock. Use the broker's commission table shown on page 273. Save your answers for later exercises.

Stock	Market Price of 1 Share	Shares Bought	Market Price of 100 Shares	Broker's Commission on 100 Shares	Broker's Total Commission	Market Price of Stock	Total Cost
1. AAA	$ 7.00	400	$ 700	$ 24.30	$ 97.20	$ 2,800	$ 2,897.20
2. CAX	14.00	300					
3. AirC	20.00	500					
4. UnR	26.00	900					
5. RxSe	32.50	200					

Complete these exercises to find the total cost of each odd lot. Use the broker's commission table shown on page 273. Save your answers for later exercises. (If necessary, round off the odd lot charge to the nearest cent.)

Stock	Market Price of 1 Share	Shares Bought	Market Price of 100 Shares	Broker's Commission on 100 Shares	Odd Lot Charge	Broker's Total Commission	Market Price of Stock	Total Cost
6. AMX	$ 8	50	$ 800	$ 26.70	$ 6.25	$ 32.95	$ 400	$ 432.95
7. AmWa	15	65						
8. XXX	21	40						
9. Ref	27	75						
10. DED	44	30						

Reading Stock Market Reports

Stock prices change almost daily. Often world and national events affect stock market trading. A company's stock may climb in value because many investors want to buy the shares. It may go down when a lot of investors sell their shares. To get information on their investments, stockholders read stock market reports in their daily newspapers.

STOCK MARKET SCHEDULE

19-- High	19-- Low	Stocks and Div in Dollars		P/E	Sales in 100s	High	Low	Last	Net Chg
39 3/8	32 3/8	ACF	2	9	32	36 1/2	36 1/4	36 1/4	......
23 3/8	18 3/8	AMF	1.24	10	143	19 1/8	19	19 1/8	......
15 3/8	12 7/8	APL Cp	1	6	27	14	13 1/2	14	+ 3/8
50 3/4	36 3/4	ARASv	1.32	11	115	42 3/4	42 1/2	41 1/2	+ 1/4
23 5/8	17 1/4	ASALtd	.80	..	153	19 3/8	19	19	- 1/8
12 3/8	9 3/8	ATOInc	.40	6	118	11 5/8	11 1/4	11 1/2	......
49 1/8	38 7/8	AbbtLb	1.20	13	271	46 1/4	45 1/2	46	+ 3/8
13 1/4	9 1/2	AcmeC	.50	17	23	12 1/8	11 7/8	12 1/8	......
3 1/2	2 5/8	AdmDg	.04	5	33	3	2 7/8	3	+ 1/8
13 1/4	11 5/8	AdmEx	1.15e	..	35	12 1/8	12	12	- 1/8
5	3 7/8	AdmMI	.10e	8	8	4 3/8	4 3/8	4 3/8	+ 1/8
15 3/8	9 7/8	Addrsg	.10e	22	160	13 3/4	13 3/8	13 3/4	+ 1/2
37 1/2	28 3/8	AetnaLf	1.60	8	615	36 1/2	36	36 1/2	+ 1/4
56	44 5/8	AetnaLf pf	2	..	1	54	54	54	- 1/2
16	10 1/2	Aguirre		..	5	15 1/2	15 3/8	15 1/2	......
20	15 1/8	Ahmans	.40	5	137	17 7/8	17 3/4	17 7/8	+ 1/8
3 7/8	2 3/4	Aileen		68	18	3 3/8	3 1/4	3 3/8	......
35 7/8	21 1/8	AirPrd	.20b	10	546	21 3/4	21 3/4	21 3/4	+ 1/4
15 1/2	11 1/2	AirbFrt	.60	11	39	12 3/8	12 1/4	12 3/8	+ 1/4
34 1/8	28	Airco	1.15	6	124	29 3/4	29 3/8	29 5/8	+ 1/4
19 1/8	15 3/4	Akzona	1.20	68	17	16	15 3/4	15 3/4	- 1/4
16 7/8	14 3/8	AlaGas	1.28	8	7	16 1/4	16 1/8	16 1/8	+ 1/8
94 3/8	89 1/2	AlaP pf	8.16	..	z1000	92 3/4	92 3/4	92 3/4	- 1/4
21 1/2	15	Alaskln	.66	8	250	19 7/8	19 1/8	19 7/8	+ 7/8
20 1/8	17 1/4	Albany	.80	6	11	17 5/8	17 5/8	17 5/8	- 1/8
8 1/8	6	Alberto	.36	20	18	7 3/8	7 1/4	7 1/4	......
24	19 3/8	Albertsn	.80	9	284	u24 1/4	23 5/8	24	+ 1/4
29 1/2	23 1/8	AlcanAl	.80	14	174	26 5/8	26 3/8	26 1/2	- 1/8
23 3/4	18 1/8	AlcoStd	.96	6	28	22 7/8	22 3/8	22 1/2	- 1/2
23 1/8	16 1/8	AlconLb	.32	14	42	19 1/2	19 3/8	19 3/8	......
8 1/8	5 5/8	Alexdr	.40e	7	40	6 3/4	6 5/8	6 5/8	- 1/8
15 1/8	11 7/8	AllgCp	.60a	7	11	14 1/2	14 1/2	14 1/2	......
25 1/8	18 5/8	AllgLd	1.28	8	51	19	18 3/4	19	+ 1/4
43 1/8	39 1/4	AllgLd pf	3	..	1	39 3/4	39 3/4	39 3/4	......
22 5/8	19 7/8	AllgPw	1.68	8	175	21 3/4	21 1/2	21 1/2	......
14 1/2	12 3/4	AllenGp	.70	7	37	14 1/2	14 1/8	14 1/2	+ 1/8
24	20	Allergan	.40	11	14	23 1/2	23	23 3/8	+ 1/4
51 3/8	38 3/4	AlldCh	1.80	12	606	49 1/4	48 1/2	48 1/2	- 5/8
14 5/8	12 1/4	AlldMnt	.64	8	14	13 1/2	13 1/8	13 1/2	+ 1/2
12 1/2	10	AlldPd	.45e	22	3	11	11	11	......
23 1/2	19 5/8	AlldStr	1	7	115	22 5/8	22 1/4	22 1/4	- 3/8
4 1/8	2 3/4	AlldSup		..	39	3 3/4	3 1/2	3 3/4	- 1/8
33 3/4	23 1/2	AllisCh	1.10	6	584	30 1/2	30	30 1/4	+ 1/4
10 1/4	8 5/8	AllrtAut	.60	10	12	10	10	10	......
19	14 1/2	AlphPrt	.72	4	4	17 1/8	16 7/8	16 7/8	- 3/8
59 1/2	50 1/2	Alcoa	1.80	11	786	51 3/4	51 1/4	51 3/4	+ 5/8
36 3/4	25	AmlSug	2	6	13	26 1/8	25 3/4	25 3/4	- 3/8
59 3/4	41 1/8	Amax	1.75	10	351	41 3/8	d41	41 1/8	- 1/8
141	101 1/2	Amax pf	5.25	..	1	101 1/2	101 1/2	101 1/2	......
59 3/4	45 1/2	Amax pf	3	..	127	45 3/8	d44 1/2	44 1/2	- 1
29 7/8	21 5/8	AMBAC	1	9	43	28 7/8	28 3/8	28 3/8	- 1/2
13 1/8	10 3/8	Amcord	.60	9	84	12 7/8	12 3/4	12 7/8	......
24 7/8	17 1/2	Amrce	1.20	8	117	24 3/8	23 5/8	23 7/8	- 1/4
41 1/4	33 3/4	Amrc pf	2.60	..	2	41	40 3/4	40 3/4	+ 1/8
37 3/8	29 1/2	AHess	.80b	8	802	36 1/4	35 3/4	36	......
82	66 1/2	AHes pf	3.50	..	40	79 3/8	78 3/4	79	......
24	18 1/8	AAirFilt	.56	10	70	22 1/4	22	22 1/4	+ 1/8
14 3/4	10	AmAir		5	318	10 5/8	10 1/4	10 1/2	+ 1/8
5	2 3/4	AmAir wt		..	98	3 7/8	3 3/4	3 3/4	......
22 1/4	21	AAir pf	2.18	..	88	22	21 7/8	22	......
16 1/4	13 1/8	AmBaker	1	6	47	15 5/8	15 1/2	15 1/2	- 1/8
48 1/8	43	ABrnds	2.92	10	167	47	46 3/4	47	+ 1/4
26	23 1/2	ABrd pf	1.70	..	5	24 1/2	24 1/2	24 1/2	- 1/8
46 3/4	37	ABdcst	1	10	464	45 1/2	44 3/4	45 1/2	+ 1
12 1/2	10 1/8	ABldM	.50	7	29	12 1/4	12 1/8	12 1/8	- 1/8
41 3/8	38 1/4	AmCan	2.50	8	94	41 3/8	41 1/8	41 3/8	+ 1/8
24 1/8	22 1/4	ACan pf	1.75	..	7	23 5/8	23 1/2	23 1/2	- 3/8
2 7/8	1 7/8	ACentry		..	9	2	1 7/8	1 7/8	......
19 1/2	16	ACredt	1.16	5	9	18 3/8	18 1/8	18 3/8	+ 1/4

The way to read a stock market table is shown below. Note that prices are quoted in mixed numbers and written as a whole number and a fraction. The fraction is read as part of \$1. For example, if a stock is quoted as $62\frac{1}{2}$, then the price is read as \$62.50. The fractions are multiples of $\frac{1}{2}$(\$.50), $\frac{1}{8}$(.125), and $\frac{1}{4}$(\$.25). To help you do the math in this chapter, you may wish to memorize the aliquot parts table on page 165 of Chapter 8. It lists the decimal equivalents of the fractions used in stock reports.

Each column across the top of the stock market table is explained on this and the next page. Look at the first listing.

1	2	3	4	5	6	7	8	9	10
High	Low	Stocks and Div in Dollars		P/E	Sales 100s	High	Low	Last	Net Chg
$39\frac{3}{8}$	$32\frac{3}{8}$	ACF	2	9	32	$36\frac{1}{2}$	$36\frac{1}{4}$	$36\frac{1}{4}$	. . .

1. *High.* Highest price paid for the stock since the beginning of the year ($39\frac{3}{8}$ *or* \$39.375).

2. *Low.* Lowest price paid for the stock since the beginning of the year ($32\frac{3}{8}$ or $32.375).

3. *Stocks.* Name of the company (ACF). Sometimes an abbreviated name is given. For example, *AmCan* is the abbreviation of American Can.

4. *Div in Dollars.* Dividend in dollars. Annual dividend, or payment, made by the company to stockholders. (Dividends are discussed in more detail on pages 278 and 279.) The dividend for ACF was $2 a share.

5. *P/E.* Price-Earnings Ratio. This is the price of a share of stock divided by earnings per share for the last four reported quarters of earnings. The price-earnings ratio for ACF was 9.

6. *Sales 100s.* Numbers of shares traded in a day, expressed in hundreds. The number 32 in this column reads as 3,200 shares.

7. *High.* Highest price paid for the stock during the day's trading ($36\frac{1}{2}$ or $36.50).

8. *Low.* Lowest price paid for the stock during the day's trading ($36\frac{1}{4}$ or $36.25).

9. *Last.* Last price of the stock for that day ($36\frac{1}{4}$ or $36.25).

10. *Net Chg.* Net change. Difference between that day's last price and the previous day's last price. This is shown by a plus sign (+) if today's last price was higher and by a minus sign (−) if today's last price was lower. If this column read $+\frac{1}{2}$, it would mean that the stock had increased by $.50 a share. As you can see, there was no net change for ACF.

Exercises

For each stock, compute the number of shares traded and the dollar value of each share. (Do not round off any numbers.)

Stock	Sales 100s	Year's High	Year's Low	Day's High	Day's Low	Day's Last	Net Chg
1. Asarco	736	$23\frac{5}{8}$	$16\frac{1}{4}$	$19\frac{1}{8}$	$18\frac{7}{8}$	19	$-\frac{1}{2}$
	73,600	$ 23.625	$ 16.25	$ 19.125	$ 18.875	$ 19	Down $.50
2. Armada	15	$8\frac{1}{8}$	$4\frac{3}{4}$	7	$6\frac{7}{8}$	7	. . .
	____	____	____	____	____	____	____
3. ApecoCp	29	$2\frac{1}{8}$	$1\frac{5}{8}$	$1\frac{3}{4}$	$1\frac{1}{8}$	$1\frac{5}{8}$	. . .
	____	____	____	____	____	____	____
4. AtlRich	2,038	$61\frac{7}{8}$	50	$58\frac{1}{2}$	57	$58\frac{3}{8}$	$+1\frac{1}{8}$
	____	____	____	____	____	____	____
5. ArkLGs	101	$35\frac{1}{2}$	$28\frac{7}{8}$	35	$34\frac{3}{4}$	35	$+\frac{1}{8}$
	____	____	____	____	____	____	

Bill Adams received a bonus at the end of the year. He decided to invest the money in stocks. He bought 100 shares of Airborne Freight (AirbFrt) at the low one day. How much money did he pay for this stock? Look at the stock market table on page 276. In the Stocks and Dividends in Dollars column, read down to the listing for AirbFrt. Now read across to the Low column to find the price of the stock. (In this example, we will not include the broker's commission or fees.)

Low price a share	$12\frac{1}{4}$ or $12.25
Number of shares of stock	100
Cost of 100 shares	$100 \times \$12.25 = \$1,225$

Exercises
Use the stock market table on page 276 to compute the cost of buying each stock. Do not include brokerage fees.

Stock	Number of Shares Bought	Price of 1 Share		Total Cost
1. AdmMl	200	Year's low:	$3.875	$775
2. Aguirre	300	Day's high:	_____	_____
3. Airco	100	Day's low:	_____	_____
4. Albany	400	Year's high:	_____	_____
5. AllgLd	600	Day's low:	_____	_____

Finding Dividends—Preferred Stock

Companies are in business to earn money. When companies earn a profit, they often pay out a part of this profit to their stockholders in the form of dividends. Usually, if profits are good, stock dividends will also be good. Many companies in growing industries, however, reinvest the profits in the company.

Two types of stock:
Preferred.
Common.

Most companies issue two types of stock, preferred and common. Dividends on *preferred* stock must be taken from the profits before any dividends on common stock can be paid. Owners of preferred stock are paid dividends based on the *par value* of the stock, which is the original value of the stock. The par value is often printed on company stock certificates and referred to as the *face value*. *Market value* is the price stocks are worth when they are traded. The dividend rate on a preferred stock is set by the company when the stock is issued. It can never be higher than the rate stated on the preferred stock certificate. The dividend is computed with the simple interest formula. For example, what is the dividend on 5-percent preferred stock with a par value of $75 a share?

Par value:
original value of a stock or bond, assigned when it is first issued. Also called *face value*.

Market value:
price stocks are worth when traded.

Par value of one share	$75			
5-percent rate	.05			
Dividend a share	$75 × .05 = $3.75			

If a stockholder owns 60 shares, the total dividend would be $225 ($3.75 × 60 = $225).

Exercises

Complete these exercises to find the total amount each shareholder earns in dividends on the preferred stocks whose par value is listed below. (If necessary, round off the total dividend to the nearest cent.)

Par Value of Share	Number of Shares Owned	Dividend Rate	Dividend a Share	Total Dividend
1. $55	110	$4\frac{3}{4}\%$	$ 2.6125	$287.38
2. 40	60	5%		
3. 75	85	$5\frac{1}{2}\%$		
4. 60	100	$4\frac{1}{4}\%$		
5. 35	200	$4\frac{1}{2}\%$		

Finding Dividends—Common Stock

After preferred stock dividends are paid, a company's board of directors may declare dividends on *common* stock, if there are enough profits left. These annual dividends may vary depending on how much profit a company makes. Sometimes, a company omits dividends to holders of common stock if it wants to reinvest the money in its business. When dividends are declared, they are frequently paid to stockholders quarterly or semiannually.

Turn to the stock market table on page 276. Find AlldCh (Allied Chemical) under the Stocks and Dividends in Dollars column. Next to this listing is the annual dividend in the amount of $1.80. If you owned 200 shares of common stock in Allied Chemical, you would have received $360 in dividends last year ($1.80 × 200 = $360).

Making or Losing Money on Stocks

A few years ago Meg Reilly bought 50 shares of common stock priced at $27 a share. Meg sold the stock a few years later when it was worth $36 a share. When she purchased her shares and when she sold them, Meg paid a broker's commission. Remember that the commission is computed on the market value of 100 shares (in addition to an odd-lot charge). Use the broker's commission table on page 273 to compute how much she paid for the 50 shares.

Number of shares of common stock	50
Market value of 1 share	$27
Market value of 50 shares	$50 \times \$27 = \$1{,}350$
Market value of 100 shares	$100 \times \$27 = \$2{,}700$
Broker's commission on 100 shares	$(.011 \times \$2{,}700) + \$26$ $= \$29.70 + \$26 = \$55.70$
Additional odd lot charge ($.125 a share)	$\$.125 \times 50 = \$6.25$
Total broker's commission	$\$55.70 + \$6.25 = \$61.95$
Total cost	$\$1{,}350 + \$61.95 = \$1{,}411.95$

Brokerage firms may be members of stock exchanges that list and trade stocks of companies. The largest stock exchange is the New York Stock Exchange (NYSE) shown here. The NYSE is a kind of marketplace about the size of a football field. This is where members of brokerage firms carry out the orders of customers to buy and sell stocks. Over 2,000 stocks are listed in the NYSE, and most are traded here every day.

Now the market value of Meg's stock is $36. If she decides to sell her shares, what would be the proceeds? *Proceeds* are the amount the stockholder receives from a sale of stock after a broker's commission and other fees are deducted.

Number of shares of common stock	50
Market value of 1 share	$36
Market value of 50 shares	50 × $36 = $1,800
Market value of 100 shares	100 × $36 = $3,600
Broker's commission on 100 shares	(.011 × $3,600) + $26 = $39.60 + $26 = $65.60
Additional odd lot charge ($.125 a share)	$.125 × 50 = $6.25
Total broker's commission	$65.60 + $6.25 = $71.85
Proceeds from sale of 50 shares	$1,800 − $71.85 = $1,728.15

Meg's profit is computed using the following formula.

$$\text{Profit} = \text{Proceeds} - \text{Total cost of buying shares}$$

What would Meg's profit be on the sale of 50 shares at $36?

Total proceeds	$1,728.15
Total cost of 50 shares	$1,411.95
Profit	$1,728.15 − $1,411.95 = $316.20

Suppose the value of Meg's stock had gone down to $20 a share. Then the proceeds would be less than the total cost of buying the shares. Meg would have lost money. Her loss would be computed as follows.

$$\text{Loss} = \text{Total cost of buying shares} - \text{Proceeds}$$

Perform the necessary computations yourself to find what Meg's loss would be. (Base your computations on a market value of $20 a share. Use the commission table on page 282.) Is your answer $463.20? If not, recheck your work.

Exercises

Use the broker's commission table on the next page to complete the ten exercises. Find the proceeds from selling each stock. Use your answers from Exercises 1 to 5 on page 275, which give the total cost of buying the shares, to compute the total profit or loss.

Dollar Value of Sale or Purchase	Broker's Commission*
Less than $100	7.5% of price for 100 shares
$100 to and including $800	2.4% of price for 100 shares + $7.50
Above $800 to and including $2,500	1.5% of price for 100 shares + $15.00
Above $2,500 to and including $5,000	1.1% of price for 100 shares + $26.00

*Commission based on 100 shares. Shares bought in multiples of 100 shares are determined by commission for 100 shares multiplied by the multiple. If less than 100 shares are traded, the same commission is charged as for 100 shares, and in addition, there is an extra charge of $.125 a share.

Stock	Market Price of 1 Share	Number of Shares Sold	Market Price of 100 Shares	Broker's Comm. on 100 Shares	Broker's Total Comm.	Market Price of Stock Sold	Proceeds	Profit (P) or Loss (L)
1. AAA	$ 9	400	$ 900	$ 28.50	$ 114	$ 3,600	$ 3,486	$ 588.80 (P)
2. CAX	14	300						
3. AirC	18	500						
4. UnR	30	900						
5. RxSe	35	200						

Use the broker's commission table shown above to complete these exercises. Find the proceeds from the sale of these odd lots. Then use your answers from Exercises 6 to 10 on page 275 to compute the total profit or loss. (If necessary, round off your answer to the nearest cent.)

Stock	Market Price of 1 Share	Number of Shares Sold	Market Price of 100 Shares	Broker's Comm. on 100 Shares	Odd Lot Fee	Broker's Total Comm.	Market Price of Stock Sold	Proceeds	Profit (P) or Loss (L)
6. AMX	$10	50	$ 1,000	$ 30	$ 6.25	$ 36.25	$ 500	$ 463.75	$ 30.80 (P)
7. AmWa	16	65							
8. XXX	23	40							
9. Ref	27	75							
10. DED	49	30							

Computing Rate of Return, or Yield

Consumers investing money in stocks like to know how much that money will earn for them. They can determine the earnings in

Rate of return:
The percent of earnings on the investment. Also called yield.

much the same way they would find out how much interest will be earned on a savings account.

To determine what percent you are earning on your stock investment, simply take the amount of the annual dividend and divide by the amount you paid for the stock. The result is called the *rate of return,* or the stock's *yield.* The following formula is used.

$$\text{Yield} = \frac{\text{Annual dividend} \times \text{Number of shares}}{\text{Total cost}}$$

For example, Meg Reilly held her 50 shares for two years. During that time, she received the following annual dividends: first year, $2.25 a share; second year, $2.50 a share.

How much was the yield on her investment each year? Remember that Meg's investment was $1,411.95. Round off the total cost of the stock to the nearest whole number ($1,412).

Annual dividend, first year	$2.25 a share
Number of shares of common stock	50
Total cost of 50 shares	$1,412
Yield, first year (rounded off to nearest tenth of a percent)	$\dfrac{\$2.25 \times 50}{\$1,412} = 7.96\%$ *or* 8%
Annual dividend, second year	$2.50 a share
Number of shares of common stock	50
Total cost of 50 shares	$1,412
Yield, second year (rounded off to nearest tenth of a percent)	$\dfrac{\$2.50 \times 50}{\$1,412} = 8.85\%$ *or* 8.9%

If Meg had put her money into a savings account, it would have earned about 5.25-percent compound interest. In this case, Meg's investment in stock was more profitable. Be aware, however, that not all stocks return dividends at a rate of 8 or 9 percent. Indeed, many do not offer dividends at all. Remember, too, that while Meg was earning this high rate of return, the market value of her stock might have gone up or down.

Exercises for Section One

On the next page, find the yield each investor earned to the nearest tenth of a percent. (Round off the total stock cost to the nearest whole number of dollars.)

Investor	Shares Owned	Annual Dividend a Share	Total Cost of Stock	Yield
1. A. Norton	200	$1.15	$2,852.70	8.1%
2. P. Black	400	0	1,625.90	_____
3. R. Freund	50	.66	1,133.24	_____
4. C. Koll	100	.40	2,617.05	_____
5. C. Rask	150	1.80	8,916.66	_____
6. K. Munson	300	2.60	12,716.10	_____
7. R. Brooks	250	1.16	4,290.20	_____
8. D. Lotto	400	.32	8,110.80	_____
9. R. Nunzio	900	.96	16,312.55	_____
10. J. Faber	500	1.00	11,950.33	_____

Harvey Thurmond bought 300 shares of Alaskin at the year's low and sold it at today's low. (If necessary, round off to the nearest cent.)

11. Use the stock market table on page 276 and the broker's commission table on page 282 to answer the following questions.

   a. What was the price for each share when Harvey bought Alaskin?

   b. What was the price for each share when Harvey sold Alaskin?

   c. What was the annual dividend on 300 shares of Alaskin?

   d. What was the total cost for buying 300 shares of Alaskin?

   e. What were the proceeds from selling 300 shares of Alaskin?

12. Did Harvey make a profit or loss on his investment? How much?

13. Find the yield on Harvey's investment for 1 year. (Round off your answer to the nearest tenth of a percent. Round off the total stock cost to the nearest whole number of dollars.)

Section Two
Investing in Bonds

Bonds:
promissory
notes for money
that investors
lend to
companies or
government
agencies for a
period of time.

Suppose you suddenly inherited $5,000. How could you invest it in order to make money? One way would be to invest it in bonds. *Bonds* are promissory notes for money lent to a corporation or to the government for a certain period of time. At the end of this specified time, the owner of a bond may cash the bond for its par value. The par value, or face value, of a bond is written on it. Bonds are usually issued in thousand-dollar amounts ($1,000, $5,000, and so on).

Until your bond is repaid, you earn a fixed amount of interest on the bond. Interest on bonds is computed with the simple interest formula and is paid semiannually. Bonds are usually long-term investments. The time when the bond is due to be repaid is called the *maturity date*. It can be as much as 25 years or more from the time of purchase.

Maturity date: The date when a bond must be repaid.

Tax-free: bearing interest that is not subject to federal, and sometimes state, income tax. Also called *tax-exempt*.

Three types of bonds:
1. Corporate.
2. Municipal.
3. Federal.

Some bonds, such as local government bonds, are called *tax-free*, or *tax-exempt*, bonds. This means you do not have to pay federal income tax on the interest you receive from these bonds. The interest on some tax-free bonds may also be exempt from state tax. Three important types of bonds are discussed below.

Corporate Bonds. These bonds are issued by corporations that need to raise huge amounts of money to expand their operations.

Municipal Bonds. These bonds are issued by local and state governments and government agencies to raise money for improving community services. These include schools, city water systems, and housing. Interest from these bonds is tax-free.

Federal Bonds. These bonds are issued by the federal government. The most popular federal bonds are Series E and Series H savings bonds. These are issued in amounts as low as $25. There are other federal bonds, but their cost is much higher. Interest from federal bonds is not exempt from federal income tax. It is usually exempt from state and local income tax, however.

DO YOU KNOW

these tips on bond investing? Investing bonds is a good way to earn money if you keep the following things in mind.

1. Know the basics of bond yields, maturity dates, and ratings before you invest.
2. Buy only top-grade, quality bonds. Check a reliable broker or bank for credit ratings on bonds.
3. Avoid low-grade bond issues, even if they're paying high interest. There's always a chance that a corporation or municipal bond issuer might default. If the issuer of a bond *defaults*, that means it is unable to pay bondholders interest on their loan. It may also mean that the issuer cannot pay bondholders the par of their bonds when the bonds mature.

Not all bondholders keep their bonds until the maturity date. Bondholders sometimes sell their bonds before they are paid off by a corporation or government. These sellers do not always receive the par value of the bond. Instead they receive the market value. This is the price at which the bond is then being sold. The market value may be above or below the par value.

Bonds are bought and sold in much the same way as stocks are traded. Current bond prices are listed in newspapers daily. A bond trading table is shown below. The first entry from the table is explained.

BOND TRADING TABLE

Bonds	Current Yield	Sales in $1,000s	High	Low	Last	Net Chg
GM 8.05s85	7.7	16	104 1/4	104	104 1/4	+ 1/4
GM 8 5/8 05	8.1	3	107	107	107	+ 5/8
GTelE 4s90	cv	2	72 1/4	72 1/4	72 1/4	....
GTelE6 1/4 91	6.8	11	92 1/2	92 1/8	92 1/8	3/8
GTelE9 3/4 95	9.1	1	107 1/4	107 1/4	107 1/4	+ 1/4
GTelE6 1/4 96	cv	97	98 1/2	98	98	- 3/8
Gene10 3/8 84	10.	4	100 1/2	100 1/8	100 1/8	- 3/8
GaPac5 1/4 96	cv	70	106 1/2	105 1/2	105 1/2	-1
GaPac6 7/8 82	6.9	10	99 1/2	99 3/8	99 3/8	- 5/8
GaPw8 7/8 00	8.8	7	101 1/4	101 1/4	101 1/4	+ 1/4
GaPw8 1/8 01	8.6	10	94	94	94	- 1/8
GaPw7 1/2 02J	8.5	23	87 3/4	86 1/2	87 3/4	+ 1/2
GaPw7 1/8 03	8.6	9	91 3/8	91 1/4	91 1/4	- 1/8
GaPw8 5/8 04	8.7	53	99	98 7/8	99	....
GaPw11s79	10.	11	106 1/2	106 1/8	106 1/2	+ 3/8
GaPw11 3/4 05	10.	69	112 5/8	112 1/2	112 5/8	....
Gdrch8 1/4 94	8.3	10	99 1/4	99 1/4	99 1/4	+ 3/4
Gdrch9 3/4 82	9.1	6	107 3/8	107 3/8	107 3/8	- 1/2
Grace4 1/4 90	cv	6	73 3/4	73 1/2	73 3/4	+ 3/4
Grace6 1/2 96	cv	66	102 1/2	102 1/8	102 1/2	....
GtNoN7 1/8 98	8.6	5	92	92	92	+1 1/8
Greyh6 1/2 90	cv	12	90 1/4	90	90	+ 1/4
GreyF9.7 84	9.3	5	104 5/8	104 5/8	104 5/8	....
Grum4 1/4 92	cv	21	70 1/2	70 1/2	70 1/2	- 1/2
GlfWn 6s88	7.5	11	79 1/2	79 1/2	79 1/2	....
GlfWn5 1/2 93	cv	48	82	81 1/2	81 1/2	- 1/2
GlfWn7s03A	9.7	197	72 5/8	72 3/8	72 1/2	- 1/4
GlfWn7s03B	9.6	41	72 3/4	72 1/4	72 5/8	- 1/8
HamP 5s94	cv	7	76 3/8	76 3/8	76 1/8	- 1/8
Harra 7 1/2 96	cv	33	110	110	110	....
Harra9 1/2 96	9.0	13	105 7/8	105 1/2	105 7/8	....
HarBk7.2s80	7.2	5	100	100	100	- 5/8
Hartfd8 1/2 96	9.0	5	94 3/4	94 3/4	94 3/4	- 1/4
Hellr 9 1/8 91	9.0	5	101 1/8	101 1/8	101 1/8	- 7/8
Hercul6 1/2 99	cv	23	88 1/4	87 5/8	88 1/4	+ 1/4
Heubn 4 1/2 97	cv	39	66	65 1/2	65 1/2	- 1/2
Heubn8 3/8 85	8.1	4	103	103	103	- 3/4
HiltnH 5 1/2 95	cv	13	84 1/4	83 5/8	84 1/4	+ 3/4
HonyF 7s78	7.0	5	100	100	100	....
HosAff10s99	9.8	5	102 1/2	102	102 1/2	+ 1/2
HosAff10s91	9.5	5	105 1/8	105 1/8	105 1/8	- 7/8
Hostin 5 1/4 94	cv	2	65	65	65	....
HousF 4s78	4.1	1	98	98	98	+7-32
HousF 5s82	5.6	10	90	90	90	....
HousF 8.386	8.0	10	103 5/8	103 5/8	103 5/8	+ 1/8
Human 6s89	cv	5	92	92	92	+2
ITTF 10 1/2 95	9.3	2	112 1/2	112 1/2	112 1/2	+ 1/4
IllBel 2 3/4 81	3.1	2	88	88	88	....
IllBel 8s04	8.0	32	99 7/8	99 3/4	99 7/8	- 1/8
IllPw 7.6s01	8.1	10	94 7/8	94	94	- 3/8
IllPw 8 5/8 06	8.3	14	104 1/2	104 1/2	104 1/2	+1
InMic 11s83	10.	11	108	107 3/4	107 3/4	-1
InMP 10 7/8 84	10.	12	108 1/2	108 1/8	108 1/8	- 7/8
IndBel8 1/8 11	8.1	5	100 5/8	100 5/8	100 5/8	....
IndNtl8 1/4 96	8.6	10	95 1/2	95 1/2	95 1/2	+ 3/4
InNtl 7.4s03	7.5	15	98 1/8	98 1/8	98 1/8	....
InldStl6 1/2 92	7.0	5	92 1/2	92 1/2	92 1/2	- 1/2
InldStl8 3/4 95	8.4	7	103 7/8	103 7/8	103 7/8	- 1/8
Insilco9 3/4 99	cv	17	117 1/4	117 1/2	117 1/2	- 1/4
InsInv7 7/8 80	11.	5	73	73	73	....
Intrik 8.8s96	8.7	2	101 1/2	101 1/2	101 1/2	+3 1/8
IntHrv4 5/8 88	6.0	7	76 3/8	76 3/8	76 3/8	....
IntHrv4.8s91	6.6	2	72 3/8	72 3/8	72 3/8	+ 1/8
IntHrv8 5/8 95	8.5	10	101 3/4	101 5/8	101 3/4	+ 3/4
InHvC 4 3/4 81	5.3	1	90 1/8	90 1/8	90 1/8	+ 1/2
InMin 4s91	cv	13	112	112	112	+2
IPap 4 1/4 96	cv	1	64 1/4	64 1/4	64 1/4	- 3/4
IntTT8.9s95	8.6	5	104	104	104	+1
IntTT 11s82	9.7	5	113	113	113	+ 1/2
IntTT8 5/8 00	cv	52	139 1/2	139	139	....
JoneL6 3/4 94	9.1	2	74	73 3/8	74	....
JoneL9 7/8 95	9.6	7	103	103	103	+1
K mart 6s99	cv	131	103 1/4	103	103 1/4	+ 1/4
Kane 9 1/2 90	9.7	8	98	98	98	+1
Kellog8 5/8 85	8.2	8	105 3/4	105 3/4	105 3/4	....
KerrMa8s83	7.8	5	102 1/2	102 1/2	102 1/2	- 1/2
Kraft 7.6s07	7.8	11	98	98	98	....
Krogr 9s95	8.7	3	103 3/4	103 3/4	103 3/4	+1
Krogr 9 7/8 83	9.1	20	108	107 1/2	108	....
LTV 5s88	8.0	102	63 1/4	62 7/8	62 7/8	....
LTV 9 1/4 97	11.	55	86 1/2	86 1/4	86 3/8	+ 3/8

1	2	3	4	5	6	7
Bonds	Current Yield	Sales In $1,000s	High	Low	Last	Net Chg
GM 8.05s85	7.7	16	$104\frac{1}{4}$	104	$104\frac{1}{4}$	$+\frac{1}{4}$

1. *Bonds.* The abbreviated name of the company (GM). The number after the abbreviation is the annual interest rate that the

company pays on the par value of these bonds (8.05%). The next two digits tell the date of maturity (85 means 1985).

2. *Current Yield.* The percent that the interest payment is of the current market value (7.7%). The yield is often different from the annual interest rate. The letters *cv* shown in many lines in this column mean that the bonds can be converted into common stock. Current yield is discussed in more detail below and on page 288.

3. *Sales in $1,000s.* The sales of bonds for the day expressed in thousands of dollars. The number 16 reads as $16,000 in sales.

4. *High.* The highest price paid for the bond during the day's trading. The price is expressed as a percent of the $1,000 par value. Thus, $104\frac{1}{4}$ does not mean $104.25. It means 104.25% of $1,000, or $1,042.50. To find this amount, change the fraction to a decimal, and multiply by 10 to find the sale price $(104.25 \times 10 = 1{,}042.50)$.

5. *Low.* The lowest price paid for the bond during the day's trading (104 *or* $1,040).

6. *Last.* The last price of the bond for that day ($104\frac{1}{4}$ *or* $1,042.50).

7. *Net Chg.* The difference between that day's last price and the last price of the previous day. The $+\frac{1}{4}$ means the bond is now being sold for $2.50 more than it was being sold for at the end of the previous day $(.25 \times 10 = 2.50)$.

Exercises

Use the bond trading table on page 286 to complete **these** exercises.

Bond	Rate of Interest	Maturity Date	Current Yield	Number of $1,000s Sold	Day's High	Day's Low	Day's Last	Net Chg
1. GaPac 6⅞82	6.875%	1982	6.9%	10	$ 995	$ 993.75	$ 993.75	$ Down $6.25
2. GM 8⅝s05		20						
3. GlfWn 6s88		19						
4. Hartfd 8¼96		19						
5. Heubn 8⅜85		19						
6. HousF 8.386		19						
7. IllBel 8s04		20						
8. IntTT 8⅝00		20						
9. Kane 9½90		19						
10. LTV 5s88		19						

Computing Rate of Return, or Yield

The interest paid on a bond is based on the par value of the bond when it was first issued. The yield is based upon its market value when it was purchased.

The buyer of a bond may pay more or less for the bond than its par value. But interest continues to be computed on the par value of the bond. Investors who buy $1,000 par value bonds for less than $1,000 will have a higher percent of return on the bonds than those who buy them for $1,000 or more. This percent is the rate of return, or the bond's yield. The yield is computed using the following formula.

$$\text{Current yield} = \frac{\text{Interest paid}}{\text{Amount paid for bond}}$$

For example, suppose Frank Avarone bought a bond for $1,000. It pays 6.5-percent annual interest. What yield can he expect?

Par value	$1,000
Interest rate	6.5% *or* .065
Interest	$1,000 × .065 = $65
Amount paid for bond	$1,000
Yield (rounded off to the nearest tenth of a percent)	$\frac{65}{1,000}$ = .0065 *or* 6.5%

As you can see, when the bond is bought at par value, the yield is the same as the interest rate. If, however, the bond is bought at more or less than par value, the yield will not be the same as the interest rate. For example, if Frank bought this same bond at $920, he would continue to receive the same amount of interest, 6.5 percent of par value, or $65. What would be his yield?

Interest	.065 × $1,000 = $65
Amount paid for bond	$920
Yield (rounded off to nearest tenth of a percent)	$\frac{65}{920}$ = .0706 *or* 7.1%

Now, suppose that Frank had paid $1,040 for this bond. What would be his yield on this investment?

Interest	.065 × $1,000 = $65
Amount paid for bond	$1,040
Yield (rounded off to nearest tenth of a percent)	$\frac{65}{1,040}$ = .0625 *or* 6.3%

Savings Bonds

Savings bonds are issued by the United States government in amounts of $25 to $10,000. They are a safe, easy way to save small amounts of money regularly. The current yield is fixed at the time of purchase and does not rise and fall with the stock market.

The most familiar type of savings bond is called Series E. Series E bonds mature in 5 years from their date of issue. The Series E savings bonds are sold at a *discount*. This means that the bonds are sold at less than their face value. The face value is paid at maturity. The difference between the lower purchase price and the maturity value is the earned interest. The interest rate for Series E bonds is 6% compounded semiannually.

Discount: price that is lower than face value.

Savings bonds are one of the safest investments you can make. Most experts on bond investments agree that you should have at least $5,000 over and above your regular savings before you invest in corporate or municipal bonds. But savings bonds are guaranteed by the federal government and involve almost no risk.

Exercises for Section Two

Complete these exercises to find the yield on each bond if it had been purchased at a market value of $1,000, $980, or $1,020. (Round off your answer to the nearest tenth of a percent.)

Bond	Annual Interest Rate	Annual Interest Payment	Yield ($1,000 Paid for Bond)	Yield ($980 Paid for Bond)	Yield ($1,020 Paid for Bond)
1. Hostin 5$\frac{1}{4}$94	5.25%	$ 52.50	5.3%	5.4%	5.1%
2. GM 8$\frac{5}{8}$s05					
3. GTelE 6$\frac{1}{4}$91					
4. GreyF 9.7 84					
5. HamP 6s94					
6. HosAff 10s99					

Find the listing for IllBel 8s04 in the bond trading table on page 286. Then solve these problems. Assume a par value of $1,000.

7. What is the annual interest rate? How much interest is earned each period on 7 bonds if interest is paid semiannually?

8. How many $1,000s in bonds were sold that day? What was the high sale for the day? The low sale for the day? The net change from the day before?

9. What is the current yield listed in the table? What would be the yield if the bond had been bought at a market price of $970? At a price of $1,030? (Round off your answers to the nearest tenth of a percent.)

10. Joan Hawkins bought one IllBell 8s04 bond, and Jerry Hawkins bought one IllBell $2\frac{3}{4}$81 bond. Who made more in interest in one year, Joan or Jerry? How much more?

11. James Nunez bought one HosAff 10s91 bond, and Julia Nunez bought one HosAff 10s99 bond. Who made more in interest in one year, James or Julia?

REVIEW FOR CHAPTER 14
INVESTING MONEY

Use the stock market schedule on page 276 for Exercises 1 to 7.

1. How many shares of Aguirre were traded that day? What is the year's highest price? The day's lowest price?

2. How much annual dividend is paid on 1 share of AlcoStd? On 400 shares of AlcoStd? What is the yield (to the nearest tenth of a percent) on 400 shares of AlcoStd if the total cost is $9,152?

3. What is the cost of 600 shares of AmlSug at the day's high if the broker's fees are *not* included?

4. Patsy Jones bought 200 shares of Alberto at the day's low. What is the total cost if broker's fees are included? (Use the broker's commission table on page 282.)

5. Patsy sold 200 shares of Alberto at the year's high. What are her total proceeds? (Use the broker's commission table on page 282. Round off your answer to the nearest cent.)

6. Use Exercise 4 to decide if Patsy made a profit or loss. How much of a profit or loss?

7. What is the cost of buying 70 shares of AllgLd at the last price of the day if broker's fees are included? (Use the broker's commission table on page 282.)

Use the bond trading schedule on page 286 for Exercises 8 to 10.

8. What were the sales in $1,000s of Grace $6\frac{1}{2}$96 bonds that day? What is the day's highest price? The day's lowest price?

9. How much interest a year is paid on 1 Human 6s89 bond? On 8 Human 6s89 bonds?

10. What is the current yield of GaPac $5\frac{1}{4}$96 at the day's high? Of HamP 5s94 at the day's low? Of GlfWn $5\frac{1}{2}$93 at par value? (Round off your answer to the nearest tenth of a percent.)

CHAPTER 15

Buying Insurance

If you suddenly become ill and must go to the hospital, who will pay your medical bills? If there's a fire or theft in your home, will you have enough money to replace all the things that you and your family value? How can your family best protect itself financially in case the main wage earner dies?

These are crises that anyone could experience. If you want protection against the high costs of such events, plan to invest in insurance. And that means life insurance, homeowners' (or tenants') insurance, and health insurance.

Section One
Life Insurance

A lot of families invest in life insurance. Tom and Regina Major were married for five years when Tom suddenly became ill. He died within a few months, and Regina was left with two young children to support, a small savings account, and a house mortgaged for 20 years. There was not enough money to raise the two children and pay all the bills without Tom's income. Even if Regina returned to her old job, there still wouldn't be enough money. But the Majors' life insurance investment paid off. Because of the insurance, Regina had enough income to keep her family together and to continue to live a somewhat normal life.

Types of Life Insurance

Insurance policy: written contract between the person being protected and the company selling the protection.

The Majors had a variety of policies to choose from when they first shopped around for life insurance. An *insurance policy* is a written contract between the *insured*, the person being protected, and the *insurer*, the company selling the protection.

The amount of money the insured pays for a life insurance policy is called the *premium*. It is figured on an annual basis. (Premium costs are discussed in more detail on pages 295 to 297.)

Some basic life insurance plans are explained below.

Premium: amount of money paid for insurance.

Beneficiary: person named to receive payment from an insurance policy.

Face value: total amount of insurance stated in the policy.

Cash value: amount of money that you can get for a policy before its term is over or before it becomes payable by death.

Term Insurance. Gives protection against loss of life for a certain period of time, or term. Usually term insurance is for 5 years or 10 years. You may also buy term life insurance for the period of time until you reach a specified age. At the end of each term, you can renew your policy. It will, however, cost you more because insurance premiums increase as you get older. If you should die during the term of the insurance policy, your *beneficiary*, the person (or persons) you name in the contract, will get the *face value*, the total amount of insurance of your policy. Term insurance is inexpensive for young, healthy people who want to make sure their young children will be taken care of if they die.

There is no cash value to a term policy, however. *Cash value* is the amount of money that you can get for an insurance policy before its term is over or before it becomes payable by death.

Straight Life Insurance. One kind of permanent life insurance. It protects you for your whole life, and the premium never goes up. When you're younger, the cost of straight life insurance is higher than the cost of term insurance, but the premium remains the same as you grow older. In other words, you pay more for straight life insurance than you would for term insurance when you're young, and less when you're older. You pay an average premium for life, and it builds up a cash value. Thus, if you decide to cancel the policy, you can get back some of the money you have paid in. Also, you can borrow money against the cash value of the policy.

Limited-Payment Life Insurance. Another kind of permanent life insurance. With this type of insurance policy, you pay premiums for a certain number of years—for 20 years, perhaps, or until you reach the age of 65. After that time you don't pay any more premiums but you continue to be covered for the rest of your life. The premiums for limited-payment insurance are higher than those for straight life.

Endowment Insurance. Similar to an insured savings plan. You are guaranteed a certain amount of money within a certain time. For example, after 20 years of paying premiums, the cash value of your policy is equal to its face value and the insurance expires. If you die before the 20 years expire, your beneficiary gets the face value of the insurance policy. If you are alive, you get the money for yourself as an endowment. You can take the complete amount, or lump sum, or take a series of monthly payments. Premiums are higher for endowment insurance than for other kinds of life insurance.

When Tom Major was five years old, his father took out a $2,000 straight life policy on Tom. The cost was $23 a year. As an adult, Tom continued to pay the premium on this policy each year. When Tom was 25, he married Regina. Tom worked as a draftsman earning $13,500 a year. His company offered him a group life insurance plan at a cost to Tom of $67.50 a year. The face value of the new insurance policy was $13,500, the same as Tom's annual salary. The company's insurance plan was written on a term basis. Tom bought the group life insurance and also purchased an additional $15,000 straight life insurance policy at a yearly cost of $200.25. Tom's total coverage was for $30,500 ($2,000 + $13,500 + $15,000 = $30,500).

How much was the cost of Tom's life insurance coverage for one year?

$2,000 straight life policy premium	$23
$13,500 group life policy premium	$67.50
$15,000 straight life policy premium	$200.25
Total cost of premiums	$23 + $67.50 + $200.25 = $290.75

What percent of Tom's yearly income is the cost of the insurance?

Cost of life insurance (rounded off to the nearest dollar)	$290.75 *or* $291
Tom's annual salary	$13,500
Percent of income (rounded off to the nearest tenth of a percent)	$291 \div \$13,500 = .0215$ *or* 2.2%

that if you are a policyholder of life insurance (except for term insurance) for one year or longer, and you find yourself in financial difficulty, you can get a loan from your insurance company? The amount you can borrow depends on the amount of premiums you have paid. Your policy serves as collateral for the loan. A table in your policy contract shows exactly how much you can borrow at any time. Interest rates are low, about 5- to 6-percent simple interest on the unpaid balance.

Insurance companies cannot refuse their customers policy loans if they need cash. Nor can the company demand repayment at any time. Usually, such loans are paid back in a lump sum or in installments at any time. In the meantime, your coverage remains good. However, if a claim becomes payable under your policy, the company will deduct the amount of the loan and the interest due. Your beneficiary will receive the face value of the policy minus these deductions.

Exercises

Given below are the amount of insurance coverage and the cost of insurance for ten persons.

1. C. Baylor: Term, $3,000 ($14.97 a year); Straight life, $20,000 ($231 a year); Limited-payment life, $10,000 ($198.40 a year); Endowment, $5,000 ($212.75 a year).
2. F. Ginack: Term, $30,000 ($212.70 a year).
3. W. Horton: Straight life, $8,000 ($268.88 a year).
4. A. Watkins: Limited-payment life, $15,000 ($328.95 a year).
5. S. Lane: Endowment, $12,000 ($311 a year).
6. K. Neil: Term, $20,000 ($124 a year); Straight life, $20,000 ($313 a year).
7. R. Shaver: Term, $15,000 ($137.50 a year); Limited-payment life, $16,000 ($477 a year).
8. K. Parr: Term, $8,000 ($148.72 a year); Endowment, $8,000 ($397.20 a year).
9. J. Reta: Straight life, $15,000 ($200.25 a year); Limited-payment life, $7,000 ($154.49 a year).
10. N. Bingley: Term, $25,000 ($144.25 a year); Straight life, $18,000 ($281.70 a year); Endowment, $5,000 ($215.05 a year).

Use the above information to compute the percent of annual income spent on insurance. (Round off the cost of insurance to the nearest dollar and the percent to the nearest tenth of a percent.)

Person	Annual Income	Total Insurance Coverage	Total Cost of Insurance	Percent of Annual Income Spent on Insurance
1. C. Baylor	$19,000	$ 38,000	$ 657	3.5 %
2. F. Ginack	8,000	_____	_____	_____
3. W. Horton	12,500	_____	_____	_____
4. A. Watkins	14,000	_____	_____	_____
5. S. Lane	9,500	_____	_____	_____
6. K. Neil	11,000	_____	_____	_____
7. R. Shaver	16,000	_____	_____	_____
8. K. Parr	13,500	_____	_____	_____
9. J. Reta	15,000	_____	_____	_____
10. N. Bingley	19,000	_____	_____	_____

Finding Premiums

Life insurance is bought in units of $1,000. You are billed for that premium annually, semiannually, quarterly, or monthly. Your life insurance premium is based primarily on estimates of how long you will live at the time you take out the policy. The longer you are likely to live, the lower the premiums. In other words, the premiums are lower when you're younger.

Different companies charge different premiums for similar policies. You must decide which policy is best suited to your needs and best fits into your whole budget situation. Shown on page 296 is a table of typical premium rates charged by life insurance companies for the four kinds of policies.

Suppose Regina Major took out a 10-year term insurance policy for $10,000 at age 28. What would be the approximate annual premium for this insurance policy?

Look at the table on page 296. Locate the Age column under *Female*. Move down the column to age 28. Next, follow along this line to the 10-year Term column. The amount quoted here is $5.19 per $1,000 of insurance.

To compute the annual cost of Regina's term insurance premium, multiply the premium per $1,000 of insurance by the number of $1,000s covered in her policy.

Annual premium per $1,000	$5.19
Number of $1,000s	10
Annual premium	$5.19 $\times$ 10 = $51.90

APPROXIMATE ANNUAL PREMIUMS PER $1,000 OF INSURANCE

Age		Term		Straight Life	Limited-Payment		Endowment	
Male	Female	10-year	15-year		20-year	30-year	20-year	30-year
15				$10.11	$17.97	$13.80	$42.47	$25.90
20	23	$ 4.99	$ 5.42	11.55	19.84	15.26	42.55	26.15
25	28	5.19	5.63	13.35	22.07	17.03	42.69	26.50
30	33	5.77	6.20	15.65	24.73	19.20	43.01	26.92
35	38	7.09	7.42	18.61	27.93	21.93	43.63	27.50
40	43	9.18	9.67	22.55	31.80	25.38	44.76	29.85
45	48	12.74	13.44	27.58	36.49	29.79	46.67	33.33
50	53	18.59	19.03	33.61	42.19	35.52	49.65	37.77
55	58	24.89		41.57	42.25		54.14	
60	63			52.71	58.68		61.26	

Policies under $10,000 are a little higher in premiums. Premiums are lower for policies of $25,000 and over. Policies for women are lower because women generally live longer.

Exercises

Use the rate table above to complete these exercises. Find the amount each person pays annually in insurance premiums.

Person	Age	Type of Insurance	Annual Premium per $1,000	Total Premium
1. John Shah	20	$12,000 straight life	$ 11.55	$ 138.60
2. Eva Trib	33	$11,000 of 15-year term	_____	_____
3. Jim Wolf	25	$15,000 of 30-year limited-payment life	_____	_____
4. Joan Ward	23	$18,000 straight life	_____	_____
5. Mel Safer	35	$18,000 of 20-year endowment	_____	_____
6. Amy King	38	$16,000 of 10-year term	_____	_____
7. Cal Jay	15	$10,000 of 30-year endowment	_____	_____
8. Rose Little	48	$13,000 of 15-year term	_____	_____
9. Frank Drake	40	$20,000 of 20-year limited-payment life	_____	_____
10. Lucy Quinn	43	$25,000 of 20-year endowment	_____	_____

Periodic Premium Payments

If you pay premiums monthly, quarterly, or semiannually, you pay more for insurance than if you paid these same premiums annually. One reason for these higher costs is that insurance companies have more work to do in processing these payments.

The periodic premium table below is used by most insurance companies to compute premiums other than those paid annually.

PERIODIC PREMIUM TABLE

Period	Percent of Annual Premium
Semiannual	51%
Quarterly	26%
Monthly	8.7%

To find the monthly, quarterly, or semiannual premium, multiply the annual premium by the percent listed in the table above. For example, what is the monthly premium on a $15,000 straight life policy if issued for a male at age 20? (Use the table on page 296.)

Annual premium per $1,000	$11.55
Number of $1,000s	15
Annual premium	$11.55 × 15 = $173.25
Monthly premium (rounded off to the nearest cent)	$173.25 × .087 = $15.07275 or $15.07

Exercises for Section One

At age 30, Max Walton bought $20,000 worth of 15-year term insurance and a $14,000 straight life policy. His wife Kelly bought a 30-year endowment policy for $16,000 and a 20-year limited-payment life insurance worth $22,000 when she was 28. (For the exercises below, use the tables above and on page 296. Round off to the nearest cent, if necessary.)

1. How much would Kelly pay for life insurance the first year if she paid her premiums annually? If she paid semiannually? Quarterly? Monthly? How much would she pay annually for life insurance the twenty-first year?

2. Find out how much Max paid for life insurance the first year if he paid his premiums annually. If he paid semiannually. Quarterly. Monthly. How much would he pay annually for life insurance the sixteenth year?

3. Use Exercises 1 and 2 to determine how much the Waltons paid for life insurance the first year if premiums were paid annually.

4. Use Exercise 3 to determine what percent of the Waltons' annual income was spent for life insurance the first year. They earned $26,000, and they paid an annual premium. (Round off to the nearest tenth of a percent.)

5. How much total coverage will the Waltons have when Max is 40 years old? 47 years old?

Use the rate table on page 296 and the periodic premium table on page 297 to find the amount each person pays in premiums for each period. (If necessary, round off your answer to the nearest cent.)

Person, Age, Type of Insurance	Annual Premium	Semi-annual Premium	Quarterly Premium	Monthly Premium
6. Hal Agee, 45, $20,000 of 20-year limited-payment life.	$ 729.80	$ 372.20	$ 189.75	$ 63.49
7. Nancy Chu, 48, $20,000 of 30-year limited-payment life.	_____	_____	_____	_____
8. Tom Shannon, 25, $15,000 of 10-year term insurance.	_____	_____	_____	_____
9. June Leon, 28, $15,000 of 15-year term insurance.	_____	_____	_____	_____
10. Ted Doran, 30, $18,000 of 20-year endowment insurance.	_____	_____	_____	_____
11. Nina Marsh, 33, $18,000 of 30-year endowment insurance.	_____	_____	_____	_____
12. Fred Hayes, 60, $10,000 of straight life insurance.	_____	_____	_____	_____
13. Mary Ali, 58, $10,000 of straight life insurance.	_____	_____	_____	_____
14. Paul Dillon, 50, $12,000 of 10-year term insurance.	_____	_____	_____	_____
15. Sue River, 53, $12,000 of 20-year endowment insurance.	_____	_____	_____	_____

Section Two
Homeowners' Insurance

In only one year, financial losses caused by fire in this country amounted to $3.5 billion. And fire is only one of the causes of property damage. As a homeowner, you can buy different kinds of insurance to protect your home from losses caused by fires, floods, theft, and so on. (Although this section will deal primarily with homeowners, people who rent houses and apartments can get special tenants' insurance.)

A *standard fire policy* insures your home and its contents against loss by fire or lightning. For an additional premium, you can have *extended coverage* that protects not only against fire and lightning, but also theft, wind, hail, smoke, explosions, riots, and falling aircraft. *Liability insurance* protects you against lawsuits for injuries suffered by another person on your property. And as you learned in Chapter 11, it covers you for damage caused by you to another person's property and for injuries caused by you to another person. You can buy these policies separately, or you can select a *homeowners' insurance policy* that includes fire protection, extended coverage, and liability all in the same policy.

Appurtenant structure: structure other than a dwelling place on a person's property.

Most homeowners' policies cover damage to other structures on a person's property, such as tool sheds, garages, and so on. These are called *appurtenant structures*. Living expenses when you are unable to live in your home (because of a fire, for example) can also be provided for. These are called *additional living expenses*. In some sections of the country, you may also qualify for flood or earthquake insurance. A homeowners' policy usually costs less than the same coverage provided by several policies for fire, theft, liability, and so on.

Additional living expenses: amounts the insurer will provide for living expenses when you are unable to live in your home.

Amounts of Coverage

How much insurance on your home should you carry? Suppose your house is worth $25,000. You know it would cost as much to replace it. It's a good idea to have coverage equal to your home's full value. But if you carry maximum insurance on your home, you will pay higher premiums. You may be tempted to insure your home for less than its full value. It's important to know, therefore, about the "80 percent clause." This is a statement which is found in most homeowners' policies. It says that in order to receive full payment for any partial loss or damage, you have to insure your home for at least 80 percent of its full value.

The amount of coverage you buy on your home determines the amounts of coverage you will have on appurtenant structures, on your personal property, and for additional living expenses. The basic amount of personal liability coverage is $25,000, but you can buy larger amounts. Look at the table on the next page. It shows the different amounts of property coverage when property is insured to full value and when it is insured at 80 percent of full value. The property is valued at $25,000.

	Insured to Full Value	Insured at 80%
PROPERTY COVERAGE		
Dwelling	$25,000 (full value)	$20,000 (80% of full value)
Appurtenant structures	$2,500 (10% of dwelling)	$2,000 (10% of dwelling)
Personal property	$12,500 (50% of dwelling)	$10,000 (50% of dwelling)
Additional living expenses	$5,000 (20% of dwelling)	$4,000 (20% of dwelling)
LIABILITY COVERAGE		
Personal liability	$25,000 (each occurrence)	$25,000 (each occurrence)
Medical payments to others	$500 (each person)	$500 (each person)
Damage to property of others	$250 (each occurrence)	$250 (each occurrence)

Here is how coverage can be computed with the use of the table. Regina Major's home has an assessed value of $30,000, and she has a homeowners' policy covering the home's full value. How much coverage does she have for each type of risk? What is her total coverage?

Full value of dwelling	$30,000
Appurtenant structures	.10 × $30,000 = $3,000
Personal property	.50 × $30,000 = $15,000
Additional living expenses	.20 × $30,000 = $6,000
Total coverage	$30,000 + $3,000 + $15,000 + $6,000 = $54,000

Exercises

Complete Exercises 1 to 5 for property valued at $21,000. Use the percents given in the homeowners' policy table above.

Property Coverage	Insured to $21,000	Insured at 80%
1. Dwelling	$ 21,000	$ 16,800
2. Appurtenant structures	_____	_____
3. Personal property	_____	_____
4. Additional living expenses	_____	_____
5. Total amount covered	_____	_____

Deductibles

At least one-third of all losses for damage to homes and personal property amounts to less than $100. These losses are too numerous and too small for insurance companies to handle without great cost. So most insurance policies include a deductible of $100. Suppose your plumbing leaks and causes property damage amounting to $82.50. With a $100 deductible, you would pay the full amount. You are responsible for any losses up to $100.

Although a $50 deductible is available in a few states, most homeowners' policies have a $100 deductible.

The 80 Percent Clause

As mentioned earlier, you must insure your home for a minimum of 80 percent of its full value in order to receive full payment for any partial loss or damage. Insurance companies use the following formula to compute how much of the damage they must pay if your property is insured for less than 80 percent of full value.

$$\frac{\text{Amount of insurance carried}}{\text{80 percent of full value}} \times \text{Amount of damage}$$

Let's look at two examples: one in which the owner insured her home for 80 percent of its value, and one in which the owner insured her home for less than 80 percent of its value. (For the purpose of these examples, we will not consider deductibles.)

Nora Santi has a house valued at $25,000. It's insured against fire for $20,000. If fire destroys the kitchen, with damages of $4,000, how much of the loss must the insurance company pay? We must know if her coverage is 80 percent or more of the home's full value.

Home's full value	$25,000
80 percent of home's full value	.80 × $25,000 = $20,000

Since Nora Santi's house *is* insured for exactly 80 percent of its value, the insurance company must pay the full cost of the damage, which is $4,000. Nora pays nothing.

Lucy Frisino owns a house valued at $22,500. She has insurance in the amount of $16,000. A small fire in the basement caused damages amounting to $2,700. How much of the loss must the insurance company pay? How much will Lucy pay? Again, we first determine if her coverage is 80 percent of the home's full value.

Home's full value	$22,500
80 percent of home's full value	.80 × $22,500 = $18,000

The amount of coverage Lucy carries on her home, $16,000, is not 80 percent of its full value. The next step is to determine the insurance company's payment, using the formula given on page 301. What will Lucy's payment then be?

Amount of damage	$2,700
Amount paid by insurance company	$\dfrac{16,000}{80\% \text{ of } 22,500} \times \$2,700$
	$= \dfrac{16,000}{18,000} \times \$2,700$
	$= \dfrac{8}{9} \times \$2,700 = \$2,400$
Amount paid by Lucy	$\$2,700 - \$2,400 = \$300$

Of course, you can never collect more than your actual loss or more than the insurance carried, whichever is less. This is so even if you insured your property for more than its value.

FURNITURE INVENTORY RECORD		
ITEM	DATE OF PURCHASE	COST
Desk	Oct. 1, 19–	$321.42
Sofa	Oct. 1, 19–	$513.00
Rocking Chair	Oct. 3, 19–	$49.00
Television	Oct. 5, 19–	$355.50

In case of fire or theft, a list (or inventory) of your belongings will be helpful. You will be able to tell the insurance company exactly what has been damaged or destroyed. Photographs of expensive items can also be used for insurance purposes.

Exercises for Section Two

Complete these exercises to find the amount of damages paid by the insurance company and the amount paid by the insured. When the insured has full coverage, use $\frac{1}{1}$ as the fraction of the loss that the insurance company pays. As you work these exercises, do not consider the deductible. Round off your answers to the nearest cent if necessary.

Property Value	Amount of Property Loss	Amount of Insur.	Amount of Insur. Needed for Full Payment	Fraction of Loss Insur. Co. Pays	Amount Paid by Insur. Co.	Amount Paid by Insured
1. $15,000	$1,200	$12,500	$ 12,000	$\frac{1}{1}$	$ 1,200	$ 0
2. 15,000	1,200	10,000				
3. 18,000	2,400	14,000				
4. 18,000	2,400	16,000				
5. 22,000	1,500	18,000				
6. 22,000	1,500	15,000				
7. 30,000	2,800	24,000				
8. 30,000	2,800	20,000				
9. 32,500	4,000	25,000				
10. 32,500	4,000	30,000				

11. The Tehrats' homeowners' policy includes the value of the dwelling, appurtenant structures at 15 percent of the value of the dwelling, personal property at 40 percent of the value of the dwelling, and additional living expenses at 25 percent of the value of the dwelling. If they are insured at 80 percent and the property is valued at $32,000, how much is their total coverage?

12. Jerry Carp's homeowners' policy has a $100 deductible. How much does his insurance company pay on apartment damages of $45 if he is fully insured?

13. Carla Hamilton's beach house is valued at $12,000. What minimum amount of insurance must she have in order to receive full payment for damages?

14. Mandi Rudolph's $38,000 house had fire damages of $4,080. Her house is insured for $32,000. What amount of the damages was paid by the insurance company? By Mandi?

15. The Harlows' $30,000 house had damages of $2,000 after a big storm. They carried insurance in the amount of $20,000. What amount of the damages was paid by the insurance company? By the Harlows?

Section Three
Health Insurance

Accident and sickness can cut off family income. They can wipe out savings in no time and leave you with a pile of debts. Medical care is so expensive that many families cannot afford all the medical services they need. Fortunately, insurance companies have plans to help people avoid financial problems such as these.

What are some medical and health insurance plans?

Disability Income Insurance. Pays benefits when you are unable to work because of sickness or accident. Under group policies, benefits are usually paid for periods of 13 to 26 weeks. Long-term coverage protects you for periods of two years to life.

Hospital Expense Insurance. Helps to pay the cost of a room in the hospital. Other in-hospital expenses such as X-rays, the use of the operating room, and medicine are also covered. You are allowed a certain amount a day for your hospital room (usually at full coverage) up to a maximum number of days, generally from 21 to 180 days.

Surgical Expense Insurance. Pays all or part of a surgeon's fee for an operation.

Physicians Expense Insurance. Usually offered as an extra benefit in a hospital or surgical expense insurance policy. It pays for a certain number of in-hospital visits by your doctor. This policy sometimes pays for house calls or visits to your doctor's office as well.

Major Medical Expense Insurance. Protects you against most other medical expenses. It takes over where basic hospital and surgical plans stop or when they do not apply. For example, major medical expense insurance usually covers the cost of blood transfusions, a cost that is not included in hospital expense plans. Most major medical expense insurance plans include the following features.

1. A high maximum limit of $100,000, $250,000, or more. This limit is the highest amount the insurance company will pay during an individual's lifetime.
2. There is a deductible, anywhere from $50 to $1,000. The higher the deductible, the lower the premium.
3. There is a *coinsurance clause,* which requires the insured to pay part of the bill, usually 20 or 25 percent. If there is a 20-percent coinsurance clause, for example, the insurer pays 80 percent of expenses after the deductible has been paid.

Coinsurance clause: requires that the insured pay a part of the bill.

Health insurance can be bought individually or through a group.

Health insurance can be bought either individually or through a group. Many employers and organizations offer group insurance plans. As a group member, you may not have to have a medical examination to qualify for insurance, and you will usually have lower premiums. The premiums you pay as a group member may be as much as 25 percent less than those paid by an individual. Your employer may pay part or all of the cost.

Faith Hayes joined a group health insurance plan at work. She developed a heart condition, but she was able to remain at home while getting well. Her major medical policy covered most of her expenses during this long illness although she was not in the hospital. Below is a list of Faith's medical expenses.

Physician's fee	$ 525.00
Consultant's fee	200.00
Private nurses—	
5 days at $115 a day	575.00
Laboratory	85.00
Medicines	45.00
Hospital bed rental	450.00
Total	$1,880.00

Faith's policy pays 80 percent of her "reasonable and customary" medical charges after a $300 deductible is paid. How much of Faith's expenses were paid by the insurance company? How much did Faith pay?

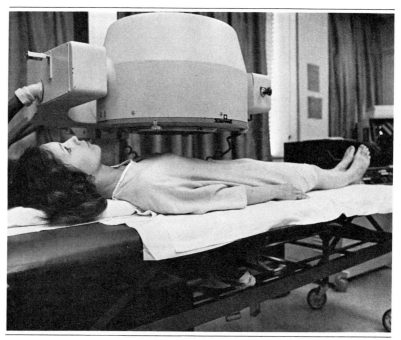

Since no one can predict when illness will occur, some form of health insurance is a must for everybody.

STEP 1: *Determine how much the insurance company paid.*

Deductible	$300
Total expenses	$1,880
Amount covered by coinsurance	$1,880 − $300 = $1,580
Amount paid by insurance company at rate of 80 percent	$1,580 × .80 = $1,264

STEP 2: *Determine how much Faith paid.*

Deductible	$300
20-percent coinsurance	$1,580 − $1,264 = $316 *or* $1,580 × .20 = $316
Total amount paid by Faith	$300 + $316 = $616

One of the most important decisions in your life will be to select sufficient life, home, and health insurance. Intelligent choices can protect you and your family against the high costs of death, perils to your home, and sickness. Inadequate insurance protection could cause you unnecessary financial hardship.

Exercises for Section Three

Find the amount of medical expenses that each person pays and the amount paid by major medical in each case. (If necessary, round off your answer to the nearest cent.)

Person	Medical Expenses	Deductible	Coinsur. Rate for Insur. Co.	Amount Paid by Insured	Amount Paid by Insur. Co.
1. F. Dahl	$ 1,068.19	$500	75%	$ 642.05	$ 426.14
2. D. Evans	956.00	200	80%		
3. K. Fold	870.00	50	80%		
4. R. Hess	1,570.80	100	75%		
5. A. Klass	420.55	50	80%		
6. H. Miller	1,358.00	400	75%		
7. S. Flick	3,542.60	500	80%		
8. V. Picher	5,280.00	100	80%		
9. G. Raskin	10,330.00	200	75%		
10. K. Ross	15,405.60	100	80%		

11. Kevin Lahr's disability income insurance paid 55 percent of his weekly gross earnings for the 18 weeks he missed work following a car accident. His annual income is $13,780. How much did the insurance company pay a week? For the entire 18 weeks?

12. Selma Jones' hospital expense insurance paid $75 a day for her room for the 3 weeks she was in the hospital after surgery. The daily cost of her hospital room was $88. How much did the insurance company pay for the room? How much did Selma have to pay?

13. Peter Ganzio can buy an individual health insurance policy for $67.70 a month, or he can join a group health plan at work for 80 percent of that. How much would the individual policy cost Peter annually? How much would the group policy cost him annually?

14. Leslie Brandt's major medical policy pays 80 percent of his medical expenses after a $300 deductible is paid. How much of a $3,185.75 medical bill does the insurance company pay? How much does Leslie pay?

15. Sonia Morrison's major medical policy pays 75 percent of her medical expenses after a $200 deductible is paid. How much of a $2,200.50 medical bill does the insurance company pay? How much does Sonia pay? (Round off your answer to the nearest cent.)

REVIEW FOR CHAPTER 15 BUYING INSURANCE

1. Timothy Bauer bought 10-year term life insurance worth $16,000 when he was 35. When he was 40, he bought $10,000 of straight life insurance. His premiums were computed using the table on page 296. How much did Timothy pay annually for life insurance coverage when he was age 35? Age 41? Age 46?

2. At age 41, Timothy's yearly income was $14,000. What percent of his annual income was spent on life insurance that year?

3. Frances Haworth bought a 20-year endowment policy worth $14,000 when she was 23 years old. She paid the premium quarterly. Her premium was computed using the tables on pages 296 and 297. How much did Frances pay for life insurance the first year? The tenth year? The twenty-first year?

4. At age 23, Frances's yearly income was $8,000. At age 33, her yearly income was $18,000. What percent of her yearly income was spent on insurance at age 23? At age 33?

5. The Harpers have a house valued at $25,000, for which they are considering homeowners' insurance. What amount of insurance must they carry so that the company will make full payment for any partial damages?

6. Suppose the Harpers' home is insured for $16,000 when fire causes damage of $2,500. How much must they pay? How much must the insurance company pay?

7. How much coverage will the Harpers have if they decide to insure their property at 80 percent of its value, their appurtenant structures at 5 percent of the value of the dwelling, their personal property at 45 percent of the value of the dwelling, and their additional living expenses at 15 percent of the value of the dwelling?

8. John Morgan's homeowners' policy includes the value of the dwelling, appurtenant structures at 10 percent of the value of the dwelling, personal property at 40 percent of the value of the dwelling, and additional living expenses at 25 percent of the value of the dwelling. If he is insured at 80 percent, and the property is valued at $45,000, how much is his total coverage?

9. Christopher Lake's disability income insurance pays 60 percent of his weekly earnings of $280 for up to 21 weeks. How much does the insurance company pay for the 17 weeks Christopher could not work after knee surgery?

10. Christopher's major medical plan pays 80 percent of his medical expenses after a $100 deductible is paid. How much of Christopher's $13,300 in medical expenses does his insurance company pay? How much does he pay?

CHAPTER 16

Paying Income Taxes

At the beginning of each year, millions of taxpayers are mailed a set of federal income tax forms. Many of these taxpayers also receive a second set of income tax forms from their state governments. Some taxpayers are even mailed a third set for city income taxes. Most taxpayers are wage earners. Their tax deductions from their paychecks are collected by their employers. You learned about this in Chapter 2. Wage earners, however, are still required by law to file annual federal and, in many states, state income tax returns.

Have you held your first part-time or summer job? If so, you have made a step toward becoming a taxpayer. You applied for a social security number, which is used as your taxpayer identification number. You have also filled out an Employee's Withholding Allowance Certificate (Form W-4) that tells your employer the number of allowances you claim. The number of allowances you claim is related to the amount of tax to be withheld from your earnings. Soon after the end of the year during which you worked, your employer sent you a Wage and Tax Statement (Form W-2). If you worked for more than one employer that year, you should have received a Form W-2 for each job. The Form W-2 provides the following information.

1. A record of the wages you were paid.
2. The amount of income tax withheld from your wages, including federal, state, and city, if applicable.
3. The amount of social security tax (FICA) deducted from your pay.

If you are required to file income tax returns, you must attach copies of Form W-2 to your federal and state returns. Your employer sends a copy of your Form W-2 to the Internal Revenue Service (IRS) and keeps one for its own files. You keep a copy for your records too.

Section One
Federal Income Tax

Before choosing the form to use, check the instruction booklets.

How do you know if you are required to file a federal income tax return? Since the requirements may be changed, check with the IRS. Instruction booklets that come with tax forms also give details on who must file and on which forms taxpayers should use.

Separate returns: a married couple files two returns.

Married couples required to file returns have a choice of filing separate returns or joint returns. With *separate* returns, the husband and wife file two returns. With a *joint* return, the couple files only one return. All income, exemptions, and deductions are included in this one return, even if one spouse earned all the money. How the return is filed determines which tax table is used.

Joint return: a married couple files one return.

"Short Form"—Form 1040A

Almost half of the 75 million taxpayers in the United States fill out the U.S. Individual Income Tax Return, Form 1040A, known as the "short form." Taxpayers may file Form 1040A when they receive their income from wages, salaries, tips, and no more than $400 in dividends or $400 in interest. To use Form 1040A, taxpayers must also have income of $20,000 or less ($40,000 or less if they are married and filing a joint return). They also may not itemize their deductions. (Itemized deductions are discussed on page 314.)

To get a better idea of how to prepare Form 1040A, look at the form filled out by Juan Mendez on page 312. Juan works as a salesclerk for Tru-Best Products Inc. When he first got his job at Tru-Best, Juan filed a Form W-4 on which he claimed one withholding allowance. During the past year, Juan earned $9,600. Juan's employer mailed him the Wage and Tax Statement (Form W-2) opposite. In addition to Juan's gross income of $9,600, the form also reports $1,290 of income tax withheld. Juan uses the information from his Wage and Tax Statement to complete his tax return.

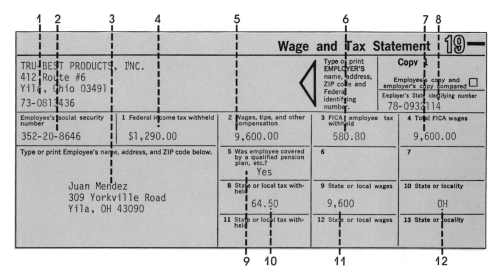

| 1 | 2 | 3 | 4 | 5 | 6 | 7 | 8 |

Wage and Tax Statement 19—

TRU-BEST PRODUCTS, INC.
412 Route #6
Yila, Ohio 03491
73-0813436

Type or print EMPLOYER'S name, address, ZIP code and Federal identifying number.

Copy
Employee's copy and employer's copy compared ☐
Employer's State identifying number
78-0932114

Employee's social security number	1 Federal income tax withheld	2 Wages, tips, and other compensation	3 FICA employee tax withheld	4 Total FICA wages
352-20-8646	$1,290.00	9,600.00	580.80	9,600.00

Type or print Employee's name, address, and ZIP code below.	5 Was employee covered by a qualified pension plan, etc.? Yes	6	7
Juan Mendez 309 Yorkville Road Yila, OH 43090	8 State or local tax withheld 64.50	9 State or local wages 9,600	10 State or locality OH
	11 State or local tax withheld	12 State or local wages	13 State or locality

| 9 | 10 | 11 | 12 |

The Form W-2 contains the following information.
1. Employer's name, address, and federal identifying numbers.
2. Employee's social security number.
3. Employee's name and address.
4. Federal income tax withheld from the employee's wages.
5. Total wages paid that were subject to federal income tax.
6. FICA tax withheld from the employee's wages.
7. Total wages paid that were subject to FICA tax.
8. Employers' state identifying number.
9. Pension plan coverage.
10. State or local tax withheld from employee's wages.
11. Total wages paid that were subject to state or locality tax.
12. Name of state or locality for which tax is withheld.

Since Juan filed Form 1040A last year, the Internal Revenue Service sent him the short form again this year. Juan can use this again. Here are the steps Juan followed to complete his Form 1040A.

1. He printed his name, address, social security number, and occupation at the top of the form.
2. On line 1, Juan checked the Single box to indicate his filing status.
3. On Line 5a, Juan took an exemption for himself. In the box to the right, he entered the one exemption. He did the same in the box on line 6, since he was claiming no other exemptions.
4. Juan entered $9,600 on line 7. This is the amount of total wages shown on his Form W-2 from the Tru-Best Company.
5. Juan has a savings account which earned $110.75 interest. Juan

Form **1040A**	Department of the Treasury—Internal Revenue Service **U.S. Individual Income Tax Return**	**19—**		

Use IRS label. Otherwise, print or type.

First name and initial (if joint return, give first names and initials of both)
Juan T.

Last name
Mendez

Your social security number
352 20 8646

Present home address (Number and street, including apartment number, or rural route)
309 Yorkville Road

For Privacy Act Notice, see page 9 of Instructions.

Spouse's social security no.

City, town or post office, State and ZIP code
Yila, Ohio 43090

Occu-pation	Yours ▶ *Salesclerk*
	Spouse's ▶

— 1

Presidential Election Campaign Fund ▶

Do you want $1 to go to this fund? . . . .   Yes ☐   No ☐

If joint return, does your spouse want $1 to go to this fund?   Yes ☐   No ☐

Note: Checking "Yes" will not increase your tax or reduce your refund.

— 2

Filing Status

Check Only One Box

1 ☒ Single   2 ☐ Married filing joint return (even if only one had income)

3 ☐ Married filing separately. If spouse is also filing, give spouse's social security number in the space above and enter full name here ▶

4 ☐ Unmarried Head of Household. Enter qualifying name ▶   . See page 6 of Instructions.

Exemptions

Always check the "Yourself" box. Check other boxes if they apply.

5a ☒ Yourself   ☐ 65 or over   ☐ Blind

b ☐ Spouse   ☐ 65 or over   ☐ Blind

Enter number of boxes checked on 5a and b ▶ *1*

c First names of your dependent children who lived with you ▶ . . . .

Enter number of children listed ▶

— 3

d Other dependents: (1) Name	(2) Relationship	(3) Number of months lived in your home.	(4) Did dependent have income of $750 or more?	(5) Did you provide more than one half of dependent's support?

Enter number of other dependents ▶

6 Total number of exemptions claimed . . . .

Add numbers entered in boxes above ▶ *1*

(Left margin, vertical: Please Attach Copy B of Forms W–2 Here)

7	Wages, salaries, tips, and other employee compensation. (Attach Forms W–2. If unavailable, see page 11 of Instructions)	7	*9,600 00*	— 4
8	Interest income (see page 4 of Instructions).	8	*110 75*	— 5
9a	Dividends. . . . . 9b Less exclusion . . . . Balance ▶ (See pages 4 and 11 of Instructions)	9c		— 6
10	Adjusted gross income (add lines 7, 8, and 9c). If under $8,000, see page 2 of Instructions on "Earned Income Credit." If eligible, enter child's name ▶	10	*9,710 75*	

11a Credit for contributions to candidates for public office. Enter one-half of amount paid but do not enter more than $25 ($50 if joint return) 11a

IF YOU WANT IRS TO FIGURE YOUR TAX, PLEASE STOP HERE AND SIGN BELOW.

b Total Federal income tax withheld (if line 7 is larger than $16,500, see page 12 of Instructions) 11b *1,290 00*

— 7

c Earned income credit (from page 2 of Instructions) 11c

— 8

12	Total (add lines 11a, b, and c)	12	*1,290 00*	
13	Tax on the amount on line 10. (See Instructions for line 13 on page 12, then find your tax in Tax Tables on pages 14–25.)	13	*1,161 00*	— 9
14	If line 12 is larger than line 13, enter amount to be **REFUNDED TO YOU** . . . . ▶	14	*129 00*	—10
15	If line 13 is larger than line 12, enter **BALANCE DUE.** Attach check or money order for full amount payable to "Internal Revenue Service." Write social security number on check or money order . . ▶	15		

(Left margin, vertical: Please Attach Check or Money Order Here)

Under penalties of perjury, I declare that I have examined this return, including accompanying schedules and statements, and to the best of my knowledge and belief, it is true, correct, and complete. Declaration of preparer (other than taxpayer) is based on all information of which preparer has any knowledge.

— 11

(Left margin, vertical: Please Sign)

▶ *Juan T. Mendez*   *April 10, 19—*
Your signature   Date

Paid preparer's signature and identifying number (see instructions)

▶
Spouse's signature (if filing jointly, BOTH must sign even if only one had income)

Paid preparer's address (or employer's name, address, and identifying number)

☆ U.S. GOVERNMENT PRINTING OFFICE : —O-235-359

entered this amount on line 8. (Although amounts on tax forms can be rounded off to whole dollars, Juan wrote the exact amount.)

6. Juan skipped line 9 because he has no interest from dividends. He added lines 7 and 8 and entered the total on line 10 ($9,600 + $110.75 = $9,710.75). This is Juan's adjusted gross income.

7. Juan skipped line 11a. On line 11b he entered $1,290, his income tax withheld as reported on his Form W-2.

8. Juan has no earned income credit. Thus he skipped line 11c and entered $1,290 again on line 12.

9. Then Juan determined the amount of tax owed on his adjusted gross income of $9,710.75 (line 10). To do this, he checked the tax tables included with the instructions for filing Form 1040A. Juan checked box 1 (single) in the Filing Status section, so he used Tax Table A—Single, shown below. In the table, Juan found the line for his adjusted gross income—over $9,700 but not over $9,750. He went across this line to the column for taxpayers claiming one exemption. The amount of tax shown here is $1,161. Juan wrote this amount on line 13.

10. Since the amount on line 12 is larger than the amount on line 13, Juan subtracted line 13 from line 12 to find how much the Internal Revenue Service owes him. He entered the amount on line 14 ($1,290 − $1,161 = $129). The amount of $129 will be refunded to Juan by the IRS.

11. Juan made sure to sign and date his return.

19—Tax Table A—SINGLE

If line 10, Form 1040A is—		And the total number of exemptions claimed on line 6 is—			If line 10, Form 1040A is—		And the total number of exemptions claimed on line 6 is—		
Over	But not over	1	2	3	Over	But not over	1	2	3
		Your tax is—					Your tax is—		
8,400	8,450	890	748	580	9,200	9,250	1,051	900	748
8,450	8,500	900	757	590	9,250	9,300	1,062	909	758
8,500	8,550	909	767	601	9,300	9,350	1,073	919	769
8,550	8,600	919	776	611	9,350	9,400	1,084	928	779
8,600	8,650	928	786	622	9,400	9,450	1,095	938	790
8,650	8,700	938	795	632	9,450	9,500	1,106	947	800
8,700	8,750	947	805	643	9,500	9,550	1,117	957	811
8,750	8,800	957	814	653	9,550	9,600	1,128	966	821
8,800	8,850	966	824	664	9,600	9,650	1,139	976	832
8,850	8,900	976	833	674	9,650	9,700	1,150	985	842
8,900	8,950	985	843	685	9,700	9,750	1,161	996	852
8,950	9,000	996	852	695	9,750	9,800	1,172	1,007	862
9,000	9,050	1,007	862	706	9,800	9,850	1,183	1,018	871
9,050	9,100	1,018	871	716	9,850	9,900	1,194	1,029	881
9,100	9,150	1,029	881	727	9,900	9,950	1,205	1,040	890
9,150	9,200	1,040	890	737	9,950	10,000	1,216	1,051	900

Exercises

The people listed in Exercises 1 to 10 qualify for Form 1040A. All of them are single. Use the tax table on page 313 to find the amount of tax owed in each case.

Taxpayer	Taxable Income (Line 10)	Number of Exemptions	Amount of Tax Owed
1. K. Raymond	$ 8,925.00	2	$ 843
2. S. Joyce	9,015.25	1	_____
3. M. Rowe	8,447.19	1	_____
4. N. Chen	9,655.00	2	_____
5. Y. Hardy	8,805.15	3	_____
6. C. Kandler	8,690.00	1	_____
7. B. Mellon	9,680.00	3	_____
8. R. Forrest	8,950.49	2	_____
9. A. Lendman	8,777.00	2	_____
10. J. Good	9,230.40	1	_____

DO YOU KNOW

that if you meet certain requirements, the Internal Revenue Service will figure your tax? The specific IRS requirements you must meet in order to get this help are listed in the instruction booklet that comes with your tax forms.

The service is free. All you must do is fill in a few lines of your return, and send them the information they request. They will compute your tax and send you a refund check if you paid too much or bill you if you did not pay enough.

Long Form 1040

Many taxpayers do not meet the requirements for using Form 1040A. They use the U.S. Individual Income Tax Return, Form 1040, which is also called the "long form." Taxpayers who must use Form 1040 include those who receive over $400 in dividends or interest. Taxpayers who *itemize*, or list, expenses must also use Form 1040. These taxpayers list certain expenses that are then subtracted from their income before any tax is computed. Examples of deductible expenses are medical and dental expenses, state and local income taxes, sales taxes, interest payments, and church and charity contributions.

Itemize: to list specific amounts which should not be taxed.

The IRS sets a fixed amount which is not taxed for each filing status. Always check your instruction booklet for the current amount. Taxpayers have a choice of using the fixed amount (called

Zero bracket amount: fixed amount set by the IRS which is not taxed.

the "zero bracket amount") or of itemizing their deductions. If you itemize your deductions and the total is greater than the current zero bracket amount, your taxable income will be lower. And the lower your taxable income, the less taxes you will pay.

Last year, according to Jonas Todd's Form W-2, he earned $12,400. The amount of federal income tax withheld was $1,159.60. Elsie Todd earned $8,050.33 and had $681.20 withheld for federal income tax. The Todds are filing a joint return. They must use Form 1040 because they received over $400 income in interest. Their joint return is shown on pages 316 and 317. Look at the return as you note the steps they followed in preparing it.

1. At the top of their return, the Todds printed their names, address, social security numbers, and occupations.
2. They checked box 2 in the Filing Status section to show that they are filing a joint return.
3. In the Exemptions section, the Todds first checked boxes 6a and b, indicating that they took an exemption for each of them. They entered the two exemptions in the box to the right. On line 6c they wrote the names of their two dependent children. They took an exemption for each child and entered the number of these exemptions in the box to the right of line 6c. The Todds have no other dependents, so they entered a zero in the box to the right of d. They entered the four exemptions in the box on line 7.
4. On line 8 the Todds listed their income from wages ($12,400 + $8,050.33 = $20,450.33).
5. On line 9 they entered $597.50 for interest income. This is the total interest earned on their bank account and savings bonds. They also entered their interest income in Part 1 of Schedule B—Interest Income. This form is shown on page 318. The Todds had no income from dividends, so they left line 10c blank.
6. Since the Todds had no other income, they skipped lines 11 to 20. They entered the total of lines 8 and 9 on line 21. This amount is their total income.
7. The Todds had no adjustments to their total income. They skipped lines 22 to 27 and entered a zero on line 28.
8. The Todds subtracted the amount on line 28 from the amount on line 21 and entered $21,047.83 on line 29. They left line 30 blank and entered their adjusted gross income of $21,047.83 on line 31.
9. First the Todds copied their adjusted gross income from line 31 onto line 32 of page 2. Next they found their tax table income, which is the figure taxpayers use when they consult a table or

Form 1040 Department of the Treasury—Internal Revenue Service
U.S. Individual Income Tax Return 19—

For the year January 1–December 31, 19—, or other taxable year beginning _____ , 19— ending _____ , 19 _____

Use IRS label. Otherwise, print or type.

First name and initial (if joint return, give first names and initials of both): **Elsie B. and Jonas W.** Last name: **Todd**

Your social security number: **105 62 5927**

Present home address (Number and street, including apartment number, or rural route): **411 Front Street**

For Privacy Act Notice, see page 3 of Instructions.

Spouse's social security no.: **211 32 4002** — 1

City, town or post office, State and ZIP code: **Falls City, Nebraska 68355**

Occupation — Yours ▶ **nurse** Spouse's ▶ **lathe operator**

Presidential Election Campaign Fund ▶ Do you want $1 to go to this fund? . . . . | Yes / No

If joint return, does your spouse want $1 to go to this fund? . | Yes / No

Note: Checking "Yes" will not increase your tax or reduce your refund.

Filing Status — Check Only One Box — 2

1 ☐ Single
2 ☒ Married filing joint return (even if only one had income)
3 ☐ Married filing separately. If spouse is also filing, give spouse's social security number in the space above and enter full name here ▶ ....
4 ☐ Unmarried Head of Household. Enter qualifying name ▶ .... See page 7 of Instructions.
5 ☐ Qualifying widow(er) with dependent child (Year spouse died ▶ 19 ____). See page 7 of Instructions.

Exemptions — 3

Always check the "Yourself" box. Check other boxes if they apply.

6a ☒ Yourself   ☐ 65 or over   ☐ Blind
b ☒ Spouse   ☐ 65 or over   ☐ Blind

Enter number of boxes checked on 6a and b ▶ **2**

c First names of your dependent children who lived with you ▶ **Carol, John**

Enter number of children listed ▶ **2**

d Other dependents:

(1) Name	(2) Relationship	(3) Number of months lived in your home.	(4) Did dependent have income of $750 or more?	(5) Did you provide more than one-half of dependent's support?

Enter number of other dependents ▶ **0**

7 Total number of exemptions claimed . . . .

Add numbers entered in boxes above ▶ **4**

Income — (Please Attach Copy B of Forms W-2 Here)

8	Wages, salaries, tips, and other employee compensation. (Attach Forms W-2. If unavailable, see page 5 of Instructions.)	8	20,450 33 — 4
9	Interest income. (If over $400, attach Schedule B.)	9	597 50 — 5
10a	Dividends (If over $400, attach Schedule B) .... , 10b less exclusion .... , Balance ▶	10c	

(See pages 9 and 17 of Instructions)

(If you have no other income, skip lines 11 through 20 and go to line 21.)

11	State and local income tax refunds (does not apply if refund is for year you took standard deduction) . . .	11	
12	Alimony received	12	
13	Business income or (loss) (attach Schedule C)	13	
14	Capital gain or (loss) (attach Schedule D)	14	
15	50% of capital gain distributions not reported on Schedule D	15	
16	Net gain or (loss) from Supplemental Schedule of Gains and Losses (attach Form 4797) . .	16	— 6
17	Fully taxable pensions and annuities not reported on Schedule E	17	
18	Pensions, annuities, rents, royalties, partnerships, estates or trusts, etc. (attach Schedule E) .	18	
19	Farm income or (loss) (attach Schedule F)	19	
20	Other (state nature and source—see page 9 of Instructions) ▶ .... ▶	20	
21	Total income. Add lines 8, 9, and 10c through 20	21	21,047 83

Adjustments to Income *(if none, skip lines 22 through 27 and enter zero on line 28.)* — 7

22	Moving expense (attach Form 3903)	22		
23	Employee business expenses (attach Form 2106)	23		
24	Payments to an individual retirement arrangement (from attached Form 5329, Part III)	24		
25	Payments to a Keogh (H.R. 10) retirement plan	25		
26	Forfeited interest penalty for premature withdrawal	26		
27	Alimony paid (see page 11 of Instructions)	27		
28	Total adjustments. Add lines 22 through 27 . . . . ▶	28	—0—	
29	Subtract line 28 from line 21	29	21,047 83	— 8
30	Disability income exclusion (sick pay) (attach Form 2440)	30		
31	Adjusted gross income. Subtract line 30 from line 29. Enter here and on line 32. If you want IRS to figure your tax for you, see page 4 of the Instructions . . . . ▶	31	21,047 83	

316   Part 5 MANAGING MONEY

Form 1040 (19—)   **Page 2**

Tax Computation

32 Amount from line 31	32	21,047	83
33 If you itemize deductions, enter excess itemized deductions from Schedule A, line 41			
If you do NOT itemize deductions, enter zero.	33	-0-	

Caution: If you have unearned income and can be claimed as a dependent on your parent's return, check here ▶ ☐ and see page 11 of the Instructions. Also see page 11 of the Instructions if:
● You are married filing a separate return and your spouse itemizes deductions, OR
● You file Form 4563, OR
● You are a dual-status alien.

} —9

34 Tax Table Income. Subtract line 33 from line 32	34	21,047	83

Note: See Instructions for line 35 on page 11. Then find your tax on the amount on line 34 in the Tax Tables. Enter the tax on line 35. However, if line 34 is more than $20,000 ($40,000 if you checked box 2 or 5) or you have more exemptions than those covered in the Tax Tables for your filing status, use Part I of Schedule TC (Form 1040) to figure your tax. You must also use Schedule TC if you file Schedule G (Form 1040), Income Averaging.

35 Tax. Check if from ☒ Tax Tables or ☐ Schedule TC	35	2,786	00	—10
36 Additional taxes. (See page 12 of Instructions.) Check if from ☐ Form 4970, ☐ Form 4972, ☐ Form 5544, ☐ Form 5405, or ☐ Section 72(m)(5) penalty tax	36			} —11
37 Total. Add lines 35 and 36 . . . . ▶	37	2,786	00

Credits

38 Credit for contributions to candidates for public office	38			
39 Credit for the elderly (attach Schedules R&RP)	39			
40 Credit for child and dependent care expenses (attach Form 2441) .	40			
41 Investment credit (attach Form 3468)	41			
42 Foreign tax credit (attach Form 1116)	42			
43 Work Incentive (WIN) Credit (attach Form 4874)	43			
44 New jobs credit (attach Form 5884)	44			
45 See page 12 of Instructions	45			
46 Total credits. Add lines 38 through 45	46	-0-	
47 Balance. Subtract line 46 from line 37 and enter difference (but not less than zero) . . . . ▶	47	2,786	00

} —12

Other Taxes

48 Self-employment tax (attach Schedule SE)	48		
49 Minimum tax. Check here ▶ ☐ and attach Form 4625	49		
50 Tax from recomputing prior-year investment credit (attach Form 4255)	50		
51 Social security tax on tip income not reported to employer (attach Form 4137)	51		
52 Uncollected employee social security tax on tips (from Form W–2)	52		
53 Tax on an individual retirement arrangement (attach Form 5329)	53		
54 Total tax. Add lines 47 through 53 . . . . ▶	54	2,786	00	—13

Payments

55 Total Federal income tax withheld (attach Forms W–2, W–2G, and W–2P to front)	55	1,840	80	
56 1977 estimated tax payments (include amount allowed as credit from 1976 return)	56			
57 Earned income credit. If line 31 is under $8,000, see page 2 of Instructions. If eligible, enter child's name ▶...................	57			
58 Amount paid with Form 4868	58			
59 Excess FICA and RRTA tax withheld (two or more employers) . . .	59			
60 Credit for Federal tax on special fuels, etc. (attach Form 4136) . .	60			
61 Credit from a Regulated Investment Company (attach Form 2439)	61			
61a See page 13 of Instructions	61a			
62 Total. Add lines 55 through 61a . . . . ▶	62	1,840	80

} —14

Refund or Due

63 If line 62 is larger than line 54, enter amount OVERPAID . . . . ▶	63		
64 Amount of line 63 to be REFUNDED TO YOU . . . . ▶	64		
65 Amount of line 63 to be credited on 1978 estimated tax . . . . ▶	65		
66 If line 54 is larger than line 62, enter BALANCE DUE. Attach check or money order for full amount payable to "Internal Revenue Service." Write social security number on check or money order . . . ▶	66	945	20	—15
(Check ▶ ☐ if Form 2210 (2210F) is attached. See page 14 of Instructions.)			

Please Sign Here

Under penalties of perjury, I declare that I have examined this return, including accompanying schedules and statements, and to the best of my knowledge and belief, it is true, correct, and complete. Declaration of preparer (other than taxpayer) is based on all information of which preparer has any knowledge.

▶ *Elsie B. Todd*   *April 3, 19—*
Your signature   Date

Jonas N. Todd   *April 3, 19—*
Spouse's signature (if filing jointly, BOTH must sign even if only one had income)

▶ Paid preparer's signature and identifying number (see instructions)

▶ Paid preparer's address (or employer's name, address, and identifying number)

} —16

☆ U.S. GOVERNMENT PRINTING OFFICE :   —O-235-331

Part I	Interest Income		
1 If you received more than $400 in interest, complete *Part I*. Interest includes earnings from savings and loan associations, mutual savings banks, cooperative banks, and credit unions as well as interest on bank deposits, bonds, tax refunds, etc. Interest also includes original issue discount on bonds and other evidences of indebtedness (see page 17 of Instructions). **(List payers and amounts.)**			
First Guarantee Trust		560	00
U.S. savings bonds		37	50
2 Total interest income. Enter here and on Form 1040, line 9		597	50

rate schedule to determine their taxes. Their deductible expenses were low, so they did not itemize. Thus, the Todds entered zero on line 33. They subtracted the amount on line 33 from the amount on line 32 and entered their tax table income ($21,047.83) on line 34.

10. The Todds completed the Tax Computation section by first entering the amount of tax they owed ($2,786) on line 35. How did they find this figure? They consulted their instruction booklet. Then they looked up their tax table income in Tax Table B—Married Filing Jointly. Look at the tax table on page 319 to see how the Todds found the tax amount of $2,786. First the Todds found the set of numbers in the left column that covered their tax table income shown on line 34—over 21,000 but not over 21,050. They read to the right until they came to the column for four exemptions, the number they claimed on line 7 of page 1. The amount in this column, $2,786, is the tax they owe. They checked the box indicating how they found their taxes.

11. They don't owe additional taxes (line 36), so they entered $2,786 on line 37.

12. The Todds have no credits (lines 38 to 46). Thus, they entered zero on line 46 and $2,786 on line 47.

13. They have no other taxes (lines 48 to 53). Thus, they entered $2,786 again on line 54.

14. The Todds entered $1,840.80, the total federal taxes withheld from the sum of their gross earnings, on line 55. They added the amounts withheld from their Forms W-2 ($1,159.60 + $681.20 = $1,840.80). The Todds have no other tax payments. They left lines 56 to 61a blank and entered $1,840.80 again on line 62.

15. The total tax owed on the Todds's earnings (line 54) is greater than the total tax withheld (line 62). The Todds subtracted the amount on line 62 from their total tax and entered the balance due on line 66 ($2,786 − $1,840.80 = $945.20). This is the amount of income tax the Todds still owe.

If line 10, Form 1040A is—		And the total number of exemptions claimed on line 6 is—							
Over	But not over	2	3	4	5	6	7	8	9
		Your tax is—							
18,800	18,850	2,611	2,424	2,236	2,053	1,858	1,658	1,458	1,258
18,850	18,900	2,624	2,436	2,249	2,064	1,869	1,669	1,469	1,269
18,900	18,950	2,636	2,449	2,261	2,075	1,880	1,680	1,480	1,280
18,950	19,000	2,649	2,461	2,274	2,086	1,891	1,691	1,491	1,291
19,000	19,050	2,661	2,474	2,286	2,099	1,902	1,702	1,502	1,302
19,050	19,100	2,674	2,486	2,299	2,111	1,913	1,713	1,513	1,313
19,100	19,150	2,686	2,499	2,311	2,124	1,924	1,724	1,524	1,324
19,150	19,200	2,699	2,511	2,324	2,136	1,935	1,735	1,535	1,335
19,200	19,250	2,711	2,524	2,336	2,149	1,946	1,746	1,546	1,346
19,250	19,300	2,724	2,536	2,349	2,161	1,957	1,757	1,557	1,357
19,300	19,350	2,736	2,549	2,361	2,174	1,968	1,768	1,568	1,368
19,350	19,400	2,749	2,561	2,374	2,186	1,979	1,779	1,579	1,379
19,400	19,450	2,761	2,574	2,386	2,199	1,990	1,790	1,590	1,390
19,450	19,500	2,774	2,586	2,399	2,211	2,001	1,801	1,601	1,401
19,500	19,550	2,786	2,599	2,411	2,224	2,012	1,812	1,612	1,412
19,550	19,600	2,799	2,611	2,424	2,236	2,023	1,823	1,623	1,423
19,600	19,650	2,811	2,624	2,436	2,249	2,034	1,834	1,634	1,434
19,650	19,700	2,824	2,636	2,449	2,261	2,045	1,845	1,645	1,445
19,700	19,750	2,836	2,649	2,461	2,274	2,056	1,856	1,656	1,456
19,750	19,800	2,849	2,661	2,474	2,286	2,069	1,867	1,667	1,467
19,800	19,850	2,861	2,674	2,486	2,299	2,081	1,878	1,678	1,478
19,850	19,900	2,874	2,686	2,499	2,311	2,094	1,889	1,689	1,489
19,900	19,950	2,886	2,699	2,511	2,324	2,106	1,900	1,700	1,500
19,950	20,000	2,899	2,711	2,524	2,336	2,119	1,911	1,711	1,511
20,000	20,050	2,911	2,724	2,536	2,349	2,131	1,922	1,722	1,522
20,050	20,100	2,924	2,736	2,549	2,361	2,144	1,933	1,733	1,533
20,100	20,150	2,936	2,749	2,561	2,374	2,156	1,944	1,744	1,544
20,150	20,200	2,949	2,761	2,574	2,386	2,169	1,955	1,755	1,555
20,200	20,250	2,961	2,774	2,586	2,399	2,181	1,966	1,766	1,566
20,250	20,300	2,974	2,786	2,599	2,411	2,194	1,977	1,777	1,577
20,300	20,350	2,986	2,799	2,611	2,424	2,206	1,988	1,788	1,588
20,350	20,400	2,999	2,811	2,624	2,436	2,219	1,999	1,799	1,599
20,400	20,450	3,011	2,824	2,636	2,449	2,231	2,010	1,810	1,610
20,450	20,500	3,024	2,836	2,649	2,461	2,244	2,021	1,821	1,621
20,500	20,550	3,036	2,849	2,661	2,474	2,256	2,034	1,832	1,632
20,550	20,600	3,049	2,861	2,674	2,486	2,269	2,046	1,843	1,643
20,600	20,650	3,061	2,874	2,686	2,499	2,281	2,059	1,854	1,654
20,650	20,700	3,074	2,886	2,699	2,511	2,294	2,071	1,865	1,665
20,700	20,750	3,087	2,899	2,711	2,524	2,306	2,084	1,876	1,676
20,750	20,800	3,101	2,911	2,724	2,536	2,319	2,096	1,887	1,687
20,800	20,850	3,115	2,924	2,736	2,549	2,331	2,109	1,898	1,698
20,850	20,900	3,129	2,936	2,749	2,561	2,344	2,121	1,909	1,709
20,900	20,950	3,143	2,949	2,761	2,574	2,356	2,134	1,920	1,720
20,950	21,000	3,157	2,961	2,774	2,586	2,369	2,146	1,931	1,731
21,000	21,050	3,171	2,974	2,786	2,599	2,381	2,159	1,942	1,742
21,050	21,100	3,185	2,986	2,799	2,611	2,394	2,171	1,953	1,753
21,100	21,150	3,199	2,999	2,811	2,624	2,406	2,184	1,964	1,764
21,150	21,200	3,213	3,011	2,824	2,636	2,419	2,196	1,975	1,775
21,200	21,250	3,227	3,024	2,836	2,649	2,431	2,209	1,986	1,786
21,250	21,300	3,241	3,036	2,849	2,661	2,444	2,221	1,999	1,797
21,300	21,350	3,255	3,049	2,861	2,674	2,456	2,234	2,011	1,808
21,350	21,400	3,269	3,061	2,874	2,686	2,469	2,246	2,024	1,819
21,400	21,450	3,283	3,074	2,886	2,699	2,481	2,259	2,036	1,830
21,450	21,500	3,297	3,087	2,899	2,711	2,494	2,271	2,049	1,841
21,500	21,550	3,311	3,101	2,911	2,724	2,506	2,284	2,061	1,852
21,550	21,600	3,325	3,115	2,924	2,736	2,519	2,296	2,074	1,863
21,600	21,650	3,339	3,129	2,936	2,749	2,531	2,309	2,086	1,874
21,650	21,700	3,353	3,143	2,949	2,761	2,544	2,321	2,099	1,885
21,700	21,750	3,367	3,157	2,961	2,774	2,556	2,334	2,111	1,896
21,750	21,800	3,381	3,171	2,974	2,786	2,569	2,346	2,124	1,907
21,800	21,850	3,395	3,185	2,986	2,799	2,581	2,359	2,136	1,918
21,850	21,900	3,409	3,199	2,999	2,811	2,594	2,371	2,149	1,929
21,900	21,950	3,423	3,213	3,011	2,824	2,606	2,384	2,161	1,940
21,950	22,000	3,437	3,227	3,024	2,836	2,619	2,396	2,174	1,951
22,000	22,050	3,451	3,241	3,036	2,849	2,631	2,409	2,186	1,964
22,050	22,100	3,465	3,255	3,049	2,861	2,644	2,421	2,199	1,976
22,100	22,150	3,479	3,269	3,061	2,874	2,656	2,434	2,211	1,989
22,150	22,200	3,493	3,283	3,074	2,886	2,669	2,446	2,224	2,001
22,200	22,250	3,507	3,297	3,087	2,899	2,681	2,459	2,236	2,014
22,250	22,300	3,521	3,311	3,101	2,911	2,694	2,471	2,249	2,026
22,300	22,350	3,535	3,325	3,115	2,924	2,706	2,484	2,261	2,039
22,350	22,400	3,549	3,339	3,129	2,936	2,719	2,496	2,274	2,051

16. The Todds completed their Form 1040 by writing their signatures and the date. Before they mail their return, they must attach Copy B of each of their Form W-2s to the first page of their return. They must also attach a check for the balance due. Tax returns have to be filed on or before April 15.

Exercises for Section One

Complete these exercises by deciding whether the taxpayer must pay more tax or get a refund. Determine the amount.

	Tax Owed	Tax Withheld	Balance Due	Amount Overpaid
1. G. Como	$1,578.02	$1,391.70	$ 186.32	$ 0
2. N. Sonny	1,856.10	1,902.00		
3. E. Johnson	977.53	824.75		
4. A. Fuller	903.19	1,010.50		
5. M. Moto	2,358.17	1,917.05		

The people in Exercises 6 to 10 are all married couples who filed joint Form 1040 returns. Use Tax Table B on page 319 to find out the amount of tax owed in each case.

	Taxable Income	Exemptions	Tax Owed
6. R. and S. Marsh	$18,951.75	2	$ 2,649
7. F. and R. Candy		2	
8. D. and J. Goodie	18,955.06	9	
9. W. and J. James	21,090.00	3	
10. S. and L. Chin	22,155.00	7	

11. This year Kevin Crass received a Form W-2 for his job at the Second Avenue Restaurant with $643.07 withheld for federal income taxes. He also received a Form W-2 with $815.80 in federal tax withheld for his job at the Eighth Street Grocery. What should he write on line 11b and line 12 of Form 1040A?

12. The tax table shows that this year Marjorie Hopkins' income tax is $1,377.20. Her Form W-2 shows that her employer withheld $1,280.60 for federal taxes during the year. What should she enter on line 11b of Form 1040A? On line 12 (assuming she had nothing entered for lines 11a and 11c)? On line 15?

13. Lisa and Manuel Feliciano file a Form 1040 joint return. Last year Lisa earned $10,135.96. Manuel earned $10,208.40. Their interest income was $748.32. What amount should they enter on line 8 of their Form 1040? On Line 9? On Line 21?

14. Jerry Moss is filing a Form 1040A this year. His taxable income is $8,851.70. The amount of federal tax his employer withheld is $1,592.60. Use Tax Table A on page 313 to find if he still owes or if he is due a refund. How much? (Use one exemption.)

15. Hans and Rita Dussel are filing a joint return this year. Their taxable income is $20,640.35. The amount of tax withheld by their employers is $2,870.50. The Dussels have three dependents. Use Tax Table B on page 319 to find if they still owe taxes or if they are due a refund. How much?

Section Two
State Income Tax

Many states require their residents to pay a state income tax. The system for filing this annual tax is very much like the system for filing federal income tax. However, the rates are not the same as the federal rates.

Tax support for the arts has made it easier for many young artists to further their studies.

SINGLE PERSON and
SEPARATE RETURN OF A MARRIED PERSON

Taxable Income	Tax Rate	
	Base	Percentage
$0 to $2,000		1%
2,000 to 3,500	$20 plus	2% of amount over $2,000
3,500 to 5,000	50 plus	3% of amount over 3,500
5,000 to 6,500	95 plus	4% of amount over 5,000
6,500 to 8,000	155 plus	5% of amount over 6,500
8,000 to 9,500	230 plus	6% of amount over 8,000
9,500 to 11,000	320 plus	7% of amount over 9,500
11,000 to 12,500	425 plus	8% of amount over 11,000
12,500 to 14,000	545 plus	9% of amount over 12,500
14,000 to 15,500	680 plus	10% of amount over 14,000
15,500 and over	830 plus	11% of amount over 15,500

JOINT RETURN OF MARRIED COUPLE and
WIDOW(ER) WITH DEPENDENT CHILD

Taxable Income	Tax Rate	
	Base	Percentage
$0 to $4,000		1%
4,000 to 7,000	$40 plus	2% of amount over $4,000
7,000 to 10,000	100 plus	3% of amount over 7,000
10,000 to 13,000	190 plus	4% of amount over 10,000
13,000 to 16,000	310 plus	5% of amount over 13,000
16,000 to 19,000	460 plus	6% of amount over 16,000
19,000 to 22,000	640 plus	7% of amount over 19,000
22,000 to 25,000	850 plus	8% of amount over 22,000
25,000 to 28,000	1,090 plus	9% of amount over 25,000
28,000 to 31,000	1,360 plus	10% of amount over 28,000
31,000 and over	1,660 plus	11% of amount over 31,000

For example, Bella Lutz is a single resident of California. Last year Bella's taxable income as a manager at Adventure World was $17,510. To compute her state income tax, Bella used the State Tax Rate Schedule shown above. She referred to the schedule for single persons and located the line where her taxable income falls—$15,500 and over. According to the schedule, her tax is $830 plus 11 percent of the amount of earnings over $15,000. What is Bella's total tax?

Earnings over $15,500	$17,510 − $15,500 = $2,010
11 percent tax on earnings over $15,500	.11 × $2,010 = $221.10
Total tax	$830 + 221.10 = $1,051.10

In all tax matters, it is essential that you keep complete records of expenses. When it comes time to file your tax return, remember to

Remember: Tax returns must be mailed on or before April 15. read the instructions that accompany the tax form. Tax computations are changed from year to year. And, unless you file a separate form requesting an extension of the filing date, you must file your income tax return no later than April 15 each year.

Exercises for Section Two

Use the State Tax Rate Schedule on page 322 to compute the amount of state income tax owed in each case.

Taxpayers	Filing Status	Taxable Income	Base	Percentage	Total Tax
1. N. Flynn	Single	$ 9,380	$ 230	$ 82.80	$ 312.80
2. T. Lavin	Single	1,950	0		
3. A. and R. Hoey	Married (joint return)	3,600			
4. J. and E. Troy	Married (joint return)	16,470			
5. P. Lakis	Married (separate return)	650			
6. U. Miller	Widow with dependent child	10,400			
7. K. Olson	Widower with dependent child	3,009			
8. T. Puritz	Widow with dependent child	16,820			
9. T. and E. Howe	Married (joint return)	35,900			
10. Y. Spira	Single	19,780			

Use the State Tax Rate Schedule on page 322 to solve these problems. (If necessary, round off your answers to the nearest cent.)

11. Alvin and Val Coole are filing a joint state tax return. Alvin's taxable income is $8,340, and Val's taxable income is $8,130. What is their combined taxable income? Their state tax rate? Their total state tax owed?

12. Julia Travis is married and filing a separate state tax return. Her taxable income from a part-time job is $6,400. Her taxable income from a free-lance job is $1,780. What is her total taxable income? Her state tax rate? Her total state tax owed?

13. David Hanson is a widower with a dependent child. His taxable income is $9,310. What is his state tax rate? His total state tax owed?

REVIEW FOR CHAPTER 16
PAYING INCOME TAXES

Jack Flannagan is a single person who qualifies for Form 1040A. He makes $8,550 a year as a baker's apprentice, and his interest income is $243.10. Use this information, the form on page 312, and Tax Table A on page 313 to solve Exercises 1 to 3. (Use one exemption.)

1. What amount should he enter on line 7 of Form 1040A? On line 8? On line 10?

2. What amount should he enter on line 13 of Form 1040A?

3. His Wage and Tax Statement shows that $1,034 in federal taxes were withheld. Should he complete line 14 or line 15? What amount should he enter?

The people in Exercises 4 to 8 are married and filing jointly. They qualify for Form 1040. Use Tax Table B on page 319 to complete these exercises.

4. Carol and Jim Levy have a taxable income of $19,715 and claim three exemptions. How much should they pay in federal income taxes?

5. Marsha and Ted Rudley have the same taxable income as the Levys. The Rudleys, however, have five exemptions. Who pays more taxes, the Levys or the Rudleys? How much more?

6. Naomi and George McGregor filed a joint Form 1040 tax return. Naomi earned $10,300 last year, and George earned $9,640. Their interest income was $814.32. What amount should they enter on line 8 of Form 1040? On line 9? On line 21?

7. What amounts should Naomi and George enter on lines 35, 37, 47, and 54 if they claim five exemptions?

8. What amounts should Naomi and George enter on line 66 if $1,210.14 in federal taxes was withheld from Naomi's salary and $1,006.49 was withheld from George's salary?

Use the State Tax Rate Schedule on page 322 to solve Exercises 9 and 10.

9. Barbara and Tony Adams file a joint state return. Barbara's taxable income is $9,210, and Tony's taxable income is $10,430. What is their state tax rate? Their total state tax owed?

10. Margaret Dees is a single person with a taxable income of $13,240. Her friend, Carol Fitzgerald, has the same taxable income but files her return as a widow with a dependent child. Who pays the most state tax? How much more?

PART WRAP-UP

Consumer Challenge

Bill Radler has $5,000 in his savings account earning 5.25-percent interest compounded quarterly. However, he wants to invest his money in something with a higher return. But what? Stocks? Bonds? As he was walking to work, he saw a woman holding up an envelope and exclaiming, "Look what I found! It's just a plain envelope, but there's $3,000 in it! And even better, there's a bond worth $100,000. What good luck!" Bill expected her to take the envelope to the police, but the woman, named Kathy, said she wasn't going to. "After all, there's no name written on it. No one knows whose it is. I know someone who will cash the bond for me, but he charges $6,000, and I don't have that much money. I may have to wait until I save another $3,000."

Bill really envied Kathy's luck. Why couldn't that happen to him? Then, as if she'd read his mind, she offered to split everything with him, *if* he would lend her $3,000 to get the bond cashed. At first Bill wasn't sure. Kathy wouldn't show him what was inside the envelope. She stated, "If you want to be partners, you have to trust me."

Bill was convinced; he'd share her luck and put up $3,000. He returned to his bank, withdrew the money, but then hesitated before giving it to his new partner. "What happens now?" he asked. She answered, "No problem. I go to my friend. He cashes the bond. Presto—we're rich." Bill still hadn't seen the cash or the bond. "I'd like to come with you," he said. She objected, "My friend will cash it only if I go alone. But don't worry. I'll be back in an hour with everything."

Bill hesitated again. He wasn't sure what to do. To make a wise decision, Bill asked himself the questions listed below. What do you think Bill should decide? Explain your answers.

1. How much would Bill's $3,000 earn if he left it in the bank for a year? How much would he earn if Kathy returned with the cashed bond? What rate of return would that be on his $3,000?

2. Is it likely that someone would find an unmarked envelope with such valuable contents? What do you think about Kathy's not taking the envelope to the police?

3. What do you think about Kathy's offer to Bill? How would you feel if you were Bill? Would you insist on seeing the contents of the envelope? Would you insist on going with her when she cashed the bond?

4. Does Kathy sound like an honest person? (It is illegal to cash a bond that you do not own. A reputable broker will not do it.) Do you think she's being honest with Bill? If he trusts her with his money, do you think she'll come back? What do you think Bill should do?

For You To Solve

1. Tom and Mary Brill want to buy their own home. Tom works as a plumber's helper and nets $155 a week. Mary works as an office manager and nets $150 a week. At present they are regularly saving 5 percent of their weekly net income. They put this amount in a savings bank paying 5.25-percent interest compounded quarterly. They examined their budget carefully to see where they might be able to save some additional money. Mary said she would give up guitar lessons at a savings of $7.50 a week, and Tom said he would give up his bowling night for a weekly savings of $5.25. If these amounts go into their weekly savings, what will their savings amount to? Answer the questions below. (Use the compound interest table on page 269.)

   a. How much do Tom and Mary save in one year based on saving 5 percent of their weekly net income?

   b. How much more will Mary be able to save in one year by giving up guitar lessons?

   c. How much more will Tom be able to save in one year by giving up bowling?

   d. How much will Tom and Mary be able to save in one year with their new savings plan? How much interest will they earn in that year?

   e. The home they wish to buy will cost at least $32,800. The Brills must make a down payment of 20 percent, and the closing costs will be $1,600. How long will it take Tom and Mary to save enough money for the down payment and closing costs? Remember to include the interest their money will earn. (Round off your answer to the nearest month.)

2. Lily Wilcox inherited $20,000 when her aunt died. She decided to invest the money. She put half of it in tax-exempt municipal bonds paying 5-percent annual interest and half in preferred stock with a par value of $100 a share paying 7.5-percent annual interest.

   a. How many municipal bonds selling at a discount rate of 15 percent with a face value of $1,000 each, paying 5-percent interest, can Lily buy? (Round off your answer to the closest bond.)

b. How much will Lily earn in 5 years if she is able to sell the bonds at face value? (Don't compute the broker's commission in your answers.)

c. How much will Lily earn on her preferred stock?

d. How much will Lily earn in 5 years from her investments?

3. Roy Harris is 25 years old. He wanted to find out the actual cost a year of different kinds of life insurance policies. His insurance agent gave him the following rates.

> *Term Insurance* for 10-year periods. If bought at age 25, it costs $5.19 a year for $1,000 of insurance. If bought at age 35, it costs $7.09 a year. There is no cash value for this type of insurance.
> *Straight Life Insurance.* If bought at age 25, it costs $13.35 a year for each $1,000 of insurance. There is a cash value of $285 for each $1,000 of insurance.
> *Limited-Payment Life Insurance* for a 20-year term. If bought at age 25, it costs $22.07 a year for each $1,000 of insurance. There is a cash value of $489 for each $1,000 of insurance after 20 years.
> *Endowment Insurance* for a 20-year term. If bought at age 25, it costs $42.69 for each $1,000 of insurance. The cash value of the policy after 20 years is the face value of the policy.

Roy would pay premiums on an annual basis. As you answer the questions below, assume that Roy will live at least 20 years from the time he buys the insurance. He will buy insurance totaling $25,000.

a. What would be Roy's total premium cost for 20 years of term insurance bought at age 25 for 10 years and renewed at age 35 for 10 years?

b. What would be Roy's average annual cost?

c. What would be Roy's total premium cost for a straight life policy?

d. What would be the cash value of a $25,000 straight life policy if Roy cashed it in at the end of 20 years?

e. What would be Roy's total cost or gain? His average annual cost or gain?

f. What would be Roy's premium cost for a 20-year limited-payment life policy? What would be the cash value?

g. What would be Roy's total cost or gain? His average annual cost or gain?

h. What would be the premium cost of a 20-year endowment policy? What would be the cash value?

i. What is the total cost or gain? The average annual cost or gain?

j. Assuming that Roy could afford to pay any premium he chooses, which policy do you think Roy should buy? Why?

Basic Math Skills

A. Identifying the Place Value of Whole Numbers

A. THE PROBLEM	4,683,572

a. The digit in the ones place is "2." A "2" in the ones place means two, or 2.

b. The digit in the tens place is "7." A "7" in the tens place means seventy, or 70.

c. The digit in the hundreds place is "5." A "5" in the hundreds place means five hundred, or 500.

d. The digit in the thousands place is "3." A "3" in the thousands place means three thousand, or 3,000.

e. The digit in the ten thousands place is "8." An "8" in the ten thousands place means eighty thousand, or 80,000.

f. The digit in the hundred thousands place is "6." A "6" in the hundred thousands place means six hundred thousand, or 600,000.

g. The digit in the millions place is "4." A "4" in the millions place means four million, or 4,000,000.

millions	hundred thousands	ten thousands	thousands	hundreds	tens	ones
4,	6	8	3,	5	7	2

Exercises

Write the digit in the tens place for each number.

1. 659   **2.** 81   **3.** 3,476,112   **4.** 4,345   **5.** 90,473

Write the digit in the thousands place.

6. 5,892   **7.** 76,319   **8.** 884,692   **9.** 70,367   **10.** 1,468,932

Write the digit in the hundreds place.

11. 1,956   **12.** 724   **13.** 4,589,236   **14.** 81,452   **15.** 740,317

B. Identifying the Place Value of Decimals

a.   The digit in the tenths place is "7." A "7" in the tenths place means seven tenths, or $\frac{7}{10}$.

b.   The digit in the hundredths place is "1." A "1" in the hundredths place means one hundredth, or $\frac{1}{100}$.

c.   The digit in the thousandths place is "5." A "5" in the thousandths place means five thousandths, or $\frac{5}{1,000}$.

d.   The digit in the ten thousandths place is "8." An "8" in the ten thousandths place means eight ten thousandths, or $\frac{8}{10,000}$.

	tenths	hundredths	thousandths	ten thousandths
4.	7	1	5	8

Exercises

Write the digit in the thousandths place.

1. 4.7389   **2.** .305   **3.** 16.592   **4.** .4132   **5.** 73.9248

Write the digit in the tenths place.

6. 31.5   **7.** 429.86   **8.** .1837   **9.** 2.4986   **10.** 356.8207

Write the digit in the hundredths place.

11. .5893   **12.** .407   **13.** 67.81   **14.** 3.052   **15.** 513.624

C. Rounding Off

a.   Locate the digit in the tenths place (7), and then locate the digit to its right (6).

b.   If the digit to the right is 5 or greater, add 1 to the digit in the tenths place (7). If the digit to the right is less than 5, leave the 7 in the tenths place. Drop any digits to the right of the tenths place.

1.8

Here is how to round off when a 9 is involved, such as 3.98. Add 1 to the digit in the tenths place (9). Then write zero in the tenths place, and add 1 to the digit in the ones place.

Answer: 4.0 or 4.

Exercises

Round off to the nearest tenth.

1. 3.57   **2.** 5.12   **3.** .492   **4.** 617.083   **5.** 24.34

C.2. THE PROBLEM   Round off 259.638 to the nearest hundredth.

a. Locate the digit in the hundredths place (3), and then locate the digit to its right (8).
b. If the digit to the right is 5 or greater, add 1 to the digit in the hundredths   259.64
    place (3). If the digit is less than 5, leave the 3 in the hundredths place.
    Drop any digits to the right of the hundredths place. (You would round
    off to the nearest cent in the same way as you round off to the nearest
    hundredth.)

Exercises
Round off to the nearest hundredth (or to the nearest cent).
1. 4.561   2. .0792   3. $31.4608   4. $597.242   5. .835

C.3. THE PROBLEM   Round off .05126 to the nearest thousandth.

a. Locate the digit in the thousandths place (1), and then locate the digit to its right (2).
b. If the digit to the right is 5 or greater, add 1 to the digit in the thousandths   .051
    place (1). If the digit is less than 5, leave the 1 in the thousandths place.
    Drop any digits to the right of the thousandths place. (You would round off
    to the nearest tenth of a cent just as you rounded off to the nearest
    thousandth.)

Exercises
Round off to the nearest thousandth (or to the nearest tenth of a cent).
1. 8.1287   2. $44.34732   3. .9196   4. $1.42853   5. 4,760.3189

C.4. THE PROBLEM   Round off $279.58 to the nearest dollar.

Locate the first digit to the right of the decimal point (5). If the digit is 5 or $280
greater, add 1 to the dollars. If the digit is less than 5, leave the dollars
unchanged. Drop the cents.

Exercises
Round off to the nearest dollar.
1. $33.76   2. $33.06   3. $589.81   4. $10,246.49   5. $.62

The vocabulary of addition

$$4 \leftarrow \text{addend}$$
$$+\ 9 \leftarrow \text{addend}$$
$$\overline{13} \leftarrow \text{sum, or total}$$

D.1. THE PROBLEM
$$\begin{array}{r} 42 \\ +25 \\ \hline \end{array}$$

---

a. Add: 2 + 5, answer 7.
b. Add: 4 + 2, answer 6.

$$\begin{array}{r} 42 \\ +25 \\ \hline 67 \end{array}$$

Exercises

1. $\begin{array}{r} 56 \\ +21 \\ \hline \end{array}$
2. $\begin{array}{r} 34 \\ +20 \\ \hline \end{array}$
3. $\begin{array}{r} 41 \\ +44 \\ \hline \end{array}$
4. $\begin{array}{r} 62 \\ +\ 5 \\ \hline \end{array}$
5. $\begin{array}{r} 23 \\ +16 \\ \hline \end{array}$

D.2. THE PROBLEM
$$\begin{array}{r} 43 \\ +29 \\ \hline \end{array}$$

---

a. Add: 3 + 9, answer 12. Write 2 below the line. Remember 1 or write
it above the next column to the left.
b. Add: 1 + 4, answer 5. Remember 5.
c. Add: 5 + 2, answer 7.

$$\begin{array}{r} 1 \\ 43 \\ +29 \\ \hline 72 \end{array}$$

Exercises

1. $\begin{array}{r} 35 \\ +38 \\ \hline \end{array}$
2. $\begin{array}{r} 46 \\ +19 \\ \hline \end{array}$
3. $\begin{array}{r} 59 \\ +21 \\ \hline \end{array}$
4. $\begin{array}{r} 23 \\ +18 \\ \hline \end{array}$
5. $\begin{array}{r} 27 \\ +57 \\ \hline \end{array}$

D.3. THE PROBLEM
$$\begin{array}{r} 5,217 \\ 1,045 \\ 2,461 \\ +2,583 \\ \hline \end{array}$$

Begin at the right (with the ones column),
and add each column.

$$\begin{array}{r} 1 \\ 5,217 \\ 1,045 \\ 2,461 \\ +2,583 \\ \hline 6 \end{array} \qquad \begin{array}{r} 21 \\ 5,217 \\ 1,045 \\ 2,461 \\ +2,583 \\ \hline 06 \end{array} \qquad \begin{array}{r} 1\ 21 \\ 5,217 \\ 1,045 \\ 2,461 \\ +2,583 \\ \hline 306 \end{array} \qquad \begin{array}{r} 1\ 21 \\ 5,217 \\ 1,045 \\ 2,461 \\ +2,583 \\ \hline 11,306 \end{array}$$

Exercises

1.	23	**2.**	603	**3.**	5,426	**4.**	2,198	**5.**	1,825
	38		419		+3,513		4,803		6,798
	+51		327				1,735		3,627
			+483				2,529		2,124
							+2,384		2,440
									+1,812

D.4. THE PROBLEM $327 + 862 + 47 =$

Write the problem in column form, and then add.

$$\begin{array}{r} 327 \\ 862 \\ +\ 47 \\ \hline 1,236 \end{array}$$

Exercises

1. $42 + 31 + 27 =$ **2.** $56 + 8 + 33 =$ **3.** $119 + 236 + 404 =$

4. $827 + 325 + 210 =$ **5.** $4,103 + 2,717 + 3,548 =$

Check the sum.

$$\begin{array}{r} 495 \\ 28 \\ +1,337 \\ \hline 1,760 \end{array}$$

D.5. THE PROBLEM

a. Add the numbers in a different order.

b. If the new sum matches the original sum, your answer is correct. This sum does not match. There is a mistake. You must recheck your addition.

$$\begin{array}{r} 1,337 \\ 28 \\ +\ 495 \\ \hline 1,860 \end{array}$$

Exercises

Add. Then check your answer.

1.	29	**2.**	4,200	**3.**	460	**4.**	8	**5.**	293
	68		3,205		149		1,601		8,322
	+421		1,726		38		523		607
			+2,183		+295		14		4,259
							7,268		+3,174
							394		
							+ 26		

332   BASIC MATH SKILLS

E. Adding Decimals

		47.3
		1.508
E.1. THE PROBLEM		+ .493

a. Be sure the decimal points are lined up one above the other. Begin at the right, and add each column. (Fill in zeros if you wish.)

b. Show the decimal point in the sum, below the other decimal points.

$$
\begin{array}{r}
47.300 \\
1.508 \\
+ \ \ .493 \\
\hline
49.301
\end{array}
$$

Exercises

1.	2.	3.	4.	5.
2.8	14.239	.4127	4.9	437.02
3.71	27.36	.3651	.12	26.0593
+ .42	+ 5.092	+3.2	.07	31.4
			+6.2	+ 20.266

E.2. THE PROBLEM $\quad 2.1 + 3.25 + 12.8 + .068 =$

Write the problem in column form, keeping the decimal points one above the other. Add. Show the decimal point in the sum, below the other decimal points.

$$
\begin{array}{r}
2.1 \\
3.25 \\
12.8 \\
+ \ \ .068 \\
\hline
18.218
\end{array}
$$

Exercises

1. .26 + .34 + .28 = $\qquad$ **2.** .3 + .48 + .315 + .6 =

3. 19.7 + 3.6 + 44.1 + 59.3 = $\qquad$ **4.** 6.85 + 3.02 + 75.1 =

5. 28.1 + 375.6 + 59.34 =

	6.3	1.3914	28.374
	2.5	.0724	1.245
E.3. THE PROBLEMS	+3.2	+ .4362	+ 7.086

In adding decimals, zeros to the right of the decimal point can be dropped unless another numeral follows the zero.

$$
\begin{array}{r}
6.3 \\
2.5 \\
+3.2 \\
\hline
12.0
\end{array}
$$

The sum
is 12.

$$
\begin{array}{r}
1.3914 \\
.0724 \\
+ \ .4362 \\
\hline
1.9000
\end{array}
$$

The sum
is 1.9.

$$
\begin{array}{r}
28.374 \\
1.245 \\
+ \ 7.086 \\
\hline
36.705
\end{array}
$$

The sum
is 36.705.

Exercises

1.   5.32
     .65
     .48
 +3.05

The sum is _____.

2.   4.37
    62.2
 + 4.938

The sum is _____.

3.   36.1
   1.17
   2.046
 + .584

The sum is _____.

4.   441.329
 + 38.671

The sum is _____.

E.4. THE PROBLEM

$3,715.26
+   291.54

Add, and show the dollar sign and the decimal point in the sum. Cents are always shown with two decimal places, so the zero is not dropped.

  $3,715.26
+   291.54
  $4,006.80

Exercises

1. $726.32
+ 119.29

2. $47.69
+ 31.78

3. $924.53
+ 35.27

4. $558.45
+ 104.56

5. $209.18
    37.25
    42.61
+ 357.12

F. Subtracting Whole Numbers

The vocabulary of subtraction

   8 ← minuend   (number subtracted from)
−5 ← subtrahend (number being subtracted)
   3 ← difference (answer)

F.1. THE PROBLEM

  847
−613

---

a. Begin at the right (with the ones column), and subtract in each column. Subtract: 7 − 3, answer 4.

b. Subtract: 4 − 1, answer 3.

c. Subtract: 8 − 6, answer 2.

  847
−613
  234

Exercises

1.   56
−23

2. 458
−127

3. 992
−431

4. 674
−214

5. 37,586
−10,245

$$\begin{array}{r} 42 \\ -17 \\ \hline \end{array}$$

a. You cannot subtract 7 from 2. Take 1 from the next column (the tens column). That leaves 3 in the tens column.
Add the 1 from the tens column to the 2 in the ones column. That changes the 2 to 12 (10 + 2 = 12).

b. Subtract: 12 − 7, answer 5.

c. Subtract: 3 − 1, answer 2.

$$\begin{array}{r} 3\,12 \\ \cancel{4}\cancel{2} \\ -17 \\ \hline 25 \end{array}$$

Exercises

1.	2.	3.	4.	5.
56	87	61	92	73
−29	−58	−53	−34	−18

$$\begin{array}{r} 367 \\ -182 \\ \hline \end{array}$$

a. Subtract: 7 − 2, answer 5.

b. You cannot subtract 8 from 6. Take 1 from the next column (the hundreds column). That leaves 2 in the hundreds column. Add the 1 from the hundreds column to the 6 in the tens column (10 + 6 = 16).

c. Subtract: 16 − 8, answer 8.

d. Subtract: 2 − 1, answer 1.

$$\begin{array}{r} 2\,16 \\ \cancel{3}\cancel{6}7 \\ -182 \\ \hline 185 \end{array}$$

Exercises

1.	2.	3.	4.	5.
833	678	754	549	846
−271	−393	−560	−292	−495

$$\begin{array}{r} 572 \\ -286 \\ \hline \end{array}$$

a. You cannot subtract 6 from 2. Change 7 to 6, and change 2 to 12.

b. Subtract: 12 − 6, answer 6.

c. You cannot subtract 8 from 6. Change 5 to 4, and change 6 to 16.

d. Subtract: 16 − 8, answer 8.

e. Subtract: 4 − 2, answer 2.

$$\begin{array}{r} 16 \\ 4\,6\,12 \\ \cancel{5}\cancel{7}\cancel{2} \\ -286 \\ \hline 286 \end{array}$$

Exercises

1.	2.	3.	4.	5.
433	605	9,428	8,114	65,017
− 78	−246	−5,734	−2,629	−37,283

F.5. THE PROBLEM $4,821 - 436 =$

Write the problem in column form, and then subtract.

$$\begin{array}{r} 4,821 \\ -436 \\ \hline 4,385 \end{array}$$

Exercises

1. $321 - 110 =$ **2.** $85 - 68 =$ **3.** $219 - 203 =$

4. $421 - 89 =$ **5.** $8,911 - 4,222 =$

F.6. THE PROBLEM   Check the difference.

$$\begin{array}{r} 5,238 \\ -2,743 \\ \hline 2,295 \end{array}$$

Add the subtrahend and the difference. If the sum matches the top number in the subtraction example, your work is correct. If the numbers do not match, you made a mistake. There is a mistake here. You must recheck your subtraction.

$$\begin{array}{r} 2,743 \\ +2,295 \\ \hline 5,038 \end{array}$$

Exercises

Subtract. Then check the difference.

1.	**2.**	**3.**	**4.**	**5.**
$\begin{array}{r} 409 \\ -157 \\ \hline \end{array}$	$\begin{array}{r} 6,548 \\ -2,603 \\ \hline \end{array}$	$\begin{array}{r} 5,184 \\ -327 \\ \hline \end{array}$	$\begin{array}{r} 98,612 \\ -47,931 \\ \hline \end{array}$	$\begin{array}{r} 82,495 \\ -6,287 \\ \hline \end{array}$

G. Subtracting Decimals

G.1. THE PROBLEM

$$\begin{array}{r} 15.632 \\ -2.814 \\ \hline \end{array}$$

Begin at the right, and subtract. Proceed as in F.3. and F.4. when you find numbers that cannot be subtracted. Show the decimal point in the answer below the other decimal points.

$$\begin{array}{r} 15.632 \\ -2.814 \\ \hline 12.818 \end{array}$$

Exercises

1.	**2.**	**3.**	**4.**	**5.**
$\begin{array}{r} 25.386 \\ -11.572 \\ \hline \end{array}$	$\begin{array}{r} 6.024 \\ -3.279 \\ \hline \end{array}$	$\begin{array}{r} 75.863 \\ -28.175 \\ \hline \end{array}$	$\begin{array}{r} 9,137.4 \\ -5,286.2 \\ \hline \end{array}$	$\begin{array}{r} 5,831.4 \\ -2,176.9 \\ \hline \end{array}$

Write the problem in column form, keeping the decimal points one above the other. Show the decimal point in the answer, below the other decimal points. Subtract.

$$\begin{array}{r} 197.23 \\ -3.56 \\ \hline 193.67 \end{array}$$

Exercises

1. 36.75 − 19.82 =   **2.** 4.67 − 2.83 =   **3.** .529 − .317 =

4. 813.2 − 47.8 =   **5.** 7.106 − .549 =

Think of a zero in the hundredths place. Then subtract.

$$\begin{array}{r} 7.42 \\ -1.30 \\ \hline 6.12 \end{array}$$

Exercises

1. $\begin{array}{r} 8.39 \\ -4.2 \\ \hline \end{array}$ **2.** $\begin{array}{r} 6.834 \\ -2.6 \\ \hline \end{array}$ **3.** $\begin{array}{r} 427.95 \\ -38.1 \\ \hline \end{array}$ **4.** $\begin{array}{r} 90.2 \\ -17 \\ \hline \end{array}$ **5.** $\begin{array}{r} 84.39 \\ -6.1 \\ \hline \end{array}$

a. Write zeros to fill decimal places in the top number.
b. Then subtract.

$$\begin{array}{r} 85.500 \\ -7.368 \\ \hline 78.132 \end{array}$$

Exercises

1. $\begin{array}{r} .57 \\ -.248 \\ \hline \end{array}$ **2.** $\begin{array}{r} 25.7 \\ -9.33 \\ \hline \end{array}$ **3.** $\begin{array}{r} .8 \\ -.1672 \\ \hline \end{array}$ **4.** $\begin{array}{r} 42.2 \\ -8.519 \\ \hline \end{array}$ **5.** $\begin{array}{r} 5. \\ -.06 \\ \hline \end{array}$

```
  .35
-.26
   9
```

There should be two decimal places in the difference. You must add a zero to the answer to make two decimal places. Write the zero to the left of the 9, and add a decimal point.

```
  .35
-.26
  .09
```

Exercises

1.	2.	3.	4.	5.
.87	35.46	.253	7.636	463.71
−.79	−12.38	−.247	−4.629	−370.68

```
 4.2963
-2.1563
```

a. Zeros to the right of the decimal point can be dropped when they are not followed by another numeral.
b. The answer is 2.14.

```
 4.2963
-2.1563
 2.1400
```

Exercises

1.	2.
27.38	629.47
−14.58	− 31.57
The answer is _____.	The answer is _____.

3.	4.
.8153	53.7149
−.2153	−24.2849
The answer is _____.	The answer is _____.

```
$7,129.53
−   236.19
```

Subtract. Then show the dollar sign and the decimal point in the answer.

```
$7,129.53
−   236.19
$6,893.34
```

Exercises

1.	2.	3.	4.	5.
$12.58	$325.69	$441.36	$7,265.84	$5.827.73
− 4.76	− 174.39	− 112.28	− 5,193.41	− 3,912.90

338 BASIC MATH SKILLS

H. Multiplying Whole Numbers

The vocabulary of multiplication

$$\begin{array}{r} 6 \leftarrow \text{multiplicand} \\ \times\ 7 \leftarrow \text{multiplier} \\ \hline 42 \leftarrow \text{product (answer)} \end{array}$$

H.1. THE PROBLEM

$$\begin{array}{r} 32 \\ \times\ 4 \\ \hline \end{array}$$

a. Start at the right. Multiply each number at the top by 4. Multiply: 2 × 4, answer 8.

b. Multiply: 3 × 4, answer 12.

$$\begin{array}{r} 32 \\ \times\ 4 \\ \hline 128 \end{array}$$

Exercises

1.	41	2.	52	3.	70	4.	63	5.	34
	× 8		× 3		× 4		× 3		× 2

H.2. THE PROBLEM

$$\begin{array}{r} 12 \\ \times\ 7 \\ \hline \end{array}$$

a. Multiply: 2 × 7, answer 14. Write 4 below the line. Remember 1 or write it above the next column.

b. Multiply: 1 × 7, answer 7. Remember 7.

c. Add: 7 + 1, answer 8.

$$\begin{array}{r} 1 \\ 12 \\ \times\ 7 \\ \hline 84 \end{array}$$

Exercises

1.	28	2.	14	3.	35	4.	827	5.	546
	× 2		× 4		× 3		× 2		× 3

H.3. THE PROBLEM

$$\begin{array}{r} 425 \\ \times 423 \\ \hline \end{array}$$

a. Multiply: 425 × 3, answer 1,275.

b. Multiply: 425 × 2, answer 850. Begin to write the answer below the 2 in 423.

c. Multiply: 425 × 4, answer 1,700. Begin to write the answer below the 4 in 423.

d. Add the answers. Show commas when necessary.

$$\begin{array}{r} 425 \\ \times 423 \\ \hline 1\ 275 \\ 8\ 50 \\ 170\ 0 \\ \hline 179{,}775 \end{array}$$

Exercises

1.	224	2.	416	3.	39	4.	4,173	5.	5,028
	×132		× 25		×42		× 626		× 753

Rewrite the problem with one numeral below the other. (Put the ones below the ones, the tens below the tens, and so on.) Then multiply.

$$\begin{array}{r} 317 \\ \times 482 \\ \hline 634 \\ 25\ 36 \\ 126\ 8 \\ \hline 152{,}794 \end{array}$$

Exercises

1. $47 \times 3 =$ **2.** $514 \times 9 =$ **3.** $418 \times 26 =$

4. $2{,}307 \times 45 =$ **5.** $329 \times 457 =$

$$\begin{array}{r} 32 \\ \times 69 \\ \hline 288 \\ 1\ 82 \\ \hline 2{,}108 \end{array}$$

H.5. THE PROBLEM   Check the product. 2,108

a. Reverse the order of the two numbers. Multiply.

b. If the new product matches the original product, your work is correct. These products do not match. There is a mistake. You must recheck the multiplication.

$$\begin{array}{r} 69 \\ \times 32 \\ \hline 138 \\ 2\ 07 \\ \hline 2{,}208 \end{array}$$

Exercises

Multiply. Then check the product.

1.	**2.**	**3.**	**4.**	**5.**
21	271	222	6,932	3,228
$\times 35$	$\times 394$	$\times\ 38$	$\times\ \ 341$	$\times\ \ 497$

I. Multiplying Decimals

$$\begin{array}{r} 32.6 \\ \times\ .04 \end{array}$$

I.1. THE PROBLEM

a. Multiply.

b. Count the number of places to the right of the decimal point in each of the numbers multiplied. There are three.

c. Moving from right to left, count off the same number of places in the product. Put the decimal point to the left of the three digits.

$$\begin{array}{r} 32.6 \\ \times\ .04 \\ \hline 1.304 \end{array}$$

1. 24.9	**2.** .08	**3.** 268.3	**4.** 14.75	**5.** 48.19
$\times$ .07	$\times$356	$\times$ .7	$\times$ .82	$\times$ .64

	.012
	$\times$ .8
I.2. THE PROBLEM	96

There should be four decimal places in the product. You must add two zeros to the answer to make four decimal places. Write the zeros to the left of the numerals, and add a decimal point.

.012
$\times$ .8
.0096

Exercises

1. .021	**2.** .118	**3.** .876	**4.** .09	**5.** .0025
$\times$ .3	$\times$ .3	$\times$.004	$\times$.07	$\times$ 6.1

	$41.26
I.3. THE PROBLEM	$\times$ 8

Multiply as before. Show the decimal point and the dollar sign in the product.

$41.26
$\times$ 8
$330.08

Exercises

1. $7.12	**2.** $43.50	**3.** $251.68	**4.** $17.75	**5.** $38.57
$\times$ 9	$\times$ 27	$\times$ 8	$\times$ 49	$\times$ 365

J.   Multiplication Shortcuts

	617
J.1. THE PROBLEM	$\times$403

a. Multiply by 3.
b. Write 0 under the 0 in 403.
c. Continue and multiply by 4. Write the result on the same line as the 0. Complete the solution by adding.

617
$\times$403
1 851
246 80
248,651

1.   251
    × 302

2.   648
    × 401

3.   325
    × 207

4.   269
    × 3.05

5.   8.72
    × 60.3

J.2. THE PROBLEMS

   43
  × 50

   43
  × 250

   78
  × 200

   319
  × 6,000

a. Rewrite the problem with 0 far to the right.

    43
× 50
2,150

    43
× 250
2 150

    78
× 200
15,600

    319
× 6,000
1,914,000

b. Write 0 below the line, in the product.

    86
10,750

c. Multiply.

Exercises

1.   72
    × 40

2.   47
    × 230

3.   58
    × 400

4.   3.71
    × 800

5.   19
    × 6,000

K. Multiplying by 10, 100, or 1,000

K. THE PROBLEMS $5.398 \times 10 =$ $13.7 \times 100 =$ $6 \times 1,000 =$

Count the number of zeros in the multiplier. Move the decimal point that number of places to the right in the multiplicand. Add zeros if necessary.

$5.398 \times 10 = 53.98$
$13.7 \times 100 = 1,370$
$6 \times 1,000 = 6,000$

Exercises

1. $6.231 \times 10 =$ **2.** $45.3 \times 100 =$ **3.** $4.928 \times 100 =$
4. $5 \times 1,000 =$ **5.** $2.5 \times 1,000 =$

L. Dividing Whole Numbers

The vocabulary of division

$3 \leftarrow$ quotient (answer)
$5\overline{)15} \leftarrow$ dividend (number being divided)
 ↑
divisor (number doing the dividing)

L.1. THE PROBLEM $7\overline{)19}$

a. Find the multiple of 7 that is 19 or nearest to 19, but not more than 19. Think of these facts: $0 \times 7 = 0$; $1 \times 7 = 7$; $2 \times 7 = 14$; $3 \times 7 = 21$; $4 \times 7 = 28$; $5 \times 7 = 35$; $6 \times 7 = 42$; $7 \times 7 = 49$; $8 \times 7 = 56$; $9 \times 7 = 63$. 14 is nearest to 19 but not more than 19. Use the number that multiplied by 7 equals 14. Answer: 2. Write 2 above the line, in the quotient.

$$\begin{array}{r} 2 \text{ r.5} \\ 7\overline{)19} \\ \underline{14} \\ 5 \end{array}$$

b. Multiply: 2×7, answer 14. Write 14 under the dividend.
c. Subtract: $19 - 14$, answer 5. 5 is $r.$, the remainder.

Exercises

1. $3\overline{)17}$ 2. $4\overline{)23}$ 3. $6\overline{)27}$ 4. $8\overline{)32}$ 5. $7\overline{)55}$

L.2. THE PROBLEM $5\overline{)317}$

a. Divide: $5\overline{)31}$. (Follow the same method as in problem L.1.) Answer is 6 with a remainder of 1.

$$\begin{array}{r} 63 \text{ r.2} \\ 5\overline{)317} \\ \underline{30} \\ 17 \\ \underline{15} \\ 2 \end{array}$$

b. Bring down the 7, and write it next to the remainder.
c. Divide: $5\overline{)17}$. (Follow the same method as in problem L.1.) Answer is 3 with a remainder of 2. Write this answer above the 7 in the quotient.

Exercises

1. $2\overline{)133}$ 2. $7\overline{)178}$ 3. $5\overline{)207}$ 4. $8\overline{)1,344}$ 5. $4\overline{)33,871}$

L.3. THE PROBLEM $30\overline{)645}$

a. Find the multiple of 30 that is 64 or nearest to 64 but less. Since $2 \times 30 = 60$, use 2. Write 2 above the 4. Multiply: 2×30, answer 60. Write 60 under 64.

$$\begin{array}{r} 21 \text{ r.15} \\ 30\overline{)645} \\ \underline{60} \\ 45 \\ \underline{30} \\ 15 \end{array}$$

b. Subtract: $64 - 60$, answer 4. Write 4 under the 60, and bring down 5 next to the 4.
c. Find the multiple of 30 that is 45 or nearest to 45 but less. Since $1 \times 30 = 30$, use 1.
d. Multiply, and then subtract as in the first two steps.

Exercises

1. $60\overline{)681}$ 2. $30\overline{)687}$ 3. $40\overline{)838}$ 4. $20\overline{)618}$ 5. $20\overline{)485}$

L.4. THE PROBLEM   42)907

a. To find the number in the quotient, think of 42 as 40. Find the multiple of 40 that is 90 or nearest to 90. Since 2 × 40 = 80, use 2.
b. Multiply: 2 × 42, answer 84. Subtract: 90 − 84, answer 6. Write 6 under 84 and bring 7 down next to 6.
c. Again, think of 42 as 40. Find the multiple of 40 that is 67 or nearest to 67. Since 1 × 40 = 40, use 1.
d. Multiply: 1 × 42, answer 42. Subtract: 67 − 42, answer, remainder 25.

```
   21 r.25
42)907
   84
   67
   42
   25
```

Exercises

1. 31)976   2. 46)532   3. 81)860   4. 23)515   5. 52)614

L.5. THE PROBLEM

```
    2
42)816
   84
```

a. Sometimes, even if you work correctly, the number you decide to use in the quotient will be too great. After multiplying you will have a number which cannot be subtracted. You will have to correct the number in the quotient. Instead of 2, try 1.
b. Continue to solve as before.

```
   19 r.18
42)816
   42
   396
   378
    18
```

Exercises

1. 24)458   2. 31)914   3. 43)514   4. 22)610   5. 56)661

L.6. THE PROBLEM

```
      2
41)8,446
   82
   24
```

a. To find the number in the quotient, think of 41 as 40. Find the multiple of 40 that is 24 or less than 24, but not greater than 24. 0 × 40 = 0; 1 × 40 = 40. Use 0.
b. Multiply 41 × 0, answer 0. Then subtract. Bring down the 6, and continue to solve as before.

```
    206
41)8,446
   82
   24
    0
   246
   246
     0
```

Exercises

1. $36\overline{)3{,}733}$ **2.** $72\overline{)7{,}438}$ **3.** $25\overline{)7{,}661}$ **4.** $39\overline{)7{,}839}$ **5.** $43\overline{)8{,}870}$

L.7. THE PROBLEM $325\overline{)5{,}892}$

a. To find the number in the quotient, think of 325 as 300. Find the multiple of 300 that is 589 or nearest to 589, but not more than 589. $0 \times 300 = 0$; $1 \times 300 = 300$; $2 \times 300 = 600$. Use 1.

b. Multiply: 1×325, answer 325. Subtract: $589 - 325$, answer 264. Write 264, and bring down 2.

c. Again, think of 325 as 300. Find the multiple of 300 that is 2,642 or nearest to 2,642. Use 8.

d. Multiply: 8×325, answer 2,600. Subtract.

```
      18 r.42
325)5,892
    3 25
    2 642
    2 600
       42
```

Exercises

1. $421\overline{)7{,}583}$ **2.** $664\overline{)9{,}856}$ **3.** $739\overline{)12{,}492}$ **4.** $548\overline{)36{,}194}$ **5.** $203\overline{)4{,}928}$

L.8. THE PROBLEM $4{,}106 \div 522 =$

a. Rewrite the problem with a division bar. Show the divisor on the left.

b. Show the dividend under the bar.

c. Divide.

```
      7 r.452
522)4,106
    3 654
      452
```

Exercises

1. $38 \div 2 =$ **2.** $356 \div 4 =$ **3.** $972 \div 12 =$
4. $564 \div 47 =$ **5.** $8{,}064 \div 384 =$

L.9. THE PROBLEM   Check the answer. $27\overline{)5{,}764}$ (213 r.13)

a. Multiply the quotient by the divisor.

b. Add the remainder to the product you got in the first step.

c. If the answer matches the dividend, your quotient is correct. This quotient is correct.

$213 \times 27 = 5{,}751$
$5{,}751 + 13 = 5{,}764$

Exercises

Check the answers.

1. $\dfrac{112 \text{ r.}13}{53\overline{)5{,}944}}$ 2. $\dfrac{158 \text{ r.}4}{37\overline{)5{,}793}}$ 3. $\dfrac{204 \text{ r.}35}{46\overline{)9{,}419}}$ 4. $\dfrac{446 \text{ r.}18}{21\overline{)9{,}588}}$

M. Dividing Decimals

M.1. THE PROBLEM $3\overline{)21.6}$

Divide as before. Show the decimal point in the quotient above the decimal point in the dividend.

$$\dfrac{7.2}{3\overline{)21.6}}$$

Exercises

1. $4\overline{)20.4}$ 2. $7\overline{)24.5}$ 3. $8\overline{)289.6}$ 4. $6\overline{)1.962}$ 5. $5\overline{)4.655}$

M.2. THE PROBLEM $2.3\overline{)3.91}$

a. Move the decimal point in the divisor to the far right. Use a caret ($\wedge$) to show that you have moved it.
b. Move the decimal point in the dividend the same number of places to the right. Show this with a caret.
c. Divide as with whole numbers. Show the decimal point in the quotient above the caret in the dividend.

$$\dfrac{1.7}{2.3_{\wedge}\overline{)3.9_{\wedge}1}}$$

Exercises

1. $1.5\overline{)4.95}$ 2. $4.6\overline{)41.86}$ 3. $.9\overline{)814.5}$ 4. $.22\overline{)8.888}$ 5. $3.42\overline{)20.6568}$

M.3. THE PROBLEM $.45\overline{)18}$

a. Add as many zeros in the dividend as needed to move the same number of decimal places as in the divisor.
b. Continue to solve as before.

$$\dfrac{40}{.45_{\wedge}\overline{)18.00_{\wedge}}}$$

Exercises

1. $.7\overline{)490}$ 2. $8.6\overline{)774}$ 3. $.34\overline{)95.2}$ 4. $.76\overline{)1{,}527.6}$ 5. $.05\overline{)635}$

M.4. THE PROBLEM   Find the answer to the nearest tenth. $7\overline{)59}$

a. Find the quotient to the nearest hundredth. Use zeros to fill the   *8.42 or 8.4*
    places through the hundredths place in the dividend. $7\overline{)59.00}$
b. Divide.
c. Round off to the nearest tenth. (See C.1. on page 329 if you need
    help with rounding.)

Exercises
Divide. Find the answers to the nearest tenth.
1. $6\overline{)79}$ 2. $42\overline{)913}$ 3. $328\overline{)1{,}706}$ 4. $1.8\overline{)53}$ 5. $2.6\overline{)453.1}$

M.5. THE PROBLEM   Find the answer to the nearest hundredth. $8\overline{)63}$

a. Find the quotient to the nearest thousandth. Use zeros to fill the   *7.875 or 7.88*
    places through the thousandths place in the dividend. $8\overline{)63.000}$
b. Divide.
c. Round off to the nearest hundredth. (See C.2. on page 330 if you
    need help with rounding.)

Exercises
Divide. Find the answer to the nearest hundredth.
1. $9\overline{)80}$ 2. $421\overline{)6{,}257}$ 3. $3.5\overline{)92}$ 4. $58\overline{)8.3}$ 5. $0.9\overline{)7.04}$

N. Dividing by 10, 100, or 1,000

N. THE PROBLEMS $187.34 \div 10 =$ $4 \div 100 =$ $50 \div 1{,}000 =$

Count the number of zeros in the divisor. Move the deci- $187.34 \div 10 = 18.734$
mal point that number of places to the left. Use zeros to $4 \div 100 = .04$
the right of the decimal point if necessary. $50 \div 1{,}000 = .050$ *or* .05

Exercises
1. $53.89 \div 10 =$ 2. $7 \div 100 =$ 3. $298.3 \div 100 =$
4. $46.8 \div 1{,}000 =$ 5. $5{,}924 \div 10{,}000 =$

BASIC MATH SKILLS   347

O. Finding Averages

O. THE PROBLEM   Find the average of 41, 28, 13, and 74.

a. Add the numbers. $41 + 28 + 13 + 74 = 156$
b. Count the numbers added. There are 4. Divide $156 \div 4 = 39$
    the sum by that number. The average is 39.

Exercises

1. Find the average of 18, 65, and 46.
2. Find the average of 125, 78, 136, and 93.
3. Find the average of 32, 17, 55, 41, 62, and 45.
4. Find the average of 258, 631, 422, and 513.
5. Find the average of 62.3, 91.04, and .038.

P. Operations with Denominate Numbers

P.1. THE PROBLEMS

```
  14 minutes 20 seconds
+ 20 minutes 18 seconds
```

```
  7 hours 23 minutes
+ 10 hours  5 minutes
```

```
  6 feet 4 inches
- 4 feet 3 inches
```

Add or subtract each column.

```
  14 minutes 20 seconds        7 hours 23 minutes        6 feet 4 inches
+ 20 minutes 18 seconds      + 10 hours  5 minutes     - 4 feet 3 inches
  34 minutes 38 seconds        17 hours 28 minutes        2 feet 1 inch
```

Exercises

1.   30 minutes 4 seconds   **2.**   5 hours 6 minutes   **3.**   10 hours 40 minutes
      + 12 minutes 7 seconds   + 7 hours 8 minutes   − 8 hours 9 minutes

4.   2 feet 6 inches   **5.**   13 feet 7 inches
      + 11 feet 3 inches   − 9 feet 2 inches

P.2. THE PROBLEMS

$$22 \text{ minutes } 40 \text{ seconds}$$
$$+26 \text{ minutes } 53 \text{ seconds}$$

$$35 \text{ hours } 57 \text{ minutes}$$
$$+14 \text{ hours } 42 \text{ minutes}$$

$$12 \text{ feet } 11 \text{ inches}$$
$$+ 4 \text{ feet } 9 \text{ inches}$$

a. Add each column as you did in the addition problems in P.1.

b. Since 60 seconds = 1 minute 93 seconds = 1 minute 33 seconds. Add 1 minute 33 seconds to 48 minutes. Answer: 49 minutes 33 seconds.

$$\begin{array}{l} 22 \text{ minutes } 40 \text{ seconds} \\ +26 \text{ minutes } 53 \text{ seconds} \\ \hline 48 \text{ minutes } 93 \text{ seconds} \\ \qquad\qquad or \\ 49 \text{ minutes } 33 \text{ seconds} \end{array}$$

c. In the same way, 99 minutes = 1 hour 39 minutes. Add 1 hour 39 minutes to 49 hours. Answer: 50 hours 39 minutes.

$$\begin{array}{l} 35 \text{ hours } 57 \text{ minutes} \\ +14 \text{ hours } 42 \text{ minutes} \\ \hline 49 \text{ hours } 99 \text{ minutes} \\ \qquad\qquad or \\ 50 \text{ hours } 39 \text{ minutes} \end{array}$$

d. In the same way, 20 inches = 1 foot 8 inches. Add 1 foot 8 inches to 16 feet. Answer: 17 feet 8 inches.

$$\begin{array}{l} 12 \text{ feet } 11 \text{ inches} \\ + 4 \text{ feet } 9 \text{ inches} \\ \hline 16 \text{ feet } 20 \text{ inches} \\ \qquad\qquad or \\ 17 \text{ feet } 8 \text{ inches} \end{array}$$

Exercises

1. $\begin{array}{l} 13 \text{ minutes } 38 \text{ seconds} \\ +21 \text{ minutes } 45 \text{ seconds} \end{array}$

2. $\begin{array}{l} 16 \text{ hours } 49 \text{ minutes} \\ +11 \text{ hours } 34 \text{ minutes} \end{array}$

3. $\begin{array}{l} 8 \text{ minutes } 24 \text{ seconds} \\ +6 \text{ minutes } 43 \text{ seconds} \end{array}$

4. $\begin{array}{l} 27 \text{ feet } 7 \text{ inches} \\ + 3 \text{ feet } 5 \text{ inches} \end{array}$

5. $\begin{array}{l} 12 \text{ hours } 22 \text{ minutes} \\ +14 \text{ hours } 38 \text{ minutes} \end{array}$

14 minutes 26 seconds
− 8 minutes 41 seconds

21 hours 13 minutes
− 6 hours 20 minutes

23 feet   6 inches
−18 feet 10 inches

a. Subtract in the seconds column.

14 minutes 26 seconds = 13 minutes 86 seconds
− 8 minutes 41 seconds =   8 minutes 41 seconds
                              5 minutes 45 seconds

b. You cannot subtract 41 seconds from 26 seconds. Since 60 seconds = 1 minute, change 14 minutes 26 seconds to 13 minutes 86 seconds. Then subtract in each column.

c. Subtract the minutes.

d. In the same way, you cannot subtract 20 minutes from 13 minutes. Since 60 minutes = 1 hour, change 21 hours 13 minutes to 20 hours 73 minutes. Then subtract in each column.

20 hours 73 minutes
− 6 hours 20 minutes
14 hours 53 minutes

e. In the same way, you cannot subtract 10 inches from 6 inches. Since 12 inches = 1 foot, change 23 feet 6 inches to 22 feet 18 inches. Then subtract in each column.

22 feet 18 inches
−18 feet 10 inches
  4 feet   8 inches

Exercises

1.   56 minutes 32 seconds
−17 minutes 48 seconds

2.   12 hours 49 minutes
−10 hours 55 minutes

3.   15 hours 17 minutes
− 3 hours 23 minutes

4.   20 feet 2 inches
−15 feet 4 inches

5.   31 minutes   7 seconds
− 6 minutes 18 seconds

Q. Adding Fractions and Mixed Numbers

The vocabulary of fractions

$\dfrac{2}{8}$ ← numerator
      ← denominator

Q.1. THE PROBLEM $\dfrac{2}{8} + \dfrac{3}{8} =$

Since the denominators are both 8, just add the numerators. Add: 2 + 3, answer 5. Keep 8 as the denominator. $\dfrac{2}{8} + \dfrac{3}{8} = \dfrac{5}{8}$

Exercises

1. $\frac{1}{5} + \frac{2}{5} =$ **2.** $\frac{7}{9} + \frac{1}{9} =$ **3.** $\frac{3}{11} + \frac{2}{11} =$ **4.** $\frac{3}{7} + \frac{3}{7} =$ **5.** $\frac{2}{15} + \frac{11}{15} =$

Q.2. THE PROBLEM $\frac{1}{3} + \frac{4}{9} =$

a. Since the denominators are not the same, change them to be the same. Multiply both the numerator and the denominator of $\frac{1}{3}$ by 3. Multiply: $\frac{1 \times 3}{3 \times 3} = \frac{3}{9}$. Therefore, think of $\frac{1}{3}$ as $\frac{3}{9}$.

$\frac{3}{9} + \frac{4}{9} = \frac{7}{9}$

b. Now add the numerators. Add: $3 + 4$, answer 7.

Exercises

1. $\frac{3}{8} + \frac{1}{4} =$ **2.** $\frac{1}{2} + \frac{5}{12} =$ **3.** $\frac{3}{10} + \frac{3}{5} =$ **4.** $\frac{2}{15} + \frac{1}{3} =$ **5.** $\frac{1}{4} + \frac{3}{16} =$

Q.3. THE PROBLEM $\frac{1}{4} + \frac{1}{6} =$

a. Both denominators have to be changed. Since $4 \times 3 = 12$ and $6 \times 2 = 12$, change both denominators to 12. Multiply the numerator and denominator of each fraction by the number that will change the denominators to 12. Multiply: $\frac{1 \times 3}{4 \times 3} = \frac{3}{12}$. Therefore, think of $\frac{1}{4}$ as $\frac{3}{12}$. Multiply: $\frac{1 \times 2}{6 \times 2} = \frac{2}{12}$. Therefore, think of $\frac{1}{6}$ as $\frac{2}{12}$.

$\frac{3}{12} + \frac{2}{12} = \frac{5}{12}$

b. Now add the numerators. $3 + 2 = 5$.

Exercises

1. $\frac{1}{3} + \frac{1}{2} =$ **2.** $\frac{1}{3} + \frac{1}{4} =$ **3.** $\frac{2}{5} + \frac{1}{3} =$ **4.** $\frac{1}{2} + \frac{1}{7} =$ **5.** $\frac{3}{4} + \frac{2}{5} =$

Q.4. THE PROBLEM

$$\begin{array}{r} 4\frac{1}{3} \\ +2\frac{1}{5} \\ \hline \end{array}$$

a. To add the fractions, first change them to fractions with like denominators. Since $5 \times 3 = 15$ and $3 \times 5 = 15$, change both denominators to 15. Multiply: $\frac{1 \times 5}{3 \times 5} = \frac{5}{15}$. Therefore, think of $\frac{1}{3}$ as $\frac{5}{15}$. Multiply: $\frac{1 \times 3}{5 \times 3} = \frac{3}{15}$. Therefore, think of $\frac{1}{5}$ as $\frac{3}{15}$.

$$\begin{array}{r} 4\frac{5}{15} \\ 2\frac{3}{15} \\ \hline 6\frac{8}{15} \end{array}$$

b. Add the fractions and the whole numbers.

Exercises

1. $\begin{array}{r} 4\frac{1}{2} \\ +3\frac{2}{5} \\ \hline \end{array}$ **2.** $\begin{array}{r} 2\frac{3}{8} \\ +4\frac{1}{4} \\ \hline \end{array}$ **3.** $\begin{array}{r} 3\frac{1}{5} \\ +1\frac{1}{4} \\ \hline \end{array}$ **4.** $\begin{array}{r} 6\frac{7}{12} \\ +5\frac{1}{3} \\ \hline \end{array}$ **5.** $\begin{array}{r} 7\frac{1}{4} \\ +2\frac{5}{16} \\ \hline \end{array}$

Reduce answers like $\frac{8}{12}$ and $3\frac{4}{10}$.

a. Find the numeral that can be evenly divided into both the numerator and the denominator. Divide the numerator and the denominator of $\frac{8}{12}$ by 4: $\frac{8 \div 4}{12 \div 4} = \frac{2}{3}$

$$\frac{8}{12} = \frac{2}{3}$$

b. Find the numeral that can be evenly divided into both the numerator and the denominator. Divide the numerator and the denominator of $\frac{4}{10}$ by 2: $\frac{4 \div 2}{10 \div 2} = \frac{2}{5}$

$$3\frac{4}{10} = 3\frac{2}{5}$$

Exercises

Reduce these fractions and mixed numbers.

1. $\frac{6}{12}$ 2. $\frac{8}{10}$ 3. $\frac{3}{18}$ 4. $7\frac{6}{9}$ 5. $4\frac{2}{8}$

Q.6. THE PROBLEMS Reduce answers like $\frac{10}{5}$, $\frac{11}{6}$, or $9\frac{5}{3}$.

a. To reduce $\frac{10}{5}$: 5 can be subtracted from 10 exactly twice. $10 - 5 = 5$ and $5 - 5 = 0$. The answer is 2.

$$\frac{10}{5} = 2$$

b. To reduce $\frac{11}{6}$: 6 can be subtracted from 11 one time. Subtract: $11 - 6 = 5$. That leaves 5 sixths. The answer is $1\frac{5}{6}$.

$$\frac{11}{6} = 1\frac{5}{6}$$

c. To reduce $9\frac{5}{3}$: 3 can be subtracted from 5 one time. Add: $1 + 9$, answer 10. 2 is left in the numerator. The answer is $10\frac{2}{3}$.

$$\frac{5}{3} = 1\frac{2}{3}$$
$$9\frac{5}{3} = 10\frac{2}{3}$$

Exercises

Reduce these fractions and mixed numbers.

1. $\frac{7}{6}$ 2. $\frac{11}{4}$ 3. $\frac{15}{8}$ 4. $3\frac{6}{5}$ 5. $3\frac{11}{5}$

R. **Subtracting Fractions and Mixed Numbers**

R.1. THE PROBLEM $\frac{11}{13} - \frac{3}{13} =$

Since the denominators are both 13, just subtract the numerators. Subtract: $11 - 3$, answer 8.

$$\frac{11}{13} - \frac{3}{13} = \frac{8}{13}$$

Exercises

Reduce your answers as in Q.5. when possible.

1. $\frac{6}{7} - \frac{3}{7} =$ 2. $\frac{10}{11} - \frac{9}{11} =$ 3. $\frac{7}{10} - \frac{1}{10} =$ 4. $\frac{19}{20} - \frac{5}{20} =$ 5. $\frac{13}{16} - \frac{3}{16} =$

R.2. THE PROBLEM $\frac{1}{2} - \frac{3}{8} =$

a. Change the denominators to be the same. Since $2 \times 4 = 8$, multiply $\quad \frac{4}{8} - \frac{3}{8} = \frac{1}{8}$
both the numerator and the denominator of $\frac{1}{2}$ by 4.
Multiply: $\frac{1 \times 4}{2 \times 4} = \frac{4}{8}$. Therefore, think of $\frac{1}{2}$ as $\frac{4}{8}$.
b. Subtract the numerators. Subtract: $4 - 3$, answer 1.

Exercises
Reduce your answers when possible.

1. $\frac{2}{5} - \frac{3}{10} =$ **2.** $\frac{5}{9} - \frac{1}{3} =$ **3.** $\frac{5}{12} - \frac{1}{6} =$ **4.** $\frac{9}{14} - \frac{2}{7} =$ **5.** $\frac{3}{8} - \frac{5}{16} =$

R.3. THE PROBLEM $\frac{2}{9} - \frac{1}{6} =$

a. Both denominators have to be changed. Since $2 \times 9 = 18$ and $\quad \frac{4}{18} - \frac{3}{18} = \frac{1}{18}$
$3 \times 6 = 18$, change both denominators to 18. Multiply the nu-
merator and the denominator of each fraction by the number that
will change the denominator to 18. Multiply: $\frac{2 \times 2}{9 \times 2} = \frac{4}{18}$. There-
fore, think of $\frac{2}{9}$ as $\frac{4}{18}$. Multiply: $\frac{1 \times 3}{6 \times 3} = \frac{3}{18}$. Therefore, think of $\frac{1}{6}$
as $\frac{3}{18}$.
b. Subtract the numerators. Subtract: $4 - 3$, answer 1.

Exercises
Reduce your answers when possible.

1. $\frac{1}{3} - \frac{1}{5} =$ **2.** $\frac{1}{3} - \frac{1}{4} =$ **3.** $\frac{1}{4} - \frac{1}{6} =$ **4.** $\frac{4}{7} - \frac{1}{3} =$ **5.** $\frac{3}{4} - \frac{3}{5} =$

R.4. THE PROBLEM
$$\begin{array}{r} 5\frac{2}{9} \\ -3\frac{4}{9} \\ \hline \end{array}$$

a. You cannot subtract $\frac{2}{9} - \frac{4}{9}$. Since $\frac{9}{9} = 1$, subtract: $5 - 1$, answer 4. Think $\quad 4\frac{11}{9}$
of the 1 as $\frac{9}{9}$. Add: $\frac{9}{9} + \frac{2}{9}$, answer $\frac{11}{9}$. Therefore, think of $5\frac{2}{9}$ as $4\frac{11}{9}$. $\quad -3\frac{4}{9}$
b. Subtract the fractions and the whole numbers. $\quad\quad\quad\quad\quad\quad\quad\quad\quad \overline{1\frac{7}{9}}$

Exercises
Reduce your answers when possible. To solve some of these problems, you must
change the fractions to fractions with like denominators. (Refer to Q.3.)

1. $\begin{array}{r} 6\frac{1}{5} \\ -2\frac{4}{5} \\ \hline \end{array}$ **2.** $\begin{array}{r} 9\frac{7}{9} \\ -3\frac{8}{9} \\ \hline \end{array}$ **3.** $\begin{array}{r} 15\frac{1}{12} \\ -9\frac{5}{12} \\ \hline \end{array}$ **4.** $\begin{array}{r} 8\frac{1}{5} \\ -3\frac{1}{3} \\ \hline \end{array}$ **5.** $\begin{array}{r} 25\frac{1}{4} \\ -12\frac{1}{3} \\ \hline \end{array}$

BASIC MATH SKILLS

R.5. THE PROBLEM

$$\begin{array}{r} 6 \\ -4\frac{1}{3} \\ \hline \end{array}$$

a. Subtract: $6 - 1$, answer 5. Think of the 1 as $\frac{3}{3}$. Therefore, think of 6 as $5\frac{3}{3}$.

b. Subtract the fractions and whole numbers.

$$\begin{array}{r} 5\frac{3}{3} \\ -4\frac{1}{3} \\ \hline 1\frac{2}{3} \end{array}$$

Exercises

1.	**2.**	**3.**	**4.**	**5.**
3	10	16	23	18
$-1\frac{2}{7}$	$-5\frac{5}{8}$	$-7\frac{5}{12}$	$-11\frac{3}{10}$	$-9\frac{5}{16}$

S. Multiplying Fractions and Mixed Numbers

S.1. THE PROBLEM $\frac{2}{5} \times \frac{1}{3} =$

a. Multiply: 2×1, answer 2.

b. Multiply: 5×3, answer 15.

$$\frac{2}{5} \times \frac{1}{3} = \frac{2}{15}$$

Exercises

Reduce your answers when possible.

1. $\frac{2}{7} \times \frac{1}{3} =$ **2.** $\frac{1}{2} \times \frac{4}{5} =$ **3.** $\frac{5}{9} \times \frac{3}{4} =$ **4.** $\frac{2}{5} \times \frac{3}{8} =$ **5.** $\frac{1}{8} \times \frac{6}{7} =$

S.2. THE PROBLEM $1\frac{2}{3} \times \frac{1}{7} =$

a. Change $1\frac{2}{3}$ to a fraction. Multiply: 1×3, answer 3. Add: $3 + 2$, answer 5. 5 is the new numerator. Keep 3 as the denominator. Therefore, think of $1\frac{2}{3}$ as $\frac{5}{3}$.

b. Multiply the numerators.

c. Multiply the denominators.

$$\frac{5}{3} \times \frac{1}{7} = \frac{5}{21}$$

Exercises

Reduce your answers when possible.

1. $1\frac{1}{6} \times \frac{3}{8} =$ **2.** $2\frac{2}{3} \times \frac{1}{7} =$ **3.** $\frac{3}{5} \times 1\frac{1}{4} =$ **4.** $\frac{2}{9} \times 1\frac{2}{3} =$ **5.** $3\frac{1}{3} \times \frac{1}{6} =$

a. It is easier to multiply fractions if you can make the numbers smaller. Look at the denominator of the first fraction (2) and the numerator of the second (4). Try to find a number that divides each without a remainder. Both can be divided by 2. Divide: $2 \div 2$, answer 1. Show this by marking through the 2 and writing 1. Divide: $4 \div 2$, answer 2. Mark through the 4 and write 2. Then multiply the new numerators and the new denominators.

$$\frac{1}{\overset{2}{\cancel{2}}} \times \frac{\overset{2}{\cancel{4}}}{5} = \frac{2}{5}$$

b. To multiply $\frac{6}{7} \times \frac{2}{3}$, find the number that divides evenly into the numerator of the first fraction and the denominator of the second fraction. Both can be divided by 3. Divide: $6 \div 3$, answer 2. Divide: $3 \div 3$, answer 1. Multiply.

$$\frac{\overset{2}{\cancel{6}}}{7} \times \frac{2}{\underset{1}{\cancel{3}}} = \frac{4}{7}$$

c. To multiply $\frac{5}{8} \times \frac{4}{15}$, cancel twice. Divide 15 and 5 by 5. Divide 8 and 4 by 4. Multiply.

$$\frac{\overset{1}{\cancel{5}}}{\underset{2}{\cancel{8}}} \times \frac{\overset{1}{\cancel{4}}}{\underset{3}{\cancel{15}}} = \frac{1}{6}$$

d. To multiply $4\frac{2}{3} \times \frac{6}{7}$, change $4\frac{2}{3}$ to $\frac{14}{3}$. Then cancel twice. Multiply. Reduce the answer.

$$\frac{\overset{2}{\cancel{14}}}{\underset{1}{\cancel{3}}} \times \frac{\overset{2}{\cancel{6}}}{\underset{1}{\cancel{7}}} = \frac{4}{1} = 4$$

Exercises

Reduce your answers when possible.

1. $\frac{1}{6} \times \frac{3}{5} =$ 2. $\frac{1}{4} \times \frac{8}{9} =$ 3. $\frac{24}{55} \times \frac{20}{21} =$ 4. $7\frac{1}{7} \times 2\frac{4}{5} =$ 5. $2\frac{5}{8} \times 5\frac{1}{3}$

T. Dividing Fractions and Mixed Numbers

T.1. THE PROBLEM $\frac{1}{3} \div \frac{2}{5} =$

a. Change the divisor from $\frac{2}{5}$ to $\frac{5}{2}$, and change the division sign to a multiplication sign.

$$\frac{1}{3} \times \frac{5}{2} = \frac{5}{6}$$

b. Multiply.

Exercises

Reduce your answers when possible.

1. $\frac{1}{5} \div \frac{1}{2} =$ 2. $\frac{1}{9} \div \frac{2}{3} =$ 3. $\frac{2}{7} \div \frac{1}{4} =$ 4. $\frac{2}{3} \div \frac{1}{4} =$ 5. $\frac{5}{6} \div \frac{1}{3} =$

T.2. THE PROBLEM $2\frac{1}{3} \div \frac{4}{5} =$

a. Change $2\frac{1}{3}$ to $\frac{7}{3}$.

b. Change the divisor as in T.1., and change the sign to multiplication.

c. Multiply. Reduce the answer.

$$\frac{7}{3} \times \frac{5}{4} = \frac{35}{12} = 2\frac{11}{12}$$

Exercises

Reduce your answers when possible.

1. $1\frac{1}{5} \div \frac{1}{2} =$ **2.** $1\frac{3}{4} \div \frac{1}{6} =$ **3.** $2\frac{1}{2} \div \frac{3}{4} =$ **4.** $3\frac{1}{3} \div 2\frac{2}{5} =$ **5.** $2\frac{1}{4} \div 1\frac{5}{6} =$

T.3. THE PROBLEM $\frac{1}{4} \div 3 =$

Think of 3 as $\frac{3}{1}$. Change $\frac{3}{1}$ to $\frac{1}{3}$, and multiply. $\frac{1}{4} \times \frac{1}{3} = \frac{1}{12}$

Exercises

Reduce your answers when possible.

1. $\frac{2}{5} \div 6 =$ **2.** $\frac{1}{8} \div 2 =$ **3.** $\frac{3}{4} \div 3 =$ **4.** $2\frac{1}{4} \div 2 =$ **5.** $3\frac{1}{3} \div 4 =$

U. Percents

U.1. THE PROBLEM $6.834 = \underline{\quad}\%$

Move the decimal point two places to the right, and show the per- $6.834 = 683.4\%$
cent sign (%).

Exercises

Change the decimals to percents.

1. .389   **2.** .42   **3.** 5.744   **4.** .06   **5.** .071

U.2. THE PROBLEM $\frac{3}{4} = \underline{\quad}\%$

a. Divide the numerator by the denominator. $.75 \ or \ 75\%$
b. Change the decimal point as in U.1., and show the per- $4\overline{)3.00}$
cent sign.

Exercises

Change the fractions to percents.

1. $\frac{4}{5}$ **2.** $\frac{1}{4}$ **3.** $\frac{1}{2}$ **4.** $\frac{6}{10}$ **5.** $\frac{18}{25}$

U.3. THE PROBLEM   Change 36% to a decimal.

Drop the percent sign, and move the decimal point two places to the left. $36\% = .36$

Exercises
Change the percents to decimals.
1. 51%   **2.** 30%   **3.** 48.6%   **4.** 10.2%   **5.** 65.5%

U.4.   THE PROBLEM   Express 6 as a percent of 24.

a.   Divide as in U.2.

$\begin{array}{r} .25 \; or \; 25\% \\ 24\overline{)6.00} \end{array}$

b.   Move the decimal point two places to the right and show the percent sign.

Exercises
1. Express 9 as a percent of 45.   **2.** Express 12 as a percent of 24.
3. Express 10 as a percent of 25.   **4.** Express 15 as a percent of 20.
5. Express 8 as a percent of 32.

U.5.   THE PROBLEM   Express 7 as a percent of 18 (to the nearest percent).

a.   Divide 7 by 18. Obtain a decimal number to the hundredths place by adding a decimal point and three zeros. Show the decimal in the answer.

$\begin{array}{r} .388 \; or \; 38.8\% \; or \; 39\% \\ 18\overline{)7.000} \end{array}$

b.   Move the decimal point two places to the right and show the percent sign. Round off to the nearest percent.

Exercises
Round off to the nearest percent.
1. Express 3 as a percent of 45.   **2.** Express 7 as a percent of 24.
3. Express 12 as a percent of 42.   **4.** Express 8 as a percent of 26.
5. Express 18 as a percent of 64.

U.6.   THE PROBLEM   20% of 65 =

a.   Change the percent to a decimal by dropping the percent sign and moving the decimal point two places to the left.

$20\% = .20$

b.   Multiply: 65 × .20, answer 13.00 or 13.

$65 \times .20 = 13$

Exercises
1. 50% of 42 =   **2.** 80% of 40 =   **3.** 12% of 800 =
4. 24% of 100 =   **5.** 15% of 700 =

The Metric System

A. Units of Length

The four units of length commonly used with the metric system are the *meter*, the *millimeter*, the *centimeter*, and the *kilometer*.

This is 1 millimeter: . The millimeter is the smallest unit of length you will learn to use with the metric system.

Activities. Use a millimeter ruler to measure these things.

The length of a pencil.
The width of a desk.

The meter is 1,000 times the length of the millimeter.

Activities. Use a meter ruler to measure these things.

The length of a bulletin board.
The height of a bookshelf.

Use the symbol *m* for meter. Use the symbol *mm* for millimeter.

$$1 \text{ m} = 1000 \text{ mm}$$

When you need to convert from meters to millimeters, multiply the number of meters by 1,000.

$$3 \text{ m} = 3000 \text{ mm}$$
$$52 \text{ m} = 52\,000 \text{ mm}$$
$$.06 \text{ m} = 60 \text{ mm}$$

Note: For our purposes in dealing with numbers in the metric system, we do not use commas in the usual way. We do not use commas to separate groups of three digits. Instead, we separate the groups by a space. We use neither a comma nor a space when we have only four digits.

Exercises

a. 9 m = ___ mm   **b.** 17 m = ___ mm   **c.** 460 m = ___ mm
d. .05 m = ___ mm   **e.** .8 = ___ mm   **f.** 223.01 = ___ mm

Did you use any shortcuts to multiply by 1000? (See page 341 for a reminder of multiplication shortcuts.)

When you need to convert from millimeters to meters, divide the number of millimeters by 1,000. (See page 347 for division shortcuts.)

$$8 \, mm = .008 \, m$$
$$40 \, mm = .04 \, m$$
$$76 \, 530 \, mm = 76.53 \, m$$

Exercises

a. 6 mm = ___ m   **b.** 320 mm = ___ m **c.** 4809 mm = ___ m
d. 27 740 mm = ___ m **e.** .71 mm = ___ m   **f.** 5236.4 mm = ___ m

The centimeter is another unit which is smaller than the meter. This is 1 centimeter: ———. The centimeter has special uses. It is used to measure things around the home, to measure the body, and to measure clothing.

Activities. Use a centimeter ruler to measure the following.

The length of a shirt sleeve.
The width of your hand.
The depth of a glass.
The width of a pillow case.

There are 100 centimeters in a meter. Since *cm* is the symbol for centimeter, this can be shown as follows.

$$1 \, m = 100 \, cm \ \textit{or} \ 1 \, cm = .01 \, m$$

When you need to convert from meters to centimeters, multiply the number of meters by 100. Use a shortcut to multiply.

$$9 \, m = 900 \, cm$$
$$425 \, m = 42 \, 500 \, cm$$
$$3.8 \, m = 380 \, cm$$

Exercises

a. 5 m = ___ cm   **b.** 30 m = ___ cm   **c.** 429 m = ___ cm
d. .8 m = ___ cm   **e.** 17.52 m = ___ cm   **f.** .1354 m = ___ cm

When you need to convert from centimeters to meters, divide the number of centimeters by 100. Use a shortcut to divide.

$$8 \, cm = .08 \, m$$
$$143 \, cm = 1.43 \, m$$
$$952 \, 000 \, cm = 9520 \, m$$

Exercises

a. 2 cm = ___ m   **b.** 86 cm = ___ m   **c.** 127 cm = ___ m
d. 5.3296 cm = ___ m   **e.** 4.71 cm = ___ m   **f.** 300.95 cm = ___ m

One centimeter equals 10 millimeters. When you need to convert from centimeters to millimeters, multiply the number of centimeters by 10. Use a shortcut to multiply.

$$2 \text{ cm} = 20 \text{ mm}$$
$$700 \text{ cm} = 7000 \text{ mm}$$
$$.839 \text{ cm} = 8.39 \text{ mm}$$

Exercises

a. 6 cm = ___ mm   **b.** 83 cm = ___ mm   **c.** 500 cm = ___ mm
d. .6 cm = ___ mm   **e.** .68 cm = ___ mm   **f.** 41.92 cm = ___ mm

When you need to convert from millimeters to centimeters, divide the number of millimeters by 10. Use a shortcut to divide.

$$7 \text{ mm} = .7 \text{ cm}$$
$$36 \text{ mm} = 3.6 \text{ cm}$$
$$90\ 000 \text{ mm} = 9000 \text{ cm}$$

Exercises

a. 4 mm = ___ cm
c. 5389 mm = ___ cm   **d.** 6.4 mm = ___ cm
e. 43.77 mm = ___ cm   **f.** .007 35 mm = ___ cm
b. 21 mm = ___ cm

The kilometer is the unit of length used when the meter is too small. The symbol *km* is used for kilometer. The kilometer is much larger than the meter. It is 1,000 times the meter.

$$1 \text{ km} = 1000 \text{ m}$$

When you need to convert from kilometers to meters, multiply the number of kilometers by 1,000. Use a shortcut to multiply. Remember to move the decimal point three places to the right.

$$54.1 \text{ km} = 54\ 100 \text{ m}$$
$$.0082 \text{ km} = 8.2 \text{ m}$$

Exercises

a. 62 km = ___ m   **b.** 9300 km = ___ m   **c.** .1 km = ___ m
d. 8.1 km = ___ m   **e.** 957.24 km = ___ m   **f.** .007 852 km = ___ m

THE METRIC SYSTEM

When you need to convert from meters to kilometers, divide the number of meters by 1,000. Use a shortcut to divide.

$$2030 \text{ m} = 2.03 \text{ km}$$
$$6 \text{ m} = .006 \text{ km}$$

Exercises

a. 56 891 m = ___ km **b.** 317 m = ___ km **c.** 2 m = ___ km
d. 4.2 m = ___ km **e.** 7.468 m = ___ km **f.** .009 32 m = ___ km

B. Units of Capacity

The two common units of capacity used with the metric system are the *liter* and the *milliliter*. Use the symbol *L* for liter. Use the symbol *mL* for milliliter. The milliliter is small, about twenty drops. The liter is equivalent to 1,000 milliliters.

Activity. Use a liter container, and find the number of liters of water that each of the following containers can hold.

A milk carton.
A detergent bottle.
A bucket.

If you have a graduated cylinder, use it to find the number of milliliters of water that each of the following items can hold.

A soda can.
A cup.
A straw.

When you need to convert from liters to milliliters, multiply the number of liters by 1,000. Use a shortcut to multiply.

$$2 \text{ L} = 2000 \text{ mL}$$
$$.037 \text{ L} = 37 \text{ mL}$$
$$54.6108 \text{ L} = 54\,610.8 \text{ mL}$$

Exercises

a. 9 L = ___ mL **b.** 85 L = ___ mL **c.** .062 L = ___ mL
d. .1854 L = ___ mL **e.** 3.610 L = ___ mL **f.** 71.8 L = ___ mL

When you need to convert milliliters to liters, divide the number of milliliters by 1,000. Use a shortcut to divide.

$$3 \text{ mL} = .003 \text{ L}$$
$$25\,916 \text{ mL} = 25.916 \text{ L}$$

a. 5 mL = ___ L   **b.** 300 mL = ___ L   **c.** 6742 mL = ___ L
d. 8810 mL = ___ L   **e.** .2 mL = ___ L   **f.** 519.63 mL = ___ L

C. Units of Mass

The *kilogram* and the *gram* are units of mass (or weight) in the metric system. If you go to a supermarket, you'll find many products that have mass marked in kilograms and in grams.

One gram is so light you cannot feel it.

One kilogram is equivalent to 1,000 grams. Did you guess that? Maybe you have remembered that 1 kilometer equals 1,000 meters. *Kilo* means 1000; so, 1 kilogram equals 1,000 grams.

Multiply by 1,000 to convert kilograms to grams. Divide by 1,000 to convert grams to kilograms. Use a shortcut to divide.

1 kg = 1000 g	1 g = .001 kg
2 kg = 2000 g	7 g = .007 kg
.3 kg = 300 g	284.2 g = .2842 kg
15.019 kg = 15 019 g	.03 g = .000 03 kg

Exercises

a. 83 kg = ___ g   **b.** 6.59 kg = ___ g   **c.** .004 721 kg = ___ g
d. 19 g = ___ kg   **e.** .002 g = ___ kg   **f.** 8094.3 g = ___ kg

D. Temperature

Temperature is measured in *degrees Celsius*. Twelve degrees Celsius, for example, is written *12°C*. In Celsius, the freezing point of water is 0°C. The boiling point of water is 100°C. A reading above 37°C means that a person has a fever. In hot weather, the temperature is about 24°C or above.

E. Problem Solving

1. It is 46 kilometers from Greenville to Red City. How many kilometers is it from Greenville to Red City and back?

2. Bob Lane had some cloth 225 centimeters long. He used a piece that was 87 centimeters long. How much cloth did he have left?

3. A picture is 12 centimeters long and 10 centimeters wide. Can the picture fit in a frame 124 millimeters long and 109 millimeters wide?

4. A pitcher holds 2400 milliliters of juice. How many 300-milliliter glasses will the pitcher fill?

5. There are 4 cans of soup on the shelf. Each can holds 298 grams. Is the total contents of the 4 cans more than 1 kilogram or less than 1 kilogram?

Index

Reconciling balances, 76–77
Registration of cars, 218–219
Regular charge account, 128
Regular checking account, 65
Regular salary, 3, 5
Renting and leases, 171–172
Reposession, 126–127
Revolving charge account, 128
Rounding off, 329
Round lots in stocks, 274

S

Salary, 3 (*see also* Wages)
Sales (*see* Shopping, sales and)
Sales tax, computing, 220
Saving money, 256–257
  compound interest and, 264–265
    tables, 266–267
  how much to save, 257–258
  increasing savings, 258–259
  simple interest and, 260
    annual periods, 260–261
    daily periods, 263
    principal and, 261
    semiannual and quarterly periods,
      261
  watching savings grow, 268–269
Savings account, 65
Secured loans, 103
Security, 126
Security deposit, 173
Separate tax returns, 310
Service charge, 65, 67
Shareholder, 272
Shopping, 144
  complaints, 167
  for food, 144
    budgeting, 146–147
    container measurement and, 149
    estimates and, 156
    metric system and, 151–154
    money-saving tips, 150, 156
    nonfood items and, 145
    packages of different sizes and, 152–
      154

Shopping, for food (*continued*)
    preparation differences, 159–160
    price-per-serving comparisons, 157–
      158
    unit price and, 148–149, 151–154
  sales and, 163
    aliquot parts and, 165–167
    computing the amount saved,
      163–164
    computing discount rates, 164
    substitution and, 144
Short-term interest, 97
Simple interest, 88–89, 260
  annual periods and, 260
  daily periods and, 263
  formula for, 89
  principal and, 261
  semiannual and quarterly periods and,
    261
Single-payment loan, 88
Social security, 28
Special checking account, 67
Standard fire policy, 299
State income taxes, 25–26, 321
  rate schedule, 322–323
Station-to-station calls, 199–200
Sticker price of cars, 216–217
Stockbrokers, 273
  commissions of, 273–275
  proceeds and, 281
Stockholder, 272
Stocks, investing in, 273
  broker's commission and, 273–275
  common stock dividends, 278
  face value and, 278
  making or losing money, 279–281
    procceds and, 281
  market value and, 278
  odd lots, 274–275
  par value and, 278–279
  preferred stock dividends, 278–279
  price changes and, 275–276
  rate of return, 282–283
  round lots, 274
  stock market tables and, 276–277
  yield and, 282–283
Straight commission, 13
Straight life insurance, 292
Subleting, 173

Subtraction
   of decimals, 336–338
   of fractions and mixed numbers, 352–
      354
   of whole numbers, 334–336
Surgical expense insurance, 304
Surveyors, 183, 184

T

Tax-free bonds, 285
Taxes
   auto-use, 219
   income (*see* Federal income taxes;
      Social security; State income taxes)
   property, 183–186
   sales, 220
   tax-free bonds, 285
Telephones, 197
   cost of different calls, 198–199
   direct distance dialed calls, 200
   initial charges, 198
   long distance calls, 199–202
   message units, 197, 198
   operated-assisted calls, 200
   overtime charges, 198–199
   saving on bills for, 200
   station-to-station calls, 199–200
   types of phone service, 197–198
Tenant, 172
Term insurance, 292
Time-and-a-half pay, 6–7
Time zones, 246–247
Title insurance, 183
Title search, 183
Trading stocks, 273
Trains, 238
   communication tickets, 242
      rate schedule for, 243
   reading a timetable, 238–239
   train fares, 240–241
Truth-in-Lending Law, 95, 126

U

Unit pricing, 148
   measures on containers and, 148–149
   metric system and, 151–154
   multiple items in selling price and, 154
   packages of different sizes and, 152–154
U.S. Bureau of Labor Statistics, 146
Utilities (*see* Electricity; Gas, natural;
      Telephone; Water)

V

Variable expenses, 46–48
Volume, 149
Voluntary deductions, 30–32

W

Wages, 2–3
   commission plus, 14–15
   lateness and, 3–4
   overtime and, 3, 5–8
   piece-rate earnings plus, 11
Water, 205
   rate schedule for, 206
Watthours (Wh), 192
Watts (W), 192
Withholding allowances, 23–24
   Form W-4, 23–24

Y

Yield
   on bonds, 287–288
   on stocks, 282–283

Z

Zero-bracket amount, 315